Tom Gale
311 W 85th st.
New York, NY 10024

Savings Deposits, Mortgages, and Housing

Savings Deposits, Mortgages, and Housing

Studies for the Federal Reserve-MIT-Penn Economic Model

Edited by

Edward M. Gramlich
Office of Economic Opportunity

Dwight M. Jaffee
Princeton University

Lexington Books
D.C. Heath and Company
Lexington, Massachusetts
Toronto   London

To Our Families

Bunny	Annette
Sarah	Jonathan
Robert	Elizabeth

Table of Contents

List of Figures

List of Tables

Preface

Early in 1966 a group of economists at the Board of Governors of the Federal Reserve System and at the Massachusetts Institute of Technology began formulating plans for a large-scale quarterly econometric model of the United States economy. The University of Pennsylvania later became a third center for work on the model, and the model has since become known as the Federal Reserve-MIT-PENN model, or as it is referred to in this volume, the FMP model.

As work on the project proceeded, a steady stream of papers reporting on preliminary versions of the model became available. But the elusive goal of the "final" version seemed to recede as fast, or sometimes faster, than we progressed. It is now apparent that such a final state of the model is not possible in the context of the continuing development of new ideas, econometric techniques, and revised data. It is also clear that in the development of a large model it is important to reach a plateau from which the work can be viewed as a single entity. The participants in the FMP project generally agree that the model has reached such a plateau and that the work of the previous six years should be critically evaluated and the areas for future research realistically appraised.

In this spirit we are presenting here the papers reporting on the savings deposits, mortgages, and housing sectors of the FMP model. We note that the major sponsors of the project, Albert Ando (University of Pennsylvania) and Franco Modigliani (MIT), have in process a volume that will discuss the other sectors of the model and summarize the model as a whole. We have collected the discussions of these three sectors in this separate volume for several reasons. The individual markets stand closely connected both in terms of economic causality and in terms of the theoretical and econometric methodology necessary for their formulation and estimation. The analysis of each sector is relatively complex, and it takes a lengthy discussion to develop the sectors fully and to draw out the important relationships between sectors. Finally, the models of the three sectors have important implications for a number of timely questions concerning the effects of policy variables on residential construction.

Acknowledgements

As econometric models go, the FMP project has featured unusually close cooperation among participants. Virtually all of the work was done at three, or at the most, four, centers with an average of three or four people at each center. The model went through many incarnations with different people often being responsible for the different incarnations. There was a good deal of interaction among those people estimating equations and those people simulating different versions of the model. There was much experimentation with different versions of different sectors. And throughout the entire project, there were numerous conferences, short trips, letters, and telephone calls to insure close communication.

Given this close history, it is difficult to associate different sectors of the model, different variants of the underlying theory, and even different coefficients with the person basically responsible. Although each paper owes much on a general level to the cooperation, suggestions, and contributions of many participants, the authors have tried insofar as possible to single out those to whom they owe special thanks.

Certainly our greatest debt is to the three people who directed the project for most of its life span—Professor Franco Modigliani of MIT; Professor Albert Ando of the University of Pennsylvania; and Frank de Leeuw, formerly at the Federal Reserve Board in Washington and now at the Urban Institute. Each in his own way provided the intellectual insight, leadership ability, and sheer persistence necessary to keep the project going at its various regional offices.

We owe much to Jared Enzler of the Federal Reserve Board and Robert Rasche of Michigan State University, who so competently handled the actual operation and management of the model and, in addition, made considerable contributions in the way of work on the model, suggestions, and other assistance.

We are indebted also to Professor Gordon Sparks of Queen's College, who did much of the initial work on housing; Professors Patric Hendershott of Purdue and Harold Shapiro of Michigan, who did early work on savings deposits; and the many others who helped and made suggestions along the way, both at the Federal Reserve and at countless university seminars.

We would like to express a special word of gratitude to the senior staff in the Division of Research and Statistics at the Federal Reserve Board. This group, especially past and current Directors Daniel Brill and Charles Partee, and Lyle Gramley and James Pierce, have been instrumental in obtaining the Federal Reserve's financial support for the project. Perhaps even more importantly, they have contributed invaluable insights on the properties of the model. Without this sympathy and understanding on the part of the ultimate consumers of the model, the project could not have been nearly so successful.

E. M. G.
D. M. J.

Savings Deposits,
Mortgages, and Housing

1 The Main Considerations

EDWARD M. GRAMLICH and DWIGHT M. JAFFEE

The papers in this volume describe the formulation, estimation, and simulation properties of the savings deposits, mortgage market, and residential construction sectors of the Federal Reserve–MIT–Penn (FMP) econometric model. In most cases they were originally drafted as working papers and progress reports for the participants in the project. In preparation for publication, we have as editors revised the papers in terms of exposition and style, but we have not tampered with the technical content of the reports. In this form we hope that the papers may prove most useful to those studying the FMP model, and particularly these three sectors, in depth.

We also hope that the volume will remain useful to those primarily interested in a broader view of the workings of the three sectors and the implications of the results for questions of economic policy. It is primarily with this group in mind that we have attempted in this introductory chapter to outline the main considerations underlying the theoretical and empirical material of the individual papers. We have also tried to relate these sectors in general terms to the complete FMP model. We hope that this introduction, perhaps together with selective reading of the individual papers, will provide sufficient basis for an understanding of the policy implications of the simulation results discussed in the concluding chapter.

Objectives of the FMP Econometric Model

The FMP econometric model was originated in response to a need to understand better the workings of monetary policy and how it affects the real economy. From the standpoint of the Federal Reserve Board, the need manifested itself in the tremendous disparity of estimates of multipliers for the effect of open-market operations and other central-bank policies on the real economy. Whereas in 1965 most people would have agreed on the quantitative magnitude of fiscal policy multipliers, estimates of monetary policy multipliers varied widely between, for example, the estimates of Friedman and Meiselman [4] and the then existing econometric models.

1

From the standpoint of academic macroeconomic theorists, the need for a better understanding of monetary forces as they worked in the real economy manifested itself in a disturbing discrepancy between the monetary theory taught in classrooms and the monetary behavior reflected in other econometric models. Whereas classroom discussions delved into esoteric discussions of inside and outside money, risk and return and portfolio balance, the term structure of interest rates, and the effects of inflationary expectations on interest rates, 1965-vintage econometric models generally did no better than to take interest rates as one of many exogenous variables influencing the real economy.

In anything as comprehensive as an econometric model, the model builders will begin with numerous objectives in mind. They will want to improve on this model's treatment of this sector, that model's treatment of some other sector, and to adopt an entirely different approach to a third sector. In the FMP model many, though not all, of these practical objectives can be classified into five basic aims of the project:

1. To make consistent application of economic theory in deriving estimating equations.
2. To investigate more thoroughly than other models have done the way monetary policy instruments affect the monetary sector and the way in which monetary forces affect the economy.
3. To construct a more elaborate financial sector which uses supply and demand equations instead of reduced forms, which attempts to impose balance-sheet constraints and symmetry conditions on the estimating equations, and which makes a start at integrating the national income accounts of the Office of Business Economics with the flow of funds accounts of the Federal Reserve.
4. To deal more consistently and with a wider range of macroeconomic policy variables under the control of monetary and fiscal authorities.
5. To estimate accurately the short-run response patterns within the model, and to be sure that these short-run responses are consistent with reasonable long-run equilibrium properties.

Builders, sponsors, and users of the model will disagree on what weight to assign these five aims, but all will agree that all five are worthy goals and most will agree that it is worthwhile to try to accomplish all of them in one single econometric model.

This volume is not the place for an overall report on the FMP model and the degree to which it has or has not satisfied all of the above goals. Preliminary versions of the model have been reported in earlier papers (see Ando and Modigliani [1]; de Leeuw and Gramlich [2, 3]; and Rasche and

Shapiro [5]); and a forthcoming volume by Ando and Modigliani will summarize and evaluate most of this work. These goals have been mentioned here because they form a framework for evaluating each of the sectors discussed in this volume.

Savings Deposits, Mortgages, and Residential Construction in the FMP Model

If it was not apparent at the outset of the model project in 1965, it is certainly apparent now that the markets for savings deposits, mortgages, and residential construction form a crucial link in the chain that connects the monetary sector with the real sector. Although there are different views on whether monetary forces affect consumption or investment, and on whether these impacts operate through credit rationing or cost-of-capital channels, there now is a concensus that monetary forces have a strong impact, in some form, on residential construction. Thus one of the most important tasks in determining how forces affect the real economy is to determine exactly how monetary forces are transmitted through the supply and demand for savings deposits, the supply and demand for mortgages. and the supply and demand for houses.

To elaborate on this point, previous reports on the FMP model have demonstrated that this model has monetary multipliers a good deal more powerful than the monetary multipliers of other econometric models (see especially de Leeuw-Gramlich [3]). In part, these higher monetary multipliers come from treating the cost-of-capital channel more consistently and extensively than have other models. We have constructed expressions including rates of depreciation, property tax rates, corporate and income tax discounts, and expected rates of capital gains along with nominal interest rates. And we have tested these costs-of-capital in equations for all types of investment, consumer durables expenditures, and state and local capital expenditures. Housing, with its numerous relevant tax rates and discounts and its relatively good resale market, is a sector where this consistent cost-of-capital treatment probably makes a great deal of difference.

We also find that our higher monetary multipliers are partly due to our consideration of additional channels through which monetary forces can affect final demand. A second channel which is very powerful in the economy and in the housing sector is the stock market–net worth–consumption nexus—changes in monetary policy alter the present value of common stock in household net worth and also consumption. For our purposes, it is important to note that this change in permanent consumption leads to altered demand for savings deposits—both forces which in turn influence the level of residential construction.

A final channel through which monetary forces affect overall final demand expenditures is credit rationing. At this point in the work on the FMP model, the only conclusive evidence of a rationing effect is in the housing sector. We find that the ease with which builders can get mortgage commitments is an important determinant of new housing starts even apart from the general level of interest rates. Thus a properly specified linkage between savings deposits, mortgage markets, and residential construction is an essential feature of a comprehensive and consistent treatment of the impact of monetary forces on final demand.

The markets for savings deposits, mortgages, and residential construction are also instrumental in our attempt to build a true structural model of the financial and real sectors. In the first place, all three markets are developed in demand and supply terms. In the market for savings deposits, we envision depository institutions as setting the deposit rate to determine their supply of deposits, and households as setting the quantities of these deposits demanded on the basis of own and competing interest rates and other factors. The mortgage market envisions depository institutions as supplying mortgages on the basis of deposit levels and interest rates—with the supply mechanism decomposed into the new mortgage commitment stage and the gross flow of mortgages stage—and households as setting mortgage rates, at least in the short run, through their demand for mortgage liabilities. The housing market determines the implicit price for rental space by comparing the existing housing stock, or supply of housing services, with the demand for housing services. The quantity of new housing starts is evaluated by comparing the implicit asset price for houses with the supply price.

A second way in which we have tried to concentrate on structure in developing our markets for financial assets and liabilities is to rely extensively on risk-return portfolio balance considerations. Both for households and for depository institutions, we posit utility functions which make utility a positive function of return and a negative function of risk. We then transform these utility functions into estimating equations for the demand and supply for savings deposits and the demand and supply for mortgages. In some cases the implications of the utility function analysis are that the demand functions for a range of liquid assets should feature balance-sheet constraints, symmetric cross-elasticities of demand, and other prior constraints on the coefficient estimates. In these cases, we have paid attention to our theory and have imposed the coefficient restrictions in our statistical estimation. In other cases, we have used our statistical estimates of some equations to constrain the coefficients of other equations, also as suggested by the theory. In still other cases, we have been forced to use nonlinear estimation procedures to adhere strictly to our theory. Whatever technique we have used, we have often obtained results that differ substantially from those to be derived from unrestricted least squares or reduced form estimation. Econometricians may argue over the merits of these decisions, but we hope there is no argument over the fact that the decisions reflect our commitment to building a structural model.

The policy relevance of our model can be demonstrated by the range of macroeconomic policy variables with which we deal in the three sectors. In the savings deposit sector we deal with policy actions that alter the net worth of households, their disposable income, ceiling rates on time deposits and savings and loan deposits, and the rate on Federal Home Loan Bank Board (FHLBB) advances to savings and loan associations. In the mortgage sector we deal with FNMA holdings of mortgages, the quantity of FHLBB advances, and changes in commercial bank reserve requirements along with the variables which influence savings deposits. In the housing sector, we deal with property and income tax rates, accelerated depreciation provisions, and FHA ceiling rates, in addition to the variables which affect the other sectors. We should also emphasize that the structure of the underlying model is designed in such a way that in some cases it is possible for the policy maker to insert his own policy in the model and simulate its effect even if the policy instrument has not existed to this point. For example, since we use an explicit expression for the opportunity cost of owning a house, policy makers can compute the effect of an investment credit for residential construction or other similar policies simply by making appropriate adjustments to the opportunity cost expression.

It is often the case that the more obscure policies with which we deal are not found to have much independent influence, and so for practical purposes the users of this model will be forced to fall back on monetary and fiscal policies as the way to get things done. But this is not to deny the value of a structural model for evaluating the effects of various policy measures. After all, the effects of secondary policies will never be quantified and evaluated unless we deal with them explicitly in a model.

We see then that the sectors dealing with savings deposits, mortgages, and residential construction do play an important role in the achievement of all of the basic goals of the FMP model.

Theoretical Framework

One of the virtues of this model of savings deposits, mortgages, and housing is that we have imposed a consistent theory of behavior on all groups in all sectors. It might be useful, therefore, to spend some time at the outset describing in broad terms how each group behaves and how they interact in the model.

Households

The important independent variables for households are disposable income, initial net worth, initial stocks of tangible capital, and nominal and real interest rates. Consumers determine their permanent consumption on the basis of current and lagged income and net worth. Permanent consumption is defined to include the imputed services from houses and consumer durables rather than the expenditures on these items. Movements in permanent .consumption alter the demand for rental space and the housing stock as well as the demand for services from and stocks of consumer durable goods. The demand for money also depends on current income, the proxy for transactions needs, and interest rates. Having made these decisions, households are then free to allocate the remainder of their net worth to assets and liabilities on the basis of institutional constraints, risk, and return.

We assume that collateral requirements set a ceiling but not a floor on the portion of new housing expenditures which can be financed by mortgages. We also assume that as the housing stock increases in value with price inflation, households refinance these capital gains, but only very slowly. For both reasons, the mortgage stock is only loosely related to the housing stock in the short run, and at any point in time the aggregate mortgage–value ratio is very definitely interest sensitive.

Households determine quantities of savings deposits—defined to include life insurance reserves, savings and loan deposits, mutual savings bank deposits, and passbook savings deposits at commercial banks—on the basis of net worth, own and competing interest rates, expected rates of inflation, and income. The latter variable enters because savings deposits are found to be a supplementary source of liquidity. We also find that because of transactions costs, increases in net worth due to new saving influence savings deposits more promptly than increases due to capital gains in the stock market. The model views savings deposits as competing with all other assets and liabilities in net worth—demands for common stock, bonds and bills, consumer and mortgage credit. Since savings deposits are a rather small portion of net worth, and since the determinants of nonsavings-deposit demands are difficult to represent empirically, we have not explained the whole set of demand functions, but only the subset dealing with savings deposits. Knowledge of competing asset demands guides us in choosing relevant opportunity costs, in making symmetry condition constraints, and in rejecting unreasonable coefficients; but we have not explicitly used balance-sheet constraints.

Depository Institutions

Depository institutions are assumed to be price-takers in their asset markets and price-setters for their deposit liabilities. They strive to maximize profits by varying their asset composition in response to movements in market rates and by varying deposit rates.

The deposit rate determination model makes desired deposit rates a function of relevant asset rates and the parameters of the demand function for these deposits. The parameters of the demand function enter because institutions should respond more forcefully to changes in deposit rates of very close substitutes than to changes in deposit rates of remote substitutes. We might try to measure these responses on the basis of observations of intermediary behavior, but this route is closed by multicollinearity between competing interest rates. As an alternative, we constrain the deposit rate coefficients with coefficients estimated from our demand functions, thus integrating the supply and demand side of this market.

We deal with the effects of ceiling deposit rates in a fairly elaborate way. Ceiling rates are assumed to have two distinct impacts on actual deposit rates: (1) the definitional effect, according to which ceilings depress actual rates by forcing banks who would otherwise pay more than the ceiling to pay only the ceiling rate; and (2) an oligopolistic trigger effect, according to which changes in ceiling rates inspire a belief that competitors will raise deposit rates even if deposit rates are not initially at the ceiling level. We deal with the definitional effect by assuming actual deposit rates are distributed triangularly about the observed mean, estimating the parameters of the triangle nonlinearly, and then combining hypothetical desired rates in the absence of ceilings with ceilings on the basis of the triangular distribution to determine actual deposit rates.

The supply of mortgages by depository institutions is based upon the level of deposits and various interest rates. Institutions either make direct mortgage loans or they make mortgage commitments and allow commitments to mature into mortgages on the basis of partly institutional, partly economic factors. The most important decision variable in this process would be new mortgage commitments, but because of the lack of quarterly commitments data for savings and loan associations and mutual savings banks, we have to fall back on an explanation of outstanding commitments. In the case of commercial banks, we do not have any commitments data at all and thus are forced to use flows of outstanding mortgage stocks. FNMA is assumed to reduce demand pressures on the mortgage rates by adding its net holdings of mortgages to mortgages held by depository institutions and thus supplying a portion of total mortgage demand exogenously.

Relationships Within the Three Sectors

Because the discussion that follows in Chapter 2 through Chapter 6 emphasizes the structure of the savings deposit, mortgage, and housing sectors by themselves, it is worthwhile to outline briefly the main relationships that exist within the three sectors. These relationships are discussed in more detail in Chapter 7.

There are two links, acting simultaneously, between the savings deposit sector and the mortgage sector. The causal link running from the savings sector to the mortgage sector is the level of savings deposits at the principal financial intermediaries. These savings deposits are transformed into mortgages by the financial intermediaries, taking into account liquidity considerations and the yields available on alternative investment assets. In equilibrium, this relationship may be based on a quite straightforward application of the principles of financial intermediation and portfolio management. However, the relationship is significantly complicated in two respects by short-run dynamic considerations. First, intermediaries may respond to new deposits with some lag, and thus the rate of flow of deposits as well as the level of the stock may influence their mortgage activity. Second, an important proportion of new mortgage loans are anticipated by "advance commitments" which the intermediaries issue to potential demanders. Thus the main impact of savings deposit flows within the model is on the commitments of the intermediaries, although there does remain a direct link to the mortgage flows themselves.

The causal link running from the mortgage market to the savings deposit sector is the mortgage interest rate and/or the mortgage flows. The mortgage interest rate exerts its influence on the deposit sector as a determinant of the rate paid by the financial intermediaries on their deposits. This feedback is essentially a stabilizing influence on the two markets. For example, starting from a position of equilibrium, suppose that the mortgage interest rate rises. This will cause the deposit rate at the intermediaries to rise, and thus call forth a greater flow of deposits from the household sector. The inflow of deposits will then be transformed into an increased supply of mortgages and this will tend to reduce the mortgage rate toward its initial equilibrium.

The influence of mortgage flows on savings deposits works in a similar fashion, although the impact is more important in the short run. In this case, the emphasis is on temporary deviations between the growth rate of mortgages and the growth rate of deposits. For example, if mortgages suddenly were to grow less rapidly, the intermediaries would respond by reducing the deposit rate in order to slow deposit growth.

The mortgage and housing sectors of the model also interact simultaneously. The main influence of the mortgage market on the housing sector is the effect of the mortgage interest rate on housing demand. The mortgage interest rate is one of the important components of the cost of capital for investment in housing—that is, the higher this rate, the lower will be housing investment. In addition, there is also a direct link between flows in the mortgage market, nonprice rationing in the mortgage market, and the housing sector. As already noted, this influence is specified by including the flows of mortgage commitments in the housing demand equation.

Finally, the housing sector influences the mortgage sector through the effect of the stock and flow of housing on mortgage demand. As with most feedback links in the model, the effect of housing on the mortgage market is a stabilizing factor. For example, if the demand for housing and thus the housing stock should exogenously increase, then the demand for mortgages would tend to rise also. Within the mortgage market, an increase in demand forces the mortgage interest rate to rise. Then, completing the circle, the increase in the mortgage interest rate acts on the housing sector as an increase in the cost of capital and offsets the initial increase in housing demand.

Relationships Between the Three Sectors and
the Complete FMP Model

It is also helpful to note the main links between the three sectors discussed here and the remainder of the FMP model. First, considering the variables of the FMP model that effect the three sectors, the main link is the net worth of the household sector. The net worth variables, and related flow variables such as disposable income and savings, affect the savings deposit sectors as explanatory elements of the demand for savings. Similar net worth and income variables also influence the demand for housing in the housing sector. These variables do not, however, have direct impacts on the mortgage sector, since their influence is taken into account by the deposit and housing variables that influence the mortgage market.

A second main influence of the other sectors of the FMP model on our three sectors is based on the interest yield on competing assets. The most important interest rate in this respect is the yield on corporate bonds, which influences each of the three sectors. In addition, other interest rates such as the Treasury bill rate, commercial loan rate, municipal bond rate, and Federal Reserve and Federal Home Loan Bank discount rates affect specific relationships in the three sectors.

There is also a long list of miscellaneous variables within the FMP model which influence behavior in our three sectors. These variables include such things as social security contributions, demographic forces, and various mortgage market and housing sector policy control variables.

The effect of our three sectors on the other sectors of the FMP model is somewhat simpler to discuss. The most obvious and important link is the role of housing investment as a component of aggregate demand. Aggregate demand, of course, determines the equilibrium level of income, which in turn determines the various income and savings flows that influence the savings deposit and housing sectors. Demand also determines the level of market interest rates, which also feeds into our sectors. Thus the path of causation is indeed simultaneous.

There are also less important feedback links running from our three sectors to the other sectors of the FMP model. As one example, the mortgage rate determined in these sectors plays an important role in determining overall credit flows within the model. As another example, the commercial loan interest rate is determined in the FMP model partly as a function of the savings deposits at commercial banks. This commercial loan rate in turn has an impact on several relationships in the savings deposits, mortgage, and housing sectors. A more complete discussion of the feedback links of the FMP model will be provided in the forthcoming volume of Ando and Modigliani.

Plan of the Book

Since it is usually a laborious task to read about econometric models, even small sections of them, we have tried to present our sectors in as convenient a manner as is possible. In the first place, each of the contributing papers is self-contained. Thus one can read about one sector without having to read other parts of the book to follow the argument. Secondly, all the final equations used or discussed in the book are presented in Appendix B. This will provide a handy reference for the reader who may have trouble finding equations referred to in the text. Appendix A provides a glossary of symbols and a data directory. The final specifications for all estimated relationships are stated in the notation developed for the FMP project so this volume can be read along with other reports on the model. In developing the theoretical arguments in some cases, however, a simplified notation has been used.

The chapters of the book are arranged according to the recursive ordering in the model. The second chapter, written by Gramlich and David Hulett, considers the demand and supply for savings deposits. This chapter derives both demand and supply equations in terms of a risk-return maximization model and combines the parameters of the demand function with those of the supply function in a way discussed above. The demand equations feature rigid application of symmetry constraints on the interest rate coefficients. The supply equations feature a detailed treatment of the effect of ceiling rates.

The third and fourth chapters provide an alternative version for the savings sector. In Chapter 3, Franco Modigliani develops a model of the demand for savings deposits that emphasizes the dynamic aspects of household adjustment to disequilibrium conditions. In Chapter 4, Myron Slovin considers the supply of savings deposits by analyzing the rate-setting behavior of financial intermediaries. Slovin's equations are estimated to be consistent with Modigliani's savings demand model. Taken together, the Modigliani–Slovin sector can be compared with the Gramlich–Hulett sector, and this comparison is undertaken in terms of their simulation properties in Chapter 7.

We should at this point indicate why we include here two separate savings deposit sectors. In econometric models, as in econometrics generally, prior specification often turns out to be of fundamental importance in shaping the final results. One investigator may concentrate on explaining the variance of the dependent variable, while another might stress the need for statistical estimates consistent with underlying economic theory. One investigator may feel that certain variables are of fundamental importance and do everything to include them in the regression equations, while another may omit them by assumption. In one case certain variables are specified to have long-run importance, while in another to have only a short-run effect. In all of these respects, econometrics can be a very subjective matter. Thus we feel that those interested in savings deposits may want to sample two different offerings. As we state in Chapter 7, it is impossible to say objectively which sector is better, or even works better—this should be judged by individual readers.

The fifth chapter is written by Jaffee and discusses the supply and demand for mortgages. The supply side deals with the behavior of depository institutions and features a detailed treatment of the relationship between new commitments, net and gross flows of mortgages, and the effect of deposit flows and interest rates on all of these relationships. The demand side deals with household demand for new mortgages on new houses and the speed with which households either repay or refinance their mortgages on old houses.

The sixth chapter, by John Kalchbrenner, discusses the housing sector. The discussion distinguishes between the demand and supply for rental space, which determines the implicit rental price, and the demand for home ownership, which determines the implicit asset price. New houses are then constructed or not constructed according to the relationship between the implicit asset price and the supply price, or construction costs. In addition, builders are responsive to credit rationing as reflected by the ease of obtaining new mortgage commitments as determined in the mortgage sector.

The seventh chapter, by the editors, presents simulation results of the three sectors combined. Simulations of individual sectors are provided as needed by the authors in the detailed discussions to illustrate the dynamic tracking ability or the sectoral properties of individual sectors. The simulations in the seventh chapter, then, illustrate the tracking ability and properties of the three sectors combined. Given the uses to which we hope this model will be put, we also focus on the response of these sectors to important savings deposit and housing policy instruments either used in the past or under consideration for the future. Finally, it is worth repeating that appendixes A and B contain the final specifications and estimates of all the equations and a glossary of the notation used for variables in these equations.

References

[1] Ando, Albert, and Franco Modigliani. "Econometric Analysis of Stabilization Policies." *American Economic Review* 59 (May 1969).

[2] de Leeuw, Frank, and Edward M. Gramlich. "The Federal Reserve-MIT Econometric Model." *Federal Reserve Bulletin* 54 (January 1968).

[3] de Leeuw, Frank, and Edward M. Gramlich. "The Channels of Monetary Policy." *Federal Reserve Bulletin* 55 (June 1969).

[4] Friedman, Milton, and David Meiselman. "The Relative Stability of Monetary Velocity and the Investment Multiplier—The United States, 1897–1948." In *Stabilization Policies*. Commission on Money and Credit, 1963.

[5] Rasche, Robert, and Harold Shapiro. "The FRB–MIT Econometric Model: Its Special Features." *American Economic Review* 58 (May 1968).

2

The Demand for and Supply of Savings Deposits

EDWARD M. GRAMLICH and DAVID T. HULETT

It is often suggested that the strength of monetary forces in influencing final demand depends fundamentally on conditions in the market for savings deposits. Disequilibrium in the market for savings deposits is alleged to be fully as important as rises in market interest rates themselves in bringing about any desired degree of monetary restraint. This belief in the significance of conditions in the market for savings deposits has been instrumental in shaping Federal Reserve Board, F.D.I.C., and Federal Home Loan Bank Board ceiling deposit rate policies, and it has also been the basis for numerous policy proposals that attempt to insulate housing expenditures from monetary movements.

The attention that markets for savings deposits are receiving points up the need for econometric studies of these markets. In this paper we report on one such attempt—the analysis of the demand for and supply of savings deposits in the FMP econometric model. The paper investigates the market for time deposits at commercial banks, deposits at savings and loan associations, mutual savings bank deposits, and life insurance reserves less policy loans. We try to determine how these deposits and the interest rates on them react to external forces such as income, prices, market interest rates and deposit ceiling rates using quarterly postwar time-series regressions. We then examine the properties of this model with dynamic simulation experiments.

By now there have been numerous empirical studies of the demand and supply for savings deposits.[1] Our study is not unrelated or completely dissimilar to these earlier studies, but we think it does have important new features. For one thing, we develop the estimating equations both for household demands and financial intermediary supplies from portfolio balance principles somewhat more directly than previous studies have done. Secondly, we impose more prior constraints on our coefficient estimates than has been done in previous studies. Thirdly, we relate the household demand

The authors would like to thank all members of the FMP project, especially Jared Enzler, Dwight Jaffee, Franco Modigliani, and Myron Slovin for suggestions and other assistance.
[1] Some well-known examples include Feige [8], de Leeuw [6], Goldfeld [10, 11], Silber [22], Chetty [5].

13

equations and the intermediary supply equations more closely than in previous explanations of the behavior of savings deposit markets. Fourthly, we have made some innovations concerning the treatment of deposit rate ceilings. And finally, we present long-run dynamic simulation experiments of the inter-related demand and supply equations. These simulations offer a middle ground between those studies which present regression results but do not simulate interactive behavior, and those studies which simulate an entire financial sector without looking at the behavior of savings deposit markets in isolation.

Our explanation of the demand and supply for savings deposits relies on standard portfolio balance theory. We postulate that both households in determining their demands for assets and depository institutions in deter-mining their own portfolio behavior gain utility from their expectations of interest income and lose utility from uncertainty about this income or asset capital values. Carrying out the analysis in a manner first developed by Markowitz [18] and Tobin [23], and later refined by Schoner [21], Freund [9], Parkin [19], and Hendershott [14], yields estimating equations which contain coefficient restrictions dictated by the risk–return model.

Although these restrictions are a common feature of theoretical treatments of portfolio behavior, to this point there has been little attempt to make use of them empirically.[2] We find this situation somewhat surprising because one might expect notable gains in efficiency from using restrictions in time-series studies of portfolio behavior. Coefficient restrictions should tend to minimize estimating difficulties caused by multicollinearity between highly correlated independent variables such as interest rates—an important advantage in studies already severely disadvantaged by autocorrelation, errors in variables, and a paucity of observations. Rather than to employ an unconstrained estimation scheme in the hope that the wonders of econometrics would overcome these statistical difficulties and provide reasonable coefficients, we have instead constrained our coefficient estimates to conform to underlying risk–return theory. We can see below the extent to which imposing these coefficient restrictions worsens the fit of the equations, both in estimation and in simulation.

This paper contains three sections. The first discusses both the theoretical model and the statistical estimates of the demand for savings deposits, defined here as passbook savings deposits at commercial banks (excluding large CDs), savings and loan shares, mutual savings bank deposits, and life insurance reserves less policy loans. The second section discusses the model and esti-

---

[2] The exceptions we know of are Feige [8], Parkin [19], Hendershott [15], and Gramlich and Kalchbrenner [13]. Brainard and Tobin [3] have made a widely read complaint about this state of affairs.

mates of the supply side of this market, that is, the rate-setting behavior of depository institutions. The final section then gives dynamic simulation results of this model in which the demand and supply equations are allowed to interact simultaneously over a long period of time. We also present experimental multiplier simulations under the assumption that incomes, interest rates, and ceiling rates follow paths other than was actually the case.

Household Demand for Savings Deposits

The Model

The model for developing household demand functions for savings deposits follows the general outline of the risk–return portfolio balance analysis, amended at certain points to deal with the dynamics of portfolio adjustment. We first assume the existence of a hierarchy in the net worth allocation decision of households. Although, in principle, households might be expected to allocate net worth to all assets simultaneously, in practice some assets fill needs which might be considered of a higher order than the needs satisfied by other assets. An obvious parallel would be in the distinction between subsistence and other needs in consumer demand theory.[3] We deal with the recursive nature of the allocation decision by allowing households to allocate net worth first to the higher-order assets and liabilities, which we term prior claims, and then to uncommitted assets and liabilities. Prior claims may be sensitive to financial opportunity costs; but once the household has decided how much of the asset to buy, this portion of the portfolio is considered to be predetermined for the current period. The assets we view as prior claims are stocks of consumer durables and houses and stocks of money. Durable stocks are dependent on demographic considerations, income, initial stocks, price expectations, and so forth, with consumer credit terms and mortgages rates entering into decisions with a time lag. Money stocks depend on transactions needs or current income, and, again, interest rates as a measure of the opportunity cost. Having made these prior decisions, the household is then free to allocate the rest of its portfolio to savings deposits, liabilities (essentially deciding how much of the stock of durables and houses to finance on credit), other financial assets, and common stock according to risk–return considerations. In this paper we are concerned only with this latter decision.

Households are assumed to vary asset holdings so as to maximize utility,

---

[3] Brown and Heien [4] have also used this notion of a recursive decision process between committed and uncommitted goods.

subject to the constraint that the sum of all controllable net assets is identically equal to unclaimed net worth. Net worth in this context is total net worth less prior claims, and liabilities are treated as negative assets. For convenience, the entire analysis will be made homogenous in net worth, as if investors attempt to maximize the rates of return on net worth instead of the total dollar value of returns. For the n asset case, the appropriate definitions are as follows:

(i) The net worth constraint:

$$1 = i'A$$

with i' a $1 \times n$ row vector of ones and A an $n \times 1$ column vector of the n assets, each divided by unclaimed net worth.

(ii) The expected rate of return on net worth:

$$\overline{Y} = r'A$$

with r' a $1 \times n$ row vector of expected rates of return on the n assets, defined to include capital gains as well as interest income.

(iii) The variance of the rate of return:

$$S_Y = A'SA$$

with S an $n \times n$ variance–covariance matrix of expected rates of return, or

$$\begin{bmatrix} S_{11} & S_{12} & \cdots & S_{1n} \\ S_{21} & S_{22} & \cdots & S_{2n} \\ \vdots & \vdots & \vdots & \vdots \\ S_{n1} & S_{n2} & \cdots & S_{nn} \end{bmatrix}$$

Following the authors cited above, we let the utility of the return on net worth be given by the function

$$U(Y) = 1 - e^{-aY} \tag{2-1}$$

where $a > 0$ measures the household's aversion to risk, which is assumed to be constant (see Adler [1]). Differentiating equation (2-1) twice with respect to Y shows that this utility function implies positive but declining marginal utility of returns.

If Y is distributed normally with mean $\overline{Y}$ and standard deviation S_Y, the probability density function can be written as

$$P(Y) = b \exp\left[-\frac{(Y - \overline{Y})^2}{2S_Y} \right] \tag{2-2}$$

and expected utility is calculated as

$$E[U(Y)] = \int_{-\infty}^{\infty} U(Y)P(Y)\,dY = k \int_{-\infty}^{\infty} (1 - e^{-aY}) \exp\left[-\frac{(Y - \bar{Y})^2}{2S_Y} \right] dY$$

(2-3)

The result of this integration is (see Hendershott [13])

$$E[U(Y)] = 1 - \exp a\left(\frac{aS_Y}{2} - \bar{Y} \right)$$

(2-4)

which is maximized when

$$\bar{Y} - \frac{a}{2} S_Y = \bar{Y} - KS_Y$$

is minimized.

The optimization problem then becomes one of maximizing

$$\pi = r'A - KA'SA + \lambda(1 - i'A)$$

(2-5)

with respect to each of the n assets and λ. The first-order conditions are

$$\begin{bmatrix} \dfrac{\partial \pi}{\partial A} \\[2mm] \dfrac{\partial \pi}{\partial \lambda} \end{bmatrix} = \begin{bmatrix} r \\ 1 \end{bmatrix} - \begin{bmatrix} 2KS & i \\ i' & 0 \end{bmatrix} \begin{bmatrix} A \\ \lambda \end{bmatrix} = \begin{bmatrix} 0 \\ 0 \end{bmatrix}$$

(2-6)

where $\partial \pi/\partial A$ is of order $n \times 1$, $\partial \pi/\partial \lambda$ is of order 1×1, λ is a scalar, and the zero columns are of appropriate order. The second-order condition is that

$$\begin{bmatrix} -2KS & -i \\ -i' & 0 \end{bmatrix}$$

is negative definite. The reduced-form solution of (2-5) is

$$\begin{bmatrix} A \\ \lambda \end{bmatrix} = \begin{bmatrix} 2KS & i \\ i' & 0 \end{bmatrix}^{-1} \begin{bmatrix} r \\ 1 \end{bmatrix}$$

(2-7)

and by using a block inversion technique we obtain a solution similar except in minor details to that of Parkin:

$$\begin{bmatrix} A \\ \lambda \end{bmatrix} = \begin{bmatrix} \dfrac{1}{2K} S^{-1} - \dfrac{1}{2K} S^{-1}i(i'S^{-1}i)^{-1}i'S^{-1} & S^{-1}i(i'S^{-1}i)^{-1} \\[2mm] (i'S^{-1}i)^{-1}i'S^{-1} & -2K(i'S^{-1}i)^{-1} \end{bmatrix} \begin{bmatrix} r \\ 1 \end{bmatrix}$$

(2-8)

This gives the reduced-form asset demand functions:

$$A = \frac{1}{2K}\left(S^{-1} - \frac{S^{-1}ii'S^{-1}}{i'S^{-1}i}\right)r + \frac{S^{-1}i}{i'S^{-1}i} \qquad (2\text{-}9)$$

Equation (2-9) makes the demand for any asset a function of own and competing rates of return, with the coefficients depending on the variance–covariance matrix of expected rates of return. It should be pointed out that even if the own variance and covariance terms are rather small for some asset, which might be expected at the savings deposit end of the asset spectrum, the many interest rate coefficients would not disappear since they are also determined by uncertainty about the rates of return on other assets in the net worth allocation decision. We should also mention that the elements of the variance–covariance matrix may depend upon nonrate variables. If, for example, transactions needs were to rise, this might affect the variance of the expected rate of return (defined to include capital gains) on assets which could not easily be sold for full value on short notice. We must deal with this complication in our empirical work.

The asset demand equations in (2–9) have several interesting characteristics. First, if we premultiply the equation by i', we find that the column sum of the constants is unity while the column sum of the coefficients for each interest rate is zero. These are the balance-sheet restrictions discussed by Brainard and Tobin [3]. Secondly, we can postmultiply the interest rate coefficients by i to get a column vector of zeros, implying that the row sum of interest rate coefficients in each asset demand equation is also zero. Thirdly, we see that the matrix of interest rate coefficient is symmetric, that is, $\partial A_i/\partial r_j = \partial A_j/\partial r_i$ for all i and j.[4] These symmetry conditions are exactly analogous to those many people have established for the substitution effect in consumer demand theory.[5]

There is some ambiguity concerning the expected signs of the interest rate coefficients. Those along the principal diagonal, corresponding to the "own" rate in each equation, can be shown to be positive. Together with the zero column sums, this implies that an increase in the ith rate leads to an increase in the ith asset share and to a decline in the sum of all other asset shares. The off-diagonal coefficients will be unambiguously negative only if all covariances between rates of return are set equal to zero. This analysis does

---

[4] This proposition can be demonstrated in exactly the same way that Parkin did: S is symmetric and therefore S^{-1} is symmetric. $(i'S^{-1}i)$ is a scaler. Since S^{-1} is symmetric, $S^{-1}i$ is a transpose of $i'S^{-1}$, hence $S^{-1}ii'S^{-1}$ is symmetric. Then the difference between two symmetric matrices, S^{-1} and $S^{-1}ii'S^{-1}/i'S^{-1}i$ is also symmetric. The Royama and Hamada model [20] has similar properties.

[5] See Barten [2]. Notice that our model ignores the connection between interest income and changes in net worth and therefore suppresses all income effects.

not rule out the theoretical possibility that covariances between certain rates of return are such that some assets may be risk complements instead of substitutes, which would imply that some off-diagonal coefficients are positive instead of negative.[6]

Empirical Modifications

Equation (2-9) makes the proportion of net worth held in the form of various assets and liabilities a positive function of own rates of return, and, subject to the qualifications just mentioned, a negative function of competing rates of return, a positive function of forces tending to reduce the risks of holding the own asset, and a negative function of forces tending to reduce the risks of holding other assets. Although the possibility of asset complementarity is of interest in understanding the theoretical model, it is not likely to be important for savings deposits, where the covariance terms could be expected to be relatively unimportant. Hence, we have generally ignored the possibility of complementarity in our own work and have looked for strict substitution between all savings deposits and between savings deposits and other assets. In those cases where the preliminary empirical work indicated asset complementarity, we have constrained the relevant rate coefficients to equal zero.

We have also restricted our attention to the four rows of (2-9) that correspond to the four asset markets we are examining. This implies that we will not explicitly be using the balance-sheet restrictions described above. We could have used these restrictions only by including equations for all of the many omitted assets and liabilities, an extension which would take us rather far afield. But even though we estimate only four rows of the matrix (2-9), we must of course deal with all the columns in these rows—that is, we must look for interest rate effects corresponding to the assets whose demand functions we are not explicitly estimating as well as to those we are estimating. Thus, we must impose the zero-row sum constraints for each estimated equation.

The important questions that must be answered in estimating (2-9) concern the competing asset rates which seem to be most important statistically—the nonrate variables that may alter the variance–covariance matrix of expected returns and hence the coefficients of (2-9) and the dynamic pattern by which investors respond to changes in interest rates. We now take up these questions in turn.

Concerning the rates of return that should be included in (2-9), we have found that the relevant rates on omitted assets and liabilities may be

---

[6] Parkin [19] elaborates on these points.

summarized by a long rate (the corporate bond rate) which represents the opportunity cost of consumer credit, mortgages, and long-term bonds; a short rate (the three-month Treasury bill rate) which represents the opportunity cost of holding short-term assets and liabilities; and a proxy for the expected rate of inflation which measures alterations in the opportunity cost of holding nominal and real assets during inflationary periods. To the extent that it is measurable, the return on common stock may be approximated by the long rate and the inflationary expectations term. We have found that there was little additional explanatory power to be gained by inclusion of explicit stock market variables such as the dividend–price ratio or the earnings–price ratio.

We have also found some nonrate variables to be important determinants of the allocation of net worth into savings deposits. These nonrate variables affect asset demands by altering the variance–covariance matrix of expected returns, and hence, both the constants and interest rate coefficients of equation (2-9). To deal with the latter requirement we would have to include in the estimated version of (2-9) not only all nonrate variables, but also the product of each nonrate variable times each interest rate, with all variables obeying row and symmetry condition constraints. This is clearly an unmanageable task in a quarterly postwar time-series regression. We have instead adopted the convenient approximation that the nonrate variables influence the constants but not the interest rate coefficients.

Three nonrate variables appear to be especially important:

1. Disposable Income Deflated by Unclaimed Net Worth. This variable has two possible rationales. It could explain the demand for savings deposits as a liquidity supplement to monetary transactions balances, in the same sense that aggregate income explains the overall demand for money. Alternatively, it could represent a dynamic phenomenon whereby some current income and saving is temporarily allocated to liquid assets in the expectation of further portfolio shifts. If the former were true, disposable income should work well; if the latter were true, current saving should work even better. Since saving did not work as well, we are inclined to accept the former interpretation. In either case, current income or saving would be expected to increase the proportion of savings deposits in unclaimed net worth at the expense of other less liquid assets and liabilities.[7] We have deflated by unclaimed net worth to insure proper dimensionality.

---

[7] In his contribution to the Brookings-SSRC Econometric Model [6], de Leeuw also used current income rather than savings as the short-run constraint variable. While Kardouche is critical of this procedure, his own attempt to place savings in this role was only partly successful [17, pp. 66–68].

2. Recent Capital Gains on Assets in Net Worth.   Here, again, we deflate by unclaimed net worth. In the long run, increments to unclaimed net worth from any source add equally to savings deposits and other assets. But since capital gains on unclaimed net worth are received in illiquid form (mainly as stock market appreciation), transactions costs prevent households from adjusting savings deposits immediately in response to these increments to net worth. Thus we would expect the ratio of savings deposits to unclaimed net worth to be lower, the greater are recent capital gains.

3. Inverse of Time.   The time trend corrects the constants for secular changes arising from improvements in insurance for savings and loan associations and geographical shifts in population which have probably lowered savings and loan transactions costs over the period with which we are concerned. The variable is nonlinear to insure that this past trend will automatically become less important in the future.[8]

We must then consider dynamic factors in the response of investors to changes in interest rates. Households do not react instantaneously to changes in interest rates, and they do invest on the basis of expected rates of return on savings deposits and all other assets (one source of own rate uncertainty). For both reasons, we have treated the interest rate variables as distributed lags of current and past interest rates, though to conserve degrees of freedom we have only estimated lag patterns with simple shapes.

A final empirical consideration that has become very important in recent years is the difficulty of measuring appropriate marginal deposit rates. For three of the four assets we are considering, depository institutions have responded to high market interest rates by offering special high-interest accounts—commercial banks have offered consumer CD's, and savings and loan associations and mutual savings banks have offered their own special accounts. In each case, the time series is far too short for us to treat these new types of deposits separately, and we are forced to aggregate interest rates on various types of deposits at an institution to yield an appropriate overall rate. We did not want to aggregate by weighting specific rates by average stocks of

---

[8] It could be argued that the utility analysis discussed above is strictly appropriate only for a microunit. When applying such a utility function to an aggregate of units, it may not necessarily be true that interest income is added to all savings deposits at the prevailing net worth allocation rate, as we are assuming in omitting an explicit interest variable. Transactions costs might cause this income to be allocated temporarily to the asset on which it was earned. Interest income could also redistribute wealth among units and change overall portfolio shares even if each individual unit had symmetric substitution effects. We have tried to test for aggregation problems of this sort by including interest income on savings deposits as a separate explanatory variable, but this variable seemed to be so collinear with the basic interest rates that we eventually had to abandon the attempt.

deposits because the stocks of these new types of deposits would be so small as to make special account rates virtually irrelevant. The rapid growth of these special accounts indicates that their rates have been anything but irrelevant in explaining deposit flows. We have instead tried to approximate the marginal importance of special accounts by constructing a rate variable which includes as one component the rate on special deposits since their introduction at each institution, with the weight for this special deposit component being the average share of special account inflows from that point to 1970.

We can summarize all of these points by rewriting equation (2-9) in terms of the specific model we are estimating:

$$
\begin{bmatrix} A_1 \\ A_2 \\ A_3 \\ A_4 \end{bmatrix} = \frac{1}{VU} \begin{bmatrix} MIS \\ MSL \\ MMS \\ MTP \end{bmatrix} = \beta \begin{bmatrix} \mathscr{L}RI \\ \mathscr{L}RSL \\ \mathscr{L}RMS \\ \mathscr{L}RTP \\ \mathscr{L}RTB \\ \mathscr{L}RCB \\ \mathscr{L}PDOT \end{bmatrix} + \Gamma \begin{bmatrix} \dfrac{YD}{VU} \\ \dfrac{\mathscr{L}CG}{VU} \\ 1 \\ \dfrac{1}{TIME} \\ 1 \end{bmatrix} + \rho \begin{bmatrix} u_1(-1) \\ u_2(-1) \\ u_3(-1) \\ u_4(-1) \end{bmatrix} \quad (2\text{-}10)
$$

where
   MIS = life insurance reserves less policy loans (current dollars)
   MSL = savings and loan deposits (current dollars)
   MMS = mutual savings bank deposits (current dollars)
   MTP = commercial bank time deposits less large CD's, member banks (current dollars)
   VU = unclaimed net worth, or net worth less demand deposits, currency, stocks of houses, and stocks of consumer durables (all in current dollars)
   YD = disposable income at quarterly rates (current dollars)
   CG = recent capital gains on unclaimed net worth (current dollars)
   $TIME$ = one in 1947:1, increments by one every quarter thereafter
   $PDOT$ = rate of price inflation of consumption price deflator (percent per annum)
   RCB = Moody's Aaa corporate bond rate (percent per annum)
   RTB = U.S. three-month Treasury bill rate (percent per annum)
   RI = rate of return on life insurance reserves or cost of life insurance policy loans (percent per annum—assumed to be constant at 5.00 throughout the period)
   RSL = weighted average of rate of return on regular savings and loan

deposits and special accounts at savings and loans (percent per annum)

RMS = weighted average of rate of return on regular and special mutual savings bank deposits (percent per annum)

RTP = weighted average of rate of return on passbook savings accounts and consumer CDs at commercial banks (percent per annum)

$\mathscr{L}$ = distributed lag operator

β = 4 × 7 matrix of interest rate coefficients

Γ = 4 × 4 matrix of nonrate coefficients

$u_i(-1)$ = previous period residual in each equation

ρ = coefficient of autoregression

Equation (2-10) has been written so as to allow for the semi-first difference correction for autocorrelation. Because of the balance-sheet restrictions on the whole portfolio, we must assume that ρ is the same for each asset demand.[9] The value which appeared to work best, and which was used, was .8.

We take account of the other restrictions of (2-9) by substitution. Since the row sum of the interest rate coefficients is zero for each asset, we substitute for β_{11}, β_{22}, β_{33}, and β_{44} by using interest rate differentials everywhere. Since the interest rate coefficient matrix is symmetric, we then constrain $\beta_{ij} = \beta_{ji}$ for all internal rates in the first four rows.

Finally, we allow for lagged responses by using distributed lags for all interest rates and capital gains. On the basis of preliminary experimentation, we used six quarter rectangular distributions for the first six interest rates and weights which decayed according to the scheme $\frac{6}{21}$, $\frac{5}{21}$, $\frac{4}{21}$, ..., $\frac{1}{21}$ for $PDOT$ and CG.

----

[9] Assume we have the model

$$A_1 = \beta_1 + \alpha_1 X + \rho_1 u_1(-1) + \varepsilon_1$$
$$A_2 = \beta_2 + \alpha_2 X + \rho_2 u_2(-1) + \varepsilon_2$$
$$A_3 = \beta_3 + \alpha_3 X + \rho_3 u_3(-1) + \varepsilon_3$$

where $A_1 + A_2 + A_3 = 1$; $\beta_1 + \beta_2 + \beta_3 = 1$; and $\alpha_1 + \alpha_2 + \alpha_3 = 0$. We know that $u_1 + u_2 + u_3 = 0$ in every period, and hence that

$$\rho_1 u_1(-1) + \rho_2 u_2(-1) + \rho_3 u_3(-1) + \varepsilon_1 + \varepsilon_2 + \varepsilon_3 = 0$$

Rewriting the latter expression gives

$$\rho_1 u_1(-1) + \rho_1 u_2(-1) + \rho_1 u_3(-1) + \varepsilon_1 + \varepsilon_2 + \varepsilon_3$$
$$+ (\rho_2 - \rho_1)u_2(-1) + (\rho_3 - \rho_1)u_3(-1) = 0$$

where the first three terms sum to zero. Since ρ_1, ρ_2, and ρ_3 are constants and the ε_i and u_i are stochastic variables, this last expression only holds when ρ is the same for each asset, or $(\rho_2 - \rho_1) = (\rho_3 - \rho_1) = 0$.

The Estimates

The most efficient way to estimate the interdependent system of equations (2-10) is with a generalized restricted least squares estimation procedure (Zellner [23]), which takes account of all restrictions on the coefficients and of the variance–covariance residual correlation matrix. We experienced programming difficulties in our attempts to implement this procedure, however, and have not used it in deriving the estimates of this paper. We have instead used a simpler stacked regression technique developed by de Leeuw [7] which can readily be adapted to ordinary least squares programs. It imposes our coefficient restrictions and allows us to scale the equations by the principal diagonal of the residual variance–covariance matrix while estimating all demand equations in one stacked regression. Ironically, we find that scaling the various assets demand functions by their own residual variance (the principal diagonal of the residual correlation matrix) made the estimated coefficients generally less sensible, though of course scaling slightly improved the fit of the stacked regression. We did not conduct a full test to find the set of scaling weights that would optimize the reasonableness of the coefficients, but merely estimated the equations in unweighted form.

The equations estimated with sixty quarterly time-series observations extending from 1954 to 1969 are presented in chapter Appendix 2A. The table presents five different sets of equations which trace how we arrived at our preferred set. The first set estimates equation (2-10) directly, though with all row-sum and symmetry restrictions on the rate coefficients. Several variables have incorrect signs (denoted by *) and several others are not significant. The second set includes the time trend for savings and loan shares only, because extraneous evidence indicates that this is the asset which has benefitted most from secular changes such as improvements in insurance and westerly population shifts. Some interest rate coefficients still do not accord with a prior expectation, however, and two of the coefficients on capital gains are statistically insignificant. The third set uses average asset proportions to constrain all capital gains coefficients to be proportionately the same. Over the estimation period, life insurance reserves have averaged 11.4 percent of unclaimed net worth, savings and loan shares have averaged 6 percent of unclaimed net worth, mutual savings bank deposits 4 percent, and commercial bank savings deposits 7.4 percent. We have therefore assumed that a unit rise in CG/VU will alter A_1 by 1.14γ, A_2 by $.6\gamma$, A_3 by $.4\gamma$, and A_4 by $.74\gamma$, where γ is the common weighted average coefficient. This set still has many interest rate differentials with the wrong sign, though the income coefficients are very close to what they would be under proportional constraints. The fourth set imposes these proportional constraints on the income variable and indicates only negligible differences with the third set. Finally, in the fifth set we drop all incorrectly signed interest rate variables in order to obtain sensible coefficients on the remaining variables. The fifth set should be viewed as our preferred empirical version. It is interesting to note that even with all of the additional constraints we have placed on this fifth stacked regression, the coefficient of determination is nearly as high and the standard error is just as low as in the first regression, though autocorrelation is somewhat worse.[10]

An evaluation of the final set of equations reveals internal rate substitution relationships that are surprisingly weak in light of statements often made about the savings deposit industry and the apparent preconceptions of the regulatory authorities. Interest rate relationships have been carefully co-ordinated so as to keep them from disturbing the flows of funds to savings and loan associations, commercial banks, mutual savings banks, and even to some extent life insurance companies. In contrast to the high elasticities which apparently underlie this regulatory philosophy, we find relatively little evidence of strong deposit substitutability—the significant exceptions are between commercial banks and both mutual savings banks and life insurance companies.[11]

From the institution's point of view, commercial banks are the most vulnerable to interest rate competition from all assets and mutual savings banks the least vulnerable. Open-market securities have a strong impact on both bank time deposits and savings and loan deposits.

The rate of inflation term affects the demand for the life insurance company variable and savings and loan shares, possibly because it reflects sub-stitution between these assets and equities.

The income variable has a powerful effect on the demand for savings deposits. This variable is significant at a high level even in the unconstrained regressions, and the proportional constraints make very little difference in the size of the income coefficients. Since we are comparing asset stocks with

---

[10] The Durbin-Watson statistic presented in Appendix 2A is not a precise measure of autocorrelation for stacked regressions. Its overall value depends on the order of the stacks and the size of the residuals in each stack, among other things. Moreover, since it is just one overall value, it may not be a good measure of the amount of serial correlation within any of the stacks. It is nevertheless obvious from inspection of the residuals that we do have strong serial correlation in each stack even after the semi-difference correction. We did not attempt to eliminate this serial correlation with a value of ρ higher than .8 since higher values of ρ began to worsen the dynamic simulation performance of the sector significantly.

[11] It is, of course, possible that the reason we have not identified strong internal substitution effects is because the regulatory authorities have succeeded in making deposit rates very collinear. Hence their philosophy could really be correct even though their actions have made it appear incorrect. Other studies have obtained mixed results in estimating internal cross-elasticities—sometimes time deposits are seen to substitute with savings and loan shares and mutual savings bank deposits, sometimes not. Kardouche [17] has summarized these studies.

income flows, it is very difficult to determine what the income coefficients should be—among other things, this will depend on the length of the time interval over which we measure income flows (here we have used quarterly intervals). The only thing we can say *a priori* is that both the income coefficients and the equilibrium total derivatives for unclaimed net worth should be positive. Setting all rate differentials and the inverse of time at mean values for the period, evaluating, and multiplying through by VU, we see that these conditions are met by equation 5 in Appendix 2A:[12]

$$
\begin{aligned}
MIS &= .046VU + .608YD - .158CG \\
MSL &= .017VU + .321YD - .083CG \\
MMS &= .020VU + .214YD - .055CG \\
MTP &= .034VU + .396YD - .102CG
\end{aligned}
\qquad (2\text{-}11)
$$

Capital gains work tolerably well in all except the first set of equations in Appendix 2A. Comparisons of sets 2 and 3 indicate that proportional constraints on the coefficients do not change them significantly except in the case of passbook savings deposits.

The inverse of time works in three of the four equations of the first set, which may be too well. The coefficients of the first set of equations indicate that all savings deposits have grown over time apart from income, net worth, and interest rates. This finding is rather implausible, at least until we have identified assets or liabilities that are declining over time, and it seems safer to omit the time trends for all but savings and loan shares. These omissions do improve the performance of capital gains and interest rate terms. The savings and loan trend in the preferred set indicates that over the last ten years savings and loan deposits have grown by $.024VU$, entirely at the expense of omitted assets and liabilities, while over the next ten years their expected growth is only $.009VU$.

The Supply of Savings Deposits

The Model

The supply side of the market for savings deposits concerns the rate-setting behavior of depository institutions. The typical financial intermediary is assumed to maximize expected utility which, as before, is a function of

---

[12] It may be asked why in making this comparison, we did not set all interest rate differentials at zero. The reason is that instruments are not all the same, but differ according to risk and other considerations. Thus it would not be likely for all interest rates and the rate of inflation to be the same in equilibrium, and historical averages would probably provide a better approximation of equilibrium differentials.

expected returns and their variance. It buys assets in a market in which it is a price-taker and sets deposit rates in a market in which it takes the quantity of deposits the public wishes to hold. Uncertainty enters in because the institution is uncertain about asset rates of return and about the public's demand for deposits.[13] We assume that the institution identifies sources of interest rate competition for deposits in the same way that we have: that is, we create rate competition variables for each of the institutions that weight the competing interest rates by the cross-elasticities of demand we have estimated in the previous section. In this way we link our household demand equations to our intermediary supply equations, and we use this constraint to reduce multicollinearity between interest rates in our supply equations.

Let a typical financial intermediary hold two earning assets, mortgages (M) and bonds (B). Its profits can be represented as:

$$Y_1 = r_m M + r_b B - r_1 D_1 \tag{2-12}$$

where the subscripts denote appropriate expected rates of return and D_1 and r_1 refer to deposits and the interest rate in, say, the first row of (2-9). If depository institutions hold a constant proportion $(1 - \alpha)$ of their deposits in liquid form, the balance-sheet constraint can be written as

$$M + B = \alpha D_1 \tag{2-13}$$

The assumption that the institution's subjective view of interest rate elasticities and cross-elasticities agrees with our estimates implies that institutions maximize profits subject to a linearized version of the first row of (2-9).

$$D_1 = b_{11} r_1 + b_{12} r_2 + b_{13} r_3 + \cdots + b_{1n} r_n + b_{1m} + u_1' \tag{2-14}$$

where we approximate the influence of net worth and all noninterest rate variables by the constant and residual.

Substituting these three equations into the general objective function (2-5) gives

$$\pi = [r_m \quad r_b \quad -D_1]\{M \quad B \quad r_1\} - K[M \quad B \quad r_1]S\pi\{M \quad B \quad r_1\}$$
$$- \lambda[M + B - \alpha(b_{11} r_1 + b_{12} r_2 + \cdots + b_{1n} r_n + b_{1m} + u_1)] \tag{2-15}$$

where { } denotes a column vector and

$$S\pi = \begin{bmatrix} S_{MM} & S_{MB} & S_{MU} \\ S_{BM} & S_{BB} & S_{BU} \\ S_{UM} & S_{UB} & S_{UU} \end{bmatrix}$$

---

[13] Our treatment differs from that of Goldfeld and Jaffee [12] and other studies summarized therein because we deal explicitly with uncertainty.

This formulation differs from that for households in two respects. In the first place, the deposit uncertainty is associated not with the interest rate, which is under control of intermediaries, but with the level of deposits, which is controlled by households. Secondly, in this maximization exercise, the institution must recognize that its deposit rate influences the level of its deposits through the $b_{11}r_1$ term. The latter consideration complicates the maximization somewhat because now we must purge $[r_m \quad r_b \quad -D_1]$ of the $b_{11}r_1$ term before we can arrive at a reduced-form solution. The first order conditions are

$$
\begin{bmatrix} \dfrac{\partial \pi}{\partial M} \\[2mm] \dfrac{\partial \pi}{\partial B} \\[2mm] \dfrac{\partial \pi}{\partial r_1} \\[2mm] \dfrac{\partial \pi}{\partial \lambda} \end{bmatrix} = \begin{bmatrix} r_m \\ r_b \\ -\bar{D} \\ \alpha\bar{D} \end{bmatrix} - \begin{bmatrix} 2KS & X \\ \hline X' & 0 \end{bmatrix} \begin{bmatrix} M \\ B \\ r_1 \\ \lambda \end{bmatrix} = \begin{bmatrix} 0 \\ 0 \\ 0 \\ 0 \end{bmatrix} \tag{2-16}
$$

where $X' = \begin{bmatrix} 1 & 1 & -b_{11} \end{bmatrix}$, D is the exogenous component of deposits, $(D_1 - b_{11}r_1)$, and S equals $S\pi$ except that the element in the third row and third column is now $S_{UU} + b_{11}/K$. The reduced-form solution becomes

$$
\begin{vmatrix} M \\ B \\ r_1 \\ \lambda \end{vmatrix} = \frac{1}{X'S^{-1}X} \cdot \begin{bmatrix} \dfrac{S^{-1}(X'S^{-1}X) - S^{-1}XX'S^{-1}}{2K} & S^{-1}X \\[4mm] X'S^{-1} & 2K \end{bmatrix} \begin{bmatrix} r_m \\ r_b \\ -\bar{D} \\ \alpha\bar{D} \end{bmatrix} \tag{2-17}
$$

This model says that intermediary demands for both assets depend positively on own rates, negatively on uncertainty about own rates, negatively on competing asset rates, positively on uncertainty about competing rates, and positively on exogenous deposits. Deposit rates depend positively on both asset rates, positively on the rates of all assets which compete with these deposits in the household demand function, and negatively on all other factors which increase deposits. The importance of asset rates in the deposit rate function depends upon relative uncertainty: if, for example, there is relatively great uncertainty about future mortgage rates of return and relatively little uncertainty about future bond rates, the intermediary will tend to hold more bonds and fewer mortgages at each rate differential, and bond rates will tend to be more important and mortgage rates less important in setting desired deposit rates. The importance of rates of return on assets which compete in household demand functions depends upon the estimated cross-elasticities of demand in these functions: the closer substitutes we find assets to be, the more their rates influence the institution's deposit rate. Deposit rates are inversely related to exogenous shocks in the deposit demand function because increases in deposits from these sources allow intermediaries to reduce deposit rates.

We summarize these points by writing the deposit rate equation in more convenient notation:

$$r_1 = a_{11}r_m + a_{12}r_b - a_{13}(b_{12}r_2 + b_{13}r_3 + \cdots + b_{1n}r_n) \\ + a_{14} - a_{13}b_{1m} + v_1 - a_{13}u_1' \qquad (2\text{-}18)$$

where we call the term in brackets the rate competition variable—remembering that if assets are substitutes in household demand functions, b_{12} through b_{1n} will be negative—and we let $(a_{14} - a_{13}b_{1m})$ represent the regression intercept. The regression residual will be $(v_1 - a_{13}u_1')$ when we do not attempt to capture the influence of exogenous deposit shocks with nonrate independent variables, and v_1 when we do. Again we only attempt to estimate the third row of (2-17) and do not explicitly deal with the asset demand functions.

We note that since the quantities of mortgages, bonds, and deposits are endogenous in the overall decision-making model, equation (2-18) does not include these quantities. An alternative approach to estimating (2-18) would be to include quantities and estimate a structural instead of a reduced-form equation.[14] The choice of which technique would be appropriate involves the same considerations that apply to all choices between structural equation and reduced-form estimation: structural equations have the advantage that they can measure the impact of all exogenous variables in one independent variable, and thus use outside knowledge of the structure of the system, while they have the disadvantage that they are susceptible to simultaneous-equations bias. For our part, we have tried to gain the best of both worlds by using reduced-form equations, and thus avoiding obvious simultaneous difficulties, but at the same time constraining the reduced-form coefficients for competing interest rates by the estimated demand functions. We have also tried to include terms such as the rates of growth of deposits as a proxy for the influence of exogenous shocks.

---

[14] In fact, this technique has previously been used by one of us; see Hulett [16].

Interest Rate Ceilings

We turn next to the effects of interest rate ceilings on deposit rates. In the case of passbook savings deposits at commercial banks, the only case in which these ceilings were important over most of the estimation period, we have assumed that the ceiling has two distinct effects: (i) there is a definitional effect of the ceiling in holding down the deposit rates of those banks that would otherwise set a rate above the ceiling; and (ii) interest rate ceilings can represent an oligopolistic trigger for rate changes (if, for instance, changes in the ceiling inspire belief that competing deposit rates are about to increase).

We allow for the second effect by including as separate independent variables in the passbook savings rate equation the ceiling rate and the change in the ceiling rate. We allow for the first effect by constructing and trying to explain a hypothetical desired deposit rate that would have obtained in the absence of ceilings. We calculate this desired rate as a function of the ceiling rate, the observed rate, and parameters of an assumed triangular distribution of desired deposit rates about the unconstrained mean of desired deposit rates for all financial institutions.[15] The parameters of the triangular distribution are estimated nonlinearly along with the other coefficients of (2–18).

The details of the relationship between hypothetical desired rates, observed rates, and ceiling rates can best be illustrated diagrammatically. In Figure 2-1 we have portrayed the deposit rate ceiling by Q and three possible cases by the three triangles. The leftward triangle, whose mean is represented by μ_I, is the highest triangle where the observed rate equals the desired rate. If the observed rate is at this level or lower, we do not have to make any adjustment for the definitional effect of ceilings. If the desired rate distribution rises above I, say to II, we know that ceilings are exerting a depressing effect on observed rates by truncating the dotted part of the desired rate triangle and forcing this frequency onto Q. In this case, the observed rate would be somewhere between I and II, say at μ_{II}. The depressing effect becomes more and more pronounced as desired rates increase relative to the ceiling, eventually becoming completely effective when desired rates reach or exceed distribution III and the observed rate equals Q. We simulate this model by using our estimated equation, which is similar to (2-18) to explain the desired rate. The nonlinear parameters of the triangular distribution and the ceiling rate then convert this desired rate into an observed rate.

---

[15] We would like to give special thanks to Jared Enzler who initially suggested this idea and provided valuable counsel on its implementation.

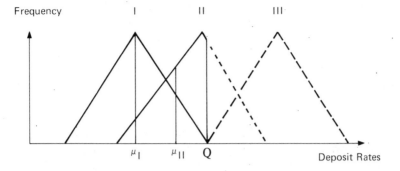

Figure 2-1. Relationship Between Desired Deposit Rates, Observed Rates, and Regulation Q Ceiling Rates.

Estimation of the Model

To estimate (2-18) we must first use the results in Appendix 2A to construct the appropriate interest rate competition expressions. In every case we have divided b_{12} through b_{1n} by

$$-b_{11} = \sum_{i=2}^{n} b_{1i}$$

to convert these rate competition expressions to a weighted average of the various component interest rates with the weights summing to plus one. Remembering that we can ignore the rate on life insurance reserves, which has remained constant over the entire period, and using steady state coefficients, the rate competition variables are

$$RSLC = \frac{.0004}{.0089} RMS + \frac{.0009}{.0089} RTP + \frac{.0071}{.0089} RCB + \frac{.0005}{.0089} PDOT$$

$$RMSC = \frac{.0004}{.0034} RSL + \frac{.0030}{.0034} RTP$$

$$RTCP = \frac{.0009}{.0061} RSL + \frac{.0030}{.0061} RMS + \frac{.0022}{.0061} RTP$$

We have also allowed the depository institution to adjust to these competitive rates in a delayed fashion by the use of Almon distributed lags.

Since the public is assumed to react to the institution's own rate with the same lag as to competing rates, delays in the institution's interest rate response imply that the institution is willing to suffer (accept) short-run losses (gains) in deposits before it raises (lowers) deposit rates.

It will be remembered that the passbook savings deposit rate to be explained is really the hypothetical desired rate in the absence of ceiling, denoted by RTP^*. The best nonlinear estimate of the base of the triangle in Figure 2-1 was sixteen basis points. We have omitted 1969 from the estimation period because of rounding errors which become important in our scheme whenever hypothetical desired deposit rates get too far above ceiling rates (or, whenever observed rates get too close to ceilings).

The three estimated equations are presented in Appendix 2B. (Again, there is no equation for the rate of life insurance reserves, which has remained constant over the entire period.) We have not reported all results of our nonlinear estimation for RTP^*, or of our unsuccessful trials with variables which did not work.

For the deposit rate of savings and loan associations, both the competing deposit rate variable ($RSLC$) and the mortgage rate (RM) enter significantly, although their impacts are distributed over time.[16] The mortgage-deposit flow variable and the FHLBB advance variable does depend, however, on the dummy shift variable (JQ) that corresponds with the introduction of certificates of deposits in 1962. Overall, the equation fits quite well with a dynamic simulation standard error (SU) of 6.2 basis points.

For mutual savings banks, the mortgage rate did work as an asset rate but the corporate bond rate did not. Nor did various terms in the rate of growth of deposits, entered with and without adjustment for CDs. The dynamic simulation standard error is 7.7 basis points and the steady-state coefficient of all interest rates is .81.

For passbook savings deposit rates, no asset rates worked; but the rate of growth of total deposits less commercial loans did have a small negative effect. The CD shift variable had only a small effect on the equation, possibly because of collinearity with CD ceilings themselves. These ceiling rates have a very important trigger effect on time deposit rates, raising observed rates by 65 percent of the ceiling change in the first quarter and 12 percent in the next quarter even if the definitional impact is absent. The dynamic standard error is 14.4 basis points and the steady-state interest rate coefficient is .57.

There is no clear pattern to these deposit rate results. Rates on competing assets are highly significant in all three rate equations, but the mean lag for this variable varies between 1.2 quarters for mutual savings banks and 4.3

---

[16] We would like to thank Myron Slovin for his help in estimating this equation.

quarters for passbook deposit rates. This means that commercial banks are willing to countenance much larger short-run fluctuations in time deposits while they slowly adjust their deposit rates to rates on competing assets. The steady-state coefficient for all freely fluctuating interest rates is reasonably close to unity for savings and loans and mutual savings banks, but much below that for passbook deposits. This discrepancy can only be eliminated if we treat deposit ceilings as a rate that varies along with other rates, which of course has been more or less the way the ceiling has been set by policy authorities over the estimation period. If authorities were to announce a drastic change in the way in which they set the ceiling, we might expect this coefficient to change. Finally, in two of the institutions there does seem to be a small but perceptible effect of balance-sheet variables, either deposits, mortgages, or loans, on deposit rates.[17]

Simulation Experiments

Predictive Simulations

We first illustrate the long-run tracking behavior of the equations described above by a set of dynamic simulations of the savings deposit sector. In these dynamic simulations we have simply let the sector run over the period of fit, 1957:1–1969:4. In each quarter we feed in actual values of exogenous variables but only initial values of endogenous variables. Starting with 1957:1, every endogenous variable is computed simultaneously within the system and these solution variables are used as lagged endogenous variables to compute subsequent solutions to the system. We calculate simulation standard errors in the usual way by comparing actual values of endogenous variables with the time path of simulated endogenous variables.

The first set of simulations is presented in chapter Appendix 2C, Figures 2C-1 to 2C-4. Here all deposit rates are exogenous and the four savings deposit demand equations are simulated dynamically. The simulations then correspond to the regressions in Appendix 2A, except that they give more meaningful standard errors. Below the simulations are printed the mean square error (MSE), the root mean square error (RMS), the coefficient of first order serial correlation of the residual (RHO), the mean error, and the mean of the variable.

These figures indicate that all equations perform reasonably well. The life insurance reserves equation makes errors of up to $5 billion in 1963 but

---

[17] This finding corresponds with the finding of one of us that general expectations of deposit volatility has an effect on deposit rates; see Hulett [16].

before and after that the errors are never much more than $2 billion. Savings and loan deposit errors also stay in the $2 billion range. Mutual savings bank deposit errors are even less, which would be expected from their smaller size. The most serious errors come in the passbook savings deposit equation. These errors get up to around $5 billion in 1962, then decline for a period before reaching a peak of $12 billion in 1968:4. After that the errors again decline and end the period at $3 billion. In all four cases there is strong serial correlation of residuals.[18]

The simulation performance of our equations indicates that these equations seem to have reasonable long-run properties, but it should not be viewed as the best performance that could be achieved in terms of fitting historic observations. There are numerous parameter constraints imposed on our estimated equations. And, while we think these parameter constraints do improve the structural usefulness and equilibrium properties of the equations, they can only be imposed at a cost in terms of the fit of the equations. One worrying simply about fitting equations well in estimation and simulation of historical periods could probably do better than we have done by relaxing many of the prior constraints.

Figures 2C-5 to 2C-11 depict the results of a dynamic simulation of the entire savings deposit sector. The first four figures show the same four deposits. The last three figures show deposit rates, all of which have long-run standard errors in the neighborhood of fourteen basis points. Strangely enough, introducing the rate equation errors does not noticeably worsen the fit of the dynamic simulation of deposits. In fact, both life insurance reserves and passbook savings deposits fit significantly better than before and mutual savings bank deposits about the same. It is only the fit of savings and loan deposits that degenerates, and this by a rather small amount due mainly to the imposition of ceiling deposit rates on SLs in 1969.[19] We notice especially that the largest errors in both life insurance reserves and passbook savings deposits have been reduced somewhat.

---

[18] Serial correlation of residuals might be expected both because there is serial correlation in the estimated equations and because the semi-difference correction factor is already relatively high. The high correction factor means that the estimated equations are improved significantly by the lagged error term. In simulation, however, the initial error is multiplied by this correction factor, which rapidly decays toward zero when the number of simulated periods (n) is large (according to ρ^n, where $0 < \rho < 1$). This means that the dynamic simulations receive almost no help from the lagged residual which was so important in the estimation. This is in fact why we have not used a higher correction factor than .8.

[19] Figure 2C-9 shows that solution deposit rates tended to get well above actual rates in 1969, because actual rates were prevented from rising by deposit rate ceilings. As these errors work into the deposit stock equation, we would expect that solution deposits would exceed actual levels. Figure 2C-6 indicates that this did happen.

Sectoral Multipliers

To compute sectoral multipliers, we compare the results of two simulations. The first, or control simulation, is a dynamic simulation done in the way described above. The second, or experimental simulation, is the same in all respects except that one or a set of exogenous variables in the simulation differs from its actual value by a specified amount in each quarter. Comparison of the two simulations enables us to determine the effect of the specified exogenous change on the endogenous variables in this block of equations over the simulation period.

Tables 2D-1 through 2D-4, in chapter Appendix 2D, present differences between endogenous variables in control and experimental simulations. The first experiment investigates the effect of a 1 percent decrease in all market rates of interest (RTB and RCB) which was assumed to be maintained over the subsequent forty-four quarters. From Table 2D-1 we see how deposit rates follow market rates down and how the net effect of a large decline in market rates and a smaller decline in deposit rates stimulates deposit inflows in three of the four cases but a deposit outflow in the case of passbook savings deposits.

We know that life insurance reserves benefit unambiguously from the decline in all competing rates because their deposit rate is assumed to be fixed. What happens to the rates and deposits of other intermediaries depends on the details of the maximization exercise and cannot be predicted a priori. Commercial banks will experience large increases in demand deposits as a result of the fall in market rates and hence they appear to countenance very slight deposit outflows in response to declining market rates. Savings and loan associations and mutual savings banks are, however, in an inherently more risky situation; and these institutions are seen to use the fall in market rates to stock up on deposits. The rate substitution is such that mutual savings banks cannot afford to cut deposit rates greatly for fear of losing deposits, but savings and loan associations can make fairly significant cuts in rates.

Table 2D-2 presents the results of an experimental rise in passbook deposit rate ceilings. The simulation beings in 1957:1—a time when the definitional depressing effect of the ceiling was absent—hence the sharp change in passbook rates is solely due to the oligopolistic trigger effect of ceiling rate changes. The initial rise in passbook savings deposit rates forces up other deposit rates as mutual savings banks and, to a lesser extent, savings and loan associations vie to avoid deposit outflows; and this in turn induces still another rise in time deposit rates. The net effect of these movements is that passbook savings deposits rise sharply at the expense of all other assets and market instruments (note that the sum of the decreases in all other assets never equals the increase in passbook savings deposits).

The experiment depicted in Table 2D-3 investigates the effect of a $10 billion increase in real disposable income (annual rates) coming in 1957:1 and maintained for forty-four quarters. In order to include the effect of saving on net worth, in this simulation we have added the consumption–net-worth sector of the FMP model to the savings deposit sector. Hence we allow the increase in disposable income to influence consumption, the implicit saving to enter net worth, and both income and net worth to affect holdings of savings deposits. Because the effect of the income change on deposit rates was trivial, we have omitted these columns from the table.

Table 2D-3 shows how real consumption gradually increases to meet increases in real income, with the cumulated savings going into unclaimed net worth. The initial rise in disposable income and the subsequent rise in unclaimed net worth stimulate continuing increases in all four deposit holdings. We also notice that in the first quarter the rise in deposit holdings is greater than the increase in unclaimed net worth because of the impact of the income variable, though these relationships are reversed in the longer run. In the first quarter unclaimed net worth rises by $1.4 billion and deposits by a total of $3.7 billion; by the forty-fourth quarter unclaimed net worth has risen $25 billion and total deposits by $8.3 billion.

The experiment in Table 2D-4 examines the effect of a sustained 1 percent increase in the dividend–price ratio on common stock, again coming in 1957:1. This increase in the dividend–price ratio, or the capitalization rate for dividends, brings about a substantial reduction in the present value of equities and an eventual reduction in all savings deposits. Again deposit rate effects were trivial.

The reduction in the present value of common stock amounts to $52 billion in the current quarter and reaches $177 billion by the forty-fourth quarter. In contrast to the previous case, however, alterations in the value of unclaimed net worth are followed by great delays in household's reduction of their savings deposits. The reason is the presence of the lagged capital gains terms reflecting allocation inertia in the regressions. In the first quarter the reduction in savings deposits is virtually nil, by the fourth quarter the reduction is but 6 percent of the reduction in unclaimed net worth, and ultimately in the forty-fourth quarter the reduction is about 15 percent of the reduction in unclaimed net worth. This is still less than the sensitivity deposits to net worth in the previous experiment because previously the maintained increase in income exerted an additional force for continued increases in deposits.

Conclusion

As was said at the outset, we think our study of markets for savings deposits has improved on earlier work in several respects. We have developed estimating equations for household asset demands and intermediary supplies directly from portfolio balance theory. We have linked these equations together, and we have dealt with the effect of ceiling deposit rates more rigorously than have previous studies. As a result, we have an empirical model of markets for savings deposits we think should be more trustworthy in policy simulations of the sector. The model also seems to fit reasonably well, both in estimation and simulation, though we do not rest our case here and we would not be surprised if the equations would fit historical observations even better if certain of the coefficient restrictions were relaxed.

We do not, of course, pretend that we have solved all of the problems concerning markets for savings deposits. Even with all of the constraints we have imposed, we are still surprised by the absence of strong internal rate substitution and by the unimportance of owned asset rates in influencing deposit rates, findings which do not agree with prevailing views on the structure of the savings deposit industry. We would be more disposed to question the conventional wisdom than our estimates, but we admit that further investigation of these conclusions would be profitable, indeed necessary. Other obvious extensions of our work would be to complete the examination of the portfolio balance problem, hopefully using balance-sheet restrictions, to estimate asset demand equations for intermediaries which are consistent with the risk–return model, and to test our notion of the sequential net worth allocation process. Possibly these examinations will shed light on the questions we may not have answered satisfactorily in this paper.

Appendix 2A:
Demands for Savings
Deposits

(Quarterly time series observations, 1954–1969.
The *t*-ratios appear below the coefficients, * denotes incorrect sign.)

$$\begin{bmatrix} A_1 \\ A_2 \\ A_3 \\ A_4 \end{bmatrix} = \frac{1}{VU} \begin{bmatrix} MIS \\ MSL \\ MMS \\ MTP \end{bmatrix}$$

Table 2A. Demand for Savings Deposits, Estimated Coefficients

Eqs.	RI – RSL	RI – RMS	RI – RTP	RI – RTB	RI – RCB	RI – PDOT	RSL – RMS	RSL – RTP	RSL – RTB	RSL – RCB	RSL – PDOT
1. A_1	.0013 (.6)	-.0034* (-1.7)	.0068 (4.8)	.0019 (2.5)	-.0002* (-.2)	.0004 (1.1)	-.0024* (-.4)	-.0012* (-.6)	.0003 (.3)	.0063 (2.8)	.0006 (1.7)
A_2	-.0013 (-.6)	—	—	—	—	—	—	—	—	—	—
A_3	—	.0034* (1.7)	—	—	—	—	.0024* (.4)	—	—	—	—
A_4	—	—	-.0068 (-4.8)	—	—	—	—	.0012* (.6)	—	—	—
2. A_1	-.0029* (-1.5)	-.0013* (-1.0)	.0089 (10.0)	.0015 (1.9)	.0001 (.1)	.0004 (1.1)	—	—	—	—	—
A_2	.0029* (1.5)	—	—	—	—	—	.0022 (.4)	.0012 (.5)	-.0002* (-.2)	.0074 (3.2)	.0007 (2.0)
A_3	—	.0013* (1.0)	—	—	—	—	-.0022 (-.4)	—	—	—	—
A_4	—	—	-.0089 (-10.0)	—	—	—	—	-.0012 (-.5)	—	—	—
3. A_1	-.0027* (-1.4)	-.0013* (-1.0)	.0080 (9.1)	.0009 (1.1)	.0006 (.4)	.0005 (1.5)	—	—	—	—	—
A_2	.0027* (1.4)	—	—	—	—	—	.0015 (.3)	.0012 (.6)	.0000 (0)	.0071 (3.2)	.0007 (2.0)
A_3	—	.0013* (1.0)	—	—	—	—	-.0015 (-.3)	—	—	—	—
A_4	—	—	-.0080 (-9.1)	—	—	—	—	-.0012 (-.6)	—	—	—
4. A_1	-.0025* (-1.3)	-.0012* (-1.0)	.0076 (9.0)	.0012 (1.5)	.0002 (.2)	.0006 (1.7)	—	—	—	—	—
A_2	.0025* (1.3)	—	—	—	—	—	.0005 (.1)	.0012 (.6)	-.0003* (-.3)	.0067 (3.0)	.0006 (1.8)
A_3	—	.0012* (1.0)	—	—	—	—	-.0005 (-.1)	—	—	—	—
A_4	—	—	-.0076 (-9.0)	—	—	—	—	-.0012 (-.6)	—	—	—
5. A_1	—	—	.0064 (12.3)	.0006 (1.1)	—	.0006 (1.9)	—	—	—	—	—
A_2	—	—	—	—	—	—	.0004 (.1)	.0009 (.5)	—	.0071 (5.2)	.0005 (1.5)
A_3	—	—	—	—	—	—	-.0004 (-.1)	—	—	—	—
A_4	—	—	-.0064 (-12.3)	—	—	—	—	-.0009 (-.5)	—	—	—

Table 2A continued

Eqs.		RMS−RTP	RMS−RTB	RMS−RCB	RMS−PDOT	RTP−RTB	RTP−RCB	RTP−PDOT	YD/VU	CG/VU	1/TIME	Constant	$\bar{R}^2$/SE/DW/ρ
1.	A_1	—	—	—	—	—	—	—	.5474 (4.8)	−.1898 (−6.1)	−.0233 (−.1)	.0417 (5.2)	.9816
	A_2	—	—	—	—	—	—	—	.3357 (2.8)	−.0979 (−3.1)	−2.3531 (−5.8)	.0832 (10.2)	.0007
	A_3	.0017 (.8)	.0001 (.2)	.0014 (.8)	.0002 (.7)	.0021 (2.7)	.0010 (.8)	.0003 (1.0)	.4444 (3.8)	.0007* (0)	−.7786 (−2.0)	.0054 (.7)	.84
	A_4	−.0017 (−0.8)	—	—	—	—	—	—	.9190 (8.4)	.0380* (1.3)	−.8657 (−2.5)	.0124 (1.6)	.8
2.	A_1	—	—	—	—	—	—	—	.4693 (6.0)	−.2057 (−8.0)	—	.0468 (6.6)	.9804
	A_2	—	—	—	—	—	—	—	.4822 (4.2)	−.0658 (−2.1)	−3.2838 (−9.6)	.0777 (9.4)	.0007
	A_3	.0005 (.2)	.0004 (.4)	−.0002* (−.1)	.0001 (.4)	.0021 (2.7)	.0000 (0)	.0002 (.6)	.2263 (2.9)	−.0482 (−1.9)	—	.0170 (2.4)	.66
	A_4	−.0005 (−.2)	—	—	—	—	—	—	.6735 (8.7)	−.0174 (−.7)	—	.0260 (3.7)	.8
3.	A_1	—	—	—	—	—	—	—	.6084 (8.9)	−.1475 (−7.5)	—	.0346 (5.5)	.9795
	A_2	—	—	—	—	—	—	—	.4455 (6.1)	−.0776 (−7.5)	−3.2055 (−10.4)	.0802 (15.0)	.0007
	A_3	.0004 (.2)	.0004 (.5)	−.0001* (−.1)	.0001 (.3)	.0030 (3.9)	−.0007* (−.5)	.0000 (0)	.2201 (4.0)	−.0518 (−7.5)	—	.0176 (3.5)	.62
	A_4	−.0004 (−.2)	—	—	—	—	—	—	.4908 (8.2)	−.0958 (−7.5)	—	.0421 (7.7)	.8
4.	A_1	—	—	—	—	—	—	—	.6532 (11.0)	−.1534 (−7.9)	—	.0305 (5.4)	.9793
	A_2	—	—	—	—	—	—	—	.3438 (11.0)	−.0808 (−7.9)	−3.0035 (−11.0)	.0871 (28.5)	.0007
	A_3	.0005 (.2)	.0004 (.5)	.0001 (.1)	.0001 (.3)	.0028 (3.7)	−.0006* (−.4)	−.0001* (−.1)	.2292 (11.0)	−.0534 (−7.9)	—	.0168 (6.6)	.59
	A_4	−.0005 (−.2)	—	—	—	—	—	—	.4240 (11.0)	−.0996 (−7.9)	—	.0479 (12.5)	.8
5.	A_1	—	—	—	—	—	—	—	.6082 (11.7)	−.1578 (−8.8)	—	.0342 (6.8)	.9793
	A_2	—	—	—	—	—	—	—	.3206 (11.7)	−.0830 (−8.8)	−2.6873 (−15.4)	.0868 (29.6)	.0007
	A_3	.0030 (2.4)	—	—	—	—	—	—	.2138 (11.7)	−.0554 (−8.8)	—	.0179 (8.9)	.56
	A_4	−.0030 (−2.4)	—	—	—	.0022 (5.0)	—	—	.3955 (11.7)	−.1024 (−8.8)	—	.0506 (16.0)	.8

Appendix 2B:
Deposit Rate
Equations

Table 2B. Deposit Rates, Estimated Coefficients

	$\bar{R}^2_u$	$\bar{R}^2_e$	SE_u	SE_e	DW	ρ
	.9896	.9974	6.16	3.07	1.37	.8
	.9883	.9978	7.68	3.32	.99	.8

Savings and Loan Rate

A.

$$RSL = -.2987 + \sum_{i=0}^{4} w_i RSLC_{-i} + \sum_{i=0}^{9} w'_i RM_{-i}$$
$$\quad (.6) \qquad\qquad (6.4) \qquad\qquad (2.5)$$

$$+ \sum_{i=0}^{9} w''_i (100) \left(\frac{\Delta MKSL}{MKSL_{-1}} - \frac{\Delta MSL}{MSL_{-1}} \right)_{-i-1}$$
$$(3.5)$$

$$+ 3.666 JQ \left(\frac{ZAFH}{MSL} \right)_{-1} + .0291 JQ$$
$$\quad (2.0) \qquad\qquad\qquad (.4)$$

$w_0 = .12$	$w'_0 = -.02$	$w''_0 = -.01$
$w_1 = .14$	$w'_1 = .00$	$w''_1 = .01$
$w_2 = .13$	$w'_2 = .03$	$w''_2 = .02$
$w_3 = .11$	$w'_3 = .04$	$w''_3 = .03$
$w_4 = .06$	$w'_4 = .05$	$w''_4 = .03$
$\Sigma w_i = .5607$	$w'_5 = .06$	$w''_5 = .04$
Mean lag 2.2 qt.	$w'_6 = .06$	$w''_6 = .04$
	$w'_7 = .05$	$w''_7 = .03$
	$w'_8 = .04$	$w''_8 = .02$
	$w'_9 = .02$	$w''_9 = .01$
	$\Sigma w'_i = .3371$	$\Sigma w''_i = .2212$
	Mean lag 5.2 qt.	Mean lag 5.2 qt.

Mutual Savings Bank Rate

B.

$$RMS = .7166 + .1418 RM + .0466 RM_{-1} + \sum_{i=0}^{5} w_i RMSC_{-i}$$
$$\quad (3.5) \quad (3.6) \qquad (2.3) \qquad\qquad (20.9)$$

$w_0 = .23$	$w_4 = .03$
$w_1 = .17$	$w_5 = .01$
$w_2 = .11$	$\Sigma w_i = .6211$
$w_3 = .07$	Mean lag 1.2 qt.

(Quarterly time series observations, 1954-1968.)

Table 2B continued

Passbook Deposit Rate

C. $RTP^* = -1.5958 - .5253 \dfrac{\Delta(MD + MTP - MCL)}{(MD + MTP - MCL)_{-1}}$
   $\qquad\quad (-10.4) \;\; (-1.1)$

   $\qquad + .7660ZCT - .1290\Delta ZCT + \sum\limits_{i=0}^{9} w_i RTPC_{-i}$ (9.6)
   $\qquad\quad (14.2) \qquad\; (-2.8)$

$\qquad$ .9788 $\qquad$ .9980 $\qquad$ 14.38 $\qquad$ 4.42 $\qquad$ 1.14 $\qquad$ .8

$w_0 = .03 \qquad w_6 = .07$
$w_1 = .05 \qquad w_7 = .06$
$w_2 = .06 \qquad w_8 = .04$
$w_3 = .07 \qquad w_9 = .02$
$w_4 = .08 \qquad \Sigma w_i = .5709$
$w_5 = .08 \qquad$ Mean lag 4.3 qt.

Note: All distributed lags are estimated with second degree Almon polynomials constrained to zero at the distant end point. The *t*-ratios are in parentheses below coefficients. Fit statistics are presented for $u = Y - \alpha X$ and $e = Y - \alpha X - \rho u(-1)$. All rates have been defined in the text, and

$\quad JQ$ = 1.00 if after 1962:1, zero otherwise
$ZAFH$ = FHLBB advances to savings and loan associations
$\quad MSL$ = savings and loan deposits
$MKSL$ = mortgages at savings and loan associations
$\quad MD$ = demand deposits at commercial banks
$\quad MTP$ = time deposits at commercial banks
$\quad MCL$ = commercial loans at commercial banks
$\quad ZCT$ = regulation Q ceiling on passbook deposits

Appendix 2C:
Behavior of Deposits and Rate Equations in Dynamic Simulations

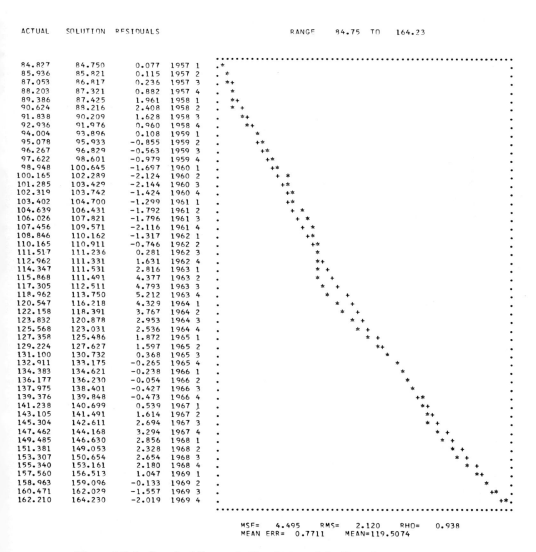

ACTUAL	SOLUTION	RESIDUALS				RANGE	84.75	TO	164.23
84.827	84.750	0.077	1957	1
85.936	85.821	0.115	1957	2
87.053	86.817	0.236	1957	3
88.203	87.321	0.882	1957	4
89.386	87.425	1.961	1958	1
90.624	88.216	2.408	1958	2
91.838	90.209	1.628	1958	3
92.936	91.976	0.960	1958	4
94.004	93.896	0.108	1959	1
95.078	95.933	-0.855	1959	2
96.267	96.829	-0.563	1959	3
97.622	98.601	-0.979	1959	4
98.948	100.645	-1.697	1960	1
100.165	102.289	-2.124	1960	2
101.285	103.429	-2.144	1960	3
102.319	103.742	-1.424	1960	4
103.402	104.700	-1.299	1961	1
104.639	106.431	-1.792	1961	2
106.026	107.821	-1.796	1961	3
107.456	109.571	-2.116	1961	4
108.846	110.162	-1.317	1962	1
110.165	110.911	-0.746	1962	2
111.517	111.236	0.281	1962	3
112.962	111.331	1.631	1962	4
114.347	111.531	2.816	1963	1
115.868	111.491	4.377	1963	2
117.305	112.511	4.793	1963	3
118.962	113.750	5.212	1963	4
120.547	116.218	4.329	1964	1
122.158	118.391	3.767	1964	2
123.832	120.878	2.953	1964	3
125.568	123.031	2.536	1964	4
127.358	125.486	1.872	1965	1
129.224	127.627	1.597	1965	2
131.100	130.732	0.368	1965	3
132.911	133.175	-0.265	1965	4
134.383	134.621	-0.238	1966	1
136.177	136.230	-0.054	1966	2
137.975	138.401	-0.427	1966	3
139.376	139.848	-0.473	1966	4
141.238	140.699	0.539	1967	1
143.105	141.491	1.614	1967	2
145.304	142.611	2.694	1967	3
147.462	144.168	3.294	1967	4
149.485	146.630	2.856	1968	1
151.381	149.053	2.328	1968	2
153.307	150.654	2.654	1968	3
155.340	153.161	2.180	1968	4
157.560	156.513	1.047	1969	1
158.963	159.096	-0.133	1969	2
160.471	162.029	-1.557	1969	3
162.210	164.230	-2.019	1969	4

MSE= 4.495   RMS= 2.120   RHO= 0.938
MEAN ERR= 0.7711   MEAN=119.5074

Figure 2C-1. Standard Dynamic Simulation of the Time Deposit Sector With Exogenous Deposit Rates: Life Insurance Reserves – *MIS*.

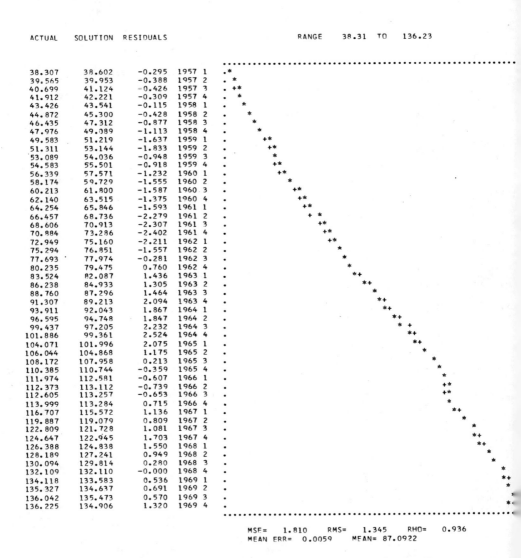

ACTUAL	SOLUTION	RESIDUALS		
38.307	38.602	-0.295	1957	1
39.565	39.953	-0.388	1957	2
40.699	41.124	-0.426	1957	3
41.912	42.221	-0.309	1957	4
43.426	43.541	-0.115	1958	1
44.872	45.300	-0.428	1958	2
46.435	47.312	-0.877	1958	3
47.976	49.089	-1.113	1958	4
49.583	51.219	-1.637	1959	1
51.311	53.144	-1.833	1959	2
53.089	54.036	-0.948	1959	3
54.583	55.501	-0.918	1959	4
56.339	57.571	-1.232	1960	1
58.174	59.729	-1.555	1960	2
60.213	61.800	-1.587	1960	3
62.140	63.515	-1.375	1960	4
64.254	65.846	-1.593	1961	1
66.457	68.736	-2.279	1961	2
68.606	70.913	-2.307	1961	3
70.884	73.286	-2.402	1961	4
72.949	75.160	-2.211	1962	1
75.294	76.851	-1.557	1962	2
77.693	77.974	-0.281	1962	3
80.235	79.475	0.760	1962	4
83.524	82.087	1.436	1963	1
86.238	84.933	1.305	1963	2
88.760	87.296	1.464	1963	3
91.307	89.213	2.094	1963	4
93.911	92.043	1.867	1964	1
96.595	94.748	1.847	1964	2
99.437	97.205	2.232	1964	3
101.886	99.361	2.524	1964	4
104.071	101.996	2.075	1965	1
106.044	104.868	1.175	1965	2
108.172	107.958	0.213	1965	3
110.385	110.744	-0.359	1965	4
111.974	112.581	-0.607	1966	1
112.373	113.112	-0.739	1966	2
112.605	113.257	-0.653	1966	3
113.999	113.284	0.715	1966	4
116.707	115.572	1.136	1967	1
119.887	119.079	0.809	1967	2
122.809	121.728	1.081	1967	3
124.647	122.945	1.703	1967	4
126.388	124.838	1.550	1968	1
128.189	127.241	0.949	1968	2
130.094	129.814	0.280	1968	3
132.109	132.110	-0.000	1968	4
134.118	133.583	0.536	1969	1
135.327	134.637	0.691	1969	2
136.042	135.473	0.570	1969	3
136.225	134.906	1.320	1969	4

MSF=   1.810   RMS=   1.345   RHO=   0.936
MEAN ERR=   0.0059   MEAN= 87.0922

Figure 2C-2. Standard Dynamic Simulation of the Time Deposit Sector With Exogenous Deposit Rates: Savings and Loan Deposits — *MSL*.

ACTUAL   SOLUTION RESIDUALS   RANGE   30.38 TO   68.31

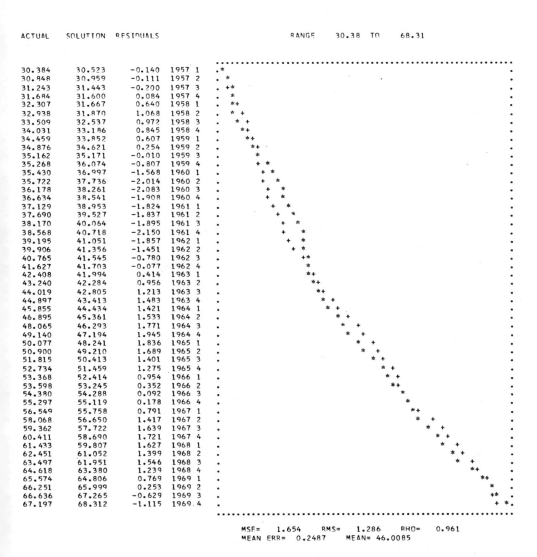

ACTUAL	SOLUTION	RESIDUALS		
30.384	30.523	-0.140	1957	1
30.848	30.959	-0.111	1957	2
31.243	31.443	-0.200	1957	3
31.684	31.600	0.084	1957	4
32.307	31.667	0.640	1958	1
32.938	31.870	1.068	1958	2
33.509	32.537	0.972	1958	3
34.031	33.186	0.845	1958	4
34.459	33.852	0.607	1959	1
34.876	34.621	0.254	1959	2
35.162	35.171	-0.010	1959	3
35.268	36.074	-0.807	1959	4
35.430	36.997	-1.568	1960	1
35.722	37.736	-2.014	1960	2
36.178	38.261	-2.083	1960	3
36.634	38.541	-1.908	1960	4
37.129	38.953	-1.824	1961	1
37.690	39.527	-1.837	1961	2
38.170	40.064	-1.895	1961	3
38.568	40.718	-2.150	1961	4
39.195	41.051	-1.857	1962	1
39.906	41.356	-1.451	1962	2
40.765	41.545	-0.780	1962	3
41.627	41.703	-0.077	1962	4
42.408	41.994	0.414	1963	1
43.240	42.284	0.956	1963	2
44.019	42.805	1.213	1963	3
44.897	43.413	1.483	1963	4
45.855	44.434	1.421	1964	1
46.895	45.361	1.533	1964	2
48.065	46.293	1.771	1964	3
49.140	47.194	1.945	1964	4
50.077	48.241	1.836	1965	1
50.900	49.210	1.689	1965	2
51.815	50.413	1.401	1965	3
52.734	51.459	1.275	1965	4
53.368	52.414	0.954	1966	1
53.598	53.245	0.352	1966	2
54.380	54.288	0.092	1966	3
55.297	55.119	0.178	1966	4
56.549	55.758	0.791	1967	1
58.068	56.650	1.417	1967	2
59.362	57.722	1.639	1967	3
60.411	58.690	1.721	1967	4
61.433	59.807	1.627	1968	1
62.451	61.052	1.399	1968	2
63.497	61.951	1.546	1968	3
64.618	63.380	1.239	1968	4
65.574	64.806	0.769	1969	1
66.251	65.999	0.253	1969	2
66.636	67.265	-0.629	1969	3
67.197	68.312	-1.115	1969	4

MSE=   1.654   RMS=   1.286   RHO=   0.961
MEAN ERR= 0.2487   MEAN= 46.0085

Figure 2C-3. Standard Dynamic Simulation of the Time Deposit Sector With Exogenous Deposit Rates: Mutual Savings Bank Deposits – *MMS*.

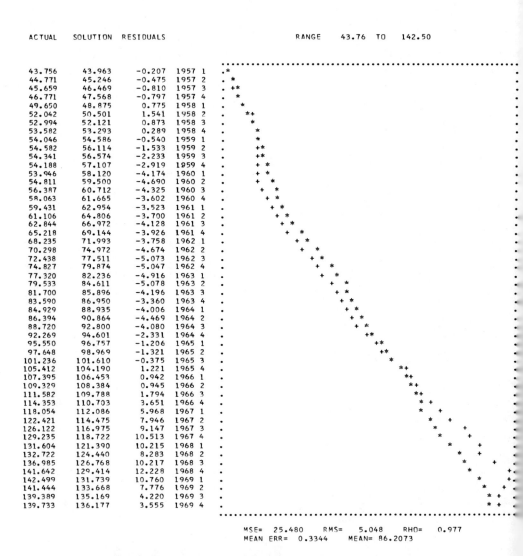

ACTUAL	SOLUTION	RESIDUALS			RANGE	43.76	TO	142.50
43.756	43.963	-0.207	1957	1
44.771	45.246	-0.475	1957	2
45.659	46.469	-0.810	1957	3
46.771	47.568	-0.797	1957	4
49.650	48.875	0.775	1958	1
52.042	50.501	1.541	1958	2
52.994	52.121	0.873	1958	3
53.582	53.293	0.289	1958	4
54.046	54.586	-0.540	1959	1
54.582	56.114	-1.533	1959	2
54.341	56.574	-2.233	1959	3
54.188	57.107	-2.919	1959	4
53.946	58.120	-4.174	1960	1
54.811	59.500	-4.690	1960	2
56.387	60.712	-4.325	1960	3
58.063	61.665	-3.602	1960	4
59.431	62.954	-3.523	1961	1
61.106	64.806	-3.700	1961	2
62.844	66.972	-4.128	1961	3
65.218	69.144	-3.926	1961	4
68.235	71.993	-3.758	1962	1
70.298	74.972	-4.674	1962	2
72.438	77.511	-5.073	1962	3
74.827	79.874	-5.047	1962	4
77.320	82.236	-4.916	1963	1
79.533	84.611	-5.078	1963	2
81.700	85.896	-4.196	1963	3
83.590	86.950	-3.360	1963	4
84.929	88.935	-4.006	1964	1
86.394	90.864	-4.469	1964	2
88.720	92.800	-4.080	1964	3
92.269	94.601	-2.331	1964	4
95.550	96.757	-1.206	1965	1
97.648	98.969	-1.321	1965	2
101.236	101.610	-0.375	1965	3
105.412	104.190	1.221	1965	4
107.395	106.453	0.942	1966	1
109.329	108.384	0.945	1966	2
111.582	109.788	1.794	1966	3
114.353	110.703	3.651	1966	4
118.054	112.086	5.968	1967	1
122.421	114.475	7.946	1967	2
126.122	116.975	9.147	1967	3
129.235	118.722	10.513	1967	4
131.604	121.390	10.215	1968	1
132.722	124.440	8.283	1968	2
136.985	126.768	10.217	1968	3
141.642	129.414	12.228	1968	4
142.499	131.739	10.760	1969	1
141.444	133.668	7.776	1969	2
139.389	135.169	4.220	1969	3
139.733	136.177	3.555	1969	4

MSE= 25.480   RMS=   5.048   RHO=   0.977
MEAN ERR= 0.3344   MEAN= 86.2073

Figure 2C-4. Standard Dynamic Simulation of the Time Deposit Sector With Exogenous Deposit Rates: Commercial Bank Deposits — *MTP*.

ACTUAL   SOLUTION   RESIDUALS   RANGE   84.71 TO   164.13

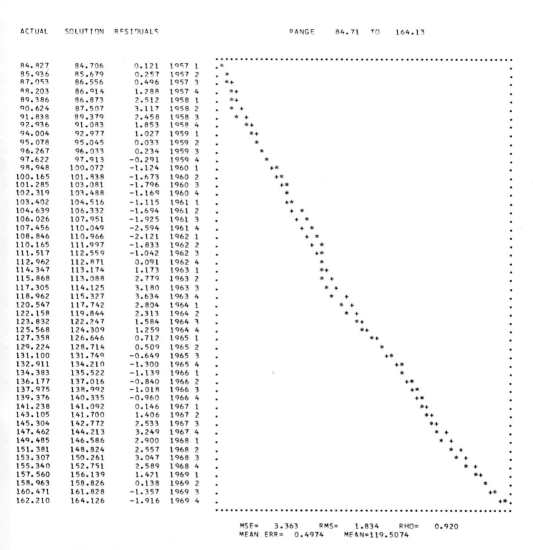

ACTUAL	SOLUTION	RESIDUALS		
84.827	84.706	0.121	1957	1
85.936	85.679	0.257	1957	2
87.053	86.556	0.496	1957	3
88.203	86.914	1.288	1957	4
89.386	86.873	2.512	1958	1
90.624	87.507	3.117	1958	2
91.838	89.379	2.458	1958	3
92.936	91.083	1.853	1958	4
94.004	92.977	1.027	1959	1
95.078	95.045	0.033	1959	2
96.267	96.033	0.234	1959	3
97.622	97.913	-0.291	1959	4
98.948	100.072	-1.124	1960	1
100.165	101.838	-1.673	1960	2
101.285	103.081	-1.796	1960	3
102.319	103.488	-1.169	1960	4
103.402	104.516	-1.115	1961	1
104.639	106.332	-1.694	1961	2
106.026	107.951	-1.925	1961	3
107.456	110.049	-2.594	1961	4
108.846	110.966	-2.121	1962	1
110.165	111.997	-1.833	1962	2
111.517	112.559	-1.042	1962	3
112.962	112.871	0.091	1962	4
114.347	113.174	1.173	1963	1
115.868	113.088	2.779	1963	2
117.305	114.125	3.180	1963	3
118.962	115.327	3.634	1963	4
120.547	117.742	2.804	1964	1
122.158	119.844	2.313	1964	2
123.832	122.247	1.584	1964	3
125.568	124.309	1.259	1964	4
127.358	126.646	0.712	1965	1
129.224	128.714	0.509	1965	2
131.100	131.749	-0.649	1965	3
132.911	134.210	-1.300	1965	4
134.383	135.522	-1.139	1966	1
136.177	137.016	-0.840	1966	2
137.975	138.992	-1.018	1966	3
139.376	140.335	-0.960	1966	4
141.238	141.092	0.146	1967	1
143.105	141.700	1.406	1967	2
145.304	142.772	2.533	1967	3
147.462	144.213	3.249	1967	4
149.485	146.586	2.900	1968	1
151.381	148.824	2.557	1968	2
153.307	150.261	3.047	1968	3
155.340	152.751	2.589	1968	4
157.560	156.139	1.421	1969	1
158.963	158.826	0.138	1969	2
160.471	161.828	-1.357	1969	3
162.210	164.126	-1.916	1969	4

MSE=   3.363   RMS=   1.834   RHO=   0.920
MEAN ERR=   0.4974   MEAN=119.5074

Figure 2C-5. Standard Dynamic Solution of the Time Deposit Sector:
Life Insurance Reserves — *MIS*.

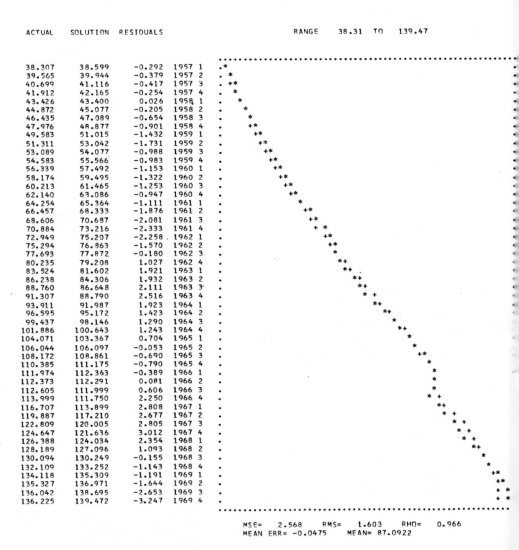

ACTUAL	SOLUTION	RESIDUALS			RANGE 38.31 TO 139.47
38.307	38.599	-0.292	1957	1	
39.565	39.944	-0.379	1957	2	
40.699	41.116	-0.417	1957	3	
41.912	42.165	-0.254	1957	4	
43.426	43.400	0.026	1958	1	
44.872	45.077	-0.205	1958	2	
46.435	47.089	-0.654	1958	3	
47.976	48.877	-0.901	1958	4	
49.583	51.015	-1.432	1959	1	
51.311	53.042	-1.731	1959	2	
53.089	54.077	-0.988	1959	3	
54.583	55.566	-0.983	1959	4	
56.339	57.492	-1.153	1960	1	
58.174	59.495	-1.322	1960	2	
60.213	61.465	-1.253	1960	3	
62.140	63.086	-0.947	1960	4	
64.254	65.364	-1.111	1961	1	
66.457	68.333	-1.876	1961	2	
68.606	70.687	-2.081	1961	3	
70.884	73.216	-2.333	1961	4	
72.949	75.207	-2.258	1962	1	
75.294	76.863	-1.570	1962	2	
77.693	77.872	-0.180	1962	3	
80.235	79.208	1.027	1962	4	
83.524	81.602	1.921	1963	1	
86.238	84.306	1.932	1963	2	
88.760	86.648	2.111	1963	3	
91.307	88.790	2.516	1963	4	
93.911	91.987	1.923	1964	1	
96.595	95.172	1.423	1964	2	
99.437	98.146	1.290	1964	3	
101.886	100.643	1.243	1964	4	
104.071	103.367	0.704	1965	1	
106.044	106.097	-0.053	1965	2	
108.172	108.861	-0.690	1965	3	
110.385	111.175	-0.790	1965	4	
111.974	112.363	-0.389	1966	1	
112.373	112.291	0.081	1966	2	
112.605	111.999	0.606	1966	3	
113.999	111.750	2.250	1966	4	
116.707	113.899	2.808	1967	1	
119.887	117.210	2.677	1967	2	
122.809	120.005	2.805	1967	3	
124.647	121.636	3.012	1967	4	
126.388	124.034	2.354	1968	1	
128.189	127.096	1.093	1968	2	
130.094	130.249	-0.155	1968	3	
132.109	133.252	-1.143	1968	4	
134.118	135.309	-1.191	1969	1	
135.327	136.971	-1.644	1969	2	
136.042	138.695	-2.653	1969	3	
136.225	139.472	-3.247	1969	4	

MSE= 2.568 RMS= 1.603 RHO= 0.966
MEAN ERR= -0.0475 MEAN= 87.0922

Figure 2C-6. Standard Dynamic Solution of the Time Deposit Sector: Savings and Loan Deposits — *MSL*.

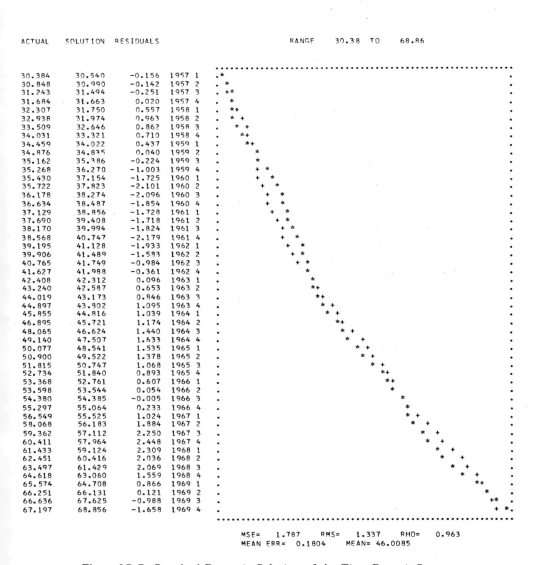

```
ACTUAL    SOLUTION   RESIDUALS                      RANGE    30.38  TO     68.86

30.384    30.540    -0.156   1957 1
30.848    30.990    -0.142   1957 2
31.243    31.494    -0.251   1957 3
31.684    31.663     0.020   1957 4
32.307    31.750     0.557   1958 1
32.938    31.974     0.963   1958 2
33.509    32.646     0.862   1958 3
34.031    33.321     0.710   1958 4
34.459    34.022     0.437   1959 1
34.876    34.835     0.040   1959 2
35.162    35.386    -0.224   1959 3
35.268    36.270    -1.003   1959 4
35.430    37.154    -1.725   1960 1
35.722    37.823    -2.101   1960 2
36.178    38.274    -2.096   1960 3
36.634    38.487    -1.854   1960 4
37.129    38.856    -1.728   1961 1
37.690    39.408    -1.718   1961 2
38.170    39.994    -1.824   1961 3
38.568    40.747    -2.179   1961 4
39.195    41.128    -1.933   1962 1
39.906    41.489    -1.583   1962 2
40.765    41.749    -0.984   1962 3
41.627    41.988    -0.361   1962 4
42.408    42.312     0.096   1963 1
43.240    42.587     0.653   1963 2
44.019    43.173     0.846   1963 3
44.897    43.802     1.095   1963 4
45.855    44.816     1.039   1964 1
46.895    45.721     1.174   1964 2
48.065    46.624     1.440   1964 3
49.140    47.507     1.633   1964 4
50.077    48.541     1.535   1965 1
50.900    49.522     1.378   1965 2
51.815    50.747     1.068   1965 3
52.734    51.840     0.893   1965 4
53.368    52.761     0.607   1966 1
53.598    53.544     0.054   1966 2
54.380    54.385    -0.005   1966 3
55.297    55.064     0.233   1966 4
56.549    55.525     1.024   1967 1
58.068    56.183     1.884   1967 2
59.362    57.112     2.250   1967 3
60.411    57.964     2.448   1967 4
61.433    59.124     2.309   1968 1
62.451    60.416     2.036   1968 2
63.497    61.429     2.069   1968 3
64.618    63.060     1.559   1968 4
65.574    64.708     0.866   1969 1
66.251    66.131     0.121   1969 2
66.636    67.625    -0.988   1969 3
67.197    68.856    -1.658   1969 4
```

MSE=   1.787   RMS=   1.337   RHO=   0.963
MEAN ERR= 0.1804   MEAN= 46.0085

Figure 2C-7. Standard Dynamic Solution of the Time Deposit Sector: Mutual Savings Bank Deposits – *MMS*.

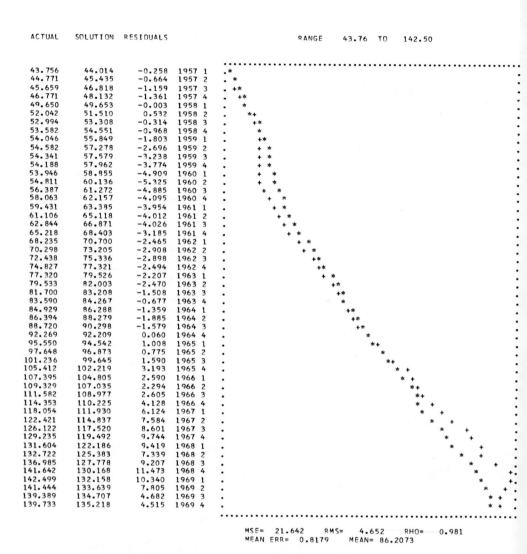

52

ACTUAL   SOLUTION   RESIDUALS   RANGE   43.76 TO   142.50

ACTUAL	SOLUTION	RESIDUALS		
43.756	44.014	-0.258	1957	1
44.771	45.435	-0.664	1957	2
45.659	46.818	-1.159	1957	3
46.771	48.132	-1.361	1957	4
49.650	49.653	-0.003	1958	1
52.042	51.510	0.532	1958	2
52.994	53.308	-0.314	1958	3
53.582	54.551	-0.968	1958	4
54.046	55.849	-1.803	1959	1
54.582	57.278	-2.696	1959	2
54.341	57.579	-3.238	1959	3
54.188	57.962	-3.774	1959	4
53.946	58.855	-4.909	1960	1
54.811	60.136	-5.325	1960	2
56.387	61.272	-4.885	1960	3
58.063	62.157	-4.095	1960	4
59.431	63.385	-3.954	1961	1
61.106	65.118	-4.012	1961	2
62.844	66.871	-4.026	1961	3
65.218	68.403	-3.185	1961	4
68.235	70.700	-2.465	1962	1
70.298	73.205	-2.908	1962	2
72.438	75.336	-2.898	1962	3
74.827	77.321	-2.494	1962	4
77.320	79.526	-2.207	1963	1
79.533	82.003	-2.470	1963	2
81.700	83.208	-1.508	1963	3
83.590	84.267	-0.677	1963	4
84.929	86.288	-1.359	1964	1
86.394	88.279	-1.885	1964	2
88.720	90.298	-1.579	1964	3
92.269	92.209	0.060	1964	4
95.550	94.542	1.008	1965	1
97.648	96.873	0.775	1965	2
101.236	99.645	1.590	1965	3
105.412	102.219	3.193	1965	4
107.395	104.805	2.590	1966	1
109.329	107.035	2.294	1966	2
111.582	108.977	2.605	1966	3
114.353	110.225	4.128	1966	4
118.054	111.930	6.124	1967	1
122.421	114.837	7.584	1967	2
126.122	117.520	8.601	1967	3
129.235	119.492	9.744	1967	4
131.604	122.186	9.419	1968	1
132.722	125.383	7.339	1968	2
136.985	127.778	9.207	1968	3
141.642	130.168	11.473	1968	4
142.499	132.158	10.340	1969	1
141.444	133.639	7.805	1969	2
139.389	134.707	4.682	1969	3
139.733	135.218	4.515	1969	4

MSE=   21.642   RMS=   4.652   RHO=   0.981
MEAN ERR=   0.8179   MEAN= 86.2073

Figure 2C-8. Standard Dynamic Solution of the Time Deposit Sector: Commercial Bank Deposits — *MTP*.

ACTUAL   SOLUTION   RESIDUALS   RANGE   3.29   TO   5.93

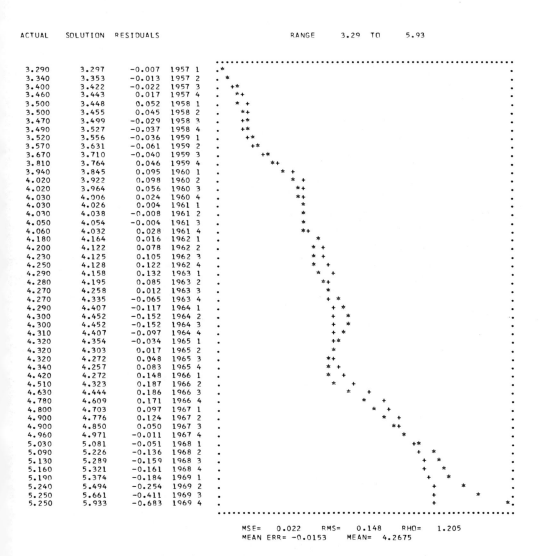

```
3.290    3.297    -0.007   1957  1
3.340    3.353    -0.013   1957  2
3.400    3.422    -0.022   1957  3
3.460    3.443     0.017   1957  4
3.500    3.448     0.052   1958  1
3.500    3.455     0.045   1958  2
3.470    3.499    -0.029   1958  3
3.490    3.527    -0.037   1958  4
3.520    3.556    -0.036   1959  1
3.570    3.631    -0.061   1959  2
3.670    3.710    -0.040   1959  3
3.810    3.764     0.046   1959  4
3.940    3.845     0.095   1960  1
4.020    3.922     0.098   1960  2
4.020    3.964     0.056   1960  3
4.030    4.006     0.024   1960  4
4.030    4.026     0.004   1961  1
4.030    4.038    -0.008   1961  2
4.050    4.054    -0.004   1961  3
4.060    4.032     0.028   1961  4
4.180    4.164     0.016   1962  1
4.200    4.122     0.078   1962  2
4.230    4.125     0.105   1962  3
4.250    4.128     0.122   1962  4
4.290    4.158     0.132   1963  1
4.280    4.195     0.085   1963  2
4.270    4.258     0.012   1963  3
4.270    4.335    -0.065   1963  4
4.290    4.407    -0.117   1964  1
4.300    4.452    -0.152   1964  2
4.300    4.452    -0.152   1964  3
4.310    4.407    -0.097   1964  4
4.320    4.354    -0.034   1965  1
4.320    4.303     0.017   1965  2
4.320    4.272     0.048   1965  3
4.340    4.257     0.083   1965  4
4.420    4.272     0.148   1966  1
4.510    4.323     0.187   1966  2
4.630    4.444     0.186   1966  3
4.780    4.609     0.171   1966  4
4.800    4.703     0.097   1967  1
4.900    4.776     0.124   1967  2
4.900    4.850     0.050   1967  3
4.960    4.971    -0.011   1967  4
5.030    5.081    -0.051   1968  1
5.090    5.226    -0.136   1968  2
5.130    5.289    -0.159   1968  3
5.160    5.321    -0.161   1968  4
5.190    5.374    -0.184   1969  1
5.240    5.494    -0.254   1969  2
5.250    5.661    -0.411   1969  3
5.250    5.933    -0.683   1969  4
```

MSE=   0.022   RMS=   0.148   RHO=   1.205
MEAN ERR= -0.0153   MEAN= 4.2675

Figure 2C-9. Standard Dynamic Solution of the Time Deposit Sector:
Savings and Loan Deposit Rate – *RSL*.

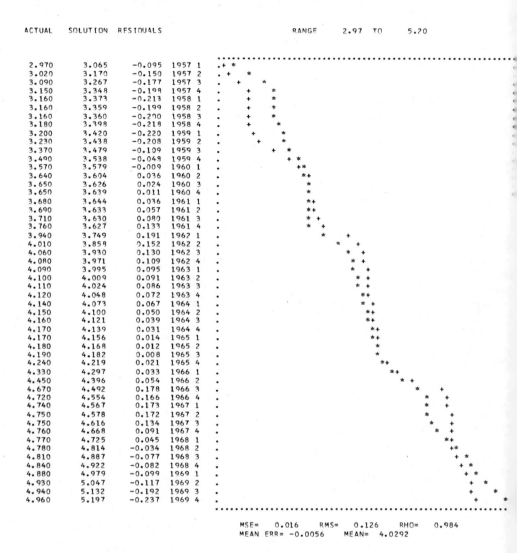

```
ACTUAL     SOLUTION   RESIDUALS                         RANGE    2.97  TO     5.20

2.970      3.065      -0.095  1957 1
3.020      3.170      -0.150  1957 2
3.090      3.267      -0.177  1957 3
3.150      3.348      -0.198  1957 4
3.160      3.373      -0.213  1958 1
3.160      3.359      -0.199  1958 2
3.160      3.360      -0.200  1958 3
3.180      3.398      -0.218  1958 4
3.200      3.420      -0.220  1959 1
3.230      3.438      -0.208  1959 2
3.370      3.479      -0.109  1959 3
3.490      3.538      -0.048  1959 4
3.570      3.579      -0.009  1960 1
3.640      3.604       0.036  1960 2
3.650      3.626       0.024  1960 3
3.650      3.639       0.011  1960 4
3.680      3.644       0.036  1961 1
3.690      3.633       0.057  1961 2
3.710      3.630       0.080  1961 3
3.760      3.627       0.133  1961 4
3.940      3.749       0.191  1962 1
4.010      3.858       0.152  1962 2
4.060      3.930       0.130  1962 3
4.080      3.971       0.109  1962 4
4.090      3.995       0.095  1963 1
4.100      4.009       0.091  1963 2
4.110      4.024       0.086  1963 3
4.120      4.048       0.072  1963 4
4.140      4.073       0.067  1964 1
4.150      4.100       0.050  1964 2
4.160      4.121       0.039  1964 3
4.170      4.139       0.031  1964 4
4.170      4.156       0.014  1965 1
4.180      4.168       0.012  1965 2
4.190      4.182       0.008  1965 3
4.240      4.219       0.021  1965 4
4.330      4.297       0.033  1966 1
4.450      4.396       0.054  1966 2
4.670      4.492       0.178  1966 3
4.720      4.554       0.166  1966 4
4.740      4.567       0.173  1967 1
4.750      4.578       0.172  1967 2
4.750      4.616       0.134  1967 3
4.760      4.668       0.091  1967 4
4.770      4.725       0.045  1968 1
4.780      4.814      -0.034  1968 2
4.810      4.887      -0.077  1968 3
4.840      4.922      -0.082  1968 4
4.880      4.979      -0.099  1969 1
4.930      5.047      -0.117  1969 2
4.940      5.132      -0.192  1969 3
4.960      5.197      -0.237  1969 4

              MSE=    0.016     RMS=    0.126     RHO=    0.984
              MEAN ERR= -0.0056      MEAN=   4.0292
```

Figure 2C-10. Standard Dynamic Solution of the Time Deposit Sector:
Mutual Savings Bank Deposit Rate — *RMS*.

55

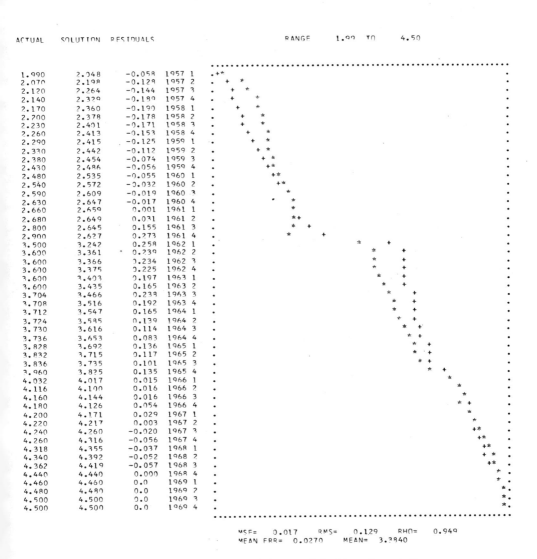

ACTUAL	SOLUTION	RESIDUALS			RANGE	1.99	TO	4.50
1.990	2.048	-0.058	1957	1
2.070	2.198	-0.129	1957	2
2.120	2.264	-0.144	1957	3
2.140	2.329	-0.189	1957	4
2.170	2.360	-0.190	1958	1
2.200	2.378	-0.178	1958	2
2.230	2.401	-0.171	1958	3
2.260	2.413	-0.153	1958	4
2.290	2.415	-0.125	1959	1
2.330	2.442	-0.112	1959	2
2.380	2.454	-0.074	1959	3
2.430	2.486	-0.056	1959	4
2.480	2.535	-0.055	1960	1
2.540	2.572	-0.032	1960	2
2.590	2.609	-0.019	1960	3
2.630	2.647	-0.017	1960	4
2.660	2.659	0.001	1961	1
2.680	2.649	0.031	1961	2
2.800	2.645	0.155	1961	3
2.900	2.627	0.273	1961	4
3.500	3.242	0.258	1962	1
3.600	3.361	0.239	1962	2
3.600	3.366	0.234	1962	3
3.600	3.375	0.225	1962	4
3.600	3.403	0.197	1963	1
3.600	3.435	0.165	1963	2
3.704	3.466	0.238	1963	3
3.708	3.516	0.192	1963	4
3.712	3.547	0.165	1964	1
3.724	3.585	0.139	1964	2
3.730	3.616	0.114	1964	3
3.736	3.653	0.083	1964	4
3.828	3.692	0.136	1965	1
3.832	3.715	0.117	1965	2
3.836	3.735	0.101	1965	3
3.960	3.825	0.135	1965	4
4.032	4.017	0.015	1966	1
4.116	4.100	0.016	1966	2
4.160	4.144	0.016	1966	3
4.180	4.126	0.054	1966	4
4.200	4.171	0.029	1967	1
4.220	4.217	0.003	1967	2
4.240	4.260	-0.020	1967	3
4.260	4.316	-0.056	1967	4
4.318	4.355	-0.037	1968	1
4.340	4.392	-0.052	1968	2
4.362	4.419	-0.057	1968	3
4.440	4.440	0.000	1968	4
4.460	4.460	0.0	1969	1
4.480	4.480	0.0	1969	2
4.500	4.500	0.0	1969	3
4.500	4.500	0.0	1969	4

MSE= 0.017   RMS= 0.129   RHO= 0.949
MEAN ERR= 0.0270   MEAN= 3.3840

Figure 2C-11. Standard Dynamic Solution of the Time Deposit Sector: Commercial Bank Deposit Rate — *RTP*.

Appendix 2D:
Differences Between
Endogenous Variables
in Control and
Experimental
Simulations

Table 2D-1. Effect of a Maintained One Percent Decrease in all Market Interest Rates, 1957: 1

| | Billions of Dollars | | | | Percentage Points | | |
| | | | | | Savings and Loan Deposit Rate | Mutual Savings Bank Deposit Rate | Passbook Savings Deposit Rate |
Quarter	Life Insurance Reserves	Savings and Loan Deposits	Mutual Savings Bank Deposits	Passbook Savings Deposits	Savings and Loan Deposit Rate	Mutual Savings Bank Deposit Rate	Passbook Savings Deposit Rate
57:1	0.082	0.742	0.006	0.258	−0.090	−0.006	−0.012
57:2	0.183	1.424	0.018	0.511	−0.177	−0.017	−0.031
57:3	0.310	2.071	0.037	0.759	−0.261	−0.033	−0.056
57:4	0.451	2.569	0.061	0.953	−0.339	−0.053	−0.099
58:1	0.616	2.992	0.091	1.112	−0.412	−0.075	−0.118
58:2	0.833	3.461	0.131	1.276	−0.477	−0.099	−0.152
58:3	1.008	3.112	0.174	1.138	−0.532	−0.122	−0.185
58:4	1.219	2.814	0.220	0.977	−0.577	−0.145	−0.216
59:1	1.449	2.542	0.266	0.790	−0.609	−0.165	−0.243
59:2	1.686	2.313	0.309	0.590	−0.628	−0.182	−0.262
59:3	1.882	2.105	0.339	0.392	−0.630	−0.195	−0.273
59:4	2.043	1.948	0.360	0.214	−0.633	−0.204	−0.282
60:1	2.151	1.828	0.370	0.063	−0.635	−0.210	−0.291
60:2	2.228	1.756	0.374	−0.055	−0.637	−0.215	−0.298
60:3	2.305	1.739	0.379	−0.145	−0.639	−0.219	−0.303
60:4	2.358	1.735	0.381	−0.215	−0.640	−0.223	−0.308
61:1	2.456	1.770	0.393	−0.281	−0.642	−0.225	−0.311
61:2	2.592	1.835	0.412	−0.346	−0.642	−0.227	−0.314
61:3	2.683	1.874	0.425	−0.397	−0.643	−0.229	−0.316
61:4	2.781	1.922	0.439	−0.443	−0.643	−0.230	−0.317
62:1	2.844	1.949	0.447	−0.476	−0.644	−0.231	−0.318
62:2	2.825	1.924	0.443	−0.490	−0.644	−0.232	−0.319
62:3	2.776	1.882	0.434	−0.494	−0.644	−0.232	−0.320
62:4	2.782	1.879	0.434	−0.504	−0.645	−0.233	−0.320
63:1	2.887	1.945	0.450	−0.531	−0.645	−0.233	−0.321
63:2	3.041	2.044	0.474	−0.565	−0.645	−0.233	−0.321
63:3	3.122	2.094	0.486	−0.585	−0.645	−0.233	−0.321
63:4	3.170	2.124	0.493	−0.598	−0.645	−0.234	−0.321
64:1	3.246	2.173	0.505	−0.615	−0.645	−0.234	−0.321
64:2	3.334	2.230	0.518	−0.634	−0.645	−0.234	−0.321
64:3	3.407	2.277	0.530	−0.650	−0.645	−0.234	−0.322
64:4	3.460	2.311	0.538	−0.662	−0.645	−0.234	−0.322
65:1	3.531	2.358	0.549	−0.676	−0.645	−0.234	−0.322
65:2	3.638	2.429	0.565	−0.698	−0.645	−0.234	−0.322
65:3	3.719	2.482	0.578	−0.714	−0.645	−0.234	−0.322
65:4	3.805	2.540	0.591	−0.731	−0.645	−0.234	−0.322
66:1	3.870	2.582	0.601	−0.734	−0.645	−0.234	−0.322
66:2	3.817	2.547	0.593	−0.718	−0.645	−0.234	−0.322
66:3	3.729	2.488	0.579	−0.702	−0.645	−0.234	−0.322
66:4	3.646	2.432	0.566	−0.719	−0.645	−0.234	−0.322
67:1	3.732	2.490	0.580	−0.759	−0.645	−0.234	−0.322
67:2	3.942	2.630	0.612	−0.791	−0.645	−0.234	−0.322
67:3	4.106	2.739	0.638	−0.801	−0.645	−0.234	−0.322
67:4	4.170	2.782	0.647	−0.802	−0.645	−0.234	−0.322

Table 2D-2. Effect of a Maintained One Percent Increase in Time Deposit Rate Ceiling, 1957: 1

	Billions of Dollars				Percentage Points		
Quarter	Life Insurance Reserves	Savings and Loan Deposits	Mutual Savings Bank Deposits	Passbook Savings Deposits	Savings and Loan Deposit Rate	Mutual Savings Bank Deposit Rate	Passbook Savings Deposit Rate
57:1	−0.485	−0.063	−0.181	0.906	0.008	0.126	0.647
57:2	−1.085	−0.135	−0.369	1.996	0.019	0.241	0.773
57:3	−1.736	−0.206	−0.541	3.197	0.029	0.320	0.782
57:4	−2.342	−0.263	−0.679	4.197	0.039	0.372	0.793
58:1	−2.954	−0.312	−0.809	5.248	0.049	0.402	0.807
58:2	−3.694	−0.364	−0.969	6.521	0.059	0.419	0.822
58:3	−3.993	−0.347	−0.950	6.954	0.067	0.428	0.838
58:4	−4.259	−0.317	−0.942	7.345	0.074	0.437	0.853
59:1	−4.543	−0.286	−0.967	7.792	0.080	0.445	0.868
59:2	−4.840	−0.257	−1.013	8.279	0.084	0.453	0.879
59:3	−5.045	−0.228	−1.049	8.618	0.086	0.459	0.888
59:4	−5.199	−0.205	−1.077	8.874	0.087	0.464	0.893
60:1	−5.264	−0.185	−1.087	8.979	0.089	0.468	0.897
60:2	−5.300	−0.172	−1.090	9.034	0.090	0.471	0.900
60:3	−5.375	−0.164	−1.101	9.156	0.091	0.473	0.902
60:4	−5.416	−0.159	−1.105	9.221	0.091	0.474	0.904
61:1	−5.569	−0.158	−1.133	9.478	0.092	0.475	0.906
61:2	−5.815	−0.160	−1.180	9.893	0.092	0.476	0.907
61:3	−5.968	−0.160	−1.210	10.153	0.093	0.477	0.908
61:4	−6.148	−0.161	−1.245	10.456	0.093	0.478	0.909
62:1	−6.256	−0.161	−1.266	10.639	0.093	0.478	0.909
62:2	−6.194	−0.158	−1.252	10.533	0.093˙	0.478	0.910
62:3	−6.070	−0.153	−1.227	10.321	0.093	0.479	0.910
62:4	−6.072	−0.152	−1.227	10.324	0.093	0.479	0.910
63:1	−6.292	−0.157	−1.271	10.698	0.093	0.479	0.910
63:2	−6.620	−0.164	−1.337	11.256	0.093	0.479	0.910
63:3	−6.790	−0.168	−1.371	11.543	0.093	0.479	0.910
63:4	−6.890	−0.170	−1.391	11.713	0.093	0.479	0.911
64:1	−7.051	−0.174	−1.423	11.986	0.094	0.479	0.911
64:2	−7.238	−0.178	−1.461	12.306	0.094	0.479	0.911
64:3	−7.395	−0.182	−1.492	12.572	0.094	0.479	0.911
64:4	−7.507	−0.184	−1.515	12.762	0.094	0.479	0.911
65:1	−7.660	−0.188	−1.546	13.021	0.094	0.479	0.911
65:2	−7.891	−0.193	−1.592	13.415	0.094	0.479	0.911
65:3	−8.066	−0.198	−1.628	13.415	0.094	0.479	0.911
65:4	−8.253	−0.202	−1.665	13.712	0.094	0.479	0.911
66:1	−8.392	−0.205	−1.693	14.029	0.094	0.479	0.911
66:2	−8.278	−0.203	−1.670	14.266	0.094	0.479	0.911
66:3	−8.085	−0.198	−1.631	14.072	0.094	0.480	0.911
66:4	−7.905	−0.193	−1.595	13.745	0.094	0.480	0.911
67:1	−8.092	−0.198	−1.633	13.438	0.094	0.480	0.911
67:2	−8.548	−0.209	−1.725	13.756	0.094	0.480	0.911
67:3	−8.901	−0.218	−1.796	14.531	0.094	0.480	0.911
67:4	−8.044	−0.221	−1.825	15.132	0.094	0.480	0.911

58

Table 2D-3. Effect of a Maintained $10 Billion Increase in Real Disposable Income, 1957: 1

			Billions of Dollars			
Quarter	Real Comsumption[a]	Unclaimed Net Worth	Life Insurance Reserves	Savings and Loan Deposits	Mutual Savings Bank Deposits	Passbook Savings Deposits
57:1	1.087	1.38	1.472	0.775	0.517	0.956
57:2	2.133	2.60	1.557	0.810	0.548	0.991
57:3	3.112	3.67	1.637	0.846	0.578	1.029
57:4	3.999	4.59	1.699	0.878	0.602	1.061
58:1	4.782	5.39	1.761	0.916	0.626	1.100
58:2	5.461	6.07	1.809	0.951	0.644	1.136
58:3	6.042	6.65	1.852	0.984	0.660	1.165
58:4	6.524	7.16	1.890	1.013	0.674	1.189
59:1	6.908	7.61	1.923	1.042	0.686	1.210
59:2	7.198	8.04	1.954	1.068	0.698	1.231
59:3	7.401	8.45	1.984	1.089	0.711	1.246
59:4	7.512	8.86	2.009	1.109	0.722	1.254
60:1	7.538	9.30	2.034	1.131	0.733	1.263
60:2	7.564	9.96	2.061	1.158	0.744	1.280
60:3	7.598	10.23	2.090	1.188	0.755	1.300
60:4	7.629	10.71	2.122	1.222	0.768	1.325
61:1	7.660	11.20	2.152	1.258	0.780	1.350
61:2	7.688	11.69	2.181	1.294	0.789	1.375
61:3	7.719	12.19	2.212	1.328	0.800	1.402
61:4	7.750	12.69	2.242	1.362	0.811	1.423
62:1	7.772	13.21	2.264	1.392	0.820	1.457
62:2	7.798	13.72	2.283	1.424	0.828	1.491
62:3	7.824	14.23	2.303	1.455	0.838	1.527
62:4	7.852	14.75	2.323	1.489	0.848	1.565
63:1	7.876	15.26	2.341	1.527	0.857	1.604
63:3	7.895	15.78	2.358	1.564	0.867	1.648
63:3	7.920	16.29	2.383	1.602	0.879	1.672
63:4	7.947	16.80	2.408	1.637	0.891	1.694
64:1	7.967	17.32	2.433	1.673	0.903	1.718
64:2	7.987	17.83	2.458	1.742	0.924	1.767
64:3	8.011	18.34	2.483	1.775	0.935	1.793
64:4	8.035	18.86	2.507	1.812	0.947	1.821
65:1	8.050	19.36	2.531	1.849	0.959	1.849
65:2	8.068	19.86	2.556	1.886	0.970	1.876
65:3	8.086	20.36	2.581	1.922	0.981	1.903
65:4	8.104	20.86	2.604	1.952	0.994	1.940
66:1	8.118	21.37	2.622	1.981	1.007	1.978
66:2	8.126	21.87	2.640	2.006	1.020	2.014
66:3	8.137	22.38	2.659	2.033	1.036	2.048
66:4	8.152	22.89	2.681	2.071	1.047	2.082
67:1	8.172	23.40	2.702	2.108	1.059	2.128
67:2	8.817	23.91	2.726	2.141	1.076	2.172
67:3	8.200	24.42	2.755	2.169	1.092	2.211
67:4	8.215	24.93	2.782	2.192	1.107	2.245

[a] Consumption here is not consumption in the GNP accounts but a concept developed by Friedman and Modigliani–Ando which includes imputed services on consumer durables instead of expenditures on durables. Thus it is much more sluggish than the GNP concept of consumer expenditures.

59

Table 2D-4. Effect of a Maintained One Percent Increase in the Dividend–Price Ratio on Common Stock, Corresponding Decline in Equity Values, 1957: 1

	Billions of Dollars				
Quarter	Unclaimed Net Worth	Life Insurance Reserves	Savings and Loan Deposits	Mutual Savings Bank Deposits	Passbook Savings Deposits
57:1	−51.58	−0.212	0.093	−0.102	0.239
57:2	−55.56	−0.672	0.009	−0.302	0.294
57:3	−50.92	−1.025	−0.212	−0.444	0.037
57:4	−46.74	−1.425	−0.529	−0.580	−0.349
58:1	−50.80	−1.766	−0.820	−0.700	−0.713
58:2	−58.29	−2.148	−1.122	−0.839	−1.032
58:3	−68.68	−2.611	−1.459	−1.011	−1.338
58:4	−80.16	−2.961	−1.749	−1.152	−1.532
59:1	−88.35	−3.166	−2.004	−1.241	−1.628
59:2	−93.79	−3.372	−2.234	−1.329	−1.750
59:3	−95.99	−3.651	−2.449	−1.454	−1.886
59:4	−92.26	−4.013	−2.693	−1.605	−2.036
60:1	−88.43	−4.356	−2.922	−1.731	−2.236
60:2	−87.45	−4.606	−3.117	−1.815	−2.438
60:3	−86.67	−4.758	−3.292	−1.867	−2.580
60:4	−94.59	−4.790	−3.415	−1.883	−2.666
61:1	−109.13	−4.847	−3.660	−1.916	−2.731
61:2	−116.20	−4.994	−4.055	−1.982	−2.844
61:3	−123.02	−5.126	−4.331	−2.040	−2.994
61:4	−125.74	−5.347	−4.648	−2.126	−3.146
62:1	−112.09	−5.531	−4.897	−2.199	−3.463
62:2	−96.40	−5.688	−4.879	−2.228	−3.769
62:3	−94.27	−5.717	−4.715	−2.216	−3.938
62:4	−105.21	−5.630	−4.726	−2.192	−4.036
63:1	−119.41	−5.505	−4.996	−2.186	−4.178
63:2	−126.93	−5.359	−5.343	−2.187	−4.396
63:3	−129.92	−5.291	−5.577	−2.198	−4.441
63:4	−135.74	−5.239	−5.701	−2.205	−4.446
64:1	−142.92	−5.324	−5.970	−2.262	−4.575
64:2	−147.48	−5.591	−6.356	−2.384	−4.848
64:3	−151.28	−5.969	−6.738	−2.529	−5.162
64:4	−155.07	−6.259	−7.056	−2.653	−5.428
65:1	−160.16	−6.447	−7.337	−2.745	−5.646
65:2	−164.02	−6.609	−7.642	−2.831	−5.860
65:3	−170.76	−6.815	−7.943	−2.921	−6.078
65:4	−171.93	−6.979	−8.929	−3.010	−6.309
66:1	−158.60	−7.016	−8.409	−3.074	−6.511
66:2	−138.64	−7.107	−8.133	−3.095	−6.577
66:3	−122.37	−7.105	−7.583	−3.046	−6.434
66:4	−128.92	−6.889	−7.025	−2.937	−6.155
67:1	−151.17	−6.585	−7.143	−2.868	−6.135
67:2	−166.34	−6.262	−7.641	−2.858	−6.380
67:3	−168.59	−5.944	−7.937	−2.843	−6.529
67:4	−177.30	−5.770	−7.905	−2.823	−6.540

References

[1] Adler, Michael. "On the Risk–Return Trade-off in the Valuation of Assets." *Journal of Financial and Quantitative Analysis* 4 (December 1969).

[2] Barten, A. P. "Evidence on the Slutsky Conditions for Demand Equations." *Review of Economics and Statistics* 49 (February 1967).

[3] Brainard, William C., and James Tobin. "Pitfalls in Financial Model-Building." *American Economic Review, Papers and Proceedings* 58 (May 1968).

[4] Brown, Murray, and Dale M. Heien. "The S Branch Utility Tree: A Generalization of the Linear Expenditure System." Discussion Paper Number 95, State University of New York at Buffalo, May 1970.

[5] Chetty, V. K. "On Measuring the Nearness of Near Moneys." *American Economic Review* 57 (June 1967).

[6] de Leeuw, Frank. "A Model of Financial Behavior." In Duesenberry, *et al.*, eds., *The Brookings Quarterly Econometric Model of the United States*. Rand-McNally, 1965. Esp. p. 523.

[7] de Leeuw, Frank. "A Portfolio Model of Household Saving and Investment." Mimeographed, 1966.

[8] Feige, Edgar L. *The Demand for Liquid Assets: A Temporal Cross Section Analysis*. Prentice-Hall, 1964.

[9] Freund, R. "The Introduction of Risk Into a Programming Model." *Econometrica* 24 (July, 1956).

[10] Goldfeld, Stephen M. *Commercial Bank Behavior and Economic Activity: A Structural Study of Monetary Policy in the Postwar United States*. North-Holland, 1966.

[11] Goldfeld, Stephen M. "An Extension of the Monetary Sector." In Duesenberry *et al.*, eds., *The Brookings Model, Some Further Results*. Rand-McNally, 1969.

[12] Goldfeld, Stephen M., and Dwight M. Jaffee. "The Determinants of Deposit-Rate Setting by Savings and Loan Association." *Journal of Finance* 70 (June 1970).

[13] Gramlich, Edward M., and John H. Kalchbrenner. "A Constrained Estimation Approach to the Demand for Liquid Assets." Federal Reserve Board Special Studies Paper No. 3. December 1969.

[14] Hendershott, Patric H. "A Flow of Funds Model of Interest Rate Determination: Theoretical and Institutional Underpinnings." Krannert Graduate School of Industrial Administration Paper No. 259. Purdue University, October 1969.

[15] Hendershott, Patric H. "Financial Models: Structure and Estimation."

Paper delivered at the Second World Congress of the Econometric Society. Cambridge, England, September 1970.

[16] Hulett, David T. "Savings Institution Behavior in Asset and Liability Markets." Mimeographed, 1970.

[17] Kardouche, George K. *The Competition for Savings*. The Conference Board Studies in Business Economics No. 107.

[18] Markowitz, H. "Portfolio Selection." *Journal of Finance* 5 (March 1952).

[19] Parkin, Michael. "Discount House Portfolio and Debt Selection." *Review of Economic Studies* 37 (October 1970).

[20] Royama, S., and K. Hamada. "Substitution and Complementarity in the Choice of Risky Assets." In D. Hester and J. Tobin, *Risk Aversion and Portfolio Choice*. Wiley, 1967. Pp. 27–40.

[21] Schoner, B. Letter to the Editor. *Management Science* 14 (August 1967).

[22] Silber, William L. *Portfolio Behaviour of Financial Institutions*. Holt, Rinehart, and Winston, 1970.

[23] Tobin, James. "Liquidity Preference as Behavior Towards Risk." *Review of Economic Studies* 25 (February 1958). Reprinted in D. Hester and J. Tobin, eds., *Risk Aversion and Portfolio Choice*. Wiley, 1967. Pp. 1–26.

[24] Zellner, Arnold. "An Efficient Method of Estimating Seemingly Unrelated Regressions and Tests for Aggregation Bias." *Journal of the American Statistical Association* 57 (June 1962).

3

The Dynamics of Portfolio Adjustment and the Flow of Savings Through Financial Intermediaries

FRANCO MODIGLIANI

This paper is concerned with the process of accumulation of household claims on the four major intermediaries dealt with in the FMP model. We account for the behavior of quarterly flows, and the stocks outstanding at the end of each quarter, for passbook savings deposits at commercial banks, savings and loan association deposits, mutual savings bank deposits, and life insurance reserves net of policy loans.

The paper is divided into four sections. The first section sets out the general form of the model we intend to test and estimate. This model is then applied to time deposits; to the other two depository institutions; and, with appropriate modifications, to life insurance reserves.

A Model of Long-Run and Short-Run Determinants of Stocks and Flows

The theory of portfolio selection would lead us to expect that, aside from transactions costs, or given time enough for adjustment, the proportion of total net worth allocated to any asset would be a function of (i) the expected rate of return on the asset, (ii) the expected rate of return on competing assets, (iii) the covariance of the rate of return on the asset with every other asset, and (iv) some appropriate measure of risk aversion which might in principle vary with per capita real net worth. If then portfolio adjustments were instantaneous and we could measure explicitly the various expectations referred to above, we would have at all times

$$A_i(t) = \alpha_i(t)V(t) \tag{3-1}$$

where $A_i(t)$ and $V(t)$ denote end of quarter values for the ith asset and net worth respectively; and where the long-run proportion α_i is related to the expected rates (r_i^e, r_j^e) and the variance, as in

$$\alpha_i(t) = \alpha_i\{r_i^e(t), [r_j^e(t)], [\sigma_{ij}^e(t)], \dots\} \tag{3-1a}$$

63

The quarterly saving flow $S_i(t)$ would then be given by

$$S_i(t) = A_i(t) - A_i(t - 1) = \alpha_i(t)V(t) - A_i(t - 1) \qquad (3\text{-}2)$$

However, even a cursory examination of the behavior of quarterly flows into the four intermediaries under consideration suggests that equations (3-1) and (3-2) are not very useful for quarterly data unless one allows properly for delayed adjustment. To see this, let us rewrite (3-2) as follows [hereafter we drop the subscripts i and t and abbreviate $(t - 1)$ by a subscript -1]:

$$S = \alpha \, \Delta V + V_{-1}(\alpha - \alpha_{-1}) \qquad (3\text{-}3)$$

The first term is the change in A resulting from the growth of wealth and the second is the flow needed to rebalance the initial portfolio in the light of changes in α. But dividing both sides of equation (3-3) by A and using equation (3-1) we can also infer that

$$\frac{S}{A} = \frac{\Delta V}{V} + \frac{V_{-1}}{V} \frac{\Delta \alpha}{\alpha} \simeq \frac{\Delta V}{V} + \gamma \frac{\Delta \alpha}{\alpha}$$

where $\gamma = V_{-1}/V$, or approximately one.

Hence the rate of growth of the asset is approximately the sum of the rate of growth of wealth and the percentage change in α. Over long periods of time the second term would average close to zero and S/A would average close to the rate of growth of wealth. But in the short run even moderate quarterly fluctuations in α should cause S/A to fluctuate fairly widely. In particular, since the long-run growth of wealth has been about 6 percent a year, or 1.5 percent a quarter, a decline in α by as little as 2 percent should lead to negative values of S/A. However, it turns out that even in the short run S/A has remained fairly close to its mean, never exceeding 4 percent per annum nor going below zero for savings and loan deposits and never exceeding 5 percent and going below zero only once for passbook savings. In view of the fact that rates of return on market instruments competing with saving deposits had sustantial short-run changes compared with the sluggish behavior of intermediary rates, we must conclude that α tends to respond very slowly to measured changes in relative rates, unless it is very inelastic with respect to these rates. The results reported in the following section will be seen to support the view of a very slow adjustment process and a fairly high elasticity.

Two basic mechanisms could account for a slow short-run response to variations in relative return. The first is that because of costs of adjustment— both pecuniary and nonpecuniary—A/V moves only gradually toward the desired ratio: we can refer to this source of delay as the *portfolio rebalancing lag*. The second is that the desired ratio might respond only gradually to measured returns, both because of inertia in habits and because the unobservable expected rates r_j^e are likely to be influenced not only by r_j but also by its past values: we can characterize this second source of lags as a *learning-expectational lag* (referred to hereafter, for brevity, as *expectational lag*).

The standard way to allow for gradual adjustments of stocks is through the so-called stock adjustment model, in which the adjustment per unit of time is hypothesized to be a fraction, say g, of the gap between the long-run equilibrium and the beginning-of-period value of the relevant variable. We can write this specification as

$$\Delta A = g(A^* - A_{-1})$$

or, on substitution,

$$S = g(\alpha V - A_{-1}) \tag{3-4}$$

This is the formulation that explicitly or implicitly underlies past empirical studies in which the current flow, or the terminal stock, is regressed on rates of return, wealth or some proxy for it like income, and the lagged stock.

But this formulation does not seem to be consistent with either the rebalancing or the expectational lag. To see its inconsistency with the rebalancing lag, rewrite (3-4) as

$$S = g\alpha \, \Delta V + g(\alpha V_{-1} - A_{-1})$$

We see that it implies an equally slow adjustment in correcting the initial stock imbalance and in the allocation of the fresh flow of wealth. However, since the adjustment lag presumably arises from the cost of shifting from previously held assets into new ones, there is no reason why it should apply to newly accumulated wealth—at least if for the moment we neglect the role capital gains.

To see the inconsistency of equation (3-4) with the notion that the delay is due primarily to the expectational lag, we denote by a^* *the optimum ratio perceived at time t* (as contrasted with α which is the true optimum) and suppose that it can be expressed as

$$a^* = g\alpha + (1 - g)a_{-1}^* \tag{3-5}$$

where $g\alpha$ can be approximated by some function of current and recently observed values of the arguments of (3-1a). One can think of α as the value of a^* generated by (3-5) when its arguments remain constant until a^* adjusts completely. Suppose further that the portfolio adjusts promptly to this currently perceived optimum value, so that

$$A = a^* V \tag{3-6}$$

implying

$$a^* = \frac{A}{V} \equiv a \qquad (3\text{-}7)$$

We can then substitute in equation (3-5) the observable ratio a for the non-observable a^*, obtaining

$$a - a_{-1} = g(\alpha - a_{-1}) \qquad (3\text{-}8)$$

This equation will be recognized as the standard form of the stock adjustment equations but now applied to the portfolio share rather than the actual stock as in (3-4).[1]

By noting that S can be written identically as $a_{-1} \Delta V + (a - a_{-1})V$, it is seen that (3-8) implies that

$$S = a_{-1} \Delta V + gV(\alpha - a_{-1}) \qquad (3\text{-}9)$$

or, also

$$S = g\alpha V - A_{-1}\left[g - \frac{(1 - g)\,\Delta V}{V_{-1}}\right] \qquad (3\text{-}9a)$$

Equation (3-9) shows that S can be expressed as the sum of a fraction a_{-1} of the increment in wealth and a portfolio rebalancing term which is a fraction g of the imbalance $(\alpha - a_{-1})V$. Expression (3-9a) is provided for comparison with the standard formulation (3-4). It shows that, under the pure expectational lag hypothesis (3-5) and (3-6), in a growing system (i.e., $\Delta V > 0$) the coefficient of A_1 is less than g. In fact, if g were small, less than $\Delta V/V$, the coefficient of the lagged dependent variable might even be positive. This may help to explain the generally surprising small "speed of adjustment" reported in past studies—i.e., a coefficient of A_{-1} very close to unity if

---

[1] One interesting property of the version of the model proposed in (3-8) is that, in contrast to the standard formulation (3-4), it allows for the possibility that *all* components of wealth adjust slowly toward their equilibrium value. Or, to put it differently, our hypothesis can be applied consistently to every asset even though it implies a gradual adjustment. It can be readily verified that if wealth has but two components, they both adjust at the same speed. Indeed, it follows from the budget equation that $a_1 + a_2 = 1$ and $\alpha_1 + \alpha_2 = 1$. But then using (3-8) we find:

$$a_2 = 1 - a_1 = 1 - (a_1)_{-1} - g[\alpha_1 - (a_1)_{-1}] = (a_2)_{-1} + g[\alpha_2 - (a_2)_{-1}]$$

which shows that asset 2 also adjusts toward the equilibrium value α_2 at the speed of g per period. By contrast, in the standard stock adjustment formulation (3-4), if one asset adjusts gradually, the other must absorb the slack. The difference arises from the fact that in the expectational model the current flow ΔV is immediately allocated according to the perceived optimum ratios a_i^*, which in turn satisfy the budget constraint

$$\sum_i a_i^* = 1.$$

the dependent variable is $A(t)$, and very close to zero if the dependent variable is $S(t)$. If our hypothesis (3-5) and (3-6) is a good approximation, this coefficient is seen to be a downward biased estimate of g.

Since equations (3-8) and (3-9) are equivalent, either one could be used to test the model and estimate its parameters [on the other hand, form (3-9a) is not a suitable one because the coefficient of A_{-1} is not a constant]. However, form (3-9) has advantages when we take into account the fact that one part of the increase in wealth $V(t)$ does not reflect current saving but rather accrues "in kind" on certain specific assets as a result of capital gains. Empirically, capital gains (which include revaluation of corporate equities reflecting in part the retention of corporate earnings) turn out to be a quite important component of V over the postwar period. On the average, two-thirds of ΔV is accounted for by capital gains and only about one-third by personal saving, though these proportions have fluctuated widely from quarter to quarter because of the volatility of the capital gains component.

It seems unlikely that these capital gains could be promptly liquidated and reallocated between assets, with the fraction a_{-1} allocated to A.[2] A more reasonable approximation is to hypothesize that only some fraction, m, would be reallocated within the period, the remaining fraction $(1 - m)$ remaining in the short run where it first accrued. Accordingly, equation (3-9) should be modified to

$$S = a_{-1}[\Delta V - (1 - m)CG] + g(\alpha - a_{-1})V$$
$$= a_{-1}SP + ma_{-1}CG + g(\alpha - a_{-1})V \qquad (3\text{-}10)$$

where SP denotes personal saving and CG capital gains. This is the main form that we shall estimate in the next section, and shall refer to as version IA.[3] In order to insure that the coefficient of the first term be unity we can

---

[2] It is even less realistic to suppose that, in case of capital losses, other assets would be liquidated in the stated proportions and the proceeds reinvested in the assets where the capital loss accrued.

[3] Equation (3-10) applies to assets on which there are no capital gains, which include those we are concerned with here. For an asset i affected by capital gains one would have to add to the right hand side of (3-10) a term $(1 - m)CG_i$, where CG_i is capital gains on asset i. Equation (3-10) could be generalized further to take into account the fact that the income earned on saving-type deposits is in part credited to the owner's account instead of being paid out in cash. One might hypothesize that, as a result, some fraction of the income earned, say $(1 - n)$, might tend initially to remain in the asset on which it accrued. To allow for this possibility, we could rewrite (3-10) in the more general form

$$S_i = (a_i)_{-1}[\Delta V - (1 - m)CG - (1 - n) \sum_j r_j(A_j)_{-1}]$$
$$+ (1 - n)r_i(A_i)_{-1} + g[\alpha_i - (a_i)_{-1}]V \qquad (3\text{-}10a)$$

where the summation extends over all relevant savings assets and r_j is the return on asset j per unit period (thus for quarterly data r_j would be $\frac{1}{4}$ the annual rate.) Equation (3-10a) transfer it to the left side. To reduce heteroscedasticity of the error term, both sides have been deflated by V. These operations yield the expression

$$\frac{S - a_{-1}SP}{V} = ma_{-1}\frac{CG}{V} + g\alpha - ga_{-1} \tag{3-11}$$

where $g\alpha$ is some function of observed rates of return on A and competing assets (and possibly other variables) appropriate to the asset under consideration. The coefficient m then provides an estimate of the proportion of current capital gains that is currently reallocated and the coefficient of $a(-1)$ an estimate of the speed of adjustment g of equation (3.5). Finally, the long-run equilibrium ratio corresponding to a maintained level of all rates of return can be inferred from the estimate of $g\alpha$ and g, $\hat{\alpha} = g\alpha/g$.

We shall also test a variant of (3-11), version IB, in which $a_{-1}SP$ remains on the right and is allowed to have a coefficient different from unity. This variant is suggested by noticing that the part of the capital gains associated with price changes and even corporate retention may be readily predictable. Thus the proportion of SP allocated to assets on which there are no capital gains, such as saving deposits, may normally be some multiple of $a_{-1}SP$ in order to maintain portfolio balance with respect to the anticipated portion of CG. We should then expect the coefficient of $a_{-1}SP$, say m', to be no less than unity and furthermore

$$m'a_{-1}SP + ma_{-1}CG < a_{-1}\Delta V$$

implying that

$$m'\frac{SP}{\Delta V} + m\frac{CG}{\Delta V} < 1 \tag{3-11a}$$

Since, as we have just noted, $SP/\Delta V$ and $CG/\Delta V$ average around $\frac{1}{3}$ and $\frac{2}{3}$ respectively, we should expect m' and m to satisfy the condition $m' > 1$ and $\frac{1}{3}m' + \frac{2}{3}m < 1$.

Version I relies on the hypothesis embodied in (3-6) or (3-7) that the

---

can be restated in the testable form

$$\frac{S_i - (a_i)_{-1}\Delta V}{V} = -(1-m)(a_i)_{-1}\frac{CG}{V} + (1-n)\left\{(a_i)_{-1}\frac{V_{-1}}{V}\left[r_i - \sum_j r_j(a_j)_{-1}\right]\right\}$$
$$+ g\alpha_i - g(a_i)_{-1}$$

and the coefficient of the second term in square brackets (which involves only observables and no unknown parameters) would provide an estimate of $(1 - n)$. Some attempts were made at testing this hypothesis but they yielded unacceptable results presumably because of multicollinearity between the term in square brackets and the lagged dependent variable, $(a_i)_{-1}$. By dropping the variable, its effect would presumably be captured by the coefficient of $(a_i)_{-1}$. Since the dropped term is positive, its omission might tend to bias down the estimated speed of adjustment given by the coefficient of $(a_i)_{-1}$ and might help to explain the very low estimates of g reported below.

portfolio adjusts quite promptly to a slowly adjusting "perceived" optimum ratio. We could instead hypothesize the coexistence of an expectational lag of the (3-5) type with a rebalancing lag applying to the second component of (3-9) which would then take the form

$$S = a^* \, \Delta V + g'(a^* - a_{-1})V_{-1}$$
$$= a_{-1} \, \Delta V + (a^* - a_{-1})[(1 - g') \, \Delta V + g'V] \qquad (3\text{-}12)$$

where g' is the speed of adjustment of the "rebalancing" component $(0 < g' < 1)$. We shall refer to this alternative hypothesis as version II. Equation (3-12) still involves the nonobservable a^* given by equation (3-5). However, at least provided α does not change very rapidly and g' is reasonably large, as one would expect, one can rely on the approximation

$$a^* - a_{-1} \simeq b(\alpha - a_{-1})$$

where b is a function of g and g' which approaches g as g' approaches unity.[4] Substituting in (3-12) we obtain

$$S = a_{-1} \, \Delta V + (\alpha - a_{-1})\gamma(\Delta V + \gamma'V) \qquad \gamma = b(1 - g'), \qquad \gamma' = g'/(1 - g')$$
$$(3\text{-}13)$$

---

[4] It follows from (3-5) that

(i) $\qquad a^* - a_{-1} = g(\alpha - a_{-1}) + (1 - g)(a^*_{-1} - a_{-1})$
$$= g(\alpha - a_{-1}) + (1 - g)(a^*_{-1} - a_{-2}) - (1 - g)(a_{-1} - a_{-2})$$

Also, from (3-12), by transposing $a_{-1} \, \Delta V$ and dividing by V, we infer that

(ii) $\qquad a - a_{-1} = g^*(a^* - a_{-1}) \qquad g^* = g' + (1 - g')(\Delta V/V)$

Therefore, $a_{-1} - a_{-2} = g^*(a^*_{-1} - a_{-2})$ and substituting in (i) and collecting terms

(iii) $\qquad a^* - a_{-1} = g(\alpha - a_{-1}) + (1 - g)(1 - g^*)(a^*_{-1} - a_{-2})$

From this basic recursive formula, one can in turn infer by appropriate manipulations

$$a^*_{-1} - a_{-2} = g(\alpha_{-1} - a_{-2}) + (1 - g)(1 - g^*)(a^*_{-2} - a_{-3})$$
$$= g(\alpha - a_{-1}) - g(\Delta\alpha - \Delta a_{-1}) + (1 - g)(1 - g^*)(a^*_{-2} - a_{-3})$$

Finally, substituting back into (iii),

$$a^* - a_{-1} = b(\alpha - a_{-1}) + R$$

where $\qquad b = g\{1 + [(1 + [(1 - g)(1 - g^*)]\}$

and

$$R = -g(1 - g)(1 - g^*)(\Delta\alpha - \Delta a_{-1}) + [(1 - g)(1 - g^*)]^2(a^*_{-2} - a_{-3})$$

should be of second order of magnitude compared with the first term if $\Delta\alpha$ is generally small and g^* is not very small.

Transposing $a_{-1} \Delta V$ and dividing by V, equation (3-13) is seen to imply

$$a - a_{-1} = (\alpha - a_{-1})\gamma \left[\gamma' + \frac{\Delta V}{V} \right] = (\alpha - a_{-1})bg' \left[1 + \frac{1 - g'}{g'} \frac{\Delta V}{V} \right]$$

(3-13a)

Comparing this expression with (3-8), it appears that replacing the adjustment process (3-7) with (3-12) still leads to a gradual adjustment of a toward α. However, the speed of adjustment—the coefficient of $(\alpha - a_{-1})$—instead of being constant as in (3-5) is now variable and increases with the rate of growth of wealth, except in the limiting case $g' = 1$ when (3-13a) reduces back to (3-8).[5]

Equation (3-13) is nonlinear in the parameter γ'. It can, however, be estimated, in the form

$$\frac{S - a_{-1} \Delta V}{\Delta V + \gamma' V} = (\gamma\alpha) - \gamma a_{-1}$$

(3-14)

by scanning over values of γ' for the value yielding the best fit for S.

If ΔV includes in part capital gains, it would seem appropriate to modify (3-12) so as to include in the first-term ΔV only the current accumulation, and to lump the capital gains component with V_{-1} in the second term. It can be verified that (3-13) and (3-14) remain unchanged except that the quantity ΔV is replaced by $\Delta V - CG$.

Application to Saving Flows into Time Deposits (MP)

The time deposits we are concerned with exclude large CDs held by corporations and foreigners (though unfortunately they include those held by state and local government).[6] We therefore expect this asset to compete most directly with money, especially demand deposits; other types of saving deposits; and with other money fixed assets, especially short-term market assets. We expect it to compete much less directly with equities and physical

---

[5] At the same time, this version shares the property of version I, that it could apply simultaneously to every component of wealth. This is because it retains the assumption that the *current* flow ΔV is allocated promptly in accordance to the perceived optimum ratios.

[6] The definition of time deposits differs slightly from Gramlich and Hulett's in Chapter 2. For Gramlich and Hulett, passbook savings deposits included all member commercial banks and is seasonally adjusted. The measure used in this study includes all commercial banks and is not seasonally adjusted.

assets held by households such as durables and houses. Also the asset is nearly risk free, as the risk of default is negligible and the rate of return is quite predictable in the short run in money terms and even in real terms, considering the sluggishness of the rate of change of prices. Accordingly, we can neglect covariance terms or, at least, approximate them as constant over time. This suggests that α might be of the form

$$\alpha = a_0 + a_1(RTP - RMON) + a_2(RTP - RSL) + a_3(RTP - RMS)$$
$$+ a_4(RTP - r_S) + a_5(RTP - r_L) + a_6(RTP - RR) \qquad (3\text{-}15)$$

where the symbols denote respectively the rate of return on time deposits (RTP), money $RMON$, saving and loan shares (RSL), mutual saving bank deposits (RMS), some index of short-term market rates (r_S), and long-term market rates (r_L), and the rate of return on equities and physical assets (RR). We should expect all the a_is to be positive and the first three or possibly four to be more important than the remaining ones, with the last the least important.

Because no cash interest is earned on money and because returns on demand deposits in the form of bank services are not readily measurable and are unlikely to have changed appreciably, at least until the last couple of years of our sample, we assume $RMON$ to be a constant $\overline{RMON}$ and thus to be impounded in a new constant term a_0'. But then α can be expressed as a linear function of all rates or

$$\alpha = b_0 + b_1 RTP + \sum_{j=2}^{n} b_j R_j \qquad (3\text{-}15a)$$

where
$$b_0 = a_0 - a_1 \overline{RMON}$$

$$b_1 = \sum_{j=1}^{n} a_j$$

$$b_j = -a_j$$

$$j = 2, \ldots, n$$

and R_j is now short for the various rates on competing assets. It should be noted that the sum of all the b coefficients, $\sum_1^n b_j$, should provide an estimate of a_1 and, hence, should be positive and measure the extent to which a rise in RTP leads to a shift from money into time deposits.

Unfortunately, because of the high collinearity of all rates, it would be virtually impossible to secure reliable estimates of the coefficients of each rate by standard OLS procedures. In what follows we have tried in a variety of ways to cut down the number of coefficients to be estimated freely—without, however, succeeding altogether in eliminating multicollinearity problems, as will soon become apparent. One step in that direction is to replace the two rates *RSL* and *RMS*—which tend to move quite closely to each other and with *RTP*—with a single composite rate *RA*, representing an average of *RSL* and *RMS* weighted by recent inflows into the two types of institutions.[7]

In chapter appendix Table 3A-1 rows 1 to 6 present the empirical results of tests of model IA with alternative specifications of the arguments of α and illustrate some of the difficulties created by the multicollinearity of the variables.

Row 1 of Table 3A-1 tests the simplest specification, namely the rate on time deposits, *RTP*, and the average rate *RA* at the two competing depository-type institutions. Both variables have the expected sign and are reasonably significant; and the sum of their coefficient is positive as expected. The proportion of capital gains reallocated currently is estimated at about $\frac{1}{4}$ (column 5) which is not unreasonably though somewhat on the high side; the estimated speed of adjustment *g* is .05 or 5 percent per quarter which, though not large, is larger than reported in other studies. Seasonal dummies for the first and fourth quarters have been added because the data for time deposits are not seasonally adjusted. (The dummy for the second quarter has been dropped since in all tests in which it was used it was negligibly small and insignificant). On the whole, then, all the estimated coefficients appear reasonable; unfortunately, the fit is rather poor as can be seen from the last three columns. Column 18 gives the standard error (SE) of the dependent variable $\Delta MP/V$, i.e., the current flow scaled by total wealth. (We do not give the conventional R^2 measure because in different tests, we use different forms of the dependent variable and, hence, the R^2 are not comparable while the SE are.) Column 19 gives the DW statistics measuring serial correlation of the residuals. Column 20 gives the root mean square (RMSE) of the difference between the actual saving flow *S* and the value computed from the estimated equation. Finally, column 21 gives the correlation coefficient between these two variables. It is seen that the *RMSE* is 1.2 billion as compared with a standard deviation of *S* of just over 1.8 billion: the independent variable accounts for not quite 60 percent of the variance. Also the serial correlation is quite high.

In equation (MP-2), Table 3A-1, we go to the opposite extreme, adding to the specifications both the short-term rate measured by the 3-months Treasury bill rate (*RTB*) and the long-term rate measured by Moody's AAA corporate bond rate (*RCB*). We have also allowed for a transient response to the rate of change of *RTP* and *RCB*. These additions result in a very substantial improvement in the fit as the RMSE measure of column 20 falls by

---

[7] See Appendix B for the precise formula.

$\frac{1}{3}$ to .8 billion, and the serial correlation declines. Furthermore, all the interest variables are seen to have the expected sign. But in every other respect, the results are very unsatisfactory. The capital gain effect is improbably small and the long-run properties of the equation are inconsistent with the basic model; not only is the sum of the interest coefficients negative but, in addition, the lagged dependent variable has a positive sign, which is inconsistent with the basic hypothesis of a gradual adjustment of the share of time deposits toward a long-run equilibrium value. The unreliability of these results is also confirmed by the very high standard errors for all coefficients—especially those of the three rates RTP, RA, and RCB—which is a well-known symptom of multicollinearity. This suggested the desirability of reducing drastically the number of rates by dropping either of the two market rates. As between the short and the long rate, we should expect the former to be the more important, especially since even for long-term instruments what should matter most should be the expected short-term holding yield which should be well approximated by the short rate. Accordingly, in equation (MP-3) we include only three rates: RTP, RA, and RTB (the rate of change of RTP was also tested but systematically turned out to be insignificant once RCB was dropped). The fit deteriorates only moderately indicating that the single rate RTB is a good proxy for the entire family of market rates; this variable is seen to contribute a good deal to the explanation as indicated by a t-ratio of over 5, whereas the role of RA is surprisingly insignificant. However, the lagged dependent variable still fails to exhibit the required negative sign.

A possible source of difficulties might be the well-known changes in the nature of the time deposit market which occurred around the early sixties with the introduction of CDs and a variety of other innovations which in part reflected and, in part, stimulated a much more aggressive competition of commercial banks for time deposits. One might expect these institutional changes to result in higher coefficients of all interest rate variables. However, since we are excluding large CDs from our measure of passbook savings deposits, it would appear that the increased competition would be primarily between interest-bearing money-fixed assets and not with money itself. This means that the sum of the coefficient of all variables which is an estimate of a_1 should not have changed significantly. To enforce this specification, we allowed for different values of the coefficient a_2, a_3, a_4, and a_5, beginning with the middle of 1962, by adding to equation (MP-3) the spread $RTP - RA$, and $RTP - RTB$, beginning with third quarter of 1962. Since a change in slope coefficients generally will be accompanied by a change in intercept, we also added a dummy on the constant, JC. Surprisingly, the spread $RTP - RTB$ turns out consistently to have no significant effect. As can be seen from equation (MP-4), even the spread $RTP - RA$ though of the right sign is barely significant, and the improvement in fit is quite marginal, while the estimate of g remains negligible.

In equation (MP-5), we have added a rather different kind of variable to the specification of α. If, as seems plausible, time deposits are a close substitute to money as a temporary abode of purchasing power, then the stock of time deposits might to some extent be controlled, just like the stock of money, by the volume of transactions. Since we are dealing basically with household holdings, we endeavored to approximate transaction requirements by disposable income. In principle, the effect of income should interact with that of interest rates; i.e., the long-run demand equation should take the form

$$MP = \alpha_v V + \alpha_y YD \qquad (3\text{-}16)$$

or

$$\frac{MP}{V} \equiv \alpha \equiv \alpha_v + \alpha_y \frac{YD}{V} \qquad (3\text{-}16a)$$

where α_v and α_y should both be functions of relative rates of return. However, not to compound further our multicollinearity problems, we were led to approximate the right side of (3-16a) by simply adding the variable YD/V to the specification (3-15a), with the expectation that the interest rate terms would capture both the effects through α_v and α_y. The coefficient of YD/V should be positive.

The results, reported as equation (MP-5), fully support this formulation. The coefficient of the YD variable (column 15) is positive with a t-ratio of 5; the fit improves considerably; DW rises; and most variables become more significant, notably the post-1962 dummy variable $RTP - RA$. Furthermore, the lagged dependent variable is now negative and indeed indicates a surprisingly large speed of adjustment of 14 percent per quarter. The only serious "casualty" is the rate RA which was already quite insignificant in (MP-4) and now has an insignificant positive sign. Also the capital gain coefficient appears now improbably high while the constant term turns negative. The result for RA suggests that, before the early sixties, time deposits were not very significantly affected by the rates offered by the other depository institution. This conclusion is somewhat hard to accept except for the evidence, to be shown below, that the other depository institutions were also little affected by the rate on time deposits. Row 6, Table 3A-1, shows that dropping the variable RA produces no significant change in fit and yields coefficients generally more in line with a priori expectation except possibly for the constant term, to which we shall return presently. Note that though the equation implies no significant effect of RA before the early sixties, it does indicate a very strong effect thereafter.

The last three rows of Table 3A-1 present some salient results of a test of variant B of the model, in which we allow the coefficient of $a_{-1}SP$ to differ from unity. Row 7 presents a test of the specification of α underlying row 4. The fit is appreciably better and most coefficients are more reasonable; notably the lagged dependent variable has the expected negative sign. But the coefficient of the new variable in column 4 is much too large to satisfy the inequality (3-11a). However, in row 8, where we add the variable YD/V and drop RA (repeating the specification of row 6) we find that the coefficient of column 4 falls a good deal and is only slightly too large—though it has a very large standard error, making the estimate rather unreliable. The interest rate coefficients also seem quite plausible: since the early sixties an increase in RTP by 1 percent (100 basis points) would tend to increase MP and hence the current saving flow by $4.4 \times 10^{-3} \times V$ or, with V presently running at roughly \$3 trillion, by \$1.3 billion. The implied short-run elasticity of demand for the stock is $4.4 \times 10^{-3} (RTP/a)$ or, with RTP currently at around 4.5 and the share at about .06, just about $\frac{1}{3}$. The corresponding effect for a one percentage point change in RA is \$.75 billion with a cross-elasticity of about .2; for RTB it is \$.15 billion with an elasticity of .05. We also observe that the sum of all rate coefficients, an estimate of the parameter a_1, is positive as hypothesized and amounts to 1.34×10^{-3}. It implies that a rise by 100 basis points in RTP, and in all other rates so as to keep all spreads unchanged, would tend to increase MP \$4 billion presumably through a reduction of cash balances. This implies a short-run elasticity of time deposits of about .1 and also an elasticity of demand for money with respect to RTP of $-.1$, which is not unreasonable when compared with the estimates obtained from most money demand studies. All these elasticities are, however, much higher in the long run, as can be seen by using row 8 of Table 3A-1 to compute the long-run equilibrium demand function. It is seen from equation (3-10) that, provided (3-11a) holds, which is roughly the case, the equilibrium ratio α can be inferred by dividing the coefficients of columns 7 through 15 by the speed of adjustment g, which is the coefficient of column 6 with sign reversed. Thus

$$MP = \alpha V = .64YD + \begin{cases} -.117V + V(.017RTP - .0048RTB) \\ \qquad\qquad\qquad\qquad t < 1962{:}3 \\ -.107V + V(.040RTP - .0048RTB - .023RA) \\ \qquad\qquad\qquad\qquad t > 1962{:}3 \end{cases}$$

(MP-8a)

Thus, the long-run slopes and elasticities are some nine times larger than the impact ones; in particular, for RTP a change of 100 basis points would increase the share by .04 (from the current .06) the elasticity of demand being roughly 3, while the elasticity with respect to RA is just below 2. These figures do not seem unreasonable, though the implicit long-run elasticity of demand for money with respect to RTP, about .9, does seem on the high side.

The one serious shortcoming of equations (MP-8) and (MP-8a) is the very high positive coefficient of current income YD and the very high negative coefficients of current wealth V which do seem rather unreasonable, if taken at face value. The first thing to observe in this regard is that, in practice, the income and wealth term largely cancel each other since the ratio of income to wealth has fluctuated fairly narrowly around $\frac{1}{5}$. Furthermore there are good reasons to expect this ratio to be roughly preserved under normal conditions.[8] Thus $.64YD/V$ is roughly .13 and when we add to this the constant term $-.117$ or $-.107$ we get a positive number rather close to zero—about .01 in the first and .02 in the second period. This constant measures the equilibrium share of time deposits when all rates are zero; and there is nothing wrong with the share being just about zero under these limiting conditions, for with zero rates, there would be no reason not to hold all money-fixed assets in the form of money. Yet the results obtained for the individual coefficients cannot be rationalized; they would seem to be seriously biased as a result of the high collinearity between the constant and the very stable variable YD/V, compounded by collinearity between the three variables YD/V, a_{-1}, and $a_{-1}SP$, and even $a_{-1}CG/V$. As a result, the coefficients of these five variables are individually not very reliable; and this hypothesis receives some support from the lack of stability of the estimated coefficients of these variables as one changes the detailed specifications of the equation.

There is little one can do about this problem short of expanding the sample through the passage of time or by some other method. One such method has been attempted and underlies the estimates presented in row 9 of Table 3A-1. There are strong a priori reasons for holding that several of the coefficients of the time deposit equation should have the same value for the other two deposit variables. This holds clearly for the spread $RA - RTP$ which should have the same numerical value, though the opposite sign, for the sum of savings and loans and saving banks deposits. It also holds for the capital gains variable (for the proportion of capital gains currently reallocated is not related to any specific asset), and by the same token for the coefficient of $a_{-1}SP$. Finally, one might conjecture, though with less assurance, that even the speed of adjustment should be roughly the same for

---

[8] If income rises, the increase in personal saving will gradually increase net worth. If net worth rises, it stimulates higher consumption and income. These effects are important for the simulation properties of the sector discussed in Chapter 7.

this group of assets. On the basis of these considerations, all the coefficients of equation (MP-8) have been reestimated simultaneously with those of the remaining two assets subject to the constraint that the above five coefficients should be the same (or the same except for sign in the case of $RTP - RA$). Further details of the procedure are best postponed until we have presented our analysis of the other two deposit assets. The results are shown in row 9 while the implications for the long-run equilbrium share α are shown below.

$$\alpha = \frac{MP}{V} = 1.18\,\frac{YD}{V} + \begin{cases} -.234 + .036RTP - .016RTB & t < 1962{:}3 \\ -.211 + .089RTP - .053RA - .016RTB \\ \qquad\qquad\qquad\qquad\qquad t \geq 1962{:}3 \end{cases}$$

$$\text{(MP-9a)}$$

In some respects, the alternative estimates appear more reasonable, notably that of capital gains and the smaller speed of adjustment. All impact elasticities (except that of RTB) are smaller by about $\frac{1}{3}$; however, because the speed of adjustment is only $\frac{1}{3}$ as large, the implied long-run elasticities are systematically larger. For example, the elasticity with respect to RTP rises from 3.0 to 3.6, and the implied elasticity of demand for money which appeared already high rises further to almost 1.5. Finally, while both the coefficients of Y and the constant are closer to zero, the long-run coefficients rise further, that of income to 1.14 and the constant to $-.225$ and $-.21$ in the first and second period respectively. The sum of the two terms still largely cancels out, leaving on the average a positive value of just .01 and .03; but the individual coefficients appear to have changed in the wrong direction. We have nonetheless adopted equation (MP-9) as our preferred equation, primarily because of its consistency with the equations for the other two saving deposits. But we retain serious qualms about the reliability of the equation with respect to its long-run properties. Clearly, because of multi-collinearity and the slow speed of adjustment, these long-run properties are hard to estimate. At the same time, just because of the slow speed, these properties do not exert a controlling influence on saving flows and, hence, these flows might be tracked reasonably well over a reasonable length of time even lacking a solid estimate of the long-run demand.

In the equations of Table 3A-1, including the "final" equation (MP-9), we have omitted the last term of equation (3-15) or (3-15a) involving the rate of return on nonmoney-fixed assets. As indicated earlier, we do not expect the substitution with these assets to be close enough for this term to contribute significantly to the explanation of saving flows. Furthermore, we were unable to construct an operational measure of the expected rate of return which could be made endogenous to the model and be adequate to capture presumably minor effects: even a measure of return on equity, such as the dividend price ratio possibly adjusted for pay-out, did not seem satisfactory, partly, because we are inclined to the view that the downward trend in the relation of this measure to the prevailing rate of return on money-fixed assets is likely to reflect a shift in risk preferences which would be hard to measure separately. One possible approach is to suppose that the real rate of return has tended to remain relatively stable and to infer the expected money rate of return from some measure of the expected rate of changes of prices. Along these lines we endeavored to add to the specification (3-15a) or (3-16a) a proxy for this expected rate, either in the form of an Almon distributed lag or by using the distributed lag suggested by the long-term rate equation. However, the results both for time deposits and for the other saving deposits were uniformly disappointing—this variable was insignificant and frequently the point estimate of its coefficient was positive instead of negative. This result, which we attribute to multicollinearity of the indicated measure with the family of interest rates already included in the equation, led us to abandon hope of capturing the effect of the last term. We shall comment later on some possible biases resulting from this failure.

Finally, some attempts were made to test and estimate the more refined model II, with distinct speed of adjustments for expectations and portfolio rebalancing. These attempts met with little success, for in scanning over alternative values of g' it was found that the RMSE was hardly affected by the choice of g'. To be more precise, for the limiting value $g' = 0$ (which is really inconsistent with the model as it implies no portfolio adjustment) the RMSE was larger than that shown in Table 3-1, which corresponds to $g' = 1$. But for positive values of g', even if quite small, say, beginning with .02 or .03 and up to unity, the RMSE was somewhat larger for model II if we drop the capital gains term, as seems appropriate for small g'. On the other hand, adding that term, the RMSE hardly changed over the entire range of positive g'. A likely explanation for this disappointing result is suggested on page 85. We thus conclude that our data and estimation procedure are not, at present, sufficiently refined to estimate the more ambitious model II and, hence, decide to rely on model I underlying Table 3A-1.

**Deposits at Mutual Saving Banks and
Savings and Loan Associations**

One could, in principle, apply our model individually to each of these two assets. We did not, however, regard this approach as desirable because these two assets are so similar that one should expect their response to variations in rates on competing assets to be essentially the same. In order to insure this symmetry, we propose to estimate a single demand for the sum of the two assets, denoted hereafter by MS. The distribution of this total between the two components in turn would seem to be controlled not by portfolio theoretic considerations of risk diversification but much more by institutional factors—notably the historical differences in the geographic location of these institutions and the difference in the rate at which these parts of the country have grown. These locational factors, combined with the costs and other disadvantages of distant banking, the resulting imperfection of information, and habit inertia tend to limit the elasticity of substitution, especially in the short run, but even in the longer run. Accordingly, once we have accounted for the behavior of MS, the behavior of each component will be accounted for by a "distribution" equation, incorporating as far as possible the considerations set out above.

Aggregate Savings and Loan Association and Mutual Savings Bank Deposits

One would expect the specification of α to be similar to that applying to time deposits except possibly for a less close substitution with money and short-term market instruments and a closer one with long-term money-fixed claims.

Table 3A-2, rows 1 to 4, reports the results of tests of model IA with alternative specifications of α. Equation (MS-1) tests the very simple specification involving only the own rate RA, RTP, and the long rate measured by RCB. All variables have the expected sign and order of magnitude and high t-ratios, with the conspicuous exception of RTP which is insignificant and has the wrong sign. Also the fit is not very good and the DW quite low. The result for RTP is typical; in every test run this variable is insignificant and mostly with a small positive coefficient. This is illustrated by equation (MS-2) in which we have added the spread $RA - RTP$ beginning with the 1962:3. The coefficient of this variable has the expected positive sign and an order of magnitude similar to that found for time deposits, and adds substantially to the explanatory power as indicated by the statistics of the last four columns. But somewhat surprisingly, it has the effect of reducing the estimated speed of adjustment g of column 6 to an improbably low level of 1 per thousand per quarter, while the coefficient of RTP remains insignificantly positive. This last result appears to corroborate the indication already supplied by our time deposit analysis that, up to the early sixties, the distribution of deposits between time and other deposits was rather insensitive to the spread in rates, but that the situation changed drastically since then. Accordingly, in equation (MS-3), and thereafter, we drop *RTP* and we test instead the responsiveness to short-term rates as measured by *RTB*, allowing also for the possibility of a higher elasticity in the more recent period. The results confirm the importance of this variable, especially since the early sixties, and indicate an improvement in fit and in DW. But some other estimates become less reliable and less credible, presumably because of multicollinearity; in particular, the speed of adjustment becomes insignificant and of the wrong sign—a peculiar result that always seems to accompany the elimination of *RTP*. Also the capital gain coefficient becomes small and not very significant and so does that of *RA*, though the latter result is not entirely surprising since the coefficient of column 7 relates now only to the earlier period. The coefficient for the second period—the sum of columns 7, 11, and 12—remains instead rather high.

Equation (MS-4) adds the income variable to the specification of α. The sign of this variable cannot be established with confidence from theory, though a negative sign seems more likely, especially in view of the results obtained for time deposits. One might, in fact, conjecture that for a given level of interest rates the total share of wealth invested in all deposit-type assets would be irresponsive or only slightly responsive to transaction requirements. If so, the total of saving deposits might tend to decrease as income rises relative to wealth because, in view of larger transaction requirements, a larger portion·of deposits would take the form of demand deposits. If, in addition, the time deposit component itself tends to respond positively to *YD* then the remaining deposit-type assets would be expected to decline. As can be seen from equation (MS-4), the estimated coefficient of YD/V is actually negative and rather significant, and the variable helps to improve the fit appreciably and reduce serial correlation. However, the speed of adjustment coefficient has again an insignificantly positive sign, and the sum of all interest coefficients, an estimate of a_1, becomes negative.

In addition to the above tests of model IA, we made a few tests of model IB, in which the coefficient of the variable $a_{-1}SP$ is estimated freely instead of being forced to unity. These tests did not appear too promising as the coefficient of a_{-1} was generally smaller, instead of larger, than one, as called for by the model. It is also rather unstable under alternative specifications and subject to large error of estimation—while at the same time the remaining coefficients are largely unaffected. This is illustrated by equation (MS-5), in which the remaining specifications are the same as in (MS-4). The coefficient in column 4 is only .26 with a standard error 5 times larger, while the other coefficients suffer from the very same shortcomings noted in equation (MS-4).

In particular, the estimated speed of adjustment coefficient is still insignificantly negative.

It thus appears that, as in the case of time deposits, it is difficult to secure reliable estimates of individual coefficients because of multicollinearity between the variables YD/V, the constant, $a_{-1}SP/V$, $a_{-1}CG/V$, and a_{-1} on the one hand, and between the various rates on the other. In view of this problem and our firm a priori belief that the coefficient of a_{-1} must be negative—though presumably not very large in view of the above results—we made some experiments forcing this coefficient to assume negative values between $-.02$ and $-.05$. We were encouraged to find that this resulted in much more reasonable and fairly stable estimates of the other coefficients, while at the same time the fit was hardly affected as long as the assumed value was no larger than .03 or .04. In equation (MS-6) we show the result for an assumed speed, g, of .03 per quarter, a value that was suggested also by some results obtained by shortening the period of fit to the sixties. It is seen that all the coefficients have the hypothesized sign and a sensible order of magnitude, including the estimated coefficient a_1, the sum of all interest rate coefficients, which is $.25 \times 10^{-3}$. This is $\frac{1}{3}$ as large as that for time deposits, which is sensible, and implies a short-run elasticity of money with respect to RA of about .04 (though the corresponding long-run elasticity of over 1 appears actually too large).

While equation (MS-6) appears quite usable, the imposed value for the speed of adjustment is clearly somewhat arbitrary; furthermore, the parameter estimates are not necessarily consistent with those of the time deposit equation. Accordingly, as explained above, we reestimated this equation simultaneously with the time deposit equation, thus forcing the coefficients of columns 4, 5, 6, and 11 to be the same. The result is shown as equation (MS-7). Because the resulting estimate of g (i.e., $-.036$) is quite close to the value assumed in (MS-6), the estimates of the coefficients are little changed. We give below the long-run share equation implied by row 7, Table 3A-2:

$$\frac{MS}{V} = -.32\frac{YD}{V} + \begin{cases} .113 + .027RA - .015RCB - .002RTB \\ \qquad\qquad\qquad\qquad\qquad\qquad t < 1962{:}3 \\ 0.85 + .084RA - .053RTP - .015RCB - .006RTB \\ \qquad\qquad\qquad\qquad\qquad\qquad t \geqslant 1962{:}3 \end{cases}$$

$$\text{(MS-7a)}$$

A comparison of (MS-7) with (MP-9), or of the above with (MP-9a), is instructive and indicates that on the whole the relation between the coefficients is eminently reasonable, making it unnecessary to have recourse to more complex constrained estimation. Incidentally, since the stock of time deposits, of *MS*, and of money all happen to have had roughly the same value around the end of 1969, about \$200 billion, the elasticities of the stock in each equation are proportional to the slope coefficients. We note in particular that the overall elasticity with respect to the own rate is similar though somewhat larger for *MP* as expected; the same holds for the elasticity with respect to *RTB* and for the elasticity of substitution with money. However, the sum of the coefficients of *YD* is substantially positive. This is contrary to our hypothesis and in our view confirms the suspicion that the estimate of this coefficient in the time deposit equation is substantially upward biased. Fortunately, as noted, this need not be fatal to the explanatory power of the equation because it is likely to be offset by a downward biased estimate of the constant term. Some bias in the coefficients may also result from our inability to estimate the effect of the expected rate of change of prices— probably reflecting the difficulty of measuring this variable adequately. In view of the positive correlation between all interest rates and the rate of change of prices over the period of observation, one would expect a downward bias in the coefficient of the own rate and/or an upward bias in the coefficients of other rates. We doubt that this bias is serious enough to create major difficulties in extrapolation since the estimated long-run response to the own rate or to all rates changing simultaneously do not appear obviously small, and also because the correlation between interest rates and the rate of growth of prices may be expected to continue.

Allocation Between Savings and Loan
Association and Mutual Savings Bank Deposits

In order to account for the allocation of *MS* between its two components, we can rely on our basic model I or II, replacing total wealth *V* by the total *MS*. Furthermore, because *MS* can only change by adding to (or withdrawing from) the initial stock but not through capital gains or losses, the capital gain term is identically zero and the distinction between version *A* and *B* disappears.

Since *MS* consists of only two components, once we have determined one component the other can be obtained as a residual. It is immaterial which of the two we choose to explain in the sense that the result would be the same; that is, if we denote by α_1, the function determining the share going into asset 1, then the function determining the other share is simply $\alpha_2 = 1 - \alpha_1$. In what follows we have chosen to deal explicitly with the savings and loan component.

As indicated at the beginning of this section the specification of α should be a relatively simple matter, at least in so far as the rates of return component is concerned, for we should expect only the differential between the two rates, $RSL - RMS$, to matter. However, because of inertia and the time involved in the spreading of information we were led to test a fairly long distributed lag on the spread, and this time with considerable success. In choosing the form of the distributed lag we allowed for the possibility that the response would depend not only on the level of the spread but also on its rate of change. As is well known, under these circumstances the coefficient of the current variable is positive but the coefficient of the variable lagged one is much smaller and may be negative and followed by coefficients either approaching zero monotonically or first rising to positive values and then falling toward zero. This rather complex shape can most conveniently be accommodated within the Almon polynomial distributed lag approach by freeing the co-efficient of the current variable; the rest of the distribution can then usually be adequately described by a second- or third-degree polynomial.

Table 3A-3 equation (MSL-1) shows the results obtained when α is specified to involve only a distributed lag on $RSL - RMS$. These results strongly support the importance of the rate of change effect as the coefficient of the current variable is very significantly positive while the rest of the distribution begins with a very significant negative value and is hump-shaped. The weighting function is approximated by a second-degree polynomial forced to zero at the end; however, very similar results were obtained with a third-degree polynomial as long as the distributed lag was allowed to include a period of around twelve quarters.

Our very simple hypothesis is seen to fit the data rather well as indicated by the high correlation between the actual and computed flow and by a RMSE of less than $100 million. However, the speed of adjustment g is even smaller than those reported in Tables 3A-1 and 3A-2, whereas one might have expected a faster response in view of the similarity of the assets. The long-run equilibrium share, corresponding to an indefinitely maintained level of the spread, can be inferred by dividing by g the sum of the coefficients of the spread shown in column 6, namely $\alpha = .33 + 2.3(RSL - RMS)$. This result seems to imply a somewhat improbably large substitution between the two instruments. Given enough time, a spread of less than 30 basis points in favor of savings and loans, which actually materialized for a great portion of the period, including the terminal quarter, would eventually lead to the whole of MS taking the form of claims on savings and loans. Similarly a spread of half as much in favor of mutual saving banks would lead to these institutions attracting all of MS.

Equation (MSL-1) makes no explicit allowance for the institutional forces mentioned earlier. We should expect those forces, on balance, to have favored the growth of savings and loan associations, though very likely at decreasing rates as the postwar period unfolded. It seemed desirable to make some allowances for these forces not only to improve our understanding of the process but also because failure to do so could bias the spread coefficient: since the share of savings and loan associations grew substantially from about $\frac{1}{2}$ to $\frac{2}{3}$, and at the same time the spread was, for the most part markedly in their favor, equation (MSL-1) could attribute to the spread an effect which was really due to other forces, thus overestimating the substitution.

There are a variety of ways one could try to account for the institutional forces. However, since any adequate procedure would call for variables that could not be readily endogenized in the model, we have fallen back on the less intellectually satisfying, but hopefully practically adequate, device of some simple time trend. Expecting that the forces favoring the relative growth of savings and loan associations were decreasing in importance, we initially tested a quadratic time trend for evidence of negative curvature. It was indeed found that when a linear and square term in time are added to the distributed lag specification, the linear term has a very significant positive coefficient, and the square term an even more significant negative coefficient—while the shape of the lag distribution was basically unchanged. The estimated time trend reached its peak shortly before the end of the period of observation, around early 1966. Since we have no reason to believe that there actually was a reversal of trend thereafter, and the estimated trend was of necessity very flat until the end of the period of observation which is still close to the peak, it appeared appropriate to suspend the time trend at the date of the estimated peak, namely the second quarter of 1966. The results of this specification are shown in equation (MSL-2). One notes immediately a substantial improvement in the fit and a reduction in the serial correlation. The distributed lag retains pretty much of its original shape and significance, but the speed of adjustment increases appreciably to over 7 percent per quarter; as a result, the long-run properties are rather different as can be seen from the following equation for α.

$$
\alpha = \begin{cases}
.48 + 6.4 \times 10^{-3}(TIME) - 6.75 \times 10^{-5}(TIME)^2 + .29(RSL - RMS) \\
\qquad\qquad\qquad\qquad\qquad\qquad\qquad\qquad t \leqslant 43 \ (1966{:}1) \\
\\
.63 + .29(RSL - RMS) \qquad\qquad\qquad t > 43 \qquad\qquad \text{(MSL-2a)}
\end{cases}
$$

This alternative estimate is seen to attribute a good deal of the observed shift to savings and loan associations to the trend forces, while the estimated long-run coefficient of the spread is only about $\frac{1}{8}$ as large as in equation (MSL-1), though it still is of respectable magnitude (a spread of 100 basis points would cause the institution with the higher rate to increase its share by 29 percent of the total). On the whole, we regard the estimates of row 2 as more reliable, though it is conceivable that this equation may attribute too much to the trend and not enough to the substitution effect.

The last two rows of Table 3A-3 report the results obtained with the more ambitious version II of the model. In row 3, the specification of α is the same as in row 1; while in row 4, we have added the time trend as in row 2. Because we regard the latter specification as more satisfactory, we concentrate our comments on a comparison of (MSL-2) and (MSL-4).

To estimate the parameters of model II, we made use of equation (3-14) and scanned over alternative values of γ' at intervals of .05 for the value minimizing the RMSE. As reported in column 10, that value turned out to be .15, implying a value of g' (the speed of adjustment of the initial portfolio imbalance) of .13 percent per quarter. However, once more the RMSE turned out to be surprisingly insensitive to variation in γ' (or, equivalently, g'). When g' is forced to unity as in row 3, the RMSE is .0796; whereas for the best value of g', the RMSE of row 4 is reduced only to .07915, a rather negligible difference. Taking the point estimate of γ' at face value, we can infer from equation (3-13a) that the overall speed of adjustment instead of being .074 per quarter is

$$.44\left(.15 + \frac{\Delta MS}{MS}\right) = .066\left[1 + 7\frac{\Delta MS}{MS}\right]$$

Since $\Delta MS/MS$ averages around .02 (corresponding to an annual growth rate of about 8 percent), the alternative estimate again implies an average speed of .075. Of course, in row 4, the speed of adjustment is a variable and is faster the larger $\Delta MS/MS$. But since over the period of observation $\Delta MS/MS$ is not only small but fairly stable, it is apparent that the refinement of a variable speed cannot really "buy" very much, and this presumably explains why the RMSE improves so little. It is only if g' is small relative to $\Delta MS/MS$ and the latter quantity is fairly variable that the refinement could make an appreciable difference. It also turns out, not surprisingly, that the long-run share equation α implied by (MSL-4) is almost identical to that implied by (MSL-2), as can be verified by dividing the coefficients of columns 3, 6, 8, and 9 by the coefficient of column 5.

On the whole, we feel that the results in rows 3 and 4 of Table 3A-3 mildly support the reasonable hypothesis that there is both an expectational and an adjustment lag. However, the sophistication appears to add little to the explanation of the phenomenon because of the appreciable speed of portfolio rebalancing and the relative stability of the rate of growth of MS. For this reason we regard the simpler equation, (MSL-2), as adequate for the purpose of the FMP model. The corresponding equation for mutual saving banks is then determined by subtracting savings and loan deposits from total savings deposits.

Life Insurance Reserves

In accounting for the behavior of life insurance reserves (MIS), we find it desirable to rely on a model somewhat different from that developed for the depository-type institutions. This decision is based on a number of factors and primarily on the consideration that saving in the form of life insurance is largely of the contractual type. As a result, one would expect the flow to be little affected by transient fluctuations in income and concommitant magnified fluctuations of personal saving, or by erratic movement of wealth reflecting capital gains and losses. This suggests that the flow of MIS, ΔMIS, should be related to "permanent" income, rather than to either saving, the change in wealth, or wealth itself, and that permanent income might be operationally approximated by consumption as measured in the FMP model.[9]

In formulating the nature of the relation between consumption and the flow and stock of life insurance, we started from the notion that the accumulation of this type of asset should be controlled by the very forces which provide the foundations for the life-cycle hypothesis of saving. As is well known, that model, with certain additional reasonable assumptions, leads to the conclusion that saving and the stock of accumulated wealth are proportional to income, and hence to consumption, with the proportionality factor depending on the growth trend of real income. Applying this proposition to MIS and recalling that the trend growth of income and consumption, say ρ, has been reasonably stable over the postwar period, we write the long-run equilibrium relation as

$$MIS = \alpha PC \tag{3-17}$$

where MIS is the stock of life insurance claims in current dollars, C is real consumption, P the price index of consumption, and α should again be a function of the rate of return on life insurance, and on other assets and possibly of other variables, to be specified presently.

Assuming for the moment a stable price level, it also follows from (3-17) that

$$\Delta MIS = \alpha \, \Delta CP = \alpha \rho C_{-1} P \tag{3-18}$$

A cursory examination of the data appears to support the usefulness of

---

[9] Consumption is defined as expenditures on nondurables and services plus the imputed consumption (interest plus depreciation) on the stock of consumer durables, measured in current dollars.

hypothesis (3-17) as a point of departure since, up to the mid-sixties, the ratio of *MIS* to *CP* appears to fluctuate quite narrowly around a level of 29 percent, except possibly for a mild declining trend. Since 1965, however, and especially in the last two years, the downward drift is more pronounced, carrying the ratio down to 25.5 percent by the end of 1969. Even these fluctuations are not inconsistent with the hypothesis since they could reflect variations in α. Furthermore, if α and/or P change in time, the long-run relations (3-17) and (3-18) need not hold in the short run for we should, as usual, expect that it will take some time to bring the stock back into its equilibrium relation; and this rebalancing will have to be accompanied by appropriate transient changes in the flow. Accordingly, in formulating a short-run model, we can again visualize the current flow as consisting of two components. A first component reflects the accumulation appropriate to the current level of permanent income or consumption. If prices were constant, this component would be given by the right side of (3-18). However, if the price level is subject to at least partly unforseen changes, it seems appropriate to allow for some lag in the adjustment of contracts by replacing P by the average level of prices over some earlier period, say $\bar{P}$. The second component should reflect the flow necessary to rebalance the stock and for this portion we propose to rely again on the standard stock adjustment formulation. These considerations lead to

$$\Delta MIS = \rho\alpha C_{-1}\bar{P} + g(\alpha C_{-1}P_{-1} - MIS_{-1})$$

For purpose of empirical testing, this can be conveniently restated in the scaled form

$$\frac{\Delta MIS}{P_{-1}C_{-1}} = (\rho + g)\alpha - ga_{-1} - b\frac{P_{-1} - \bar{P}}{P_{-1}} \tag{3-19}$$

where $a \equiv MIS/PC$, and $b = \rho\alpha$ can be taken a constant as long as α is not subject to wide fluctuations. We may also note that $(P_{-1} - \bar{P})/P_{-1}$ can be expressed as a weighted sum of the rate of change of prices over the period of averaging: namely

$$\frac{1}{n}\sum_{1}^{n-1}\tau\dot{p}(t - n + \tau) = \frac{n-1}{2}\frac{\sum\tau\dot{p}(t - n + \tau)}{\sum\tau}$$

where $\dot{p}(t)$ is the rate of change of P in period t, and n is the averaging period.

Turning now to the specification of α, we should clearly include among its arguments some measure of the spread between the return on life insurance reserves, say *RI*, and the return on other money-fixed claims, say, *RO*. Unfortunately, there is no readily available explicit information on the rate of return on *MIS*. As an approximation, we propose to use a distributed lag on the mortgage rate *RM* on the ground that mortgages are a major component of life insurance portfolios and the mortgage rate should also provide a good indicator of the return on the rest of the portfolio. Unfortunately, this rate may also be a good measure of the return available on competing long-term assets, *RO*, especially since it is highly correlated also with *RA*, the return on savings and loan and mutual saving bank deposits. The resulting multicollinearity makes it very hard to use *RA*, or some other rate of return on long-term assets like the corporate bond rate (*RCB*), as an explicit measure of *RO*, as will be shown presently. We were thus generally led to approximate $b(RI - RO)$ by

$$b_1 RM + b_2 \sum_1^m w_\tau RM(-\tau)$$

expecting b_2 positive as reflecting primarily *RI*, and b_1 negative as reflecting primarily the return on competing assets.

This formulation is also supported by the consideration that the behavior of *MIS* and ΔMIS are very significantly affected both in the short and in the long run by the behavior of policy loans. The incentive to borrow against accumulated equity should depend again on the relation between the rate of interest charged on such loans, say *RIL*, and the cost of alternative sources of financing, say *RO'*. This consideration suggests adding to the specification of α a term $c(RO' - RIL)$ with $c < 0$. The rate on policy loans, *RIL*, is set by contract and has apparently remained constant at a conventional level throughout the period covered by our data. As for the alternative cost *RO'*, we conjecture that *RM* may again provide a good proxy. Thus the term $c(RO' - RIL)$ can be reduced to $b_3 RM + b_4$, $b_3 < 0$, $b_4 > 0$ and the specification of α to

$$\alpha = c_0 + c_1 RM + c_2 \sum_1^m w_\tau RM(-\tau)$$

with $c_1 = b_1 + b_3 < 0$, $c_2 = b_2 > 0$. Note that while b_1 and b_2 might be roughly equal in absolute value—meaning that in the long run the return on life insurance will tend to match that on alternative money-fixed assets—the coefficient c_1 should exceed c_2 in absolute value because of the policy loan effect. In other words, as long as *RIL* is unresponsive to change in market rates of return, one should expect that a rise of all rates will, on balance, tend to reduce α.

A case can also be made for adding to the specifications of α some measure of the expected rate of change of prices, $\dot{p}^e$. Even though this variable should not affect the attractiveness of *MIS* versus other money-fixed assets, it should reduce it in comparison with physical assets or claims to such; hence, the sign of $\dot{p}^e$ should be negative. But we should hardly expect it to be very important, for, except in the presence of very large and unpredictable variations in prices, there should be very limited substitution between real assets and such a specialized asset as life insurance reserves.

One further factor that should have appreciably affected the attractiveness of life insurance reserves in the postwar period is the marked growth in various retirement schemes including both (i) the increase in Social Security coverage and benefits and (ii) the spread of private pension funds. The first mentioned development should clearly have an adverse effect; the second is more complex for, in so far as private pension funds are managed by life insurance companies, it could even have increased α. However, since non-insured pension funds have grown distinctly faster than the insured ones, on balance the effect is likely to have been unfavorable; and, when coupled with the growth of Social Security, it could partly account for the declining trend of MIS/PC noted earlier. Because noninsured pension funds are not treated separately in the FMP model, we ended up by trying to capture this last factor by merely adding to the specification of α the ratio of Social Security benefits $(OASI)$ to consumption.

Inserting all of the above specifications into equation (3-19) we are led to the following hypothesis as a basis for our empirical tests:

$$\frac{\Delta MIS}{\$C_{-1}} = (\rho + g)\left[c_0' + c_1'RM + c_2'\sum_{\tau=1}^{m} w_\tau RM(-\tau) + c_3'\dot{p}^e + c_4\frac{OASI}{\$C_{-1}}\right]$$
$$-g\frac{MIS_{-1}}{\$C_{-1}} + c_5'\sum_{\tau=1}^{n} v_\tau\dot{p}(-\tau) \tag{3-20}$$

where $\$C$ denotes consumption in current dollars. This equation can be further simplified by combining like terms and consolidating unknown coefficients. Note in this connection that the only operational way of measuring $\dot{p}^e$ is through a distributed lag on past $\dot{p}$, which could not be disentangled from the other distributed lag associated with c_5'. We thus arrive at the following hypothesis which is directly usable for estimation:

$$\frac{\Delta MIS}{\$C_{-1}} = c_0 + c_1RM + c_2\sum_{\tau=1}^{m} w_\tau RM(-\tau) + c_3\sum_{\tau=0}^{n} v_\tau\dot{p}(-\tau)$$
$$+ c_4\frac{OASI}{\$C_{-1}} + c_5\frac{MIS}{\$C_{-1}} \tag{3-21}$$

The considerations used in deriving this equation imply $c_0, c_2 > 0$, c_1, c_3, $c_4, c_5 < 0$, and also $c_1 + c_2 < 0$.

To this basic hypothesis we also added one further component aimed at improving the specification of the short-run dynamics of policy loans. An examination of the evidence shows that the flow of such loans is subject to very sharp short-run swings. We conjecture that such swings represent a response not only to the behavior of the alternative cost but also to swings in the stringency of credit rationing in all markets, including the mortgage and the commercial loan market. To capture this effect one might rely on some direct measure of credit rationing such as that developed by Jaffee and Modigliani.[10] We do not follow this course because that variable is not included in the FMP model. However, the above-mentioned study suggests that a significant increase in rationing tends to be accompanied by a substantial narrowing of the spread between the commercial loan rate, RCL, and short-term market rates such as the commercial paper rate, RCP. A cursory examination of the available evidence confirms that in every period in which a substantial increase in RCP brought the spread $RCL - RCP$ to well below 100 basis points, the flow of policy loans exhibits a marked transient increase with a lag of no more than one quarter. This phenomenon is strikingly apparent in 1966:1 to 1967:1, 1967:4 to 1968:3 and 1969:1 to 1969:4 and also, on a more moderate scale, in 1959:4 to 1960:2 and 1965:2 and 1965:3 when the spread did not get quite as narrow.

These considerations suggest that the effect of rationing on the flow of policy loans and thus finally on ΔMIS might be captured through a variable coming into play whenever the spread $(RCP - RCL)$ exceeds some threshold value. To see how such a variable might be constructed, we may start from the following hypothesis about the behavior of policy loans (PL):

$$PL/MIS = k^*[(RCP - RCL) - TR] + k_0 \qquad (3\text{-}22)$$

where TR denotes the threshold level,

$$k^* = \begin{cases} k > 0 & \text{if } (RCP - RCL) - TR \text{ is positive} \\ 0 & \text{otherwise} \end{cases}$$

and k_0 stands for the forces affecting policy loans other than spurts of credit rationing. To a first approximation MIS can be taken as proportional to $\$C$ so that we can rewrite (3-22) as

$$PL/\$C_{-1} = K_0 + K^*(RCP - RCL) - (K^*TR) \qquad (3\text{-}22\text{a})$$

---

[10] "A Theory and Test of Credit Rationing," *American Economic Review* (December 1969).

with K^* proportional to k^*. Since ΔMIS is reduced by an increase in policy loans, we conclude that the rationing effect may be measured by adding to (3-21) a term as follows:

$$c_6 J + c_7[\overline{J(RCP - RCL)}]$$

where J is a dummy variable with value 1 when abnormal rationing is in effect and is zero otherwise and $(\overline{RCP - RCL})$ is an average of the spread in the current and previous quarter, to allow for the short lag in response, mentioned earlier. The coefficient c_7 is then an estimate of $-k$ of (3-22), up to a proportionality factor, and thus should be negative, while $(-c_6/c_7)$ should provide an estimate of the threshold level, TR. The term K_0 of (3-22), on the other hand, is supposed to be already covered by the remaining arguments of (3-21). From the observed behavior of policy loans we tentatively concluded that the dummy variable J should take the value 1 whenever a rise in RCP narrowed the current spread to below $-.7$ (70 basis points) and should retain that value as long as $(\overline{RCP - RCL})$ remained in the neighborhood of $-.7$ or below. Under this rule the quarters in which J is 1 roughly coincide with those mentioned at the end of the previous paragraph.[11]

The empirical results are reported in Table 3A-4. In row 1 we test the basic specification (3-21) and the results appear, in most respects, fairly satisfactory. The statistics of columns 10 to 13 suggest that the model accounts quite well for the behavior of the flow ΔMIS as indicated by RMSE, below 100 million and a quite high correlation of ΔMIS, though the residual errors are highly serially correlated. The speed of adjustment in column 2 is again rather small, as for all other assets; though, for reasons stated earlier, this is one asset for which a slow speed is credible. In line with our hypothesis, the current rate RM is very significantly negative, the coefficient of the distributed lag is positive and smaller in absolute value, and the coefficient of $OASI$ is also negative. The sum of weights of $\dot{p}$ also has the expected negative sign, though it is insignificant and numerically smaller than expected by at least $\frac{1}{3}$.[12] Finally, the long-run implications of the equation also appear not unreasonable. From the coefficients of row 1 and equations

[11] The simple rule adopted does not encompass the quarters 1960:2 and 1968:3, coming at the tail end of a tight period, even though policy loans were still quite high; but it did not seem worthwhile to develop a more complex rule in order to accommodate these years. In addition, 1969:4 falls outside the period used for estimation.

[12] This coefficient is the sum of c_3' and c_5', both negative, of equation (3-20). Also, as suggested earlier, c_5 alone should be roughly $-\rho\alpha(n - 1)/2$. Since ρ is just about .01, α in the order of .30, and n was assumed at 12, this should amount to .018, or, since $\dot{p}$ is measured as a percentage, $.18 \times 10^{-3}$, as compared with the estimated value of $.04 \times 10^{-3}$.

(3-20) and (3-21), one can readily establish that the implied long-run equilibrium ratio is

$$\alpha = \frac{.024 - 10.7 \times 10^{-4}RM - 4.0 \times 10^{-5}\dot{p} - .012[OASI/\$C_{-1}]}{.045 + \rho}$$

(MIS-1a)

The coefficient of RM and $\dot{p}$ are the sum of the coefficients in columns 3 and 4 and in column 5 respectively. The growth trend of C was just about 1 percent per quarter so we can take ρ as .01 obtaining

$$\alpha \simeq .43 - .020RM - .7 \times 10^{-3}\dot{p} - .22\frac{OASI}{\$C_{-1}}$$

Since, at the beginning of the period (the end of 1954), RM was around 5 percent and $OASI$ some .02 of consumption (and the contribution of $\dot{p}$ is negligible), the implied value of α is around .33 or a little above the observed ratio of about .3. Our results also imply that α has declined since, because each of these variables has increased by just about 300 basis points: RM from 5 to 8 percent, and $OASI/\$C$ also from 2 to 5 percent. These increases imply a decrease in α to about .26, again a little above the actual value in 1969:3 of .255. Note that the implied effect of $OASI$—a decline in the stock of .2 billion per billion increase in the annual flow—is smaller than one might have expected, especially if $OASI$ is supposed to proxy also for the growth of noninsured pension funds. Yet the measured effect is not altogether negligible, and the relevance of the variable is further supported by the finding that its coefficient remains significant even if one adds a time trend while the time trend itself is not significant (and is positive).

In row 2 of Table 3A-4 we have added the rationing proxy and the results appear to support our formulation. The coefficient of column 8, an estimate of c_7 is negative as expected and quite significant as is the estimate of c_6 in column 7. These two coefficients imply a threshold value of $-(1.17/1.87) = -.63$ which is quite close to the assumed threshold value of $-.7$. They further imply that an increase in spread by 10 basis points would reduce the inflow by about $.1 \times 1.2 \times 10^{-3} \times \$C$ or with $\$C$ now running around \$600 billion by somewhat over 100 million, a nonnegligible amount compared with recent quarterly inflows of 1 to 1.5 billion. It is also seen that the fit improves appreciably and DW also rises, though it still remains uncomfortably small. On the other hand, the remaining coefficients are affected only to a minor degree; indeed aside from a slightly higher speed of adjustment, the only nonnegligible change is in the shape of the distributed lag on RM which no longer provides a clear indication of a rate of change effect. This change however can be accounted for by the consideration that the rate of change of RM is itself associated with, and hence a proxy for, the rationing effect. In row 1 the coefficients of RM current and lagged, to some extent capture the rationing effect which in row 2 we endeavor to measure by separate variables. On the other hand, the long-run properties of the two equations, which depend in particular on the *sum* of the coefficient c_1 and c_2, are nearly identical, as can be seen from the following equation, which gives the long-run equilibrium ratio implied by row 2

$$\alpha = .42 - .017RM - 1.3 \times 10^{-3}\dot{p} - .27\left(\frac{OASI}{\$C}\right)_{-1}$$

Finally, in row 3 we show the results of an attempt at measuring explicitly the return RO on competing money-fixed assets, by means of the corporate bond rate. To this end, RI was approximated by

$$\sum_{0}^{m} w_\tau RM(-\tau)$$

and RO by $\overline{RCB}$, an average of RCB in the current and previous two quarters. We should expect the first variable to have a positive and the second a negative coefficient.[13] This formulation fits the data about as well as that of row 2, but the coefficient of RCB is positive (though scarcely significant) while the coefficients of the distributed lag on RM start markedly negative; and, though they eventually turn positive, their sum is still quite negative. At the same time, the sum of all interest rate coefficients, an estimate of $c_1 + c_2$, remains approximately the same as in row 1 and 2, i.e., around -10×10^{-4}, so that the long-run implications are also roughly the same. The other major differences are a distinctly slower speed of adjustment and the greater role assigned both to the $OASI$ variable and to the rate of change of prices.

In summary, all the estimated equations tell roughly the same story: MIS and ΔMIS tend to increase with permanent income as measured by consumption and tend to be adversely affected by the overall level of long-term interest rates—a phenomenon that we primarily attribute to the policy loan effect—by the growth of social security benefits and, very mildly, by the rate of growth of prices. In the short run they are also adversely affected by the rate of change of long-term rates and by variations in the availability of credit, again primarily, we conjecture, through their effect on policy loans. Furthermore, this set of variables appears to account quite well for the

---

[13] We also tried to replace $\overline{RCB}$ by RCB but the results are very close to those reported in row 3.

behavior of ΔMIS and MIS in any of the alternative versions tested. On the whole, however, the version of row 2 appears to yield the most reasonable coefficient estimates and, accordingly, has been selected for inclusion in the model though we suspect that it tends to understate the depressing effect of the growth of pension funds and, therefore, probably to overstate the long-run effect of the level of rates, measured by the sum of the mortgage rate coefficients.

Appendix 3A:
The Flow of Savings

Table 3A-1. Time Deposits at Commercial Banks, Estimated Coefficients

(Standard errors are below the coefficients)

(1)	(2)	(3)	(4)	(5)	(6)	(7)	(8)	(9)	(10)	(11)
Equation	Model	Constant $(\times 10^{-3})$	$a_{-1} \dfrac{SP}{V}$	$a_{-1} \dfrac{CG}{V}$	a_{-1}	RTP $(\times 10^{-3})$	ΔRTP $(\times 10^{-3})$	RA $(\times 10^{-3})$	RTB $(\times 10^{-3})$	RCB $(\times 10^{-3})$
MP-1	IA	2.9 1.1	1.0^a —	.24 .15	-.050 .024	1.30 0.33		-.99 .51		
MP-2	IA	-0.6 1.2	1.0^a —	.016 .012	.053 .024	0.54 0.37	1.97 0.73	-.10 .75	-.45 .13	-.19 .31
MP-3	IA	0.71 0.96	1.0^a —	.035 .13	.006 .022	0.98 0.27		-.039 .43	-.494 .094	
MP-4	IA	-0.20 1.15	1.0^a —	.02 .13	.036 .026	0.90 0.43		-.38 .60	-.556 .095	
MP-5	IA	-18.0 3.8	1.0^a —	.61 .15	-.141 .042	1.51 0.38		.91 .56	-.553 .078	
MP-6	IA	-14.1 3.0	1.0^a —	.50 .15	-.105 .037	1.87 0.31			-.527 .078	
MP-7	IB	0.64 1.11	10.3 3.2	.17 .13	-.093 .051	1.12 0.41		.29 .61	-.650 .094	
MP-8	IB	-13.0 4.5	3.2 3.6	.51 .16	-.111 .042	1.88 0.31			-.539 .086	
MP-9	IB	-8.5 2.3	1.4 1.6	.175 .065	-.036 .023	1.31 0.18			-.590 .061	

Table 3A–1 continued

Equation	(12) ΔRCB $(\times 10^{-3})$	(13) $(RTP - RA)^b$ $(\times 10^{-3})$	(14) JC^b $(\times 10^{-3})$	(15) $\dfrac{YD}{V}$ $(\times 10^{-3})$	(16) $JS1$ $(\times 10^{-3})$	(17) $JS4$ $(\times 10^{-3})$	(18) SE $(\times 10^{-3})$	(19) DW	(20) RMSE ΔMP $ Billion	(21) R ΔMP
MP-1					.55 .18	−.27 .19	.574	0.82	1.19	.76
MP-2	−0.91 0.49				.45 .17	−.21 .16	.423	0.94	0.80	.90
MP-3					.56 .15	−.20 .15	.46	0.75	0.92	.85
MP-4		1.24 1.19	0.38 0.78		.64 .15	−.18 .15	.45	1.02	0.86	.88
MP-5		3.88 1.12	2.15 0.74	89.9 18.7	.56 .12	−.10 .12	.373	1.23	0.75	.91
MP-6		2.73 0.88	1.25 0.49	75.8 16.7	.57 .13	−.11 .13	.379	1.23	0.76	.91
MP-7		1.14 1.10	0.43 0.73		.60 .14	−.17 .14	.420	1.01	0.80	.90
MP-8		2.56 1.04	1.14 0.58	70.9 22.6	.57 .13	−.12 .13	.382	1.22	0.76	.91
MP-9		1.93 0.59	0.82 0.34	42.9 11.3	.60 .10	−.15 .10	—	—	0.80	.90

[a] Constrained to 1.
[b] Variable entered beginning with 1962:3. zero until then.

Table 3A-2. Other Savings Deposits, Estimated Coefficients

(Standard errors are below the coefficients)

(1)	(2)	(3)	(4)	(5)	(6)	(7)	(8)	(9)	(10)
Eq.	Model	Constant ($\times 10^{-3}$)	$a_{-1}\dfrac{SP}{V}$	$a_{-1}\dfrac{CG}{V}$	a_{-1}	RA ($\times 10^{-3}$)	RTP ($\times 10^{-3}$)	RCB ($\times 10^{-3}$)	RTB ($\times 10^{-3}$)
MS-1	IA	2.0	1.0^a	.267	−.071	1.58	.2	−.90	
		0.8	—	.053	.023	0.31	.24	.11	
MS-2	IA	1.39	1.0^a	.143	−.001	0.646	.27	−.815	
		0.76	—	.047	.025	0.034	.20	.091	
MS-3	IA	0.62	1.0^a	.083	.004	0.48		−.32	−.092
		—	—	.041	.020	0.28		.15	.059
MS-4	IA	3.45	1.0^a	.053	.012	0.23		−.30	−.093
		1.11	—	.040	.019	0.28		.14	.056
MS-5	IB	2.9	0.26	.063	.017	0.25		−.32	−.074
		1.5	1.21	.044	.020	0.28		.14	.064
MS-6	IB	4.1	1.28	.10	−.03	0.71		−.34	−.122
		1.9	1.18	.43	.02	0.20		.15	.063
MS-7	IB	4.1	1.4	.175	−.036	0.99		−.55	−.077
		2.8	1.56	.065	.023	0.43		.27	.12

	(11)	(12)	(13)	(14)	(15)	(16)	(17)	(18)
Eq.	$(RA-RTP)^b$ ($\times 10^{-3}$)	$(RA-RTB)^b$ ($\times 10^{-3}$)	JC^b ($\times 10^{-3}$)	$\dfrac{YD}{V}$ ($\times 10^{-3}$)	SE ($\times 10^{-3}$)	DW	RMSE ΔMS $ Billion	R ΔMS
MS-1					.223	0.90	.50	.81
MS-2	2.87		−1.88		.172	1.25	.38	.89
	0.57		0.40					
MS-3	1.60	.296	−1.11		.161	1.53	.362	.91
	0.58	.078	0.41					
MS-4	2.33	.206	−1.41	−11.7	.151	1.82	.335	.92
	0.60	.081	0.40	4.3				
MS-5	2.23	.205	−1.36	−7.5	.152	1.80	.334	.92
	0.63	.081	0.41	8.1				
MS-6	1.55	.223	−0.76	−11.8	.158	1.72	.341	.92
	0.57	.084	0.33	8.2				
MS-7	1.93	.15	−1.0	−11.7			.36	.92
	0.59	.15	0.42	11.7				

[a] Constrained to 1.
[b] Variable entered beginning with 62.3, zero until then.

Table 3A-3. Savings and Loan Association Deposits, Estimated Coefficients

(Standard errors are below the coefficients)

(1) Eq.	(2) Model	(3) Constant	(4) $a_{-1} \dfrac{\Delta MS}{MS}$	(5) a_{-1}	(6) Σw	(7) Distributed Lag on $RSL - RMS$ ($\times 10^{-3}$)											
						0	−1	−2	−3	−4	−5	−6	−7	−8	−9	−10	−11
MSL-1	I	.0032	1.0ᵃ	−.010	.0229	13.8	−4.7	−2.6	−.8	.6	1.8	2.5	2.9	3.0	2.8	2.2	1.3
		.0020	—	.003		2.3	1.0	0.7	.4	.2	0.2	0.2	0.3	0.3	0.3	0.2	0.1
MSL-2	I	.0355	1.0ᵃ	−.074	.0213	11.9	−5.0	−2.7	−.9	.7	1.8	2.6	3.1	3.2	2.9	2.3	1.3
		.0150	—	.030		2.4	1.1	0.7	.5	.3	0.3	0.4	0.5	0.5	0.5	0.4	0.2
MSL-3	II	.016	1.0ᵃ	−.054	.133	8.3	−2.8	−1.6	−.5	.3	1.0	1.4	1.7	1.8	1.6	1.3	0.7
		.012	—	.016		0.4	0.6	0.4	.3	.2	0.1	0.1	0.2	0.2	0.2	0.1	0.1
MSL-4	II	.210	1.0ᵃ	−.44	.122	7.1	−2.9	−1.6	−.5	.3	1.0	1.5	1.8	1.8	1.7	1.3	0.8
		.085	—	.18		1.4	0.6	0.4	.3	.2	0.2	0.2	0.3	0.3	0.3	0.2	0.1

Table 3A-3 continued

Eq.	(8) TIME $(\times 10^{-3})$	(9) $(TIME)^2$ $(\times 10^{-3})$	(10) γ'	(11) SE $(\times 10^{-3})$	(12) DW	(13) RMSE ΔMSL	(14) R ΔMSL
MSL-1				.72	1.21	.095	.98
MSL-2	0.47 0.19	−.0050ᵇ .0017		.68	1.37	.0796	.99
MSL-3			.15		1.15	.094	.99
MSL-4	2.9ᵇ 1.2	−.030ᵇ .010	.15		1.31	.0791	.99

ᵃ Constrainted to 1.
ᵇ The origin for *TIME* is 1955:1 and the trend is suspended in 1965:4 (i.e., $t = 43$ thereafter).

Table 3A-4. Life Insurance Reserves, Estimated Coefficients

(Standard errors are below the coefficients)

	(1)	(2)	(3)	(4) Distributed Lag on RM ($\times 10^{-4}$)											
Equation	Constant	$\left(\dfrac{MIS}{\$C}\right)_{-1}$	RM ($\times 10^{-4}$)	Σw	-1	-2	-3	-4	-5	-6	-7	-8	-9	-10	-11
MIS-1	.0235	−.0445	−13.2	2.5[b]	0.10	0.18	0.24	.28	.31	.32	.31	.28	.24	.18	.10
	.0031	.0085	2.3	2.9	0.11	0.21	0.28	.33	.35	.37	.36	.33	.28	.21	.12
MIS-2	.0238	−.0471	−7.0	−2.7[d]	−2.6	−1.7	−1.0	−.4	.1	.4	.6	.7	.6	.4	.1
	.0028	.0079	2.7	3.2	1.0	0.7	0.4	.3	.4	.4	.4	.4	.4	.5	.8
MIS-3	.0212	−.034	−5.8[f]	−8.2[f]	−4.2	−2.9	−1.7	−.8	−.1	.4	.6	.6	.4	.0	−.6
	.0031	.011	1.3		0.9	0.6	0.4	.4	.4	.4	.4	.4	.4	.5	.7

	(5) Distributed Lag on $\dot{p}$ ($\times 10^{-5}$)											
Equation	Σw	0	-1	-2	-3	-4	-5	-6	-7	-8	-9	-10
MIS-1	−4.0[c]	−0.83	−0.71	−0.60	−0.50	−0.40	−.31	−.24	−.17	−.11	−.07	−.03
	7.2	2.0	1.5	1.2	0.9	0.8	.8	.8	.8	.7	.6	.3
MIS-2	−7.4[e]	−1.6	−1.4	−1.2	−1.0	−0.8	−.6	−.4	−.2			
	6.4	1.4	1.2	1.1	0.9	0.7	.5	.4	.2			
MIS-3	−10.8[e]	−2.4	−2.1	−1.8	−1.5	−1.2	−.9	−.6	−.3			
	6.1	1.4	1.2	1.0	0.8	0.7	.5	.3	.2			

Table 3A–4 continued

Equation	(6) $\left(\dfrac{OASI}{\$C}\right)_{-1}$	(7) JR^a ($\times 10^{-3}$)	(8) $JR \times \overline{(RCP - RCL)}$ ($\times 10^{-3}$)	(9) $\overline{RCB}$ ($\times 10^{-4}$)	(10) SE ($\times 10^{-3}$)	(11) DW	(12) RMSE ΔMIS	(13) R ΔMIS
MIS-1	−.0119 .0082				.241	.74	.084	.94
MIS-2	−.0155 .0082	−1.17 0.34	−1.87 0.58		.207	.99	.069	.96
MIS-3	−.025 .012	−1.01 0.38	−1.60 0.63	3.3 2.8	.206	.99	.071	.96

[a] Dummy variable with value one when $(\overline{RCP - RCL}) > -.7$ (60:1, 65:2, 65:3, 66:1, to 67:1, 68:1, 69:1 to 69:3).
[b] Second degree polynomial constrained at both ends.
[c] Second degree polynomial constrained to zero at right end.
[d] Second degree polynomial, unconstrained.
[e] First degree polynomial constrained to zero at right end.
[f] Second degree polynomial unconstrained but including the current value of RM whose coefficient is given in column (3).

4

Deposit Rate Setting at Financial Institutions

MYRON B. SLOVIN

The subject of deposit rate setting at financial institutions has thus far attracted relatively little interest in monetary economics. Research in the area of financial intermediary behavior has instead been primarily concerned with the specific problem of the allocation of intermediary funds among competing assets. Partially as a result of this orientation, early econometric models of financial activity devoted detailed attention to these portfolio allocation problems, while regarding deposit rate setting as a rather peripheral concern.[1] As econometric models of the United States economy have grown in scale, however, and attempted to delineate more complicated financial interrelations, the need for more explicit analysis of the yields offered on intermediary liabilities has become clear. Indeed, such rate setting should be viewed as an essential factor in the explanation of the distribution of deposits among financial institutions.[2] Given, moreover, the substantial institutional differences in the asset-holding patterns characteristic of American financial intermediaries, such an explicit treatment of rate setting can provide useful insight into the short-run impact of policy actions on the relative supply of various types of lending.

This paper seeks to specify and estimate such explicit deposit rate functions for savings and loan associations, mutual savings banks, and commercial banks as a component for the FMP econometric model. The first section of the paper will review a few basic theoretical results obtained from a simple rate setting model, which provide some perspective for empirical analysis. In the second section the estimated equations for savings and loan associations and mutual savings banks are detailed, while the third section presents the corresponding results for commercial banks. The paper concludes with a short discussion of the behavior of the estimated equations in a dynamic simulation of the entire deposit sector of the econometric model.

---

[1] See, for example, Goldfeld [1], and Silber [4].

[2] For examples, see Chapters 2 and 3. The case for the importance of other factors to the flow of deposits can be found in Teck [5].

A Simple Model of Deposit Rate Setting

The theoretical work currently available in the area of deposit rate setting has concentrated on a simple comparative-statics, profit-maximization model of a savings institution.[3] The intermediary is presumed to issue essentially homogeneous time deposits and maintain a portfolio of earning assets that is primarily devoted to mortgages, a relatively long lived asset with a poor secondary market. Such a model admittedly represents an extremely simplified view of intermediary activity, especially in the case of commercial banks. Nevertheless it is not without insight as to the direction in which empirical work might usefully proceed.

The general assumptions of the model employed by Weber and Meyer, and Goldfeld and Jaffee are:

1. The mortgage holdings of the institution are assumed to represent an exogenously determined percentage, k, of its deposits. Thus, there is no simultaneous portfolio decision-making; instead, $M = kD$ where M is the stock of mortgages and D the level of deposits.

2. The demand by the public for the deposits of the intermediary is a positive function of the deposit rate, i, as well as exogenous factors such as wealth and competing rates, assumed constant for the moment. Thus deposits can be written as $D = f(i)$ with $\partial D/\partial i > 0$.

3. The mortgage market is assumed to be characterized by perfect competition. Thus the individual institution accepts the current mortgage rate, r, as given and can purchase any quantity of mortgages that it desires at that rate. Such a behavioral assumption could, however, also be justified on the basis that there exist significant institutional restraints on the level of mortgage rates (such as various types of ceilings) and that, as a result, the mortgage market is characterized by excess demand (that is, the rationing of loan funds to customers).

4. There are no ceilings on deposit rates and no advances from the central bank or a similar institution.

The profits of the institution under these conditions can be written as

$$\pi = rkD - iD \tag{4-1}$$

or, if there is initial equity C which it treats in a fashion identical to deposits, as

$$\pi = rk(D + C) - iD \tag{4-1a}$$

[3] See Goldfeld and Jaffee [2], Meyer [3], and Weber [6].

In either case the first order condition for a profit maximum, assuming a one period planning horizon, is

$$\frac{\partial \pi}{\partial i} = (rk - i)\frac{\partial D}{\partial i} - D = 0 \qquad (4\text{-}2)$$

This expression implicitly defines the optimal deposit rate, i^*, as a function of the asset rate, assuming that the parameters of the demand function are constant. The second order condition for a maximum at $i = i^*$ is

$$\frac{\partial^2 \pi}{\partial i^2} = (rk - i)\frac{\partial^2 D}{\partial i^2} - 2\frac{\partial D}{\partial i} < 0 \qquad (4\text{-}3)$$

The comparative-statics effect of a shift in the asset rate upon the optimal deposit rate is obtained by implicit differentiation of condition (4-2). This yields

$$\frac{di^*}{dr} = \frac{-k\,\partial D/di}{(rk - i)\,\partial^2 D/di^2 - 2\,\partial D/di} > 0 \qquad (4\text{-}4)$$

which is positive by virtue of the second-order condition. This result was first shown by Weber and later clarified by Meyer.[4]

Goldfeld and Jaffee noted that the above formulation implicitly assumes initial conditions appropriate to a newly established intermediary. They then demonstrated that the results obtained do, however, apply to the case of an intermediary which enters the planning period with a stock of older mortgages or other assets.[5] In such a case, abstracting from considerations of equity capital, the institution would seek to maximize the function

$$\pi = r_0 k D_0 + r_1 k(D_1 - D_0) - i_1 D_1 \qquad (4\text{-}5)$$

where D_0 indicates the level of deposits held prior to the first period and r_0 the average yield on its older mortgage or asset portfolio, kD_0. Inasmuch as none of these terms is affected by a change in the deposit rate, however, the first-order condition for a profit maximum will remain identical to that of the previous case.

Thus, under the general assumptions of the model, the optimal deposit rate for a profit maximizing intermediary with a single period planning horizon will be a function of the current asset rate and is unaffected by the yield which characterizes the portfolio carried over from previous periods.

---

[4] Weber [6]; Meyer [3].
[5] Goldfeld and Jaffee [2], pp. 617–619.

Thus, marginal rather than average portfolio yields determine the yield offered on deposits.

Goldfeld and Jaffee also analyzed the effect on rate setting of an exogenous shift in the demand for intermediary liabilities.[6] Such a response is likely to be induced, for example, by a change in the yield of an asset which is a close substitute for the deposit liability of the institution in question. Goldfeld and Jaffee examined the impact of such a change by introducing an explicit additive shift factor, α, in the demand function. The demand for deposits then becomes

$$D = \alpha + d(i) \qquad (4\text{-}6)$$

but the expression for profit remains the same as in equation (4-1). The optimal deposit rate is obtained from the same first order condition, equation (4-2), but is now a function of the parameter α as well as r. The effect of a change in this parameter is also obtained by implicit differentiation, which yields

$$\frac{di^*}{d\alpha} = \frac{1}{(rk - i)\,\partial^2 D/di^2 - 2\,\partial D/di} < 0 \qquad (4\text{-}7)$$

which is negative due to the second-order condition.

In general then, a profit maximizing intermediary would respond to an increase in yields on competing assets (i.e., a downward shift in the public's demand for the institution's liabilities) by increasing its deposit rate, as would be expected intuitively. The deposit rate offered is also a positive function of the current yield on the assets generally held in its portfolio.

Such a model can be extended in a variety of ways, but only two further assumptions will be presented here. First, the intermediary will be assumed to have a two period planning horizon. The institution is assumed to know r_1, the current asset rate, and to have an expectation of r_2, the future rate, which is held with certainty. Secondly, it is assumed that the demand for deposits is a function not only of the current deposit rate but of the past deposit rate as well. That is, an explicit lag in the demand for deposits is considered in the optimization process. Thus $D_2 = f(i_1, i_2)$ where $\partial D_2/\partial i_2 > 0$ and $\partial D_2/\partial i_1 > 0$, although D_1 will be assumed to be only a function of i_1.

The intermediary seeks to maximize

$$\pi = \pi_1 + \rho\pi_2 \qquad (4\text{-}8)$$

where $\rho < 1$ is a discount factor. Assuming that the intermediary also possesses some initial equity capital which it treats in a manner similar to

[6] Goldfeld and Jaffee [2], pp. 627–628.

deposits and that all profits are reinvested, the second-period profit function can be written as

$$\pi_2 = r_2 k \pi_1 + r_1 k C + r_1 k D_1 + r_2 k (D_2 - D_1) - i_2 D_2 \qquad (4\text{-}9)$$

Total discounted profits are then

$$\pi = (1 + \rho r_2 k)\pi_1 + \rho r_1 k(C + D_1) + \rho r_2 k(D_2 - D_1) - \rho i_2 D_2 \qquad (4\text{-}10)$$

The first order conditions for a profit maximum are

$$\frac{\partial \pi}{\partial i_1} = (1 + \rho r_2 k)\frac{\partial \pi_1}{\partial i_1} + \rho_1(r_1 - r_2)k\frac{\partial D_1}{\partial i_1} + \rho(r_2 k - i_2)\frac{\partial D_2}{\partial i_1} = 0 \quad (4\text{-}11)$$

$$\frac{\partial \pi}{\partial i_2} = \rho\left[(r_2 k - i_2)\frac{\partial D_2}{\partial i_2} - D_2\right] = 0 \qquad (4\text{-}12)$$

If the lagged effect of deposit rates on deposits were assumed to be trivial, then the last term in equation (4-11) would be omitted. In either case, the optimal current deposit rate i_1^* is a function of both the current asset rate and the expectation held about the future level of that rate.

The explicit derivatives for the comparative-statics effect of a change in asset rates on the optimal deposit rate can be obtained by taking the total differentials of equations (4-11) and (4-12) and employing Cramer's rule. The relevant matrixes for this procedure and the second-order conditions for a maximum can be found in chapter Appendix 4A. The resulting derivatives thus obtained are

$$\frac{di_1^*}{dr_1} = \frac{\left[-(1 - \rho r_2 k + \rho)k\dfrac{\partial D_1}{\partial i_1}\right]\left[\dfrac{\partial^2 \pi_2}{\partial i_2}\right]}{B} \qquad (4\text{-}13)$$

and

$$\frac{di_1^*}{dr_2} = \frac{\rho k\left(\dfrac{\partial D_1}{\partial i_1} - \dfrac{\partial D_2}{\partial i_1} - \dfrac{\partial \pi_1}{\partial i_1}\right)\left(\dfrac{\partial^2 \pi_2}{\partial i_2^2}\right) + \rho k \dfrac{\partial D_2}{\partial i_2}\left[(r_2 k - i_2)\dfrac{\partial^2 D_2}{\partial i_1 \partial i_2} - \dfrac{\partial D_2}{\partial i_1}\right]}{B}$$

$$\qquad (4\text{-}14)$$

where

$$B = \left[(1 + \rho r_2 k)\frac{\partial^2 \pi_1}{\partial i_1^2} + \rho(r_1 - r_2)k\frac{\partial^2 D_1}{\partial i_1^2} + \rho(r_2 k - i_2)\frac{\partial^2 D_2}{\partial i_1^2}\right]\left(\frac{\partial^2 \pi_2}{\partial i_2^2}\right)$$

$$- \rho\left[(r_2 k - i_2)\frac{\partial^2 D_2}{\partial i_1 \partial i_2} - \frac{\partial D_2}{\partial i_2}\right]^2$$

which is positive by the second-order conditions for a maximum. For the same reason, the first bracketed term of B must be negative, as indeed must $\partial^2 \pi_2 / \partial i_2^2$ as well.

It is clear that di_1^* / dr_1 is positive and thus an increase in the current asset rate increases the optimal level of the current deposit rate. In the case of di_1^* / dr_2 it seems reasonable to assume that the cross effect $\partial^2 D_2 / \partial i_1 \partial i_2$ is zero so that the second part of the numerator is negative. Moreover, $\partial^2 \pi_2 / \partial i_2^2$ is negative and

$$\frac{\partial D_1}{\partial i_1} - \frac{\partial D_2}{\partial i_1} - \frac{\partial \pi_1}{\partial i_1} = \frac{\partial D_1}{\partial i_1} - (r_1 k - i_1) \frac{\partial D_1}{\partial i_1} + D - \frac{\partial D_2}{\partial i_1}$$

will be positive since $r_1 k - i_1$ is a small fraction and $\partial D_2 / \partial i_1$ will not normally exceed $\partial D_1 / \partial i_1$. Thus the numerator is negative and the derivative di_1^* / dr_2 is negative. Consequently, a fall in the asset rate expected in the future will produce an increase in deposit rates. Intuitively, this is reasonable since the institution would have an incentive to invest in assets at current rates before the rate of return falls.

These models of deposit rate setting behavior are of course highly simplified views of intermediary behavior. They do, nevertheless, stress the basic view that it is the role of these institutions to intermediate between borrowers and lenders. Consequently, the major determinants of the yield on deposits should be the rate of return on the assets generally found in the portfolio of that institution and the yields available on assets that are close substitutes for the deposit liabilities that it offers.

Equations for Mutual Savings Banks and
Savings and Loan Associations

This section reports rate setting equations for savings and loan associations and mutual savings banks. A major problem in the estimation of such equations is the substantial multicollinearity endemic to time series data for such financial yield variables. In order to alleviate such difficulties in this study, interest rates on competitive assets have been aggregated into a single variable. Such a variable is obtained by weighting each competitive yield by its relative impact on deposit flows to the institution under consideration (with the weights summing to unity). Such a procedure was previously adopted by Gramlich and Hulett in the estimation of similar equations for one version of the FMP model (see Chapter 2). The current work obtains these weights from the deposit flow equations written by Franco Modigliani (see Chapter 3). Specifically, the steady-state effect on deposits caused by a change in a competing yield is calculated. Then the ratios of the derivatives thus obtained are used as the weights for these competitive yields in order to obtain a single compositive variable for competitive rates. This variable is then employed in the estimation of the rate setting equations.

In the work of Modigliani, deposits at an intermediary are viewed as primarily a function of competing rate differentials and income, with wealth employed as a scaling variable. Savings and loan shares and mutual savings bank deposits are combined for estimation purposes on the grounds that the major differences between these intermediaries are primarily geographical rather than economic in character. The two types of deposits are later disaggregated for purposes of the mortgage market by a share equation in which the principal independent variable is the differential between the deposit rates offered by the two institutions. An interesting property of Modigliani's equations is that several yield variables enter the specification at a point well into the estimation period; specifically in 1962:3. Especially important in this regard is the time deposit rate variable in the equation for savings deposits at mutual savings banks and savings and loan associations which suggests that commercial banks did not compete with these intermediaries for deposits until 1962. In order to take account of this property, separate pre and post composite competing rate variables were calculated for each intermediary.

The steady-state effect on savings and loan association deposits of a change in a given rate, say R_i, calculated from Modigiliani's equation is

$$\frac{\partial MSL}{\partial R_i} = \frac{\partial MS}{\partial R_i}\frac{\partial MSL}{\partial MS} = \frac{a_i V}{.0364}\frac{\partial MSL}{\partial MS} \tag{4-15}$$

while for mutual savings bank deposits, MMS, the analogue is

$$\frac{\partial MMS}{\partial R_i} = \frac{\partial MS}{\partial R_i}\frac{\partial MMS}{\partial MS} = \frac{a_i V}{.0364}\frac{\partial MMS}{\partial MS} \tag{4-16}$$

MSL and MMS are savings and loan association and mutual savings bank deposits respectively, while MS is the sum of the two; V is net worth; a_i is the coefficient of the appropriate yield variable in the relevant Modigliani deposit equation; and .0364 is the coefficient of the lagged dependent variable.

The calculation of the cross effect of a change in the deposit rate of one savings institution on the deposits of the other is somewhat more complicated. This is because such a change affects not only the share of deposits between the two institutions via the share equation (much in the manner of a substitution effect), but will also change the composite variable RA. This is a weighting of the mutual savings bank and savings and loan association deposit rates, with the weights determined by deposit flows to the two institutions over the previous four quarters. In turn, this change in RA will affect the total savings deposits at the two intermediaries (much in the manner of an income effect).

Overall, the effect of such a deposit rate change can be seen to be

$$\frac{dMSL}{dRMS} = \frac{\partial MSL}{\partial RMS} + \frac{\partial MSL}{\partial MS}\frac{\partial MS}{\partial RA}\frac{\partial RA}{\partial RMS} \tag{4-17}$$

or

$$\frac{dMMS}{dRSL} = \frac{\partial MMS}{\partial RSL} + \frac{\partial MMS}{\partial MS}\frac{\partial MS}{\partial RA}\frac{\partial RA}{\partial RSL} \tag{4-18}$$

depending upon which rate is changed, where RSL is the yield on savings and loan shares and RMS the yield on mutual savings bank deposits. In either case, the first term on the right side of the equation is the effect on the share of deposits between the two institutions from the share equation while the second expression measures the share of additional deposits generated by the resulting change in RA.

In order to evaluate these expressions as simply as possible, average values for many of these slopes and other variables were calculated for both the pre and post periods and then used to solve these equations. The values used for substitution into equations (4-15) to (4-18) and the weights thus obtained for the composite competing rate variable for savings and loan associations are shown in Table 4-1. It can be seen from the table that the analogous figures for mutual savings banks were the same (the actual calculations can be found in Appendix 4B).

The time deposit rate has no effect in the early period because it does not appear as a competing rate variable for the early period in Modigliani's deposit equation for these institutions. Nontrivial derivatives were obtained for $\partial MSL/\partial RMS$ and $\partial MMS/\partial RSL$ in the post 1962:2 period, but the value of the latter was positive, specifically 5.97. This results because the negative effect of an increase in RSL on the share of deposits to mutual savings banks was outweighed by the impact of RSL on increasing RA. The rise in the latter produces enough additional deposits to both institutions to prevent mutual savings banks from suffering a loss of deposits overall. Rather than introduce this complementarity, however, these cross effects were instead assumed to be zero.

The above weights were then used in specifying the composite competitive rate variables employed in the estimation of the deposit rate equations. The equations actually adopted for use in the model are presented in chapter Appendix Table 4C-1. Other combinations of weights were ultimately tried as well in order to test the sensitivity of these equations, but such experimental changes in relative weights had little impact on the coefficients obtained.

Table 4-1. Weights for the Composite Competing Rate Variable

Variable	Pre 1962:3	Post 1962:2
	Values Used	
V (\$ billion)	1578	2469
MS (\$ billion)	86.04	160.57
$\partial RA/\partial RSL$	0.75	0.73
$\partial RA/\partial RMS$	0.25	0.27
$\partial MSL/\partial MS$	0.61	0.67
$\partial MMS/\partial MS$	0.39	0.33
	Weights for Savings and Loan Associations Variable	
$\partial MSL/\partial RMS$	$-17.13 = .51$	0
$\partial MSL/\partial RCB$	$-14.54 = .43$	$-24.98 = .203$
$\partial MSL/\partial RTB$	$-2.02 = .06$	$-10.26 = .083$
$\partial MSL/\partial RTP$	0	$-87.68 = .713$
	-33.69	-122.92
	Weights for Mutual Savings Banks Variable	
$\partial MMS/\partial RSL$	$-11.12 = .51$	0
$\partial MMS/\partial RCB$	$-9.30 = .43$	$-12.31 = .203$
$\partial MMS/\partial RTB$	$-1.29 = .06$	$-5.05 = .083$
$\partial MMS/\partial RTP$	0	$-43.19 = .713$
	-21.71	-60.55

An important observation to be noted is that the competitive rate variables in these equations are switched in 1962:1, whereas the appropriate rate variables in the deposit flow equations of the model are not introduced until 1962:3. It seems probable that 1962:1 rather than 1962:3 witnessed this structural shift inasmuch as this was the quarter in which Regulation Q ceilings were raised substantially. In turn, time deposit rates increased dramatically, introducing a new degree of competition with nonbank intermediaries. Figure 4-1 which graphs the differential between deposit rates at savings and loan associations and commercial banks shows this clearly. Note that the substantial decrease occurs in 1962:1. There appears to be no a priori reason of equal importance to argue for a 1962:3 structural shift instead. The difference of two periods would not be likely to have a serious effect on the deposit equations of Modigliani since they are characterized by very slow speeds of adjustment. In the case of the rate equations, however, the effect was of considerable magnitude. Consequently, the shift in rate variables is at 1962:1 in these equations.

Each equation was estimated by means of ordinary least squares over the sample period 1955:2 to 1968:4. The observations for 1969 were excluded from the sample due to difficulties with the quality of deposit rate data for that period. Overall, the equations fit reasonably well. The standard errors

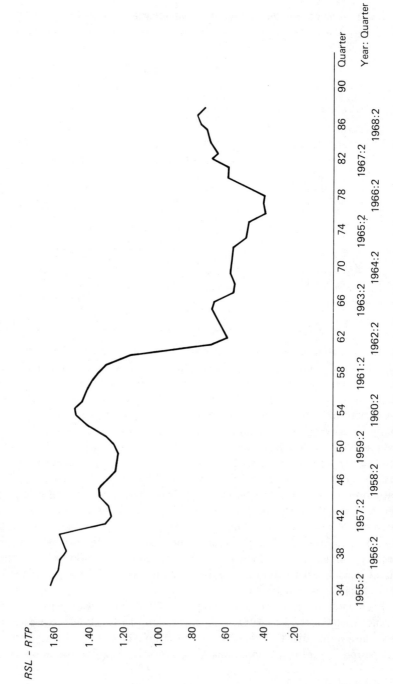

Figure 4–1. Savings and Loan Deposit Rate Minus Commercial Bank Deposit Rate: RSL – RTP.

are low and the equations tracked well when the coefficients of the lagged error terms are set equal to zero. The equations are characterized by fairly long lags, but it should be noted that there are no lagged dependent variables, so that adjustment is complete after ten quarters. The Durbin–Watson statistics, although somewhat low, are higher than is generally the case for financial equations employing time series data.

The asset rates were important in both equations. Only the mortgage rate worked well but since mortgages are dominant in the portfolios of these institutions, this should not be unexpected. In each equation the mortgage rate entered with a fairly long lag, much longer than that on competing yields. In view of the long lived nature of mortgages as an asset and the relatively unorganized character of their secondary markets, however, this is not too distressing.

The sums of the coefficients on the asset rate and the composite competitive yield come reasonably close to unity in both cases. For savings and loan associations the early period sum is 1.04 while in the post period it is .94. The similar figures for mutual savings banks are .90 and 1.13. In general then, the full impact of a change in market rates is transmitted to the deposit rates of both intermediaries.

The other major variable in these equations is the difference between the rate of growth of mortgages and deposits. This is an impact variable which transmits the effect of an imbalance in the flow of mortgages and deposits. When the intermediary's mortgage growth exceeds that of deposits (i.e., it becomes loaned up), it tends to increase yields on deposits. Analogously, when deposits grow faster than the rate at which mortgages can be disbursed, the deposit rate falls. Generally of course, since mortgages form the overwhelming proportion of portfolio holdings for these institutions, the growth rates will not differ substantially. In the steady state, moreover, this variable does not affect rate setting. It is interesting to note that when these rate equations are combined with the model's deposit equations, the overall effect of this variable is a stabilizing one. When mortgage growth exceeds that of deposits, deposit rates are raised, which in turn tends to increase deposits. This lowers the differential in the growth of assets and liabilities, tending to restore equilibrium.

In the estimation, this flow variable was entered in the savings and loan equation throughout the sample period. In the case of mutual savings banks, however, a shift in portfolio holdings from securities to mortgages occurred on a rather large scale during the period. This is revealed in Figure 4-2, which shows the steady increase in the mortgage-to-deposit ratio during the early part of the period (in contrast, the value of this variable was quite steady for savings and loan associations). Consequently, such a flow variable,

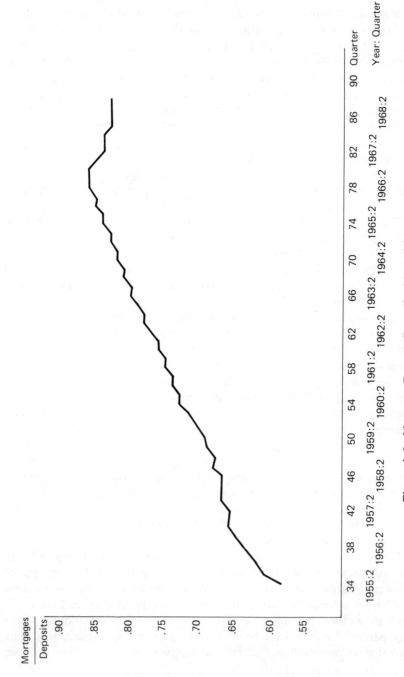

Figure 4-2. Mortgage-Deposit Ratio for Mutual Savings Banks.

if entered throughout, would capture this portfolio shift rather than the impact of changing flows. Thus for mutual savings banks the variable was entered beginning in 1963:2, by which time the proportion of mortgages in portfolio holdings had become more stable.

The resulting coefficients, 7.66 for savings and loan associations and 40.2 for mutual savings banks, indicate that deposit rate setting of the latter is extremely sensitive to changes in mortgage and deposit flows, much more so than for savings and loan associations. This should not be entirely surprising, however. First of all, these banks do not in general have access to a lender of last resort. Thus rate setting changes are their only available instrument for substantially increasing the quantity of liabilities. Savings and loan associations by contrast have access to advances from the Federal Home Loan Banks. Secondly, mutual savings banks have tended to have a much larger ratio of mortgage commitments to deposits than other institutions. This again would necessitate greater sensitivity to changing deposit flows. Note that the coefficients of the lag structure suggest that mutual savings banks begin adjusting to deposit and mortgage flow imbalances very quickly. In the case of savings and loan associations, however, no significant adjustment takes place until after about four quarters have passed.

Commitment variables were attempted but they invariably failed to have the appropriate sign or any modicum of significance. It does seem likely that the mortgage flow variable has probably captured some element of this instead, inasmuch as a large proportion of recent commitments do become new mortgages. In the case of savings and loan associations, the level of advances outstanding performed poorly and the rate on advances failed to produce a nontrivial coefficient. In both cases, the problem of multicollinearity is probably in large part responsible for this.

Deposit Rate Setting at Commercial Banks

This section reports the results of efforts directed toward the specification and estimation of a time-deposit rate-setting equation for commercial banks to complement the equations for savings banks presented in the previous section. More specifically, an equation is estimated for the yield that commercial banks would offer on savings deposits in the absence of ceiling rate restrictions.

Savings deposits are taken to include passbook savings accounts and savings certificates, but large denomination negotiable certificates of deposit are excluded. The values employed for the desired time deposit rate in the absence of ceiling restrictions are generally the actual rates that are obtained during the period. The remaining observations were calculated by Gramlich and Hulett in an attempt to adjust for the several occasions when actual rates drew sufficiently close to the Regulation Q ceilings to be affected by them. Gramlich and Hulett assumed that time deposit rates generally followed a triangular distribution. During periods when the ceilings appeared to be effective, they postulated that the upper part of the triangle would appear to be truncated with a large proportion of rates in the vicinity of the ceiling rate. Thus they viewed the desired rate as essentially the mean of the triangular distribution which would have applied normally. The calculated desired rates were then obtained as a function of the observed rate, the ceiling rate, and an estimate of the width of the base of the triangular distribution. The choice of the latter parameter was obtained, through iteration, as that value for which their desired deposit rate equation produced the best fit.[7]

The yield on demand deposits is of course established at zero by fiat, so that commercial banks cannot substantially alter this rate and must instead accept all deposits tendered to it by the public at that rate. The desired time deposit rate, however, can be viewed as primarily a positive function of the yields available on assets generally held in the portfolio and on assets which are close substitutes for the liabilities of commercial banks.

Once again a composite competitive rate variable is obtained from the competing rate coefficients in the equation for commerial bank time deposits estimated by Modigliani for the FMP model. The derivation of this variable for commercial banks is quite straightforward. In the early part of the sample period the only competing yield is the interest rate offered on short term Treasury bills. In the later period both the Treasury bill rate and the composite yield RA enter. The latter, once again, is a weighted average of the yields on savings and loan shares and mutual savings bank deposits, with the weights determined by average deposit flows to these institutions during the previous four quarters. Since the coefficients for RTB and RA are $-.00059$ and $-.00193$ respectively, the composite competitive rate variable is specified as $.23RTB + .77RA$.

The estimated equation is presented in Appendix Table 4C-2. Once again the post 1968 observations were excluded due to the lack of accurate data on deposit rates after that date. In addition, this time desired deposit rates exceeded the ceiling so much as to be effectively unobservable. The composite competitive yield variable is switched in 1962:1 as in the equations for savings and loan associations and mutual savings banks.

Overall, the equation fits the data rather well within the regression period. The equation is again characterized by fairly long distributed lags; but, as in the previous equations, there is no lagged dependent variable so that

---

[7] The procedure is explained in greater detail in Chapter 2.

adjustment is complete after ten quarters. The Durbin–Watson statistic is sufficiently high so that the use of a first order autoregressive scheme for the residuals was felt unnecessary, and thus the final specification was estimated by means of ordinary least squares.

Due to the diversified nature of commercial bank portfolio holdings, a composite variable was also employed in order to capture the effect of asset rates more efficiently. Inspection revealed that the relative proportions of commercial loans, mortgages, and municipal securities among bank holdings have been fairly stable. These are, in fact, the major earning assets of commercial banks. Figure 4-3 is a graph of the growth of these assets during the sample period. The weights used in the composite variable are the average relative share of these assets over the period (with the weights summing to unity). The actual variable found in the regression is

$$(.45RCL + .30RM + .25RMUN)$$

but the choice of different weights has only a very slight effect on the results obtained.

This asset rate does perform in an extremely vigorous manner. Its power relative to the competing rate variables is rather striking, especially in comparison with the equations for mutual savings banks and savings and loan associations. The sum of the lag coefficients is almost .90 while the competing rate coefficients in the pre and post periods produce sums of only .17 and .25 respectively. In addition, most of the t ratios for the asset rates are quite high in comparison with those for the competing rates. Nevertheless the effect of multicollinearity on the coefficients obtained is rather apparent, particularly with respect to the asset rate and the post period competitive rate variable. Consequently, much greater confidence would seem to be indicated in the estimate of the total effect of the yield variables on deposit rate setting rather than in the distribution of such an effect between the two types of variables. Once again, the sums of the coefficients for asset and competitive rate variables do come fairly close to unity. The figures are approximately 1.07 and 1.15 for the pre and post periods respectively. Thus, in the steady state the full impact of a shift in market yields is again transmitted to deposit holders by the rate setting process.

Several additional variables have also been entered in this equation. These reflect to some degree the greater complexity intrinsic to commercial banks as intermediaries and the more varied influences they must react to in comparison with other savings institutions. The differential between the composite asset rate and the discount rate is entered with a one period lag. This reflects the fact that commercial banks have access to discounting from the central bank and can thus, to some extent, substitute greater borrowings

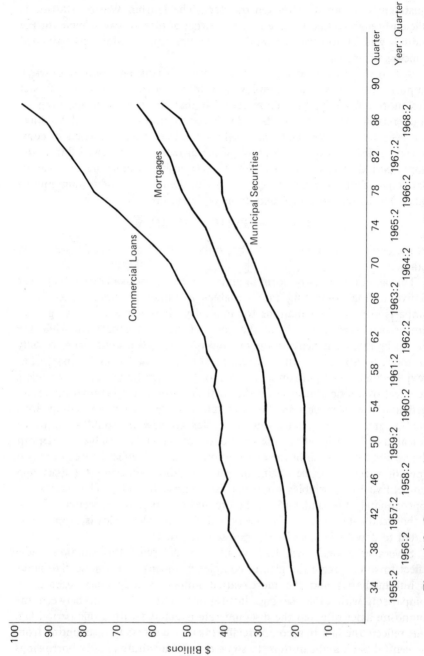

Figure 4–3. Commercial Loans, Mortgages, and Municipal Securities Held by Commercial Banks.

for increases in deposit rates. The smaller this differential becomes, the more undesirable such borrowing appears relative to changes in deposit rates, as a means for increasing the level of liabilities. The small size of the coefficient suggests that this substitutability is quite imperfect. Given the well known institutional limits applied to discounting, however, such a result does appear reasonable.

It has been suggested that changes in interest ceilings can represent an oligopolistic trigger mechanism for desired deposit rate changes if, for instance, such policy changes create the expectation that competing and asset rates are about to change (see page 30). More likely, however, such ceiling rate actions may act as a substitute for a price leader in the commercial banking industry. They might then provide a signal, tacitly recognized by all banks, that a general change in deposit rates has become appropriate. Individual institutions may have already regarded such a change as desirable, yet delayed its implementation in their rate setting policies for fear as to the course of action that competitive institutions may pursue.

Gramlich and Hulett entered the level of the Regulation Q ceiling in their desired deposit rate equation, and it did appear highly significant with a coefficient of .77 (see page 32). This would imply that a permanent change in the time deposit rate, desired in the absence of ceiling restrictions, results from ceiling changes, regardless of the level of asset or competing rates in the market. This would only be possible if the commercial banking industry is highly monopolistic in the savings deposit field. Whether this is true or not, Gramlich and Hulett's result was not confirmed with the specification used here. Instead, the final equation allows for the effect of ceiling rate changes as a trigger mechanism for deposit rate changes, with a ten period distributed lag on the change in the rate ceiling. The resulting coefficients do indicate that such changes have a sharp and fairly prolonged impact on the desired deposit rate, but there is no steady-state effect. Thus, in the absence of any change in market yields, the desired deposit rate does return to its initial level.

The remaining terms in the equation are impact variables which capture the effect on rate setting of imbalances in the flow of assets and liabilities. The specific form used is the difference between the rate of growth of deposits and commercial loans plus mortgages. Demand and time deposits are treated separately in order to allow for a difference in response to changes in the flows of these two types of deposits. Commercial loans and mortgages are the two major earning assets of commercial banks endogenously determined in the FMP model. They do, moreover, represent a substantial proportion of the investment portfolios of these institutions.

In each case, the variable worked well after 1960, but very poorly in the earlier period. Consequently these variables were omitted in the early period in the final specification. In each case, a seven quarter distributed lag was specified for the remainder of the sample period. The coefficients indicate that a change in the flow of time deposits relative to earning assets has a slightly greater impact on the desired rate than does a similar change in the flow of demand deposits.

The failure of these variables to provide any explanatory power during the early period is somewhat surprising. No very satisfactory explanation for this is immediately clear. Nonetheless, it is true that inspection of bank data does reveal that previous to 1962, commercial bank portfolios did contain much higher concentrations of cash assets and short-term Treasury liabilities relative to deposits than after that date. Figure 4-4, for example, graphs the quantity of cash assets plus Treasury notes of less than one year maturity held by commercial banks as a percentage of deposits.

No doubt such a shift in portfolio proportions represents a partial effect of the secular rise in interest rates which characterized the nineteen-sixties, as well as the low reserve requirement on time deposits, the bank liability which had the greatest growth over the same time span. In all likelihood, the growth of access to certificate of deposit offerings also played a role in lessening the desired proportion of such liquid assets in bank portfolios.

In any event, during the early period it does appear that commercial banks may have adjusted their portfolio liquidity in an active manner as a primary means by which to compensate for imbalances in asset and deposit growth. In the more recent years, however, as a consequence of this shifting portfolio behavior, a lower ratio of liquid assets to deposits has prevailed and thus possibly necessitated more active reliance on deposit rate setting for this purpose, as indicated by the regression results.

Several additional variables were tried in order to capture the possible influence of activity in certificates of deposit on the desired time deposit rate (beyond that which may already be implicit in the 1962 structural shifts present in the equation). None, however, proved to enter the final specification with significant coefficients. One attempt, for example, was a dummy variable which was entered during periods when the secondary rate on certificates of deposit exceeded the ceiling rate on new CDs. This was motivated by the belief that during such periods commercial banks would be likely to experience great difficulty issuing new certificates to replace older maturities as they expire, thus possibly producing a rise in the desired time deposit rate. Such a variable failed to obtain a significant coefficient, however, even when a distributed lag was specified. Although several theoretical explanations could be tendered, it seems more likely that this is just another example of the substantial problems that severe multicollinearity can create in the estimation of such a rate setting equation.

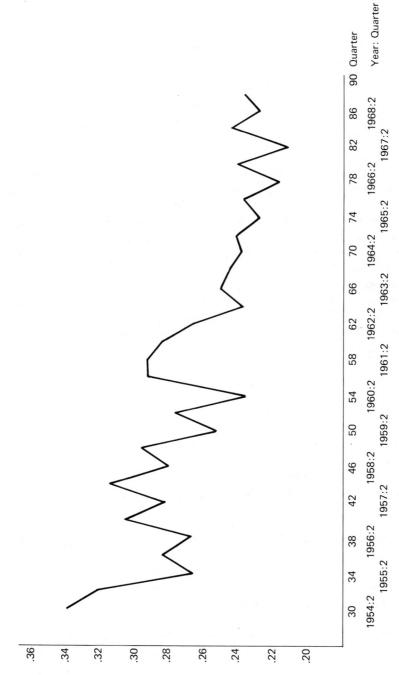

Figure 4–4. Ratio of Cash Assets Plus Short-Term Treasury Liabilities to Deposits at Commercial Banks.

Conclusion

In summary, a simple rate setting model for savings institutions has been presented, stressing their role as financial intermediaries. This perspective suggested that deposit yields could be viewed as a positive function of the yields obtained on assets held by that institution and on debt instruments which are close substitutes for the liabilities it issues. This provided the basic framework within which specific, though basically similar, equations were developed in order to explain the rate setting behavior of savings and loan associations, mutual saving banks, and commercial banks.

It is interesting to note that in each equation the sums of the coefficients on asset and competing rate variables are quite close to unity. This suggests that the full impact of a change in market yields is ultimately reflected in the yield offered on liabilities of these institutions, a result which contrasts with that of similar previous studies. It is, however, in accord with the normal theory of financial intermediation which views these institutions as basically service media by which funds are efficiently transmitted from lenders (depositors) to borrowers.

In each equation, distributed lags were specified on almost every variable and proved to be rather lengthy. This would appear to imply that expectations at these institutions adjust fairly slowly to changes in market yields. Whether these long lags continue to accurately reflect rate setting behavior after 1966 (the year of the credit crunch at these institutions) remains an open question. The lack of observations currently available after 1966 in a quarterly time series rather vitiates regression techniques as a means for analyzing the effect of such recent financial developments.

It would seem appropriate to conclude with a brief glance at the behavior of the deposit rate equations when they are simulated together with Modigliani's deposit flow equations. For current purposes, the remaining sectors of the FMP model are taken as exogenously determined. The results for such a standard dynamic simulation for the period 1957:1 to 1969:4 can be found in Appendix 4D.

In general, the equations perform rather well within the regression period (which ends at 1968:4). The mean squared errors are all rather low and the savings and loan association and commercial bank time deposit equations yield few errors of any substance at all. The mutual savings bank equation does, however, produce several misses. For example, during the period of late 1966 and early 1967 the solution values do track about ten basis points low, although this is probably due in large measure to the fact that the deposit flow equations oversimulate mutual savings bank deposits by about $1.5 billion during 1966. This growth of deposits tends thereupon to decrease the deposit rate by means of the mortgage–deposit growth variable. This in turn probably aids substantially in bringing simulated deposit flows back down to actual levels.

Beyond the regression period, the results are somewhat less pleasing. It should be borne in mind, however, that there may be inaccuracies in the actual values used for these rates since the substantial growth of consumer certificates of deposit has made the determination of a single deposit rate for these institutions very difficult. In any event, *RSL* appears substantially overpredicted, as is *RMS* for much of the period. This is probably due to the effect of ceiling restrictions which were established for these institutions several years ago. Once again, such ceilings were not in effect during a significant portion of the sample period and thus could not be easily introduced into the specification of the regressions.

The equation for the time deposit rate at commercial banks desired in the absence of ceiling restrictions also appears extremely high. Given the character of financial developments in recent years, however, this result must be interpreted with caution. In particular, it is possible that the growth of large denomination certificates of deposit has partially alleviated the need for increases in passbook yields in order to obtain the needed level of liabilities. Once again, the lack of observations precludes effective analysis of this at the current time. Moreover, the simulated values may not be entirely unrealistic during some parts of the post 1968 period. In particular, it should be recalled that during this period some commercial banks did borrow large quantities of Eurodollar deposits from subsidiaries abroad at extraordinarily high rates of interest. At the very least, the high values simulated by the desired time deposit rate equation provide some clue as to the strength of the pressures that produced such a development.

The first-order conditions for the profit maximization model are

$$\frac{\partial \pi}{\partial i_1} = (1 + \rho_2 k)\frac{\partial \pi_1}{\partial i_1} + \rho(r_1 - r_2)k\frac{\partial D_1}{\partial i_1} + \rho(r_2 k - i_2)\frac{\partial D_2}{\partial i_1} = 0 \quad (4A\text{-}1)$$

$$\frac{\partial \pi}{\partial i_2} = \rho\left[(r_2 k - i_2)\frac{\partial D_2}{\partial i_2} - D_2\right] = 0 \quad (4A\text{-}2)$$

Noting that $\partial \pi_1/\partial i_1 = (r_1 k - i_1)\,\partial D_1/\partial i_1 - D_1$, the total differentials in matrix form are

$$
\begin{bmatrix}
(1 + \rho r_2 k)\dfrac{\partial^2 \pi_1}{\partial i_1^2} + \rho(r_1 - r_2)k\dfrac{\partial^2 D_1}{\partial i_1^2} & \rho(r_2 k - i_2)\dfrac{\partial^2 D_2}{\partial i_1 \partial i_2} - \rho\dfrac{\partial D_2}{\partial i_1} \\[1em]
\quad + \rho(r_2 k - i_2)\dfrac{\partial^2 D_2}{\partial i_1^2} & \\[1em]
(r_2 k - i_2)\dfrac{\partial^2 D_2}{\partial i_1 \partial i_2} - \dfrac{\partial D_2}{\partial i_1} & (r_2 k - i_2)\dfrac{\partial^2 D_2}{\partial i_2^2} - 2\dfrac{\partial D_2}{\partial i_2}
\end{bmatrix}
$$

$$
\times
\begin{bmatrix} di_1 \\[1em] di_2 \end{bmatrix}
=
\begin{bmatrix}
-(1 + \rho r_2 k + \rho)k\dfrac{\partial D_1}{\partial i_1}\,dr_1 & \rho k\left(\dfrac{\partial D_1}{\partial i_1} - \dfrac{\partial D_2}{\partial i_1} - \dfrac{\partial \pi_1}{\partial i_1}\right)dr_2 \\[1em]
0 & -k\dfrac{\partial D_2}{\partial i_2}\,dr_2
\end{bmatrix}
$$

$$(4A\text{-}3)$$

The second-order conditions for a maximum are that

$$(1 + \rho r_2 k)\frac{\partial^2 \pi_1}{\partial i_1^2} + \rho(r_1 - r_2)k\frac{\partial^2 D_1}{\partial i_1^2} + \rho(r_2 k - i_2)\frac{\partial^2 D_2}{\partial i_1^2} < 0$$

and that B, defined as

$$
\left[(1 + \rho r_2 k) \frac{\partial^2 \pi_1}{\partial i_1^2} + \rho(r_1 - r_2)k \frac{\partial^2 D_1}{\partial i_1^2} \right.
$$

$$
\left. + \rho(r_2 k - i_2) \frac{\partial^2 D_2}{\partial i_1^2} \right] \left[(r_2 k - i_2) \frac{\partial^2 D_2}{\partial i_2^2} - 2 \frac{\partial D_2}{\partial i_2} \right]
$$

$$
- \rho \left[(r_2 k - i_2) \frac{\partial^2 D_2}{\partial i_1 \partial i_2} - \frac{\partial D_2}{\partial i_1} \right]^2 > 0
$$

The comparative statics effect of a change in current and expected asset rates on the current deposit rate are obtained by means of Cramer's rule which yields, respectively:

$$
\frac{di_1^*}{dr_1} = \frac{-(1 + \rho r_2 k + \rho)k \frac{\partial D_1}{\partial i_1} \left[(r_2 k - i_2) \frac{\partial^2 D_2}{\partial i_2^2} - 2 \frac{\partial D_2}{\partial i_2} \right]}{B} \qquad (4A\text{-}4)
$$

$$
\frac{di_1^*}{dr_2} = \frac{\rho k \left(\frac{\partial D_1}{\partial i_1} - \frac{\partial D_2}{\partial i_1} - \frac{\partial \pi_1}{\partial i_1} \right) \left[(r_2 k - i_2) \frac{\partial^2 D_2}{\partial i_2^2} - 2 \frac{\partial D_2}{\partial i_2} \right]}{B}
$$

$$
+ \frac{\rho k \frac{\partial D_2}{\partial i_2} \left[(r_2 k - i_2) \frac{\partial^2 D_2}{\partial i_1 \partial i_2} - \frac{\partial D_2}{\partial i_1} \right]}{B} \qquad (4A\text{-}5)
$$

For Savings and Loan Associations   Pre 1962:3

$$\frac{\partial MSL}{\partial RMS} = \frac{\partial RA}{\partial RMS}\frac{\partial MS}{\partial RA}\frac{\partial MSL}{\partial MS} + \frac{\partial MSL}{\partial RMS}$$

$$= (.25)\left(\frac{.00099W}{.0364}\right)(.61) - \left(\frac{.0203}{.0738}\right)MS$$

$$= (.25)(.0272)(1578)(.61) - (.2751)(86.04)$$

$$= -17.13$$

$$\frac{\partial MSL}{\partial RCB} = \frac{\partial MS}{\partial RCB}\frac{\partial MSL}{\partial MS} = \left(\frac{.00055}{.0364}\right)(1578)(.61) = -14.54$$

$$\frac{\partial MSL}{\partial RTB} = \frac{\partial MS}{\partial RTB}\frac{\partial MSL}{\partial MS} = \left(\frac{-.000077}{.0364}\right)(1578)(.61) = -2.02$$

Post 1962:2

$$\frac{\partial MSL}{\partial RMS} = (.27)\left[\frac{.00099 + .00193 + .00015}{.0364}\right](2469)(.67)$$

$$- \left(\frac{.0203}{.0738}\right)(160.57) = -6.52$$

$$\frac{\partial MSL}{\partial RCB} = \frac{-.00055}{.0364}(2469)(.67) = -24.98$$

$$\frac{\partial MSL}{\partial RTB} = \left(\frac{-.000077 - .00015}{.0364}\right)(2469)(.67) = -10.26$$

$$\frac{\partial MSL}{\partial RTP} = \frac{-.00193}{.0364}(2469)(.67) = -87.68$$

For Mutual Savings Banks

$$\frac{\partial MMS}{\partial RSL} = \frac{\partial RA}{\partial RSL}\frac{\partial MS}{\partial RA}\frac{\partial MMS}{\partial MS} + \frac{\partial MMS}{\partial RSL} = (.75)\left(\frac{.00099W}{.0364}\right)(.39) - \frac{.0203}{.0738}MS$$

$$= (.75)(.0272)(1578)(.39) - (.2751)(86.04) = -11.12$$

$$\frac{\partial MMS}{\partial RCB} = \left(\frac{-.00055}{.0364}\right)(1578)(.39) = -9.30$$

$$\frac{\partial MMS}{\partial RTB} = \left(\frac{-.000077}{.0364}\right)(1578)(.39) = -1.29$$

$$\frac{\partial MMS}{\partial RSL} = (.73)\left(\frac{.00099 + .00193 + .00015}{.0364}\right)(2469)(.33)$$

$$- \left(\frac{.0203}{.0738}\right)(160.57) = +5.94$$

$$\frac{\partial MMS}{\partial RCB} = \left(\frac{-.00055}{.0364}\right)(2469)(.33) = -12.31$$

$$\frac{\partial MMS}{\partial RTB} = \left(\frac{-.000077 - .00015}{.0364}\right)(2469)(.33) = -5.05$$

$$\frac{\partial MMS}{\partial RTP} = \left(\frac{-.00193}{.0364}\right)(2469)(.33) = -43.19$$

Appendix 4C:
Deposit Rate Equations

Table 4C-1. Savings and Loan and Mutual Savings Bank Deposit Rates, Estimated Coefficients

Equation	R^2E	R^2U	SE	SU	DW
1.	.9984	.9941	.0242	.0465	1.74

Savings and Loan Deposit Rate

$$RSL = -1.0886 + Q_1 \sum_{i=0}^{5} a_i(.51RMS + .43RCB + .06RTB)_{-i}$$
$$(-3.91)$$

$$+ Q_2 \sum_{i=0}^{4} b_i(.203RCB + .083RTB + .713RTP)_{-i} + \sum_{i=0}^{10} c_i RM_{-i}$$

$$+ \sum_{i=0}^{9} d_i \left(\frac{MKSL_{-1} - MKSL_{-2}}{MKSL_{-2}} - \frac{MSL_{-1} - MSL_{-2}}{MSL_{-2}} \right)_{-i}$$

$$+ .8232Q_2 + .74U_{-1}$$
$$(3.24)$$

$a_0 = .1513\ (4.08)$
$a_1 = .1308\ (7.43)$
$a_2 = .1084\ (7.63)$
$a_3 = .0842\ (4.49)$
$a_4 = .0580\ (3.03)$
$a_5 = .0299\ (2.30)$
$\Sigma a_i = .5626\ (8.62)$

$b_0 = .1684\ (3.32)$
$b_1 = .1261\ (7.52)$
$b_2 = .0881\ (6.82)$
$b_3 = .0545\ (2.66)$
$b_4 = .0251\ (1.51)$
$\Sigma b_i = .4622\ (10.62)$

$c_0 = .0738\ (4.46)$
$c_1 = .0686\ (5.68)$
$c_2 = .0630\ (6.92)$
$c_3 = .0572\ (7.29)$
$c_4 = .0511\ (6.48)$
$c_5 = .0447\ (5.33)$
$c_6 = .0380\ (4.39)$
$c_7 = .0310\ (3.68)$
$c_8 = .0237\ (3.17)$
$c_9 = .0161\ (2.78)$
$c_{10} = .0082\ (2.48)$
$\Sigma c_i = .4755\ (7.12)$

$d_0 = -0.6422\ (-1.10)$
$d_1 = 0.0326\ (0.06)$
$d_2 = 0.5718\ (1.07)$
$d_3 = 0.9752\ (1.62)$
$d_4 = 1.2429\ (1.90)$
$d_5 = 1.3750\ (2.06)$
$d_6 = 1.3714\ (2.15)$
$d_7 = 1.2321\ (2.21)$
$d_8 = 0.9571\ (2.25)$
$d_9 = 0.5464\ (2.28)$
$\Sigma d_i = 7.662\ (1.62)$

$$Q_1 = \begin{cases} 1.00 & \text{until } 1961{:}4 \\ 0 & \text{after } 1961{:}4 \end{cases}$$

$$Q_2 = \begin{cases} 0 & \text{until } 1961{:}4 \\ 1.00 & \text{after } 1961{:}4 \end{cases}$$

Table 4C-1 continued

Equation	R^2E	R^2U	SE	SU	DW
2. Mutual Savings Bank Deposit Rate	.9981	.9923	.0286	.0575	1.58

$$RMS = -.8252 + Q_1 \sum_{i=0}^{5} a_i(.51RSL + .43RCB + .06RTB)_{-i}$$
$$(-1.46)$$

$$+ Q_2 \sum_{i=0}^{4} b_i(.203RCB + .083RTB + .713RTP)_{-i} + \sum_{i=0}^{10} c_i RM_{-i}$$

$$+ Q_3 \sum_{i=0}^{9} d_i \left(\frac{MKMS_{-1} - MKMS_{-2}}{MKMS_{-2}} - \frac{MMS_{-1} - MMS_{-2}}{MMS_{-2}} \right)_{-i}$$

$$- .1938Q_2 - .2646Q_3 + .867U_{-1}$$
$$(-.35) \qquad (-3.08)$$

$d_0 = 0.9825 \ (0.57)$
$d_1 = 2.7819 \ (1.99)$
$d_2 = 4.1596 \ (3.10)$
$d_3 = 5.1156 \ (3.60)$
$d_4 = 5.6500 \ (3.74)$
$d_5 = 5.7625 \ (3.74)$
$d_6 = 5.4534 \ (3.70)$
$d_7 = 4.7226 \ (3.66)$
$d_8 = 3.5701 \ (3.61)$
$d_9 = 1.9959 \ (3.57)$
$\sum d_i = 40.1943 \ (3.60)$

$a_0 = .1366 \ (3.03)$
$a_1 = .1142 \ (4.12)$
$a_2 = .0917 \ (3.47)$
$a_3 = .0691 \ (2.36)$
$a_4 = .0462 \ (1.70)$
$a_5 = .0232 \ (1.31)$
$\sum a_i = .4810 \ (3.87)$

$c_0 = .0580 \ (2.32)$
$c_1 = .0558 \ (2.81)$
$c_2 = .0530 \ (3.19)$
$c_3 = .0495 \ (3.29)$
$c_4 = .0455 \ (3.11)$
$c_5 = .0408 \ (2.81)$
$c_6 = .0355 \ (2.50)$
$c_7 = .0297 \ (2.24)$
$c_8 = .0232 \ (2.03)$
$c_9 = .0161 \ (1.85)$
$c_{10} = .0083 \ (1.71)$
$\sum c_i = .4154 \ (3.25)$

$b_0 = .2834 \ (4.93)$
$b_1 = .1989 \ (8.60)$
$b_2 = .1284 \ (6.79)$
$b_3 = .0717 \ (2.92)$
$b_4 = .0289 \ (1.51)$
$\sum b_i = .7112 \ (9.71)$

$$Q_1 = \begin{cases} 1.00 & \text{until } 1961{:}4 \\ 0 & \text{after } 1961{:}4 \end{cases}$$

$$Q_2 = \begin{cases} 0 & \text{until } 1961{:}4 \\ 1.00 & \text{after } 1961{:}4 \end{cases}$$

$$Q_3 = \begin{cases} 0 & \text{until } 1962{:}1 \\ 1.00 & \text{after } 1962{:}1 \end{cases}$$

Note: All distributed lags are estimated with second-degree Almon polynomials constrained to be zero at the end point. The t ratios are in parenthesis below or beside the coefficients.

Table 4C-2. Commercial Bank Deposit Rate, Estimated Coefficients

Equation	R^2	SE	DW
	.9974	.0492	1.98

$$RTP^* = -2.0075 + Q_1 \sum_{i=0}^{4} a_i RTB_{-i}$$
$$(-15.92)$$

$$+ Q_2 \sum_{i=0}^{2} b_i \left\{ .23RTB + .77 \left[\frac{RSL(MSL_{-1} - MSL_{-5}) + RMS(MMS_{-1} - MMS_{-5})}{MSL_{-1} + MMS_{-1} - MSL_{-5} - MMS_{-5}} \right] \right\}_{-i}$$

$$+ \sum_{i=0}^{8} c_i(.45RCL + .30RM + .25RMUN)_{-i}$$

$$- .0909[(.45RCL + .30RM + .25RMUN) - ZDRA]_{-1} + \sum_{i=0}^{9} d_i(ZCT - ZCT_{-1})_{-i}$$
$$(-1.80)$$

$$+ Q_2 \sum_{i=0}^{6} e_i \left[\frac{MP_{-1} - MP_{-2}}{MP_{-2}} - \frac{(MKCB_{-1} + MCL_{-1}) - (MKCB_{-2} + MCL_{-2})}{MKCB_{-2} + MCL_{-2}} \right]_{-i}$$

$$+ Q_2 \sum_{i=0}^{6} f_i \left[\frac{MD_{-1} - MD_{-2}}{MD_{-2}} - \frac{(MKCB_{-1} + MCL_{-1}) - (MKCB_{-2} + MCL_{-2})}{MKCB_{-2} + MCL_{-2}} \right]_{-i}$$

$$+ .2194Q_2$$
$$(.59)$$

Table 4C-2 continued

Equation	R^2	SE	DW
$a_0 = .0615\ (5.06)$			
$a_1 = .0463\ (3.43)$			
$a_2 = .0325\ (2.02)$			
$a_3 = .0202\ (1.32)$			
$a_4 = .0094\ (0.94)$			
$\Sigma a_i = .1699\ (2.85)$			
$b_0 = .1832\ (1.88)$			
$b_1 = .0633\ (0.91)$			
$b_2 = .0022\ (0.02)$			
$\Sigma b_i = .2488\ (2.21)$			
$c_0 = -.0313\ (-1.47)$			
$c_1 = -.0200\ (-0.67)$			
$c_2 = .0206\ (0.74)$			
$c_3 = .0770\ (3.91)$			
$c_4 = .1358\ (15.54)$			
$c_5 = .1838\ (21.92)$			
$c_6 = .2076\ (12.06)$			
$c_7 = .1938\ (9.10)$			
$c_8 = .1291\ (7.75)$			
$\Sigma c_i = .8964^{a}\ (15.54)$			
$d_0 = 0.3804\ (6.17)$			
$d_1 = 0.3537\ (6.60)$			
$d_2 = 0.3244\ (6.16)$			
$d_3 = 0.2926\ (5.25)$			
$d_4 = 0.2583\ (4.41)$			
$d_5 = 0.2215\ (3.76)$			
$d_6 = 0.1822\ (3.27)$			
$d_7 = 0.1404\ (2.90)$			
$d_8 = 0.0961\ (2.61)$			
$d_9 = 0.0493\ (2.38)$			
$\Sigma d_i = 2.2992\ (5.25)$			
$e_0 = -0.6763\ (-0.74)$			
$e_1 = -2.2252\ (-3.28)$			
$e_2 = -3.2256\ (-4.32)$			
$e_3 = -3.6775\ (-4.33)$			
$e_4 = -3.5809\ (-4.19)$			
$e_5 = -2.9358\ (-4.06)$			
$e_6 = -1.7421\ (-3.96)$			
$\Sigma e_i = -18.0634\ (-4.32)$			
$f_0 = -2.6986\ (-2.97)$			
$f_1 = -2.7280\ (-3.73)$			
$f_2 = -2.6190\ (-3.59)$			
$f_3 = -2.3717\ (-3.12)$			
$f_4 = -1.9862\ (-2.72)$			
$f_5 = -1.4624\ (-2.42)$			
$f_6 = -0.8004\ (-2.21)$	$Q_1 = \begin{cases}1.00 & \text{until } 1961{:}4 \\ 0 & \text{after } 1961{:}4\end{cases}$		
$\Sigma f_i = -14.6663\ (-3.59)$	$Q_2 = \begin{cases}1.00 & \text{until } 1961{:}3 \\ 0 & \text{after } 1961{:}4\end{cases}$		

Note: Unless otherwise noted, all distributed lags are estimated with second degree Almon polynomials constrained to be zero at the end point. The *t* ratios are in parenthesis below or beside the coefficients.

[a] Third degree Almon polynomial tied to zero at both the end point and $c_0 + 1$.

**Appendix 4D:
Behavior of Deposit
Rate Equations**

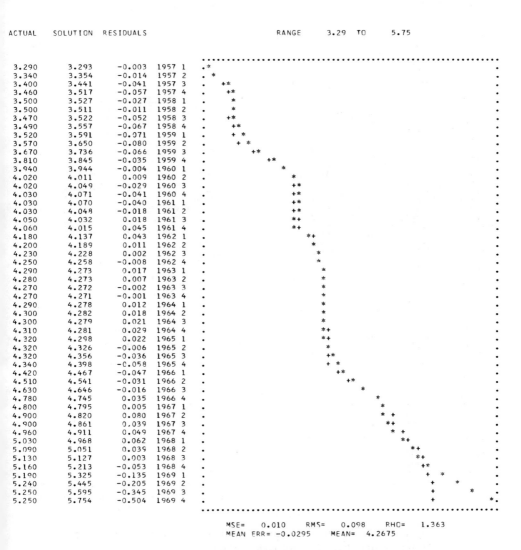

```
ACTUAL     SOLUTION   RESIDUALS                        RANGE    3.29  TO    5.75

3.290     3.293     -0.003   1957 1    .·*                                                    .
3.340     3.354     -0.014   1957 2    . *                                                    .
3.400     3.441     -0.041   1957 3    .   +*                                                 .
3.460     3.517     -0.057   1957 4    .   +*                                                 .
3.500     3.527     -0.027   1958 1    .    *                                                 .
3.500     3.511     -0.011   1958 2    .    *                                                 .
3.470     3.522     -0.052   1958 3    .   +*                                                 .
3.490     3.557     -0.067   1958 4    .   +*                                                 .
3.520     3.591     -0.071   1959 1    .   +  *                                               .
3.570     3.650     -0.080   1959 2    .    + *                                               .
3.670     3.736     -0.066   1959 3    .       +*                                             .
3.810     3.845     -0.035   1959 4    .        +*                                            .
3.940     3.944     -0.004   1960 1    .           *                                          .
4.020     4.011      0.009   1960 2    .            *                                         .
4.020     4.049     -0.029   1960 3    .            +*                                        .
4.030     4.071     -0.041   1960 4    .            +*                                        .
4.030     4.070     -0.040   1961 1    .            +*                                        .
4.030     4.048     -0.018   1961 2    .            +*                                        .
4.050     4.032      0.018   1961 3    .            *+                                        .
4.060     4.015      0.045   1961 4    .            *+                                        .
4.180     4.137      0.043   1962 1    .               *+                                     .
4.200     4.189      0.011   1962 2    .               *                                      .
4.230     4.228      0.002   1962 3    .                *                                     .
4.250     4.258     -0.008   1962 4    .                *                                     .
4.290     4.273      0.017   1963 1    .                 *                                    .
4.280     4.273      0.007   1963 2    .                 *                                    .
4.270     4.272     -0.002   1963 3    .                 *                                    .
4.270     4.271     -0.001   1963 4    .                 *                                    .
4.290     4.278      0.012   1964 1    .                 *                                    .
4.300     4.282      0.018   1964 2    .                 *                                    .
4.300     4.279      0.021   1964 3    .                 *                                    .
4.310     4.281      0.029   1964 4    .                *+                                    .
4.320     4.298      0.022   1965 1    .                *+                                    .
4.320     4.326     -0.006   1965 2    .                 *                                    .
4.320     4.356     -0.036   1965 3    .                +*                                    .
4.340     4.398     -0.058   1965 4    .                +  *                                  .
4.420     4.467     -0.047   1966 1    .                  +*                                  .
4.510     4.541     -0.031   1966 2    .                   +*                                 .
4.630     4.646     -0.016   1966 3    .                     *                                .
4.780     4.745      0.035   1966 4    .                       *                              .
4.800     4.795      0.005   1967 1    .                       *  +                           .
4.900     4.820      0.080   1967 2    .                       *+                             .
4.900     4.861      0.039   1967 3    .                       * +                            .
4.960     4.911      0.049   1967 4    .                        *+                            .
5.030     4.968      0.062   1968 1    .                        *+                            .
5.090     5.051      0.039   1968 2    .                         *+                           .
5.130     5.127      0.003   1968 3    .                          +*                          .
5.160     5.213     -0.053   1968 4    .                          +   *                       .
5.190     5.325     -0.135   1969 1    .                          +      *                     .
5.240     5.445     -0.205   1969 2    .                          +        *                   .
5.250     5.595     -0.345   1969 3    .                          +           *.               .
5.250     5.754     -0.504   1969 4    .                          +              *.            .

            MSE=    0.010   RMS=    0.098   RHO=   1.363
            MEAN ERR= -0.0295    MEAN=  4.2675
```

Figure 4D-1. Standard Dynamic Simulation of Deposit Rate Sector: Savings and Loan Deposit Rate — *RSL*.

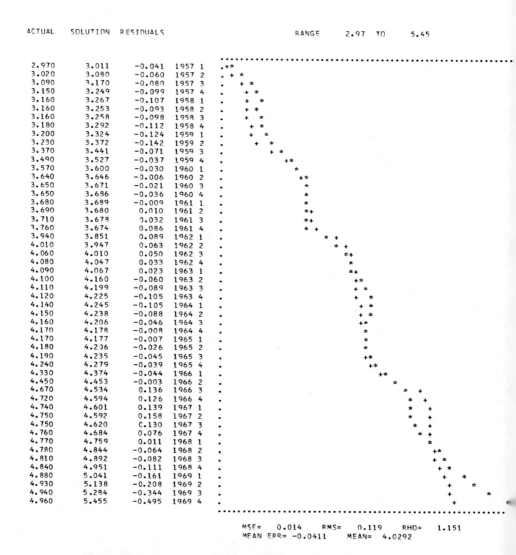

```
ACTUAL    SOLUTION   RESIDUALS                    RANGE    2.97   TO      5.45

2.970     3.011      -0.041    1957 1     .+*
3.020     3.080      -0.060    1957 2     . +  *
3.090     3.170      -0.080    1957 3     .  +  *
3.150     3.249      -0.099    1957 4     .   +  *
3.160     3.267      -0.107    1958 1     .    +   *
3.160     3.253      -0.093    1958 2     .    +  *
3.160     3.258      -0.098    1958 3     .    +  *
3.180     3.292      -0.112    1958 4     .     +  *
3.200     3.324      -0.124    1959 1     .     +   *
3.230     3.372      -0.142    1959 2     .      +    *
3.370     3.441      -0.071    1959 3     .       +  *
3.490     3.527      -0.037    1959 4     .          +*
3.570     3.600      -0.030    1960 1     .           *
3.640     3.646      -0.006    1960 2     .            +*
3.650     3.671      -0.021    1960 3     .            *
3.650     3.686      -0.036    1960 4     .            *
3.680     3.689      -0.009    1961 1     .            *
3.690     3.680       0.010    1961 2     .            *+
3.710     3.678       0.032    1961 3     .            *+
3.760     3.674       0.086    1961 4     .            *  +
3.940     3.851       0.089    1962 1     .              * +
4.010     3.947       0.063    1962 2     .               *  +
4.060     4.010       0.050    1962 3     .               *+
4.080     4.047       0.033    1962 4     .                *+
4.090     4.067       0.023    1963 1     .                *+
4.100     4.160      -0.060    1963 2     .                +*
4.110     4.199      -0.089    1963 3     .                + *
4.120     4.225      -0.105    1963 4     .                +  *
4.140     4.245      -0.105    1964 1     .                +  *
4.150     4.238      -0.088    1964 2     .                +  *
4.160     4.206      -0.046    1964 3     .                +*
4.170     4.178      -0.008    1964 4     .                *
4.170     4.177      -0.007    1965 1     .                *
4.180     4.206      -0.026    1965 2     .                *
4.190     4.235      -0.045    1965 3     .                 +*
4.240     4.279      -0.039    1965 4     .                  +*
4.330     4.374      -0.044    1966 1     .                   +*
4.450     4.453      -0.003    1966 2     .                     *
4.670     4.534       0.136    1966 3     .                     *   +
4.720     4.594       0.126    1966 4     .                      *   +
4.740     4.601       0.139    1967 1     .                      *    +
4.750     4.592       0.158    1967 2     .                      *    +
4.750     4.620       0.130    1967 3     .                       *   +
4.760     4.684       0.076    1967 4     .                        *  +
4.770     4.759       0.011    1968 1     .                         *
4.780     4.844      -0.064    1968 2     .                          +*
4.810     4.892      -0.082    1968 3     .                          + *
4.840     4.951      -0.111    1968 4     .                          +  *
4.880     5.041      -0.161    1969 1     .                           +    *
4.930     5.138      -0.208    1969 2     .                            +      *
4.940     5.294      -0.344    1969 3     .                             +        *
4.960     5.455      -0.495    1969 4     .                               +
```

```
          MSE=    0.014     RMS=    0.119     RHO=    1.151
          MEAN ERR= -0.0411     MEAN=   4.0292
```

Figure 4D-2. Standard Dynamic Simulation of Deposit Rate Sector:
Mutual Savings Bank Deposit Rate — *RMS*.

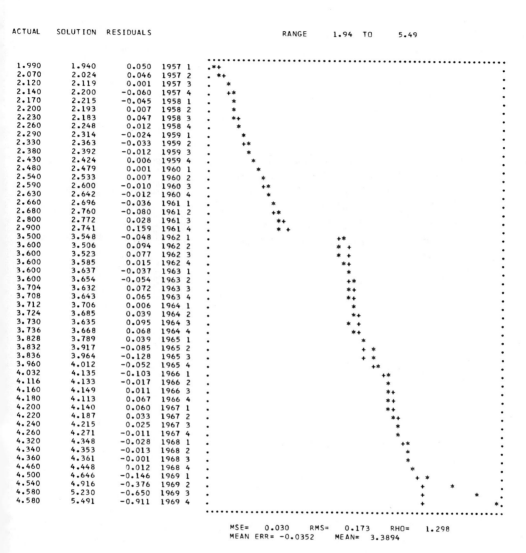

ACTUAL   SOLUTION   RESIDUALS   RANGE   1.94 TO   5.49

ACTUAL	SOLUTION	RESIDUALS		
1.990	1.940	0.050	1957	1
2.070	2.024	0.046	1957	2
2.120	2.119	0.001	1957	3
2.140	2.200	-0.060	1957	4
2.170	2.215	-0.045	1958	1
2.200	2.193	0.007	1958	2
2.230	2.183	0.047	1958	3
2.260	2.248	0.012	1958	4
2.290	2.314	-0.024	1959	1
2.330	2.363	-0.033	1959	2
2.380	2.392	-0.012	1959	3
2.430	2.424	0.006	1959	4
2.480	2.479	0.001	1960	1
2.540	2.533	0.007	1960	2
2.590	2.600	-0.010	1960	3
2.630	2.642	-0.012	1960	4
2.660	2.696	-0.036	1961	1
2.680	2.760	-0.080	1961	2
2.800	2.772	0.028	1961	3
2.900	2.741	0.159	1961	4
3.500	3.548	-0.048	1962	1
3.600	3.506	0.094	1962	2
3.600	3.523	0.077	1962	3
3.600	3.585	0.015	1962	4
3.600	3.637	-0.037	1963	1
3.600	3.654	-0.054	1963	2
3.704	3.632	0.072	1963	3
3.708	3.643	0.065	1963	4
3.712	3.706	0.006	1964	1
3.724	3.685	0.039	1964	2
3.730	3.635	0.095	1964	3
3.736	3.668	0.068	1964	4
3.828	3.789	0.039	1965	1
3.832	3.917	-0.085	1965	2
3.836	3.964	-0.128	1965	3
3.960	4.012	-0.052	1965	4
4.032	4.135	-0.103	1966	1
4.116	4.133	-0.017	1966	2
4.160	4.149	0.011	1966	3
4.180	4.113	0.067	1966	4
4.200	4.140	0.060	1967	1
4.220	4.187	0.033	1967	2
4.240	4.215	0.025	1967	3
4.260	4.271	-0.011	1967	4
4.320	4.348	-0.028	1968	1
4.340	4.353	-0.013	1968	2
4.360	4.361	-0.001	1968	3
4.460	4.448	0.012	1968	4
4.500	4.646	-0.146	1969	1
4.540	4.916	-0.376	1969	2
4.580	5.230	-0.650	1969	3
4.580	5.491	-0.911	1969	4

MSE=   0.030   RMS=   0.173   RHO=   1.298
MEAN ERR= -0.0352   MEAN= 3.3894

Figure 4D-3. Standard Dynamic Simulation of Deposit Rate Sector: Commercial Bank Deposit Rate – *RTP*.

References

[1] Goldfeld, Stephen M. *Commercial Bank Behavior and Economic Activity.* Amsterdam: North-Holland Publishing, 1966.

[2] Goldfeld, Stephen M., and Dwight M. Jaffee. "The Determinants of Deposit Rate Setting by Savings and Loan Associations." *Journal of Finance* 25 (June 1970): 615–632.

[3] Meyer, Paul A. "Comment." *Journal of Finance* 22 (September 1967): 467–470.

[4] Silber, William L. *Portfolio Behavior of Financial Institutions.* New York: Holt, Rhinehart, and Winston, 1970.

[5] Teck, Alan. *Mutual Savings Banks and Loan Associations: Aspects of Growth.* New York: Columbia University Press, 1968.

[6] Weber, Gerald S. "Interest Rates on Mortgages and Dividend Rates on Savings and Loan Shares." *Journal of Finance* 21 (September 1966): 515–521.

5

An Econometric Model of the Mortgage Market

DWIGHT M. JAFFEE

This research was financed in part by the Social Science Research Council, in conjunction with its support of the FMP model, and by the Federal Reserve Bank of Philadelphia. The author is indebted for helpful comments and suggestions to participants in the FMP project, especially Albert Ando, Edward Gramlich, and Franco Modigliani, and to colleagues, particularly Ray Fair and Stephen Goldfeld. The author is solely responsible for the views expressed and any errors that remain.

This paper develops and analyzes a quarterly econometric model of the mortgage market prepared as a component sector for the FMP model. Within the FMP model, the mortgage sector serves as the link between private savings taking the form of deposits at financial intermediaries, and investment in housing capital which is influenced by the cost and availability of mortgage credit.[1] For present purposes the flow of deposits and investment in housing are taken as exogenous. Our analysis thus focuses on the structure and workings of the mortgage sector by itself. The deposit and housing sectors for the FMP model are discussed, however, and the characteristics of the entire system are reported in other chapters of this book.

In line with the objectives of the FMP project, the mortgage sector has been designed with particular concern for the lags in the effect of variables and the quantitative effects of the available policy instruments. In this respect the model differs most notably from earlier studies[2] by incorporating the effects of Federal Home Loan Bank Board (FHLBB) and Federal National Mortgage Association (FNMA) policy[3] and by explicitly specifying the dynamic structure resulting from the institutional features of advance commitments. This emphasis is particularly timely and important with

---

[1] The financial structure of the FMP model has been summarized by de Leeuw and Gramlich [5]. Also see their references to earlier reports on the FMP project.

[2] The mortgage market has been studied by itself in papers by Huang [11], Huang and McCarthy [12], Hulett [13], and Silber [17], and in conjunction with a housing sector in papers by Smith [18] and Sparks [19], [20]. Comparisons of the present study with these works are developed in context below.

[3] The model does not reflect the September 1968 institutional changes in FNMA because they occurred at the very end of the sample period. Thus both FNMA and the Government National Mortgage Association (GNMA) are treated as exogenous.

respect to the mortgage and housing market. Although the conflict between the discriminatory effects of monetary policy on the housing sector and the concern of public policy with the availability of an adequate housing stock has long been acknowledged, the recent periods of continuing monetary tightness have brought this issue to the forefront as a major policy dilemma.

The plan of the paper is as follows. Following a brief summary of the structure of the model and notes concerning data and the method of estimation, the next section will develop the formulation and estimation of the supply of mortgages by financial intermediaries; the demand for mortgages is then treated similarly. The fourth section presents the results of a dynamic simulation of the entire mortgage market and of tests for the multiplier responses to shocks in the exogenous variables. These latter experiments also provide insight into the structure and workings of the model. The paper concludes with a summary of findings and suggestions for future research.

The final structural estimates of the model used in the simulation experiments are summarized in chapter Appendix 5A. The definitions of symbols and notation are provided at the end of the book, in Appendixes A and B The model consists of sixteen endogenous variables, twelve of which are explained by structural equations (equations 5A-1 to 5A-12) and four of which are explained by identities (equations 5A-13 to 5A-16). There are twelve exogenous explanatory variables, representing deposits at financial intermediaries, the stock of houses and investment in houses, and interest rates on nonmortgage assets. Of these twelve variables, nine are endogenous in the full FMP model, while three—the net mortgage holdings of FNMA, and the interest cost and quantity of FHLBB advances to savings and loan associations—are taken as policy instruments.

The data are entirely consistent with the variables currently in the FMP model; in particular, flow-of-funds statistics are generally used for the mortgages and deposits of the financial intermediaries. On the supply side, the model is disaggregated to the extent that the four principal suppliers—commercial banks, savings and loan associations, mutual savings banks, and life insurance companies—are treated separately.[4] On the demand side, only the aggregate demand for mortgage loans is considered. In particular, no attempt is made to separate the FHA and VA guaranteed mortgages from

---

[4] At year-end 1968 these intermediaries held mortgages in the amount of $319 billion with a distribution: savings and loan associations 41 percent, life insurance companies 22 percent, commercial banks 20 percent, and mutual savings banks 17 percent. The only other financial intermediaries of note in the mortgage market are the mortgage companies. The mortgage companies act essentially as brokers, originating mortgages which are then sold to the four major intermediaries and FNMA. Their only net contribution to the market consists of a small revolving inventory of mortgages and this has been ignored.

conventional loans, nor is there an attempt to distinguish residential and nonresidential mortgages. The main reason for not disaggregating in these two areas is the unavailability of appropriate data. The data on mortgage commitments are the main bottleneck since, except for life insurance companies, they can be obtained only as an aggregate for each of the intermediaries.[5]

The unavailability of data has also necessitated asymmetrical treatment of the supply of mortgages by the intermediaries. Data on mortgage commitments and repayments for commercial banks are not available, so that the commercial bank supply of mortgages is represented by only a single equation, (5A-8), explaining the net change in their holdings. For savings and loan associations and mutual savings banks, data are available for the stock of outstanding commitments but not for the flow of new commitments. The result of this data limitation is that equations for the new commitments of these intermediaries cannot be estimated, and thus the equations for their outstanding commitments (equations 5A-2 and 5A-3) are formulated with a structure corresponding to the equation for the new commitments of life insurance companies (equation 5A-1). For the same reason, the gross mortgage flow equations of savings and loan associations and mutual savings banks (5A-6 and 5A-7) are based on the stock of outstanding commitments, while the flow of mortgages from life insurance companies is based on new commitments (equation 5A-5). The assumptions that are made necessary by the absence of data on new commitments for the two intermediaries are discussed below.

The model has been estimated over the longest sample period compatible with the availability of data for each equation. All samples end with 1968:4 and most begin in the second half of the 1950s. Seasonally adjusted data are

---

[5] The study by Huang [11] distinguishes guaranteed and conventional residential mortgages, but because of data limitations does not separate supply by type of intermediary, and does not explicitly use data on commitments. Unfortunately, Huang could not obtain reliable estimates on the degree of substitution between the various types of mortgages; if the degree of substitution is sufficiently high then, of course, little is lost by treating mortgages as a homogenous aggregate. Furthermore Huang did not adjust the rates on FHA and VA mortgages for "points" and other methods used by suppliers in periods in which the rates on guaranteed mortgages were constrained by ceilings. These adjustments, together with the tendency for the ceilings to be raised whenever they become severely binding, significantly reduce the segmentation between conventional and guaranteed mortgage markets.

It should be further noted that the availability and nature of data on mortgage flows has been recently examined in detail by Diamond [6] at the Department of Housing and Urban Development, with the result that an organized effort is being made to obtain complete data for mortgage commitments and flows in the future.

used throughout, except for the interest rates.[6] The equations were fitted by ordinary least squares. The iterative technique of Cochrane and Orcutt [3] was used for the estimation of equations where positive serial correlation of the errors was indicated. The distributed lags in equations (5A-5) to (5A-8) were estimated with the Almon [1] technique. No correction was made for simultaneous equation bias.[7]

For brevity, in the remainder of the paper the principal intermediaries, life insurance companies, savings and loan associations, mutual savings banks, and commercial banks will be abbreviated as LICs, SLAs, MSBs, and CBs, respectively.

The Supply of Mortgages

In developing a model of mortgage supply for the four principal financial intermediaries, we will begin with general considerations and then proceed to the formulation and estimation of commitments equations (except for CBs) and mortgage flow equations for each of the financial intermediaries.

General Considerations

The economic variables and institutional factors influencing the supply of mortgages by the primary intermediaries have been outlined and discussed in several major studies. Saul Klaman's work [15] considers the mortgage market as a whole, while the intermediaries are discussed separately in the trade association monographs for the Commission on Money and Credit. Not surprisingly, one learns that there are both significant similarities and significant differences in the mortgage market activity of these institutions. We begin by considering the broadly similar characteristics of intermediary portfolio choice.

---

[6] Seasonally adjusted data has been used in order to avoid the complications related to the strong seasonal component in housing construction and hence in mortgage demand. This may provide an interesting area for further research.

[7] It is anticipated that the simultaneous equation bias will be relatively small since the mortgage rate affects both demand and supply primarily, though not solely, with a lag. This is consistent with the work of Smith [18] and Silber [17] both of whom found the ordinary and two-stage least squares fits of their models very similar; indeed Smith presents only the ordinary least squares estimates and Silber actually prefers the ordinary least squares fits in the two cases in which they differed significantly from the two-stage estimates. The model of Huang [11] was also reestimated using three-stage least squares in Huang and McCarthy [12], but the sample periods for the two sets of estimates were not the same and Huang and McCarthy do not comment on the similarity of the results.

A financial intermediary obtains deposits in the open market, and these deposits together with its equity, retained earnings, and loan repayments, provide the base for its investment activity.[8] The allocation of the intermediary's funds among the various competing assets is determined basically by the net yield and liquidity value of the assets. Thus, if the mortgage rate rises relative to the yield on government bonds, we would expect the intermediary to increase its allocation of funds to mortgages and, assuming substitution between the assets, to decrease its allocation of funds to government bonds.

In the short run, other factors may also influence the investment decision. It is frequently pointed out that intermediaries will not immediately and fully adjust their portfolio to changing conditions such as an increase in the mortgage rate. Uncertainty about the future, transactions costs, and perhaps the need to meet the immediate demands of their customers, make a more cautious and partial adjustment path essential. Furthermore, short-run cash flows may dictate the immediate depository for the intermediary's assets. For example, an intermediary may invest an unexpected deposit inflow in government bonds in the short run before it has time to allocate the proper share of these funds to mortgages.

Recent econometric studies of models of financial behavior have indicated that these considerations of portfolio allocation and adjustment may be usefully analyzed in stock adjustment models, and we use this framework as a convenient starting point.[9] The intermediary's desired level of mortgages, M^*, is specified as proportional to its stock of deposits, D, where the proportionality factor is a linear function of the rate spread between the mortgage rate, RM, and the rate on a competing asset, RC (which may vary between intermediaries):[10]

$$M^* = [a_0 + a_1(RM - RC)]D \tag{5-1}$$

Three restrictive assumptions are made in formulating the equation this way. First, only a single yield is used as the measure of the return on competing assets. This will preclude the possibility of multicollinearity which might arise if more than two interest rates were included in the equation. Second, it is assumed that the own rate and competing rate coefficients have opposite

---

[8] For LICs, deposits are defined as the sum of policy reserves and other liabilities less policy loans. Although this definition raises problems as an index of the demand for life insurance, it is suitable as the base for the portfolio allocation of the LICs. See also footnote 23.

[9] See de Leeuw [4] and Brainard and Tobin [2] for further discussion of the stock adjustment principle in relation to financial asset choice.

[10] In the following discussion it is to be understood that the variables for deposits and mortgages and the coefficients of the equations relate to a specific intermediary, although identifying superscripts have been omitted for convenience.

signs, but are equal in absolute value. Thus it is the spread between the two rates which enters the equation.[11] Third, in scaling mortgages by deposits we have neglected the intermediary's equity base and other liabilities which are sources of funds for investment. The equity base is suppressed for the practical reason that it is cumbersome to make endogenous when the mortgage market is set in the framework of a complete econometric model of the economy. The variations in equity are steady and sufficiently small so that the major effect of suppressing them will be a slightly larger coefficient for the deposit variable than would be the case with the capital accounts included. Nondeposit liabilities vary between intermediaries and these will be considered in the discussion of individual intermediaries.

The intended change in mortgage loans can now be written

$$\Delta \hat{M} = g_0(M^* - M_{-1}) + g_1 \Delta D \tag{5-2}$$

The first term represents the basic partial adjustment of mortgages toward the equilibrium level. The second term allows for an impact effect from a change in deposits. The coefficient g_1 will be positive if new deposits are initially invested in mortgages at a rate greater than indicated by the partial adjustment mechanism of the first term, and zero or negative otherwise. The reason for specifying $\Delta \hat{M}$ as the intended change, rather than the actual change as is customary, relates to the effect of advance commitments on the supply of mortgages to be discussed in the following section.

It will also be useful below to have a formulation explaining the intended gross change in mortgages $\Delta \hat{M}_g$. Adding the amount of repayments on mortgage loans, R, to both sides of equation (5-2), we obtain[12]

$$\Delta \hat{M}_g = g_0(M^* - M_{-1}) + g_1 \Delta D + R \tag{5-3}$$

It is not difficult to find fault with a model formulated in this manner. Brainard and Tobin [2] have emphasized, for example, that the coefficients of any interest rate, when summed over all the assets in the portfolio, must be zero if the model is to be estimated efficiently. By specifying an equation for only one of the assets held by the intermediary, the restrictions implied by the balance-sheet constraint must be ignored. Brainard and Tobin have

---

[11] Parkin [16] has in fact demonstrated and discussed a utility function which analytically implies asset demand functions with this property. Also, note that in equation (5-1) it is important that the interest rate spread is scaled (multiplied) by deposits. In other studies ([11], [17], and [18]) the interest rates are entered linearly with the result that the interest rate responsiveness of mortgages is independent of the level of deposits.

[12] In order to make the repayments on mortgage loans to each of the intermediaries an endogenous variable, separate repayment equations must also be estimated. These are discussed in the following section. It should also be noted that this is one form in which the noninterest rate terms on mortgages enter the supply function. Otherwise it is assumed that these terms have been constant over the sample period.

also noted, along similar lines, that short-run substitution effects between assets should be specified in the equations if the sum of the implied partial adjustments for individual assets is to equal the total change in assets. In the simplest case this may be accomplished by adding the lagged stocks of competing assets to the mortgage equation. Unfortunately most previous experiences with such specifications indicate that the multicollinearity between the lagged stocks precludes reliable estimates. Furthermore, equations for these other assets have to be estimated, if they are to be made endogenous in the model, and this posed additional problems. For both these reasons the short-run cross-substitution effects are not considered in the remainder of the discussion.

Two other weaknesses in the stock adjustment model should also be noted. First, no rationale has been provided for the partial adjustment. Although concepts such as transactions costs and uncertainty have intuitive appeal, there has been no rigorous demonstration that these lead to partial adjustment in financial decisions of the form postulated.[13] Secondly, the model assumes that current decisions depend only on the current values of deposits and interest rates, and expectations about future movements in these variables are not included. The introduction of advance commitments, to which we now turn, improves this feature of the model, but the stock adjustment mechanism is still weak in this respect.

Advance Commitments

The stock adjustment model must be further modified in the case of the mortgage market to take into account the institutional arrangements for advance or forward commitments.[14] Advance commitments arise because a builder or contractor faces the risk of not being able to sell his property should mortgage funds not be available at the time of sale. Furthermore, it is difficult for the builder to obtain even short-term bank loans to finance the construction costs, unless he can provide assurance of the availability of long-term mortgage funds upon completion of the project. In response to this problem, financial intermediaries have been willing to provide advance commitments which contain the necessary guarantee of mortgage funds for use when the structure is completed and ready for sale.

Advance commitments are important in the model because they influence

---

[13] It can be shown that short-run partial adjustment in the real investment decision may be rational if the short-run supply cost of capital is rising. Tinsley [21] has derived more general optimal adjustment paths which could be applicable to financial decision making.

[14] Klaman [15] was among the first to emphasize the importance of advance commitments for the mortgage market. Fisher [8] provides a more recent discussion of this institution.

the timing, and hence the short-run dynamics, of mortgage supply. An intermediary must decide on its supply of commitments on the basis of current information such as deposits and market interest rates. The commitments will be "taken down," that is transformed into mortgage loans, only at some future date, possibly more than a year later. In the meantime, market conditions can change substantially. The rate of growth of deposits may decline and the relative yield of mortgages may fall or vice versa. In these cases, the quantity of mortgages actually coming on the market will reflect a decision made by the intermediary predominantly on the basis of information at some past time and will not represent the volume of mortgages the intermediary would supply in the absence of the time lag created by the advance commitment institution.

In principle, the effect of advance commitments on the timing of mortgage flows can be taken into account, without explicitly entering commitments in the equations, by properly lagging the independent variables. This is in fact the method used in some earlier studies.[15] This approach raises the difficulty, however, of obtaining accurate estimates when distributed lags on as many variables as enter, say, equation (5-3) must be determined. A more efficient solution, and the one adopted here, is to make use of the available data on advance commitments by directly estimating an equation for the supply of commitments. The mortgage flows can then be formulated as a distributed lag on the commitments variable alone. The gain in efficiency from this approach is the result of specifying the *actual* amount of commitments in the mortgage flow equation. If, instead, the mortgage flow equation is specified with the *determinants* of commitments, then the error term of the implicit commitments equation enters the mortgage flow equation only as part of the general error term of the latter. The more structural approach also allows, if desired, the use of a priori restrictions on the equations.

The main difficulty in adapting the basic stock adjustment model for advance commitments is that the relevant horizon for decision making is lengthened because of the lags in the take-down of commitments. A similar problem is faced in specifying equations for new orders and investment in fixed real capital. In the formulation of Jorgenson [14], for example, it is assumed that new orders are placed such that the sum of the existing capital stock and outstanding orders in process is equal to the desired capital stock

---

[15] See for example Sparks [19] and Huang [11]. Sparks does make use of the data on advance commitments by constructing his dependent variable as the sum of outstanding mortgages and commitments. This is only a limited improvement, however, since it still assumes that deposits and interest rates influence both variables the same way. In contrast, the basis of our approach is that the timing of commitments is significantly different from that of mortgages.

Consequently, current new orders will equal the current desired change in the capital stock less orders already in process.

The corresponding result for the mortgage market is that the amount of mortgages expected to be derived from new and outstanding advance commitments should equal the desired gross change in the mortgage stock. The intended gross change in the mortgage stock, under the assumption of a one-period planning horizon, has already been derived as equation (5-3). To modify this relationship for the longer horizon consistent with the lag in take-down in commitments, it is reasonable to assume that full adjustment is attempted over the planning period and thus g_0 should be set equal to unity. We still retain, however, the short-run impact effect of the deposit flows. Thus the desired gross change in mortgages over the planning period can be written:

$$\overline{\Delta M_g} = M^* - M_{-1} + g_1 \Delta D + R \qquad (5\text{-}4)$$

This desired mortgage flow can be met in essentially three ways: (i) the intermediary can issue mortgages directly in the market, say in the amount $\overline{MM}$; (ii) the intermediary can anticipate that commitments already outstanding will be taken down during the planning period, say in the amount $\overline{MOC}$; and (iii) the intermediary can issue new commitments which lead to an expected flow of mortgages, say $\overline{MNC}$, with the actual flow and its distribution over time determined by the rate and time distribution of commitment take-downs and cancellations. The three components will be set equal to the target flow:

$$\overline{\Delta M_g} = \overline{MM} + \overline{MOC} + \overline{MNC} \qquad (5\text{-}5)$$

We have distinguished the mortgage flows derived from new and outstanding commitments ($\overline{MNC}$ and $\overline{MOC}$) from the actual levels of these commitments (NC and OC) in order to bring in the possibility of commitment cancellation. Specifically, we assume that:

$$\overline{MNC} = aNC \qquad a < 1 \qquad (5\text{-}6)$$

$$\overline{MOC} = a'OC_{-1} \qquad a' < 1 \qquad (5\text{-}7)$$

The parameter a is assumed to be less than unity because some proportion of new advance commitments will ultimately be cancelled rather than taken down into mortgages. Consequently, in aiming for a target mortgage flow of $\overline{MNC}$, the intermediary must issue a larger amount of new commitments, NC, to compensate for the cancellations. The parameter a' is assumed to be less than unity for essentially the same reason, namely that the flow of mortgages originating in commitments outstanding at the end of the previous period will be less than the actual amount of these commitments. By taking a' to be constant, we are implicitly assuming that the cancellation rate on commitments is independent of the maturity structure of outstanding commitments. We do allow, however, for the possibility that the lag in take-down or cancellation may exceed the planning horizon by distinguishing a from a'.

Equation (5-2) may now be rewritten, using (5-6) and (5-7), with new commitments as the dependent variable:

$$NC = (1/a)(\overline{\Delta M_g} - \overline{MM}) - (a'/a)OC_{-1} \qquad (5\text{-}8)$$

Since the variable OC_{-1} can be observed and $\overline{\Delta M_g}$ has been derived in equation (5-4), only $\overline{MM}$, the mortgages to be issued directly in the market during the planning period, remains to be specified. We shall assume that the planned ratio between the target flow $\overline{\Delta M_g}$ and the mortgage flow to be derived from commitments ($\overline{MNC} + \overline{MOC}$) is constant and depends on institutional factors specific to the intermediary. This implies that the planned ratio between $\overline{MM}$ and $\overline{\Delta M_g}$ is also constant:

$$\overline{MM} = b\,\overline{\Delta M_g} \qquad b < 1 \qquad (5\text{-}9)$$

The proportionality factor b will be large for intermediaries, such as SLAs which issue most of their mortgages directly in the market; and it will be, small for intermediaries, such as LICs, which rely primarily on commitments for their flow of mortgages.

By substituting (5-9) into (5-8) and then using (5-1) and (5-4), we obtain the complete specification for the supply of new commitments:

$$NC = a_0 d_0 D + a_1 d_0 (RM - RC)D + g_1 d_0\,\Delta D - d_0 M_{-1}$$
$$+ d_0 R - d_1 OC_{-1} \qquad (5\text{-}10)$$

where $d_0 = (1 - b)/a$ and $d_1 = a'/a$.

This equation can be directly estimated only for LICs because data on new commitments are not available for the other intermediaries. With further assumptions, however, the formulation can be modified to make use of the available data on outstanding commitments for SLAs and MSBs; and we now proceed to develop this alternate specification.

First note the following identity which relates outstanding commitments to new commitments:

$$OC = OC_{-1} + NC - CC - MC \qquad (5\text{-}11)$$

That is, the current stock of outstanding commitments must equal the stock of commitments at the end of the previous period, plus new commitments made during the period, less commitments cancelled during the period (CC), and less commitments which were taken down during the period (MC). Because direct data are not available for MC and CC, it is necessary to formulate a proxy for these variables. The simplest course is to assume that CC and MC are each proportional to the outstanding stock of commitments at the end of the previous period:[16]

$$CC = cOC_{-1} \qquad \qquad (5\text{-}12)$$

$$MC = mOC_{-1} \qquad \qquad (5\text{-}13)$$

Making these substitutions in (5-11) and arranging terms yields

$$NC = OC - (1 - c - m)OC_{-1} \qquad (5\text{-}14)$$

The final equation for SLAs and MSBs is then obtained by substituting equation (5-14) into equation (5-10) and solving for OC:

$$OC = a_0 d_0 D + a_1 d_0 (RM - RC)D + g_1 d_0 \, \Delta D - d_0 M_{-1} \\ + d_0 R + (1 + c - m - d_1)OC_{-1} \qquad (5\text{-}15)$$

In the empirical tests which follow, equation (5-15) is also tested for LICs and the results can be compared with the direct estimates of equation (5-10).

Mortgage Flows

Mortgage flow equations must now be specified to complete the supply side of the market. For SLAs, MSBs, and LICs we derive the gross flows of mortgages as essentially realizations of commitments made earlier. The repayments for each of these intermediaries (to be specified below) can then be used to derive the net flow of mortgages following identities (5-A13) to (5A-15) from Appendix 5A. For CBs, the absence of commitments data forces us to estimate the net mortgage flow directly. We begin with the specification of gross mortgage flows.

In constructing the commitments equations, the simplifying assumption was made that a constant percentage of the desired mortgage flow was

---

[16] This assumes that a set percentage of outstanding commitments are cancelled or taken down each period—an assumption we have already used above. An alternative scheme is to relate CC and MC to a distributed lag on new commitments. Then by recursive substitution in (3-11), new commitments can be derived as a distributed lag on outstanding commitments and a diminishing residual which can be ignored at some point. Tests with this approximation indicated that only the first two terms in the distributed lag were statistically significant and thus for practical purposes it yields essentially the same results as the approximation used in the text.

originated in commitments and that the remainder was made directly in the market. In trying to specify directly the observed mortgage flows, however, it is clearly important to take the maturity structure of the outstanding stock of commitments into account. This can be accomplished by relating the current gross mortgage flow to a distributed lag of past flows of new commitments:

$$\Delta M_g = \frac{1}{B}\left(\sum_{i=0}^{T} w_i NC_{-i}\right) \tag{5-16}$$

where

$$\sum_{i=0}^{T} w_i = 1$$

The proportionality factor B represents the percentage of the mortgage flow that can be attributed to commitments; for the moment it is assumed constant. The w_i coefficients represent the lag in take-down or realization. The distributed lag starts with the current period because NC is the total flow flow over the quarter and thus commitments made early in the quarter may be taken down later in the same period; as we shall see below, there are also other grounds for including the current new commitments in the equation.

The absence of data on new commitments for SLAs and MSBs again necessitates a modification of the basic formulation for these intermediaries. Equation (5-16) can be rewritten, using (5-14), in terms of outstanding commitments:

$$\Delta M_g = \frac{1}{B}\sum_{i=0}^{T} w_i[OC_{-i} - (1 - c - m)OC_{-i-1}] \tag{5-17}$$

or as a function of a single distributed lag on outstanding commitments:

$$\Delta M_g = \frac{1}{B}\sum_{i=0}^{T+1} v_i OC_{-i} \tag{5-18}$$

where

$$v_0 = w_0$$
$$v_i = w_i - w_{i-1}(1 - c - m) \qquad i = 1, 2, 3, \ldots, T$$
$$v_{T+1} = -w_T(1 - c - m)$$

The estimated mortgage flow equations for SLAs and MSBs are based on equation (5-18).[17]

It should now be noted that the proportionality factor B in (5-16) and

---

[17] A nonlinear estimation technique is needed to estimate either (5-17) or (5-18) with the implied restrictions on the distributed lag coefficients. Both equations were fitted without the restrictions and the results were so similar and were sufficiently close to meeting the restrictions that the restrained estimation was not pursued.

(5-18) is similar to b in (5-9), except that b relates the *planned* gross mortgage flow and the *planned* flow of mortgages arising from commitments, whereas B relates the actual amounts of the same two quantities. It is thus possible that B may exhibit significant variations over time while the planned value b remains essentially constant as assumed in (5-9). In particular, it can be expected that $1/B$ will increase—that is, the percentage of mortgages made without commitments will increase—in periods of large deposit inflows since the intermediary will be anxious to invest these funds immediately, rather than wait for commitments to be taken down. Similarly, in periods of small deposit inflows, the intermediary will be forced to make mortgages which originate from earlier commitments, but it will be able to reduce mortgages made directly in the market, thus increasing the percentage of commitment originated mortgages relative to the total flow.

As measures of this effect, we shall consider adding three different factors linearly to the specifications of (5-16) and (5-18). As a direct measure of unexpected deposit flows, the deviation of the actual deposit flow from a moving average of deposit flows is used. A second possibility is to add the current level of commitments—NC in (5-16), OC in (5-18)—to the equations on the premise that a high level of commitments indicates a desire on the part of the intermediary to immediately extend more mortgage loans. The third possibility is to add the determinants of current commitments directly to the specification for the gross mortgage flow. The specifications for the gross mortgage flow equations thus take the form of (5-16) and (5-18), but with the three factors added as indicated.

Finally we turn to the (net) mortgage flow equation for CBs. In principle, the supply function for CBs could be derived along the lines used for the other intermediaries, even without data on commitments, by directly substituting the commitments specification (5-10) into the mortgage flow specification (5-16). As we noted earlier, the problem with this method is that the resulting equation involves distributed lags on a large number of variables; and, as our preliminary tests confirmed, multicollinearity precludes reliable structural estimates under such conditions.

The alternatives which then remain open are limited. One possibility is to use a nonlinear technique with the lag structure based on prior information. The drawback here is that if the timing of lagged effects is as important for CBs as our formulation of the model for the other intermediaries would indicate, then the reliability of the estimates would still be at question. A second procedure, and the one adopted here, is to suppress many of the refinements of the stock adjustment model, and to estimate the change in CBs mortgage loans as a function of a distributed lag on past levels of deposits and interest rates and of the lagged stock of mortgages.

Specifically, the equation for the net change in CB mortgage holdings, which follows with some modifications the work of Hulett [13], is

$$\Delta MKCB = \eta_0 MDS + \eta_1 \sum_{i=0}^{T} (v_i MTM_{-i})$$

$$+ \eta_2 \sum_{i=0}^{T} [\omega_i MTM_{-i}(RM - RCL)_{-i}] - \eta_3 MKCB_{-1} \quad (5\text{-}19)$$

NOTE: We introduce at this point the FMP model notation described in Appendix A and used in the remainder of this chapter for empirically tested equations.

The demand deposits MDS and time deposits MTM are both defined net of their respective reserve requirements. Demand deposits are specified only with the current value on the expectation that they support a small percentage of CB mortgage holdings. Time deposits are entered with a distributed lag in an attempt to capture the timing effects resulting from commitments. The interest rate spread, scaled by time deposits, has a distributed lag for the same reason, and the competing yield is the commercial loan interest rate, RCL.

Estimation of Advance Commitments

Commitments equations have been estimated for LICs from equation (5-10) and for SLAs and MSBs from equation (5-15). The estimated coefficients are shown as equations (5A-1), (5A-2) and (5A-3), respectively, in chapter Appendix 5A. Before turning to the interpretation of these results, several points relating to the final specification should be made.

1. The rate of return on assets competing with mortgages, RC, has yet to be defined for each of the intermediaries. Since only a single measure of this return is to be specified, the rate of interest on long-term securities appears most appropriate for LICs and MSBs, reflecting the long-term maturity of most of their nonmortgage assets. Moody's AAA corporate bond rate, RCB, has been used as the long-term rate because it is already endogenous in the FMP model. The case of SLAs is somewhat more difficult because their nonmortgage holdings are primarily liquid assets used to meet liquidity and reserve requirements. Indeed, competing long-term rates have not been found significant in previous empirical studies of SLAs mortgage supply (see [17], [20]). This suggests that the relevant opportunity rate for SLAs should be related to their cost of liquid funds. Since the principal source of such liquid

funds for SLAs are advances from the FHLBB, we shall use the interest charge on these advances, *ZRFH*, as the competing rate.[18]

2. An important restriction on the coefficients for repayments must be taken into account in estimating the system, because repayments enter both the commitments and gross mortgage flow equations for each intermediary. The restriction arises because in long-run equilibrium, when net mortgage flows are zero, an increase in repayments must be matched by an increase in gross mortgage flows. Thus the total equilibrium effect of repayments on mortgages, calculated to include both the direct effect of the repayments variable in the gross mortgage flow equation and the indirect effect of the repayments variable in the commitments equation must be unity. This restriction was satisfied by directly estimating, for each intermediary, the repayments coefficient in the gross mortgage flow equation, then calculating the implied coefficient for repayments in the commitments equation necessary to meet the constraint, and then finally estimating the remaining coefficients in the commitments equation with repayments thus restricted.[19] As an example, for LICs, the direct effect of repayments on gross mortgage flows was estimated in equation (5A-5) as .50, thus leaving .50 as the indirect effect through commitments. Since the long-run effect of commitments on mortgages flows is estimated as about .92 in (5A-5), the long-run effect of repayments on commitments should be .54 and thus this restriction was used in estimating the LIC commitments equation (5A-1).

3. Although constants do not appear in our formulation of the commit-

---

[18] The FHLBB advances have an obvious analog in the loan discounts provided by the Federal Reserve banks. In particular, the FHLBB has placed quantitative restrictions on the availability of these advances at times. This has the implication that the borrowing rate *ZRFH* may be less than the true opportunity cost of funds for SLAs during such periods. It should be noted, however, that *ZRFH* is derived by the FHLBB from a mark-up formula over the cost of its own funds, and thus the borrowing rate will still move with the trend of market rates even when the quantity of advances is restricted.

Silber [17] uses the FHLBB borrowing rate in his SLA mortgage supply equation, but it is significant only at the 10 percent level. In Silber's specification, however, *ZRFH* is not scaled by deposits (see footnote 11) and the mortgage rate is not included. Indeed, Silber obtained a more significant coefficient for *ZRFH* when his equation was formulated in logarithmic form (which has the effect of the scaling), but the specification was rejected on other grounds.

[19] For efficiency the equations should be estimated simultaneously with the constraint holding across equations. In this particular case the constraint was nonlinear and involved the coefficients of distributed lags so that the simpler method of estimating one equation and then restricting the other equation was used. The commitments equations were restricted because the repayments, when estimated in these equations freely, were less significant than in the mortgage flow equations. It is also for this reason that the imposition of the constraint did not change the nonrepayments coefficients in the commitments equations in any important way.

ments equations, they have been included in the estimates to take at least partial account of omitted variables. In the cases of LICs and SLAs there is the additional reason that the data on commitments for these intermediaries reflects a partial sample, blown up to universe proportions by only multiplicative correction.

4. The deposit flow variable ΔMSL was not significant and obtained an essentially zero coefficient in (5A-2), and thus the variable is not included in the final specification.

5. Finally, in equation (5A-1) for LICs, the lagged dependent variable $MCNI_{-1}$ has been added to the basic specification of equation (5-10). When (5A-1) was estimated without this variable, the lagged outstanding commitments $MCOI_{-1}$ received a positive and significant coefficient, contrary to expectation. This result can be explained, however, if LICs adjust only partially to the target level for new commitments. In this case $MCNI_{-1}$ should appear in the equation with a positive coefficient, but if it is omitted, then $MCOI_{-1}$, which is determined by $MCNI_{-1}$ [see equation (5A-4)], would have its coefficient biased toward a positive value. The results of (5A-1), with $MCNI_{-1}$ included, indicate, on this interpretation, that the speed of adjustment for LICs is about 33 percent per quarter; the coefficient for $MCOI_{-1}$ is still positive, but it is not significant. Tests for a similar partial adjustment for SLAs and MSBs were made by adding OC_{-2} to equations (5A-2) and (5A-3). In both cases the estimated coefficients for the added variable were small and not significant. This is not surprising, however, since SLAs and MSBs tend to be considerably smaller than LICs on a unit basis and the speed of decision making may well be faster for the smaller enterprises.

The estimated equations for commitments (5A-1) to (5A-3) fit well, and all coefficients are significant and have the correct sign except as noted in paragraphs 4 and 5 above. Perhaps the most important aspect of these results concerns their implication for the determinants of the equilibrium stock of mortgages as given by equation (5-1). The derivation of the equilibrium coefficients a_0 and a_1 for equation (5-1) can be seen most clearly from equation (5-10). In equilibrium we must have

$$NC = d_0 R - d_1 OC_{-1}$$

and thus a_0 and a_1 can be derived by setting the first three terms of (5-10) equal to zero. As applied to the empirical estimates, this amounts to dividing the coefficients of D and $(RM - RCL)D$ by the coefficient of M_{-1}. The relative effect of the constant, included in the estimated equations, on equilibrium *NC* and *M* cannot be identified. The equilibrium relationships implied by the estimated coefficients are

$$MKSL^* = \text{constant} + [1.08 + .04(RM - ZRFH)]MSL \quad (5\text{-}20a)$$

$$MKMS^* = \text{constant} + [1.03 + .08(RM - RCB)]MMS \quad (5\text{-}20b)$$

$$MKIS^* = \text{constant} + [.61 + .04(RM - RCB)]MIS \quad (5\text{-}20c)$$

These results can be interpreted, for example for SLAs, as indicating that 108 percent of their deposits are invested in mortgages with an additional effect of about 4 percent coming from interest rate sources (assuming the rate spread is 1 percentage point).[20] The relative responsiveness of the mortgage holdings of the three intermediaries to their deposits and the interest rate spread appears in line with general expectations, although the interest rate effect for LICs is surprisingly low. It should be noted, however, that these coefficients represent marginal, not average, effects because constants were included in the estimated equations. For this reason the mortgage–deposit ratio for MSBs, estimated to be .95, may still be plausible although it is greater than the observed (average) value.[21]

Finally, it should be noted that outstanding commitments *MCOI* appear in the new commitments equation (5A-1) for LICs. Thus, to complete the commitments sector, an equation for *MCOI* must be introduced. Before turning to the specification of this equation it is worthwhile to consider the results of estimating *MCOI* using the formulation adopted for *MCOS* and *MCOM*, i.e., equation (5-15). Although the approximation implicit in this formulation is not necessary for LICs, these results are interesting for the comparison they provide between the specifications of equations (5-10) and (5-15). The estimated coefficients for equation (5-15), using LIC data, are

$$MCOI = -2.57 + .056MIS + .469\,\Delta MIS + .001(RM_{-1} - RCB_{-1})MIS$$
$$ (4.2) \quad (2.8) \qquad (2.9) \qquad\quad (.90)$$

$$ + .126MRIS - .081MKIS_{-1} + .837MCOI_{-1} \qquad (5\text{-}21)$$
$$ (2.2) \qquad\quad (14.8)$$

$$R^2 = .995 \quad \text{Mean of dependent variable} = 4.60$$
$$DW = 1.68 \quad \text{Sample 1955:2 to 1968:4}$$
$$SE = .138 \quad \rho = .473$$

The magnitude of the estimated coefficients in (5-21) cannot be directly

---

[20] As noted above, the nondeposit liabilities of SLAs have been omitted from the estimated equations and thus it is not surprising the equilibrium mortgage–deposit ratio exceeds unity.

[21] The consideration in footnote 20 applies also to the MSBs.

compared with the results in (5A-1) because the two equations have different dependent variables. The coefficients in the two equations, however, should have the same signs and roughly the same statistical significance, and indeed this is the case except that the interest rate term in (5-21) is not significant. This result can be taken as some confirmation, albeit indirect, of the usefulness of the approximations used for estimating the commitments equations for SLAs and MSBs.

In formulating the MCOI equation to be used in the simulations, it is preferable, given the availability of the data, to base the specification on new commitments of LICs. Rewriting equation (5.14), we have:

$$MCOI = MCNI + (1 - c - m)MCOI_{-1} \qquad (5\text{-}22)$$

The estimated coefficients for this relationship are shown as equation (5A-4).[22] The coefficient of $MCNI$ was constrained to unity in line with (5.22). The estimated value for $(1 - c - m)$ was about .68, implying that about 32 percent of the outstanding commitments are taken down or cancelled each period for LICs. A constant is also included in the estimated equation to allow for possible misspecification and data scaling, but its coefficient is relatively small and it is not significant.

Estimation of Mortgage Flows

The final estimates of the gross mortgage flow equations for LICs, SLAs, and MSBs are shown in chapter Appendix 5A as equations (5A-5), (5A-6), and (5A-7), respectively. The estimates for LICs were derived from new commitments following equation (5-16), and the estimates for SLAs and MSBs were derived from outstanding commitments following equation (5-18). The final form of the specification was based on the following considerations:

1. As noted in the derivation of the gross mortgage flow equations, three factors may be postulated as determinants of variations in the parameter B: deviations of deposit flows from a (four-quarter) moving average ($\overline{\Delta D}$), the current level of commitments (NC for LICs and OC for SLAs and MSBs), and the determinants of the commitments. In preliminary tests all three factors were found important in explaining gross mortgage flows and thus they have been included in the final specification. The relative importance

---

[22] An alternative formulation is to assume that outstanding commitments are directly generated by a distributed lag of new commitments. This has the advantage over (5-22) that it takes the maturity structure of outstanding commitments into account. Estimates of this relationship yielded reasonable coefficients, but (5.22) was adopted because it performed better in the simulations of the entire system to be discussed later.

of the three factors varied between intermediaries. The deposit flow variable was most important for the SLAs and MSBs, but was not significant and was omitted for LICs.[23] The relative effects of the level of current commitments are difficult to evaluate because the variable was incorporated in the specification with the first term of the distributed lag on commitments which was already in the equation. The direct determinants of commitments were included by specifying the level of deposits, repayments, and the lagged mortgage stock in the final equation. The effect of this set of variables reflects the direct influence of deposits and repayments, relative to the level of outstanding mortgages, on mortgages originated directly in the market. It is thus reasonable that these variables were most significant for SLAs which rely primarily on direct market purchase for their mortgage flows. In addition, for SLAs, the quantity of FHLBB advances, $ZAFH$, was also included in the mortgage flow equation as a determinant of variations in B. The reason for including this variable was that the increased availability of FHLBB advances should increase the flow of mortgages. This of course introduces the quantity of FHLBB advances, along with the borrowing rate on these advances which enters the SLAs commitments equation, as a policy parameter which can be varied in our simulation experiments—assuming, obviously, that the FHLBB has independent control over the two variables (see footnote 18).[24]

2. Constants have been included in the gross mortgage flow equations to allow for misspecification and data scaling as described for the estimation of the commitments equations.

3. As developed in the section on commitments, the coefficients for repayments in the gross mortgage flow equations were to be estimated without constraint. When MSB mortgage flows were estimated in this manner, however, the coefficient for repayments was so large as to imply a negative coefficient for repayments in the MSBs commitments equation. We thus experimented with reducing (by constraint) the repayments coefficient in the MSB gross mortgage flow equation (5A-7). Fortunately, the coefficient estimates for the other variables in this equation were not sensitive to these

---

[23] It should be recalled that the definition of deposits for LICs is net of policy loans. Most LICs allow policy loans in the form of borrowing by policy holders against the cash value of policies at interest rates of about 5 percent. Since the LICs have no control over the amount of such loans, they represent a prior claim on the companies' investable funds. It is thus surprising that the deposit flow variable did not work well in this case.

[24] It should also be noted that the interest rate term was tested in the gross mortgage flow equation for SLAs, as well as for LICs and MSBs, but the coefficient was small and not significant, and hence the term is not included in the final specification. This result suggests that the interest rate cost effects enter as determinants of the planned level of commitments, whereas the cash flow constraints are important in determining the ex post variations in B.

changes. A coefficient of .4 for repayments in (5A-7) was finally selected on the grounds that it implied a reasonable coefficient for repayments in the MSB commitments equation and that this magnitude was approximately the mean of the estimated repayments coefficients for LICs and SLAs in (5A-5) and (5A-6).

4. When this complete specification was estimated for the three intermediaries, the residuals for the four quarters of 1968 were negative (the fitted values exceeded the actual values) and large in all cases, and for each intermediary the four residuals were about equal in magnitude. This can be interpreted as the result of a further shift in the parameter B (see paragraph 1 above) and may be related to the uncertainty of the effects of tight money on deposit flows following the unhappy experiences in 1966. Unfortunately, it is difficult to judge the source or importance of this effect because it comes at the very end of the sample period. For present purposes it is simply taken into account by adding a dummy variable, DUM, which takes the value 1 for the four quarters of 1968 and zero everywhere else, to the specification for each intermediary. Because the 1968 residuals, estimated for each intermediary when the dummy variable was not included, were about equal, the estimates with the dummy variables are just about the same as the results obtained by estimating the equations only through the end of 1967. Omitting the dummy, but estimating the equations through 1968, of course changes the coefficients, but the main difference is that the serial correlation coefficients increase markedly. This is not surprising since a high serial correlation in the errors is often the result for an equation estimated over an unspecified structural change. In any case, high serial correlation is particularly undesirable in simulating a system, and this is an additional reason for preferring the dummy variable.

The final estimates of the gross mortgage flow equations (5A-5) to (5A-7) involve distributed lags on the commitments variables which were estimated with the Almon technique. The distributed lags were fitted using second-degree polynomials with the far end tied to zero, and the specified lag extended over 8 periods for LICs and over 7 periods for SLAs and MSBs. The results do not change significantly, however, if these lags are lengthened or shortened by one or even two periods. In particular, the mean lags for the effect of the commitments are 2.7 quarters for LICs, 1.9 quarters for MSBs, and 1.2 quarters for SLAs. These results are clearly in line with the nature of the construction projects financed by the commitments of each of the intermediaries. It might also be noted that it is consistent with the specification of equation (5-18) that the last term for the distributed lag on outstanding commitments is negative in the SLA mortgage flow equation (5A-6).

Another aspect of the relative importance of the commitments for the three intermediaries can be seen by solving the estimated equations for the steady-state ratios of gross mortgage flows to commitments. Assuming that in the steady state the contributions of the variables explaining the variations in $1/B$ are zero, we have:[25]

$$MFIS = .92MCNI \qquad (5\text{-}23a)$$

$$MFSL = 1.95MCOS \qquad (5\text{-}23b)$$

$$MFMS = .45MCOM \qquad (5\text{-}23c)$$

Thus for LICs almost all mortgage flows originate in commitments. To compare this result with the other two intermediaries, the LIC ratio must be translated from new commitments to outstanding commitments. Using the sample mean of the ratio $MCNI/MCOI$, which is .4, the ratio of mortgage flows to outstanding commitments for LICs is then

$$MFIS = .37MCOI \qquad (5\text{-}23d)$$

It is apparent that MSBs make only slightly less use of commitments than LICs, but that SLA mortgage flows originate primarily from noncommitment sources. This is of course in line with the institutional considerations noted above.

Finally we turn to the estimates for the net mortgage flow equation of CBs. The formulation has been given in equation (5-19) and the estimated coefficients are shown as equation (5A-8). Both distributed lags were estimated using second-degree polynomials with five-period lags and the tails constrained to zero. The speed of adjustment to the equilibrium solution is indicated to be about 18 percent per quarter, which is in line with other studies. The equilibrium solution is given by

$$MKCB = .028MDS + .409MTM + .091MTM(RM - RCL) \qquad (5\text{-}24)$$

These results are quite reasonable—the CBs invest only a small percentage, about 3 percent, of their demand deposits in mortgages; they invest about 41 percent of their time deposits in mortgages, which is a smaller percentage than we found for the other intermediaries as one might expect; and, the interest rate responsiveness of CBs is in line with our results for the other intermediaries. Thus, though one may have misgivings about the specification of the equation with respect to the short-run dynamics of CB mortgage holdings, the equation's equilibrium properties appear quite acceptable.

---

[25] When equations (5-16) and (5-18) are estimated with only the distributed lags on commitments as independent variables, the implied mortgage-flow–commitments ratios are very close to the corresponding values in equation (5-23). This suggests that the average effect of the variables determining variations in B is indeed close to zero.

The Demand for Mortgages

The demand for mortgages, in its most fundamental aspects, is related to the theory of portfolio choice by households. This approach is most directly applicable to owner-occupied houses, but is sufficiently general so that other structures can be analyzed in a similar fashion. The basic variable in such a formulation, at a given point in time, is the household's level of net worth. Ruling out for the moment the possibility of borrowing, the household will distribute its total net worth among various financial and real assets in order to maximize some utility function. Presumably this utility function will weight factors such as the satisfaction of wants by real assets,[26] interest income obtained from financial assets, and the liquidity or illiquidity value of both types of assets. With the optimal allocation, the marginal utility of all assets will be equal.

Now allow the household the opportunity to borrow in order to increase the level of its assets. In general, the household will borrow whenever the marginal cost (marginal disutility) of borrowing is less than the marginal utility derived from its assets. However, an important institutional fact must be recognized: in almost every case, a household can borrow only on the basis of very specific collateral requirements. Stock market credit is based on holdings of stocks and bonds, consumer credit generally requires consumer durables, and mortgages are available only with a house. One effect of these constraints is to encourage the purchase of those assets which meet the requirements. Thus, in the final equilibrium, the marginal utility of a house for example, will in general be less than the marginal utility of some asset which cannot be used for collateral.

Because of the collateral requirement, the demand for mortgages can be usefully related, at least for empirical purposes, to the total outstanding stock of houses $KH\$$. The desired ratio of mortgage debt to the stock of houses, in the aggregate, will depend on the relative cost of mortgage financing, where the alternative cost should be represented by some weighted average of rates on other assets and liabilities. As with the supply side, however, it is likely that multicollinearity between interest rates will preclude reliable estimates for more than one alternative rate. Measuring the alternative rate by Moody's AAA corporate bond rate RCB, the demand relationship may be written:

$$M^d = (e_0 + e_1 RCB - e_2 RM)KH\$ \qquad (5\text{-}25)$$

Several features of this relationship should be noted. First, this formulation

---

[26] This is not to rule out the possibility that financial assets may also directly satisfy some basic needs or wants.

need not imply that mortgage funds are literally used to purchase homes. A household may own a home without the opportunity of obtaining mortgage debt, and the additional financing provided by mortgages could be used to purchase other assets. Second, in principle, the desired mortgage–house ratio will depend on nonrate terms of the contract, such as the maturity of the loan. These factors have generally not been found important in previous empirical studies of mortgage demand, perhaps because of the quality of the data, and they are not included in our formulation. Third, for individual household units, the collateral requirement will take the form of a zero or one constraint in determining the feasibility of a specific mortgage. We have assumed in the aggregate, however, that a smooth and continuous relationship can be obtained. Viewing this relationship as the equilibrium of a stock adjustment process, the change in the demand will then be:

$$\Delta M^d = \lambda_0(e_0 + e_1 RCB - e_2 RM)KH\$ - \lambda_0 M_{-1} \qquad (5\text{-}26)$$

It is important to note that the speed of adjustment of demand to its equilibrium is likely to be quite slow in this case because of the large costs of renegotiating a mortgage once it is set.[27] Thus, starting from equilibrium, only a minimal change in demand would be expected in response to, say, a change in the mortgage rate. This has the important implication that variations in mortgage demand are likely to be primarily determined by the flow effect of additions to the stock of houses. The appropriate measure of this flow effect is the gross change in the stock of houses, but it should not include capital gains on existing structures since these represent "paper" additions to the housing stock which will typically be translated into mortgages only very slowly.

On the operational level, the flow effect can be appropriately measured by the National Income Accounts definition of gross investment in residential structures, denoted as $EH\$$.[28] Since $EH\$$ is expected to be the main determinant of changes in the demand for mortgages, we should allow its coefficient to be responsive to the same interest rates influencing the equilibrium stock demand. Furthermore, given the large costs of renegotiating a mortgage, the short-run interest rate responsiveness is unlikely to differ significantly from the long-run effect. For this reason, the constant and interest rate

---

[27] Silber [17] estimates a demand function similar to (5-26) and does find a very slow speed of adjustment. He does not consider this result plausible, however, and succeeds in raising the speed of adjustment by essentially adding a time trend to the equation. Our position is that the "locked-in" effect resulting from the high costs of negotiating and renegotiating mortgages does in fact make a slow speed of adjustment likely.

[28] Since our data include some mortgages made on nonresidential structures, the demand equation was also tested using variables for other nonresidential structures. These variables were not significant and reference to them is omitted in the text.

responsiveness have been constrained to be the same for the flow as the stock of houses. Also, the stock of houses is now lagged one period:

$$\Delta M^d = (e_0 + e_1 RCB - e_2 RM)(\lambda_0 KH\$_{-1} + EH\$ - \lambda_0 M_{-1}) \quad (5\text{-}27)$$

In equilibrium, the change in mortgage demand will of course be equal to the change in supply. This equilibrium relationship can be used in general to derive the equilibrium mortgage rate, RM^*, as a function of the parameters of the demand and supply schedules. Our estimates of the supply of mortgages (pages 000–000) indicated, however, that the supply of mortgages is relatively unresponsive to the current mortgage rate because of the reliance on advance commitments. Indeed, the mortgage rate does not enter directly in the gross mortgage flow equations, and it enters indirectly only through the current outstanding commitments for SLAs and MSBs. The consequence is that in the short run the mortgage rate can be thought of as adjusting such that it brings the current mortgage demand into line with an essentially predetermined supply. Under these circumstances, it is desirable, especially from the point of view of simulation, to normalize equation (5-27) on the mortgage rate and to set the change in demand equal to the observed mortgage flow:

$$RM^* = \frac{e_0}{e_2} + \frac{e_1}{e_2} RCB - \frac{1}{e_2}\left(\frac{\Delta M_g^T + \lambda_0 M_{-1}^T}{EH\$ + \lambda_0 KH\$_{-1}}\right) - \frac{1}{e_3}\left(\frac{OC_{-1}^T}{EH\$ + \lambda_0 KH\$_{-1}}\right)$$

$$(5\text{-}28)$$

where M^T is the total mortgage holding of the four principal intermediaries and FNMA, and ΔM_g^T is the corresponding gross mortgage flow.[29] The last term in (5-28) represents the future flow of mortgages arising from outstanding commitments (relative to the housing variable) and is included on the premise that the expectation of such mortgage flows will have a depressing effect on the mortgage rate in the same way, although perhaps not to the same degree, as actual mortgage flows.[30]

Equation (5-28) is of course predicated on the assumption that the mortgage rate is clearing the market, at least on a quarterly basis. There is substantial institutional evidence and some empirical evidence, however, that

---

[29] The variable ΔM_g^T is precisely defined in the empirical tests as the sum of the gross mortgage flows of LICs, SLAs, and MSBs, and the net mortgage flows of CBs and FNMA. The asymmetry in the definition arises because gross mortgage flows are not available for CBs, and because the gross purchases of FNMA would include double accounting since FNMA sales are made primarily to the private intermediaries. The mortgage holdings of the private household sector have been ignored because the amount is small relative to the total market and the available data is not accurate.

[30] The variable OC^T includes the outstanding commitments of LICs, SLAs, and MSBs, but omits the CBs because data on their commitments are not available.

the mortgage rate adjusts more slowly toward its equilibrium value. This can be incorporated in the specification by assuming the speed of adjustment to be a constant λ_1 and by adding a lagged dependent variable to (5-28):

$$RM = \lambda_1 \frac{e_0}{e_2} + \lambda_1 \frac{e_1}{e_2} RCB - \frac{\lambda_1}{e_2}\left(\frac{\Delta M_g^T + \lambda_0 M_{-1}^T}{EH\$ + \lambda_0 KH\$_{-1}}\right)$$
$$- \frac{\lambda_1}{e_3}\left(\frac{OC_{-1}^T}{EH\$ + \lambda_0 KH\$_{-1}}\right) + (1 - \lambda_1)RM_{-1} \qquad (5\text{-}29)$$

The allowance for a disequilibrium mortgage rate also implies the existence of credit rationing in the market. Because we have estimated the commitments equations and mortgage flows equations over the entire sample period, using the observed mortgage flows as the dependent variable in the latter, we are implicitly assuming that the market was never in a situation of excess supply—that is, the observed mortgage flows were never entirely demand determined. As a first approximation we believe this assumption is warranted over the sample period used for estimation. However, we note that the specification would have to be modified if estimation or simulation over periods of excess supply were to be attempted.[31]

The estimated coefficients for the specification of equation (5-29) are shown in equation (5A-9). The equation was estimated by scanning over least squares fits to find the value of the nonlinear parameter λ_0 yielding the lowest standard error of estimate. The estimated value of λ_0 was .03, indicating a very slow speed of adjustment of mortgage demand to its equilibrium, which is in line with the considerations discussed above. The remaining coefficients all have the right sign and, except for the coefficient of the OC variable, all are statistically significant. The implied speed of adjustment of the mortgage rate to its equilibrium level, about 45 percent per quarter, also appears quite reasonable.[32]

In order to derive the estimated equivalent of the demand relationship (5-26), we first solve equation (5A-9) for RM^* by setting $RM^* = RM =$

---

[31] General techniques for the estimation of demand and supply schedules of markets in disequilibrium are developed in forthcoming work by Fair and Jaffee [7]. Unfortunately their techniques cannot be applied to this model because of the complex nature of the supply side. It can be shown, however, that if only excess demand is observed, as assumed here, then the addition of the lagged mortgage rate to (5-28) is equivalent to one of the techniques developed by Fair and Jaffee.

[32] Tests were also performed to determine whether usury law ceilings restrained potential increases in the mortgage rate. Significant effects were not found, suggesting that the ceilings have not been generally binding on an aggregate basis, and that in those instances where they are constraining, the ceilings tend to be raised rather promptly. This conclusion must be taken as only tentative, however, since the number of sample observations in which the ceilings were likely to be important was quite small.

RM_{-1}, and then solve the resulting equation for the change in mortgages:

$$\Delta M^d = (2.65 + .574RCB - .746RM)(EH\$ + .03KH\$_{-1})$$
$$- .03M_{-1} - .006OC_{-1} \tag{5-30}$$

It is thus apparent that the implied interest elasticity of mortgage demand is quite high. A 10-basis-point increase in the mortgage rate, for example, causes the mortgage-demand–house ratio to decline by over 7 percent. The implications of this result for the response of the mortgage market to exogenous shocks will be developed in the simulation experiments in the following section.

An equally striking feature of these results is the large constant term (2.65) in the ratio of mortgage demand to houses. The constant is of course consistent with the mean values of the observed data since the estimate was determined by least squares fit; for example, if RM and RCB are evaluated at their sample means (6.18 and 4.73, respectively), then the overall mortgage-demand–house ratio attains the reasonable value of .76. The large constant does imply, however, that if the mortgage rate falls sufficiently low relative to the bond rate, then the demand for mortgages will exceed the housing stock. This is not surprising since, in the absence of a collateral requirement, mortgages would in fact be extremely attractive as a means for household borrowing. The large constant thus simply serves as a warning not to extrapolate the results of this equation to the range of interest rate spreads at which the collateral requirement, in the aggregate, becomes binding on households.

Mortgage Repayments

Mortgage repayments are defined as the difference between the total mortgage loans made (the gross mortgage flow) and the net additions to the mortgage stock (the net mortgage flow). Gross mortgage flow equations have been estimated for three of the intermediaries: LICs, SLAs, and MSBs. In order that the increments to their outstanding stocks of mortgages be endogenous in the model, it is necessary that repayments equations be estimated for each of these intermediaries.

The repayment of mortgages can be viewed, in analogy with real assets, as the depreciation of the outstanding stock of mortgages. In general the amount of repayments will be related to the maturity structure of the outstanding stock of mortgages and the rate of repayment on each maturity. As a special case, however, it may be assumed that the rate of repayment is a constant and that it is independent of the maturities of the mortgages. We then obtain a very simple aggregate relationship between repayments and the stock of mortgages:

$$R = \alpha M_{-1} \tag{5-31}$$

More generally, however, the rate of repayment is a term of the mortgage contract negotiated between the lender and borrower and thus it might vary over time. An important source of variation in the repayment rate will be related to the expectations of future mortgage rates. On the supply side, if an intermediary expects mortgage rates to rise in the future, it will favor high repayment rates so that funds will be available for reinvestment at the higher future interest rate.[33] The preferences of demanders, however, are in just the opposite direction; thus the net effect must be in doubt. Indeed, preliminary attempts to relate the variation in the repayments rate to various proxies for the expected movement in interest rates yielded no significant relationships. In particular, the long-run trend in repayments was roughly a constant percentage of the mortgage stock as assumed in equation (5-31); and the short-run variations in the repayment ratio could not be explained by interest rate expectations, at least as they were measured in these attempts.

An alternative explanation for the short-run movements in the repayment ratio is that the contractual repayment ratio has remained essentially constant over time, but that the rate of *prepayment* of mortgages has shown significant short-run variability. Prepayments come about for essentially two reasons. First, in periods of falling mortgage rates, the homeowner will obviously find it advantageous to recontract at the new and lower mortgage rate. Standard mortgage contracts allow for such prepayments, but only with a penalty fee. This penalty, together with the cost of negotiating a new mortgage, makes such renegotiation profitable only for substantial declines in the mortgage rate, and in fact there is no evidence that recontracting has occurred in significant amounts in recent years. The second reason for prepayments results from the sale of a mortgaged house. The seller of the house often will repay his mortgage and the buyer will then contract for a new mortgage. Although this may not lead to any net change in the stock of mortgages, it will generate repayments and gross mortgage flows. Consequently, we would expect repayments to rise in periods of active trading of existing houses.

As measures of the volume of trading of houses we considered both demographic and cyclical income variables and measures of the availability of mortgage credit. The former variables, however, were never significant. The mortgage credit availability was postulated on the grounds that the sale of existing homes will be reduced if mortgage credit is not available to

---

[33] See Goldfeld and Jaffee [9] for a more detailed discussion of the supply side determinants of the repayment rate.

potential buyers. Specifically, the availability of mortgage credit was assumed to be reduced in periods of rising mortgage rates. This was measured by the deviation of the mortgage rate from a twelve-quarter moving average $\overline{RM}$. The lagged value of the gross flow of mortgages was also included as an indicator of mortgage credit availability. This value should also be included in the equation because the data on mortgage loans contain at least some construction and home improvement loans made by the intermediaries. These loans have, obviously, a much shorter maturity than standard mortgage loans and thus repayments will rise as these loans mature. The final equation then takes the form:

$$R = (\alpha_0 - \alpha_1 \overline{RM})M_{-1} + \alpha_2(\Delta M_g)_{-1} \tag{5-32}$$

The estimated coefficients of this relationship for LICs, SLAs, and MSBs are shown as equations (5A-10) to (5A-12).[34] The long-run ratio of quarterly repayments to mortgages was estimated to be slightly greater than .02 for LICs and SLAs, and slightly greater than .01 for MSBs. The interest rate term is significant for LICs and SLAs but is not significant for MSBs although it has the correct sign. The mortgage flow effect was important for all three intermediaries.

Simulation of the Model

The final form of the model is summarized in the sixteen equations of chapter Appendix 5A. The first twelve equations are the estimated behavioral relationships and the last four equations are the identities defining the outstanding stock of mortgages for each intermediary. There are twelve exogenous variables in the system, and they may be grouped as follows:

Policy instruments	$ZAFH, ZMFN, ZRFH$
Interest rates	RCB, RCL
Deposits	MIS, MSL, MMS, MDS, MTM
Housing	$EH\$, KH\$$

The definition of symbols is given in Appendixes A and B.

---

[34] The equation for MSBs, (5A-12), was not estimated with the Cochrane-Orcutt procedure although the ordinary least squares estimates indicate significant serial correlation. The reason is that the dependent variable is interpolated from annual data and thus a first-order autoregressive transformation did not help.

This section presents the results of two sets of simulation experiments performed with the model. For the first experiment, a dynamic simulation is executed over the longest period consistent with data availability, 1960:4 to 1968:4. The simulation is deterministic in that the stochastic error terms are all set equal to zero. Throughout the simulation the exogenous variables are fixed at their actual historic values. The lagged endogenous variables are also set at their historic values for the initial conditions. The system then generates solution values in succeeding quarters for the endogenous variables, using the exogenous variables and the previously generated lagged endogenous variables. For purposes of comparison with other simulations described below, this experiment will be referred to as the *standard simulation* of the system.

Special care must be taken in evaluating the results of this experiment because of the nonlinear structure of the model. Howrey and Kelejian [10] have shown that the solution values generated by dynamic (and deterministic) simulation of nonlinear models may not correspond to the properties of the reduced form. In particular, the residuals (actual values–solution values) of the dynamic solution may in general be heteroskedastic and serially correlated even when this is not true for the errors of the reduced form. Consequently, the results of the dynamic simulation cannot be used to validate the model in a formal statistical sense. On the other hand, if the model is linear, and results noted below suggest this is at least approximately true, then the dynamic simulation will provide evidence on the inherent dynamic structure of the model. It is in this less formal sense that the dynamic simulation can be used to evaluate the model.

The second set of experiments determine the effects in the model of changes in the exogenous variables. The method consists of changing the exogenous variables, either singly or in groups, and then performing a dynamic simulation of the model with the new level(s) for the exogenous variable(s). By comparing the time paths of the endogenous variables generated by such simulations with the values generated by the standard simulation (with exogenous variables at their historic levels), the values for the dynamic multipliers can be derived. These experiments also provide insight into the dynamic structure and workings of the model.[35] Six groups of exogenous

---

[35] Although Howrey and Kelejian do not consider the specific question of the determination of dynamic multipliers, the issues they raise with respect to the evaluation of dynamic simulations of nonlinear models might also apply here. On the other hand, the multiplier analysis consists of the comparison of the solution values of two simulation experiments, and thus one may conjecture that the testing errors in each of the two solution series either actually cancel or at least tend to net with each other.

variables are tested in this manner: separate simulations are first run for each of the three policy instruments, and then the interest rates, deposits, and housing variables are tested as groups. Since the model is nonlinear, these results will in general not be invariant to the choice of starting point, the direction or magnitude of the shock, and the grouping of the exogenous variables. Important changes in the multipliers were not observed, however, when these factors were allowed to vary in about twenty additional simulation tests. This suggests the model may be at least approximately linear, which also has implication for the question of the evaluation of the model by dynamic simulation referred to above.

The assumed exogeneity of the interest rates (competing yields), deposits, and housing variables raises an important point of interpretation with respect to the partial-equilibrium nature of these results. The point can be made perhaps most clearly with the example of an exogenous increase in FNMA mortgage holdings, although the same considerations apply to all the multiplier experiments. The impact effect of an increase in FNMA mortgage holdings is to bid up the price of mortgages in the secondary market, and thus to reduce the mortgage rate. As the mortgage rate falls, the private intermediaries will transfer their funds away from mortgages and into other assets. The structure and stability of the model insures that the net change in mortgages, including both the increase in FNMA holdings and the decrease in the private intermediary holdings, will be positive, although the actual amount of the change will depend on the elasticities of supply and demand. Our multiplier experiment will determine the amount of this response.

Two additional effects, however, would be brought into a general equilibrium simulation of the same shock. First, as the mortgage rate falls, investment in residential structures would presumably be increased (indeed this is the likely objective of the policy), and thus the demand for mortgages would shift upward. The increased demand for mortgages would exert pressure to reduce, but not eliminate, the initial decline in the mortgage rate. Secondly, as the mortgage rate falls from the initial shock, the financial intermediaries should tend to bid less for deposit funds, and this would lead to a decrease in the flow and the stock of deposits. The decrease in deposits has the effect of shifting the mortgage supply function downward, and this also implies a higher level for the mortgage rate than indicated by the initial shock. The feedback from deposits and residential structures thus tends, in a general equilibrium context, to stabilize the response of the mortgage rate, and hence the response of the other endogenous variables, to a shock in an exogenous variable. The result is that the partial equilibrium simulations to be presented here will tend to exaggerate the effects of exogenous shocks to the system to the extent that the feedbacks from deposits and residential structures are important.

Standard Simulation with Exogenous Variables
at Historic Levels

The results of the dynamic simulation of the model, starting in 1960:4 with all exogenous variables set at their historic values, are shown in Figures 5B-1 to 5B-15 in chapter Appendix 5B. The results for the endogenous variables are shown for LICs in Figures 5B-1 to 5B-5, for SLAs in Figures 5B-6 to 5B-9, for MSBs in Figures 5B-10 to 5B-13, for CBs in Figure 5B-14, and for the mortgage rate in Figure 5B-15. The net change in CB mortgage holdings has been omitted because it can be easily derived as the change in the stock of CB mortgages which is shown in Figure 5B-14. For each variable, the actual, solution, and residual values are shown for the 33 quarters in the simulation, and the actual (+) and simulated (*) values are graphed. The following summary statistics are presented for each variable: mean squared error (MSE), root mean squared error (RMS), serial correlation coefficient (RHO), mean error (MEAN ERR), and the mean of the actual series (MEAN).

The solution values and graphs shown in the figures are basically self-explanatory and hence the commentary will be brief. In general terms, the model tracks the actual values of the endogenous variables quite well. The solutions for the stocks of mortgages held by the four intermediaries, shown in Figures 5B-5, 5B-9, 5B-13, and 5B-14, provide perhaps the best summary measures of the accuracy of the supply side predictions: the ratio of the root mean squared error of the simulation to the mean of the actual mortgage stock series is .96 percent for LICs, .57 percent for SLAs, .67 percent for MSBs, and 1.1 percent for CBs. On the demand side, the root mean squared error for the mortgage rate equation, Figure 5B-15, is only slightly greater than 9 basis points. In terms of specific periods, the tight monetary conditions of 1966 provide perhaps the most stringent test of the model. The results are encouraging in that although the actual values for commitments and mortgage flows all fell significantly in 1966, particularly during the last three quarters of the year, the solutions values all followed the general pattern quite closely. In particular, with the exception of *MCNI* (Figure 5B-1), the residuals for this period were roughly equal to the respective root mean squared errors for the sample.

On the negative side, in almost all the equations there are one- and two-period spikes in the actual series which are missed in the solution; and in several instances the solution was significantly off track for about four quarters. The weakest equation in this respect appears to be the outstanding commitments of LICs (Figure 5B-5) although, fortunately, the feedback from this variable to the rest of the system is quite small [see equations (5A-1) and (5A-9)].

The residuals in all the equations also tend to be highly serially correlated, but this is an expected property of dynamic simulations.[36]

It is thus with generally satisfactory results for the standard dynamic simulation that we now turn to an analysis of the effects of shocks in the exogenous variables. The tables in chapter Appendix 5C tabulate the results of shocking the six sets of exogenous variables. Each table shows, for impor-tant variables, the difference between the simulated value with the shock and the simulated value of the standard run. The results are presented, starting with the period of the shock (1960:4), for the first 8 periods and then for the 12th, 20th, and 32nd (1968:4) periods. The results for four endogenous variables, *MRIS*, *MRSL*, *MRMS*, and *MCOI* have been omitted from the tables to clarify the presentation: the repayments can actually be easily derived from the tabulated results by subtracting the net change in the stock of mortgages from the gross mortgage flow; and the *MCOI* equation serves essentially as a linking relationship in the model, and we shall have no need to refer to it directly. Again, the tables are basically self-explanatory, and we shall generally only briefly comment on each of the experiments. It should be stressed that the shocks to the system to be presented in the six experiments below, all take the form of increasing an exogenous variable above its historic level in the initial period, 1960:4, and then maintaining this increment throughout the simulation.

$1 Billion Increase in FNMA Mortgage Holdings

Table 5C-1 summarizes the results of increasing FNMA mortgage holdings by $1 billion starting in 1960:4. The impact effect of the FNMA purchase is to decrease the mortgage rate by 3 basis points in the initial period. The maximum decline of the mortgage rate is attained after 5 periods and its magnitude is 12 basis points.

Institutionally, an increase in FNMA mortgage holdings is obtained almost entirely from mortgage companies which originate the mortgages in the primary market in response to the FNMA demand. Consequently, an FNMA purchase has no direct effect on the mortgage holdings of the private

---

[36] See Howrey and Kelejian [10].

intermediaries. Furthermore, since the stock of houses is exogenous in this experiment, the only effect of this initial increase in FNMA mortgage holdings on the demand side is an increase in the mortgage-demand–house ratio induced by the decline in the mortgage rate. The decline in the mortgage rate causes the supply of commitments and the net mortgage flows of the intermediaries also to fall.

It should be noted, however, that the *gross* mortgage flows of LICs and SLAs actually rise for a number of periods before finally falling. The source of this unexpected result is that the repayments to these intermediaries increase in response to the falling mortgage rate [see equations (5A-10) and (5A-11)]. The increase in repayments in turn leads to a short-run increase in gross mortgage flows, although the net effect, as already noted, is a decline in the mortgage stock. This result is not observed for MSBs because the interest rate effect in the MSB repayments equation (5A-12) is very small.

The last row of Table 5C-1 shows the final response, 32 periods after the shock, of the mortgage stock holdings of the private intermediaries to the decline in the mortgage rate induced by the FNMA purchase. The mortgage stock holdings are reduced by \$.45 billion for LICs, \$.19 billion for SLAs, \$.43 billion for MSBs, and \$1.30 billion for CBs. The relative amounts of these reductions reflect the differing mortgage rate sensitivities of the intermediaries. The small response of the SLAs and the large response of the CBs are consistent with institutional considerations, although the CBs multiplier appears somewhat out of line.

In this context, it should be noted that the system has not attained a stationary solution, relative to the standard simulation, even 32 periods after the shock: the stocks of mortgages for LICs, SLAs, and CBs are still decreasing and the stock of mortgages for MSBs is cycling slightly. This result is the consequence of having scaled the interest rate variables by deposits in equations (5A-1), (5A-2), (5A-3), and (5A-8). Because of this scaling, the equilibrium responsiveness of mortgages to the interest rates is a function of the level of deposits, and since all deposits rise monotonically over the sample, the difference between the solution of the experimental simulation and the solution of the standard simulation will continue to diverge. In other words, the equilibrium response to the shock cannot be defined in absolute amounts but only relative to the level of deposits. For simulations in a growing economy this is a realistic property for the model; but it has the inconvenient aspect that experiments which change the interest rates significantly will not yield stationary solutions, although we shall still refer to the results 32 periods after the shock as the "final" response.

These results also have implications for the effectiveness of FNMA policy, since they show the degree to which the reduction in private intermediary holdings of mortgages offsets the original FNMA purchase. Taken at face value, the experiment indicates a rather remarkable finding. The final reduction in the mortgage holdings of the four private intermediaries is $2.37 billion, which more than doubly offsets the increase in the FNMA holdings. Furthermore, even if the large change in CB mortgage holdings is set to zero, the response of the remaining three private intermediaries is still a reduction of $1.07 billion in their mortgage holdings.

Now, assuming the model is stable, this response cannot be maintained indefinitely. The net reduction in the total supply of mortgages must eventually cause the mortgage rate to rise, and it will continue to rise at least until the net reduction in the mortgage supply is zero; in fact, the structure of the mortgage demand equation (5A-9) insures that in the long-run equilibrium the net change in mortgages will be positive. In Table 5C-1 it can be seen that starting 12 periods after the shock, the mortgage rate has indeed started to rise relative to the solution of the standard simulation. Although the simulation is not long enough to provide this long-run equilibrium multiplier, it seems reasonable to extrapolate on the basis of these results that the FNMA action will at least be nearly fully offset by the reactions of the private intermediaries even in the long-run equilibrium. In any case, it is certainly clear that for any realistic planning period, FNMA actions will be dominated by the reactions of the private intermediaries.

While this conclusion raises doubt about the effectiveness of FNMA in making long-run contributions to the aggregate supply of mortgages, two other considerations should be noted. First, in the short run, FNMA is able to make a net contribution to the mortgage supply; from our results it is eight quarters before the response of the private intermediaries dominates the initial FNMA purchase. Secondly, many of FNMAs policy actions are directed at a supply of mortgages for specific purposes which the private intermediaries will not handle. Although the model cannot formalize this aspect of FNMA policy, it is apparent that even if FNMA actions are offset completely in terms of magnitude, it can still achieve a desirable redistribution of mortgages. It should also be repeated that this model does not reflect the September 1968 institutional changes in the structure of FNMA and the creation of GNMA. Furthermore, the model does not take into account the fact that FNMA will issue debt to finance its mortgage purchases. In principle, this debt may be purchased either by the depositors of the financial intermediaries (substituting for their deposits) or by the financial intermediaries themselves (substituting for their own mortgages); in either case this would reinforce our conclusions. The empirical relevance of this effect, however, is doubtful in view of the overall size of the capital markets, except perhaps for a one-time shift during the 1966 money crunch.

$1 Billion Increase in Volume of FHLBB
Advances

Table 5C-2 shows the effects of increasing the advances supplied by the FHLBB to the SLAs by $1 billion starting in 1960:4.[37] The primary impact of this shock should be an increase in the mortgage holdings of the SLAs, and it can be seen that this is the case. After 33 quarters of simulation the mortgage holdings of the SLAs have increased by $.95 billion, almost equal to the amount of the increase in FHLBB advances. In terms of dynamics, over 90 percent of this final effect for SLAs was achieved after 4 quarters, reflecting the relatively quick responsiveness of the mortgage flows of the SLAs. Furthermore the mortgage flows are generated entirely by mortgages made without commitments because the volume of FHLBB advances appears only in the SLAs gross mortgage flow equation (5A-6). In fact, the commitments of the SLAs actually decline, in response to the larger stock of mortgages and the falling mortgage rate.

The effects of the FHLBB policy action on the rest of the mortgage market are essentially negligible over the period of the simulation. The increase in the SLA mortgage holdings causes a maximum decrease in the mortgage rate of only 2 basis points. This small decline in the mortgage rate has, in turn, only trivial effects on the mortgage holdings of the other intermediaries. It thus appears that FHLBB policy actions, by routing funds to the mortgage market via a private intermediary, are significantly more effective than FNMA policies which directly supply the mortgage market.

It should be stressed, however, that eventually the increase in the SLA mortgage holdings will cause a decline in the mortgage rate of the same magnitude observed for FNMA policy. This in turn will lead to a significant reduction in the mortgage holdings of the other private intermediaries. Thus, in the long run, FHLBB policy is likely to achieve primarily a redistribution of mortgages (in this case to SLAs from the rest of the market) just as was the case with FNMA policy. The FHLBB policy retains an important intermediate-run effect (for example after 32 quarters), in contrast to FNMA policy, however, because the resulting increase in the supply of mortgages by SLAs occurs only gradually. This avoids the impact effect, resulting from large mortgage flows, on the mortgage rate, and thus precludes an

---

[37] For this policy to be effective, it must be assumed that the FHLBB interest charge on advances is sufficiently low to induce the SLAs to make use of the increased availability of FHLBB funds. Over the sample period, 1960:4 to 1968:4, this generally has been the case, the borrowing rate has averaged about 1.6 percentage points less than the mortgage rate, but future conditions may present an exception.

immediate and strong reaction by the other private intermediaries.[38] Furthermore, the ultimate effects on the mortgage rate, which give rise to the long-run results, are observed only after a very long period because the speed of adjustment of mortgage demand is very slow—e.g., 3 percent per quarter in equation (5A-9).

One Percentage Point Increase in the Rate of Interest on FHLBB Advances

Table 5C-3 shows the results of increasing the FHLBB borrowing rate on advances by 1 percentage point starting in 1960:4. Qualitatively, the results are similar to the effects of a change in the volume of FHLBB advances to the SLAs as just discussed. The major impact of the shock is on the mortgage holdings of the SLAs, although it is negative of course because the cost of funds has been increased. Furthermore, the secondary effects on the rest of the market are very small.

Quantitatively, the effect of the FHLBB policy on the SLAs appears quite strong. After four quarters the mortgage holdings of the SLAs have been reduced by over $2 billion, and after 32 quarters the mortgage holdings are down by over $5 billion. Indeed, in 1968:4, the process is still continuing because of the deposit scaling effect on the interest rate sensitivity as already discussed in the first test with FNMA policy. It is well to point out, however, that this experiment assumes that other market rates of interest have remained at their historic levels. If these other market rates were to increase, with their implied effects on the mortgage rate, the final multiplier for the FHLBB policy would be significantly reduced.[39]

An Increase in Market Rates of Interest by One Percentage Point

Table 5C-4 summarizes the effects of increasing the rates of interest on assets competing with mortgages in the portfolios of the intermediaries. In our

---

[38] It may be assumed that in practice FNMA does smooth its mortgage purchases over time in order to maintain short-run stability in the mortgage market. These results suggest that such a policy may have the additional benefit of postponing the reactions of the private intermediaries, to the decline in the mortgage rate, even into the intermediate run.

[39] Silber [17] for example, finds that a 1 percentage point change in the FHLBB borrowing rate has the effect of changing the SLA mortgage holdings by $.475 billion after 4 quarters, which is a significantly smaller multiplier than our results indicate. His model is estimated without the mortgage rate in the SLA mortgage supply equation, however, and thus the offsetting effect of an additional increase in the mortgage rate is in some sense already contained in his estimates. See also footnote 18.

model these rates are the corporate bond rate for LICs and MSBs, and the commercial loan rate for CBs. The results shown in this table incorporate increases in both of these rates. It should also be stressed that the FHLBB borrowing rate is maintained at its historic levels in this experiment, and thus if the borrowing rate does tend to move with general market rates, as just suggested in the previous section, the multipliers would have to be appropriately adjusted. Furthermore, these results should not be interpreted in terms of the effects of general monetary tightness, as might be generated by Federal Reserve policy, because we have abstracted from the decreases in deposit flows which would be likely to occur under such conditions.

The final effects of the increase in the market interest rates are shown in the last row of Table 5C-4. The mortgage rate rises by about 77 basis points in its long-run response to the shock. The stock of mortgages for LICs, MSBs, and CBs all decrease as expected, whereas the stock of SLAs mortgages rises, because the mortgage rate is rising while the SLA opportunity cost, i.e., the FHLBB borrowing rate, is assumed constant. As with the FNMA and the FHLBB rate change experiments, the mortgage stocks continue to change even at the end of the simulation period because of the interest rate scaling effect. The magnitudes of the final decreases in the mortgage stock holdings are small relative to the total holdings of these intermediaries. The explanation of this result is that the interest rate spread between the mortgage rate and the market rates, which determines the portfolio allocation of the intermediaries, has been decreased by only 23 basis points.

The dynamics of the adjustment toward equilibrium appear in general to be quite smooth. The mortgage rate attains a peak gain of 82 basis points after 8 quarters and then cycles slightly, under the pressure of the decreased supply, to the final gain of 77 basis points. The approach of the CB mortgage stock toward its final value is monotonic, and the same is true for MSBs except for a small cycle at the 20-quarter mark. The pattern for LICs is more interesting. The mortgage stock for LICs actually rises through the fourth period after the shock, although LIC commitments and gross mortgage flows are both decreased during this period. The reason is that the sharp increase in the mortgage rate causes the repayments to LICs to fall [see equation (5A-10)] by an amount which is, in fact, greater than the decrease in the gross mortgage flow; the net mortgage flow is thus positive during this interval. A similar effect, it may be recalled, has already been observed in the experiment with shocking FNMA mortgage purchases. Once the mortgage rate starts to stabilize, in this case about the fifth quarter after the shock, the mortgage stock of LICs of course starts to decline, and does so monotonically except for the small cycle, similar to MSBs, observed after 20 quarters.

$1 Billion Increases in Deposits of Each
Intermediary

Table 5C-5 shows the effects of shocking the system by increasing the deposits at each of the four intermediaries by $1 billion. For CBs, it should be noted, this means that both time deposits and demand deposits have been increased by $1 billion before allowance for the reserve requirements.

The impact of the increase in deposits for each intermediary is of course an increase in commitments and mortgage flows, and subsequently an increase in the stock of mortgages. The peak gain in the stock of mortgages was about $1.11 billion for LICs (in the 7th period), $1.11 billion for SLAs (in the 5th period), $1.53 billion for MSBs (in the 8th period), and $.45 billion for CBs (in about the 20th period). In each case there was cycling, however, and at the end of the simulation the gain in outstanding mortgages was less than the peak; the final levels were about $.54 billion for LICs, $1.00 billion for SLAs, $1.00 billion for MSBs, and $.38 billion for CBs. These multipliers are quite close to the single-equation solutions already developed in equations (5-20) and (5-24), reflecting the relatively small changes in the mortgage rate. Reference is made to these earlier results for further interpretation of the multipliers.

The explanation for the cycling in the mortgage supply is to be found in the important role of commitments in the model. The LICs serve as a good example of the process. They respond to the increase in deposits by quickly increasing their flow of new commitments. This in turn leads, with some lag, to an increase in mortgage flows and an increase in the stock of mortgages. By the end of the 3rd period after the shock, however, it is apparent that they have over committed in the sense that the stock of mortgages exceeds the desired level.[40] Thus in the 5th quarter after the shock, with allowance for partial adjustment of new commitments, the flow of new commitments is actually reduced below the solution of the standard simulation. This of course leads to some reduction in the supply of mortgages. By the 32nd quarter after the shock the process has essentially reached equilibrium and the additional flow of commitments is essentially zero. The case for SLAs and MSBs is

---

[40] This result does not imply that LICs systematically over react in making commitments. For the purposes of the experiment the shock was large and occurred all at one time. In more realistic situations the change in deposits would occur gradually and cycling would be observed in only the more extreme cases.

essentially the same although it must be interpreted in terms of outstanding commitments. The cycling for CBs, on the other hand, cannot be related to commitments [see equation (5A-8)], but is simply the result of cycling in the mortgage rate which is due to the cycling in the supply of mortgages of the other intermediaries.

$1 Billion Increase in Investment in Residential Structures

As the final experiment, Table 5C-6 tabulates the results of increasing the flow of investment in residential structures by $1 billion for each year ($.25 billion for each quarter). Since the stock of houses also enters the model [see equation (5A-9)], for consistency this variable should reflect the increased investment. This was achieved by incrementing the stock of houses by an additional $1 billion each year.[41]

The results indicate only very minor effects from this shock. The impact effects are essentially nil. The long-run effects are to increase the mortgage rate by 7 basis points and the total supply of mortgages of the private intermediaries by $1.61 billion. The stock of houses, on the other hand, has been assumed to increase by about $8 billion at the end of the simulation ($1 billion per year). This raises the obvious question of how the increased stock of houses was financed. In the long run, the explanation is related to the leverage which a small change in the average mortgage–house ratio has on the availability of a large dollar amount of mortgage funds. Since the outstanding stock of houses is in the order of magnitude of $500 billion, even a 1 percentage point change in the mortgage–house ratio will make $5 billion in mortgage funds available for the financing of the additional stock of housing. Furthermore, because of the relatively high interest elasticity of the demand for mortgages, only a small change in the mortgage rate is required to induce this change in the desired mortgage–house ratio.

In the short run, there is an additional effect due to credit rationing and the partial-equilibrium nature of the experiment. Although the demand for mortgages increases with the stock of houses, in the short run the supply of mortgages responds very little, as is apparent from our results. Because the mortgage rate does not adjust to the equilibrium immediately, excess demand in the form of credit rationing will appear in the market. Now, in a general equilibrium context, the existence of such rationing would presumably

---

[41] In principle, the depreciation on the increments to the stock of houses should be taken into account, but to simplify the experiment this small effect has been ignored.

feedback on the demand for housing and thus would tend to reduce the investment to a level consistent with the short-run availability of financing. In this experiment, however, we have exogenously shifted the investment function without allowing for such feedbacks, and thus the excess demand remains in the mortgage market until the mortgage rate adjusts.

Summary and Conclusions

The model of the mortgage market developed in this paper differs most notably from earlier studies in its emphasis on the effects of policy controlled variables and the lags in timing introduced by advance commitments for mortgages. The advance commitments were introduced in the model by estimating an equation for new commitments for life insurance companies (LICs) and equations for outstanding commitments for savings and loan associations (SLAs) and mutual savings banks (MSBs), and these variables were then used in the specification of the respective gross mortgage flow equations. In terms of the general fit of the estimated model and the stability of the standard dynamic simulation, the emphasis on commitments appears to have been well placed. In addition, the introduction of commitments in the models allows for the possibility of cycling, as seen in some of the simulation tests.

Perhaps the most important aspects of the simulation experiments relate to the effectiveness of FNMA and FHLBB policy. The evaluation of FNMA policy was quite pessimistic in that FNMA purchases of mortgages were more than offset by the reductions in the private intermediaries' holdings in the intermediate run, and even in the long run it appeared the net effect of FNMA policy would be about zero. Thus, taken without qualification, these results leave only a short-run impact (which itself is very small) and long-run distributional effects as viable areas for FNMA policy influence.

The results for the FHLBB instruments provide somewhat more optimistic grounds for the likely effectiveness of its policy. Variations in the FHLBB borrowing rate have significant effects in the model in both the long run and the short run. There is an open question, however, concerning the degree to which the FHLBB is actually able to vary its borrowing rate independent of movements in the general level of market rates. In the past, the FHLBB borrowing rate has been closely tied to market rates through the use of a mark-up formula, but recently there have been suggestions that the FHLBB policy may become more flexible in this respect. The second policy tool of the FHLBB, variations in the quantity of advances made available to the SLAs, also has significant short-run and intermediate-run effects on the supply of mortgages. In the long run, however, this instrument suffers from the same dilemma facing FNMA policy, namely that the reactions of the private intermediaries are likely to reduce its effectiveness to only distributional considerations, in this case the distribution being to SLAs and away from the rest of the mortgage market.

Several of the experiments pointed to the important need to incorporate the mortgage model with housing and deposit markets in the first instance, and with a complete model of the economy in a more general context. It is only in this way that the reactions of housing investment to monetary policy generated by Federal Reserve instruments, or to fiscal policy tools for that matter, can be determined in a structural and reliable manner. This is, of course, directly related to the apparent policy trade-off between the general desirability of tight monetary conditions in periods of inflationary pressure and the specific, sometimes called discriminatory, effects of the tight money on housing investment. The results presented in Chapter 7 simulate the savings, mortgage, and housing sectors together, and results will soon be reported in the context of the complete FMP model.

Finally, there is no shortage of important projects for future research on the mortgage market. Probably the most important area for future work concerns the possibility of further dissaggregation in the model, particularly on the demand side. For example, in models of housing demand it is desirable to disaggregate the demand at least by one- to four-family and multifamily housing units, and thus it would be useful if the mortgage market reflected this same disaggregation. Along similar lines it is also desirable that the component of mortgage demand derived from nonresidential structures be separated from the aggregate. Still another possibility, which may have important policy implications, is to disaggregate government-guaranteed FHA and VA mortgages on both the demand and supply sides of the market. The primary hindrance to the incorporation of these disaggregated elements in this model, and in earlier studies, has of course been the lack of appropriate disaggregated data for the various mortgage stocks and flows and for commitments. There are indications, however, that the collection of mortgage data is being given priority by some government agencies, principally the Department of Housing and Urban Development,[42] and thus a more disaggregated model may be possible in the future.

---

[42] See Diamond [6].

Appendix 5A:
Structure and
Estimates of the
Mortgage Model

Table 5A. Structure and Estimates of the Mortgage Model

Commitments

(5A-1)

$$MCNI = -1.63 + .045MIS + .708\Delta MIS + .003(RM_{-1} - RCB_{-1})MIS$$
$$\quad (2.6) \quad (2.1) \quad\quad (3.3) \quad\quad\quad (2.3)$$
$$+ .186MRIS - .073MKIS_{-1} + .032MCOI_{-1} + .657MCNI_{-1}$$
$$(1.9) \quad\quad\quad\quad\quad (.46) \quad\quad\quad (5.2)$$

	Mean of Dependent Variable	R^2	DW	SE	ρ
	1.74	.880	1.82	.125	.337

Sample = 1955:2 to 1968:4

(5A-2)

$$MCOS = -.749 + .161MSL + .004(RM - ZRFH)MSL + .119MRSL$$
$$\quad (4.3) \quad (6.3) \quad (2.9) \quad\quad\quad\quad\quad\quad (C)$$
$$- .149MKSL_{-1} + .378MCOS_{-1}$$
$$(5.9) \quad\quad\quad (3.7)$$

	Mean of Dependent Variable	R^2	DW	SE	ρ
	2.27	.982	1.82	.121	.653

Sample = 1956:3 to 1968:4

(5A-3)

$$MCOM = -2.23 + .152MMS + .472\Delta MMS + .012(RM - RCB)MMS$$
$$\quad (2.8) \quad (2.6) \quad\quad (2.5) \quad\quad\quad (2.1)$$
$$+ .060MRMS - .148MKMS_{-1} + .955MCOM_{-1}$$
$$(C) \quad\quad\quad (2.5) \quad\quad\quad (11.0)$$

	Mean of Dependent Variable	R^2	DW	SE	ρ
	3.74	.936	1.86	.224	.220

Sample = 1959:2 to 1968:4

(5A-4)

$$MCOI = .763 + 1.00MCNI + .681MCOI_{-1}$$
$$\quad (.84) \quad (C) \quad\quad\quad (8.65)$$

	Mean of Dependent Variable	R^2	DW	SE	ρ
	4.60	.994	2.25	.133	.977

Sample = 1955:2 to 1968:4

Mortgage Flows

(5A-5)

$$MFIS = .696 - .283DUM + .026MIS + .502MRIS - .047MKIS_{-1}$$
$$\quad (2.1) \quad (3.7) \quad\quad (2.3) \quad\quad (2.8) \quad\quad\quad (2.7)$$
$$+ .922 \sum_{i=0}^{7} b_i MCNI_{-i}$$
$$(15.5)$$

$$b_0 = .17 \quad\quad b_4 = .13$$
$$b_1 = .17 \quad\quad b_5 = .11$$
$$b_2 = .16 \quad\quad b_6 = .08$$
$$b_3 = .15 \quad\quad b_7 = .04$$

	Mean of Dependent Variable	R^2	DW	SE	ρ
	1.92	.950	2.04	.083	.084

Sample = 1955:1 to 1968:4

Table 5A continued

Equation	Mean of Dependent Variable	R^2	DW	SE	ρ
(5A-6)	4.76	.995	1.73	.103	.741
	Sample = 1957:2 to 1968:4				
(5A-7)	1.76	.969	2.16	.066	
	Sample = 1960:2 to 1968:4				
(5A-8)	.832	.940	1.81	.128	.632
	Sample = 1955:1 to 1968:4				

(5A-6)
$$MFSL = .152 - .830DUM + .118\Delta\overline{MSL} + .260MSL + .190ZAFH$$
$$\quad (.47) \quad (7.1) \qquad (2.0) \qquad\quad (3.4) \qquad\quad (1.7)$$
$$+ .625MRSL - .299MKSL_{-1} + 1.95 \sum_{i=0}^{6} b_i MCOS_{-i}$$
$$\quad (5.3) \qquad\quad (3.7) \qquad\qquad (11.5)$$

$b_0 = .39$ $b_4 = .05$
$b_1 = .27$ $b_5 = .01$
$b_2 = .18$ $b_6 = -.01$
$b_3 = .10$

(5A-7)
$$MFMS = .779 - .284DUM + .334\Delta\overline{MMS} + .115MMS + .400MRMS$$
$$\quad (2.1) \quad (3.4) \qquad\quad (6.1) \qquad\quad (3.2) \qquad\quad (C)$$
$$- .132MKMS_{-1} + .449 \sum_{i=0}^{6} b_i MCOM_{-i}$$
$$\quad (3.5) \qquad\qquad (15.0)$$

$b_0 = .27$ $b_4 = .10$
$b_1 = .22$ $b_5 = .06$
$b_2 = .18$ $b_6 = .03$
$b_3 = .14$

(5A-8)
$$\Delta MKCB = .005MDS + .072 \sum_{i=0}^{4} b_i MTM_{-i} - .176MKCB_{-1}$$
$$\quad\quad (.77) \qquad (3.8) \qquad\qquad\qquad (3.3)$$
$$+ .016 \sum_{i=0}^{4} c_i (MTM_{-i})(RM - RCL)_{-i}$$
$$\quad (3.5)$$

$b_0 = .14$ $c_0 = .24$
$b_1 = .22$ $c_1 = .25$
$b_2 = .26$ $c_2 = .23$
$b_3 = .24$ $c_3 = .18$
$b_4 = .14$ $c_4 = .10$

Table 5A continued

Mortgage Demand

(5A-9)

$$RM = 1.60 + .346RCB - .601\frac{\Delta M_g^T + .03M_{-1}^T}{EH\$ + .03KH\$_{-1}} + .03KH\$_{-1}$$

$$\; (3.7)\quad (6.6)\qquad (2.5)$$

$$-\,.004\frac{MCOS_{-1} + MCOM_{-1} + MCOL_{-1} + .549RM_{-1}}{EH\$ + .03KH\$_{-1}}$$

$$\;(1.5)\phantom{MCOS_{-1} + MCOM_{-1} + MCOL_{-1} +}\;(6.6)$$

6.18   .982   1.49   .060   .531
Sample = 1958:3 to 1968:4

Repayments

(5A-10)

$$MRIS = .021MKIS_{-1} - .007(\overline{RM})MKIS_{-1} + .125MFIS_{-1}$$

$$\;(11.9)\qquad (7.5)\qquad\qquad (3.2)$$

1.14   .920   1.96   .085   .076
Sample = 1955:1 to 1968:4

(5A-11)

$$MRSL = .022MKSL_{-1} - .008(\overline{RM})MKSL_{-1} + .228MFSL_{-1}$$

$$\;(8.6)\qquad (5.0)\qquad\qquad (5.7)$$

2.68   .980   1.88   .118   .678
Sample = 1956:4 to 1968:4

(5A-12)

$$MRMS = .012MKMS_{-1} - .001(\overline{RM})MKMS_{-1} + .281MFMS_{-1}$$

$$\;(5.9)\qquad (.50)\qquad\qquad (6.8)$$

.898   .974   1.13   .033
Sample = 1958:4 to 1968:4

Mortgage Stock Identities

(5A-13) $MKIS = MKIS_{-1} + MFIS - MRIS$

(5A-14) $MKSL = MKSL_{-1} + MFSL - MRSL$

(5A-15) $MKMS = MKMS_{-1} + MFMS - MRMS$

(5A-16) $MKCB = MKCB_{-1} + \Delta MKCB$

Notes:

i. Dollar magnitudes are measured in billions of current dollars; interest rates are measured in percentage points; all flows are at quarterly rates; stocks are measured at the end of quarter.

ii. The absolute values of t-statistics are shown in parentheses; C = constrained coefficient (see text discussion, p. 157).

iii. The following distributed lags were constrained to second degree polynomials with the far end tied to zero by the Almon technique:

MCNI in equation (5A-5)
MCOS in equation (5A-6)
MCOM in equation (5A-7)
MTM in equation (5A-8)
MTM(RM − RCL) in equation (5A-8)

iv. ρ is the coefficient of serial correlation for those equations estimated with the iterative procedure of Cochrane and Orcutt. Otherwise, ordinary least squares was used.

v. Notation and variable definitions are given in Appendix A.

Appendix 5B: Behavior of the Mortgage Model Equations

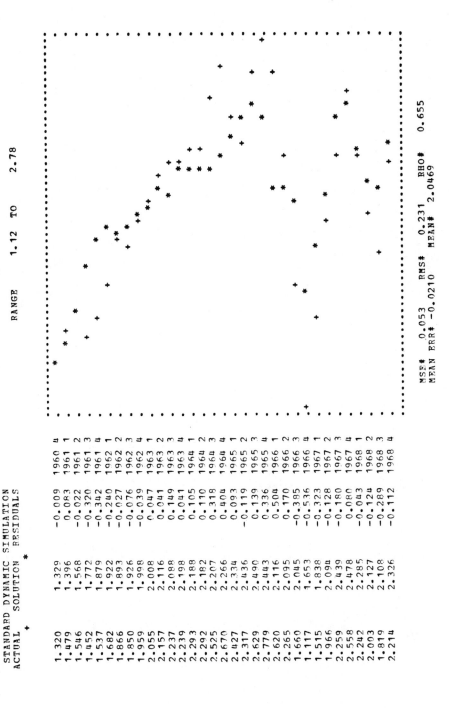

Figure 5B-1. Standard Dynamic Simulation of Mortgage Sector: Life Insurance Companies, New Commitments — *MCNI*.

186

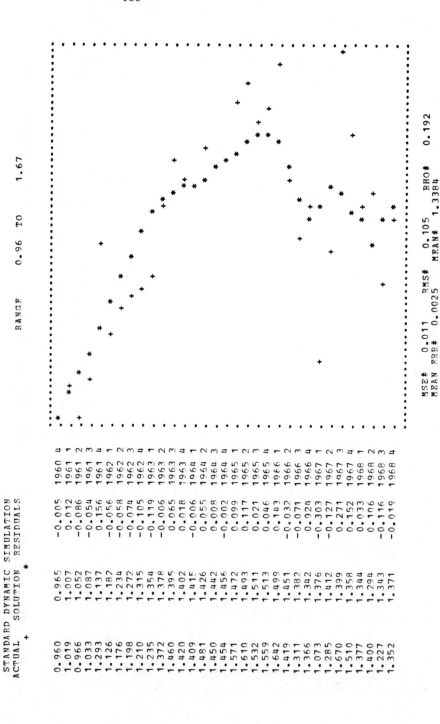

Figure 5B–2. Standard Dynamic Simulation of Mortgage Sector: Life Insurance Companies, Mortgage Repayments – *MRIS.*

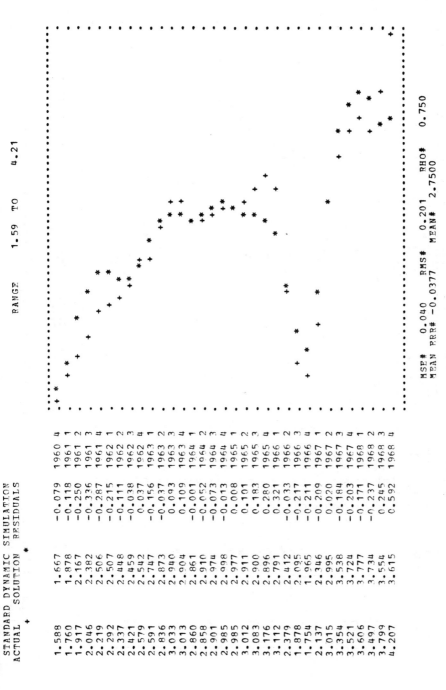

Figure 5B-3. Standard Dynamic Simulation of Mortgage Sector: Life Insurance Companies, Outstanding Commitments — *MCOI*.

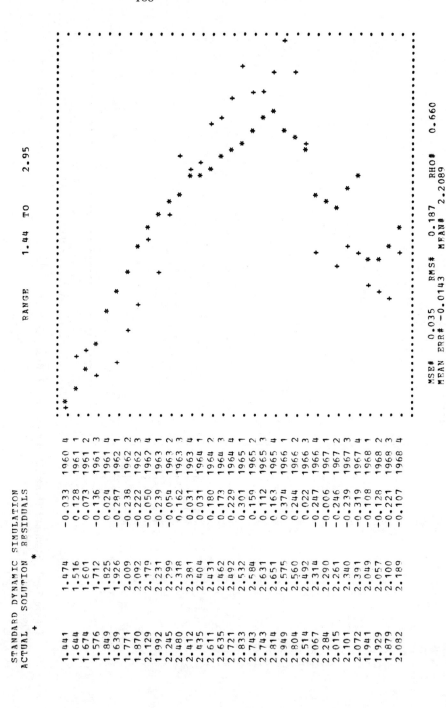

Figure 5B-4. Standard Dynamic Simulation of Mortgage Sector: Life Insurance Companies, Gross Mortgage Flows — *MFIS*.

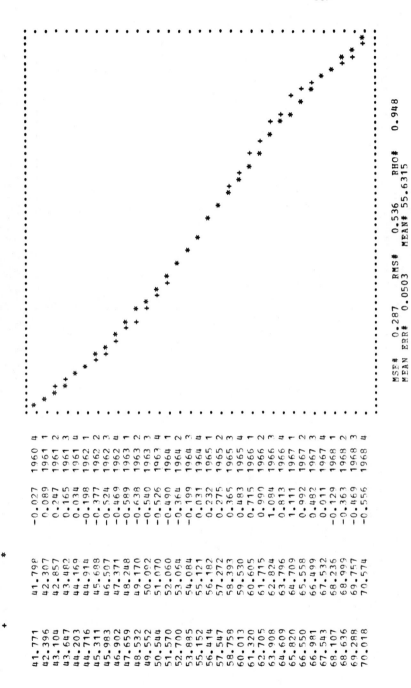

STANDARD DYNAMIC SIMULATION

RANGE   41.77 TO   70.57

ACTUAL	SOLUTION	RESIDUALS		
41.771	41.798	-0.027	1960	4
42.396	42.307	0.089	1961	1
43.104	42.857	0.247	1961	2
43.647	43.482	0.165	1961	3
44.203	44.169	0.034	1961	4
44.716	44.914	-0.198	1962	1
45.311	45.688	-0.377	1962	2
45.983	46.507	-0.524	1962	3
46.902	47.371	-0.469	1962	4
47.659	48.248	-0.589	1963	1
48.532	49.170	-0.638	1963	2
49.552	50.092	-0.540	1963	3
50.544	51.070	-0.526	1963	4
51.570	52.060	-0.490	1964	1
52.700	53.064	-0.364	1964	2
53.885	54.084	-0.199	1964	3
55.152	55.121	0.031	1964	4
56.414	56.182	0.232	1965	1
57.547	57.272	0.275	1965	2
58.758	58.393	0.365	1965	3
60.013	59.530	0.483	1965	4
61.320	60.605	0.715	1966	1
62.705	61.715	0.990	1966	2
63.908	62.824	1.084	1966	3
64.609	63.796	0.813	1966	4
65.820	64.709	1.111	1967	1
66.550	65.558	0.992	1967	2
66.981	66.499	0.482	1967	3
67.543	67.532	0.011	1967	4
68.107	68.235	-0.129	1968	1
68.636	68.999	-0.363	1968	2
69.288	69.757	-0.469	1968	3
70.018	70.574	-0.556	1968	4

MSE#   0.287   RMS#   0.536   RHO#   0.948
MEAN ERR# 0.0503   MEAN# 55.6315

Figure 5B-5. Standard Dynamic Simulation of Mortgage Sector: Life Insurance Companies, Stock of Mortgages — *MKIS*.

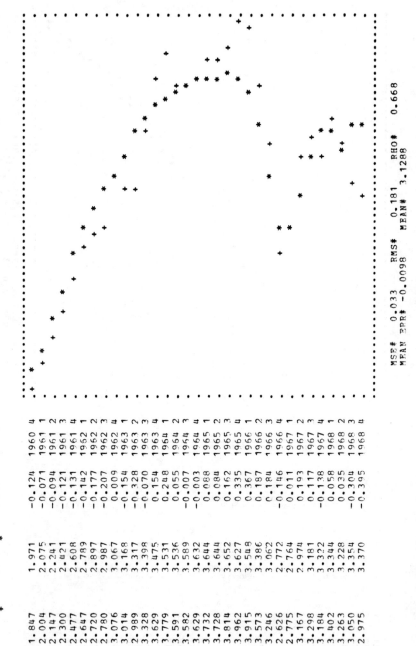

Figure 5B-6. Standard Dynamic Simulation of Mortgage Sector: Savings and Loan, Outstanding Commitments — *MCOS*.

191

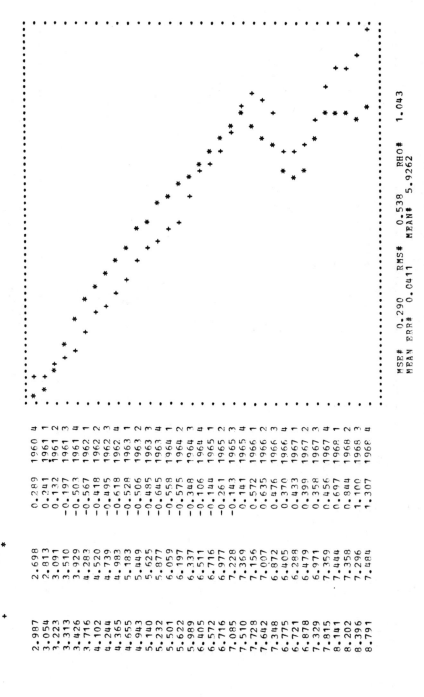

Figure 5B-7. Standard Dynamic Simulation of Mortgage Sector: Savings and Loan, Mortgage Repayments — *MRSL*.

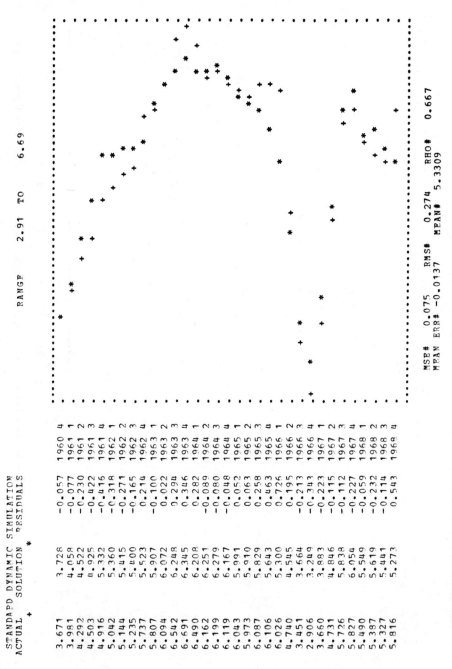

Figure 5B–8. Standard Dynamic Simulation of Mortgage Sector: Savings and Loan, Gross Mortgage Flows — *MFSL*.

RANGE 60.00 TO 131.04

STANDARD DYNAMIC SIMULATION

ACTUAL	SOLUTION	RESIDUALS		
60.070	60.002	0.068	1960	4
62.047	61.985	0.062	1961	1
64.192	64.265	-0.073	1961	2
66.395	66.770	-0.375	1961	3
68.834	69.494	-0.660	1961	4
71.229	72.064	-0.835	1962	1
73.653	74.583	-0.930	1962	2
76.108	76.996	-0.888	1962	3
78.769	79.452	-0.683	1962	4
81.562	82.191	-0.629	1963	1
84.667	84.946	-0.279	1963	2
87.881	87.796	0.085	1963	3
90.943	90.665	0.278	1963	4
93.654	93.343	0.311	1964	1
96.225	96.058	0.167	1964	2
98.842	98.747	0.095	1964	3
101.332	101.283	0.049	1964	4
103.643	103.630	0.013	1965	1
105.888	105.895	-0.007	1965	2
108.161	108.072	0.089	1965	3
110.305	110.088	0.217	1965	4
112.416	111.840	0.576	1966	1
113.583	112.999	0.584	1966	2
113.788	113.601	0.187	1966	3
114.068	114.078	-0.010	1966	4
114.953	115.197	-0.244	1967	1
116.517	117.069	-0.552	1967	2
118.945	119.727	-0.782	1967	3
121.588	122.459	-0.871	1967	4
123.676	124.663	-0.987	1968	1
125.800	127.054	-1.254	1968	2
128.077	129.142	-1.065	1968	3
130.918	131.045	-0.127	1968	4

MSE# 0.312   RMS# 0.559   RHO# 0.868
MEAN ERR# -0.2566   MEAN# 97.5371

Figure 5B-9. Standard Dynamic Simulation of Mortgage Sector: Savings and Loan, Stock of Mortgages — *MKSL*.

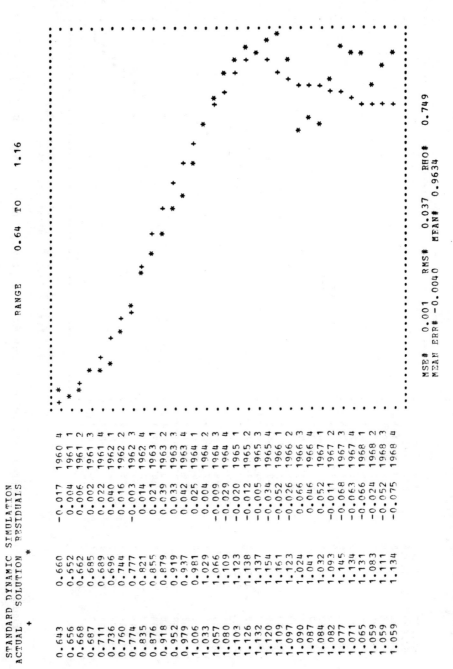

Figure 5B-10. Standard Dynamic Simulation of Mortgage Sector: Mutual Savings Banks, Outstanding Commitments — *MCOM*.

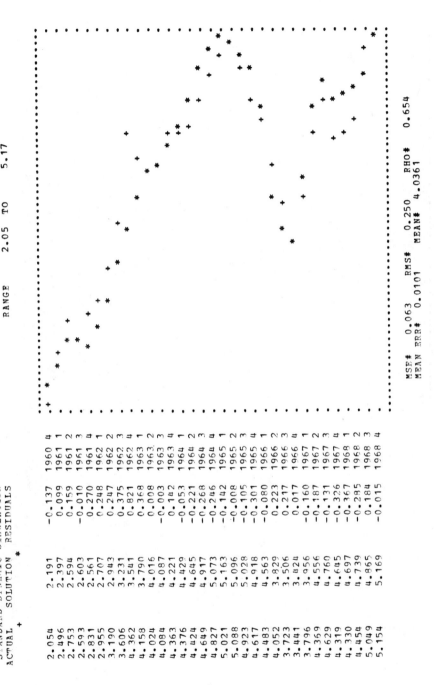

Figure 5B-11. Standard Dynamic Simulation of Mortgage Sector: Mutual Savings Banks, Mortgage Repayments — *MRMS*.

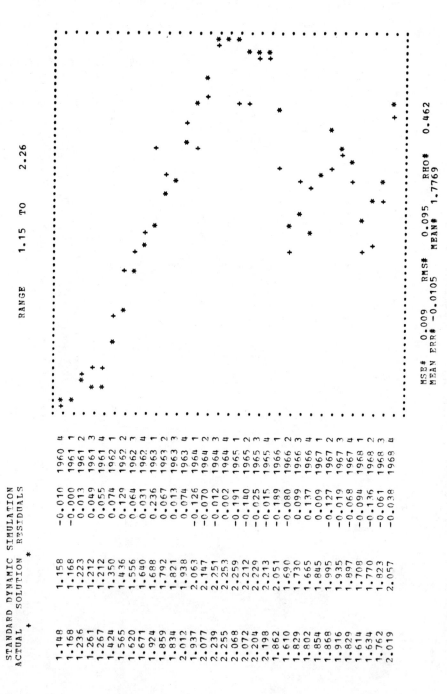

Figure 5B–12. Standard Dynamic Simulation of Mortgage Sector: Mutual Savings Banks, Gross Mortgage Flows — *MFMS*.

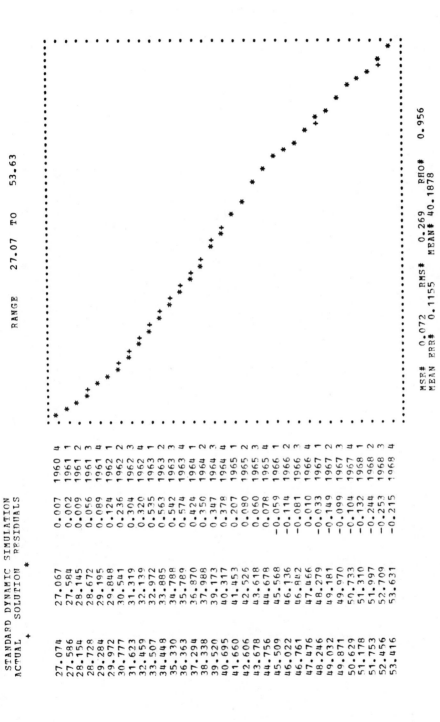

STANDARD DYNAMIC SIMULATION   RANGE   27.07 TO   53.63

ACTUAL   SOLUTION RESIDUALS
  +   *   *

ACTUAL	SOLUTION	RESIDUALS		
27.074	27.067	0.007	1960	4
27.586	27.584	0.002	1961	1
28.154	28.145	0.009	1961	2
28.728	28.672	0.056	1961	3
29.284	29.195	0.089	1961	4
29.972	29.848	0.124	1962	1
30.777	30.541	0.236	1962	2
31.623	31.319	0.304	1962	3
32.459	32.139	0.320	1962	4
33.507	32.972	0.535	1963	1
34.448	33.885	0.563	1963	2
35.330	34.788	0.542	1963	3
36.363	35.789	0.574	1963	4
37.294	36.870	0.424	1964	1
38.338	37.988	0.350	1964	2
39.520	39.173	0.347	1964	3
40.695	40.317	0.378	1964	4
41.660	41.453	0.207	1965	1
42.606	42.526	0.080	1965	2
43.678	43.618	0.060	1965	3
44.756	44.678	0.078	1965	4
45.509	45.568	-0.059	1966	1
46.022	46.136	-0.114	1966	2
46.761	46.842	-0.081	1966	3
47.476	47.466	-0.010	1967	4
48.246	48.279	-0.033	1967	1
49.032	49.181	-0.149	1967	2
49.871	49.970	-0.099	1967	3
50.629	50.733	-0.104	1967	4
51.178	51.310	-0.132	1968	1
51.753	51.997	-0.244	1968	2
52.456	52.709	-0.253	1968	3
53.416	53.631	-0.215	1968	4

MSE#   0.072   RMS#   0.269   RHO#   0.956
MEAN ERR# 0.1155 MEAN# 40.1878

Figure 5B–13. Standard Dynamic Simulation of Mortgage Sector: Mutual Savings Banks, Stock of Mortgages
– *MKMS.*

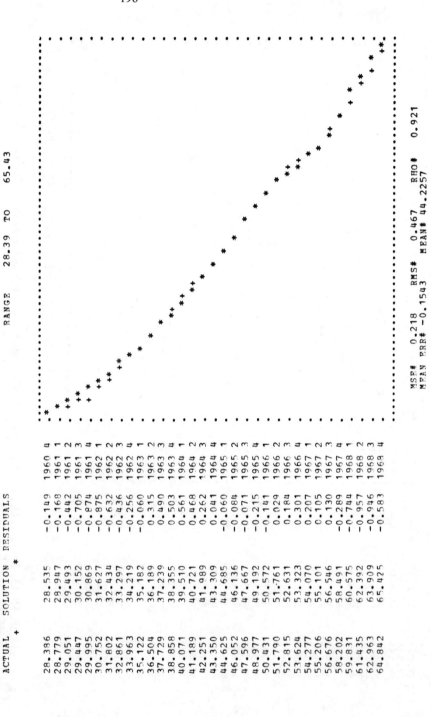

Figure 5B-14. Standard Dynamic Simulation of Mortgage Sector: Commercial Banks, Stock of Mortgages — *MKCB*.

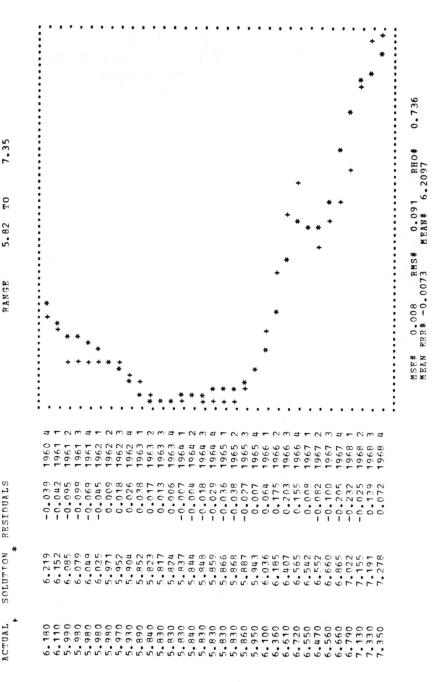

Figure 5B–15. Standard Dynamic Simulation of Mortgage Sector: Interest Rate on Mortgages — *RM*.

Appendix 5C:
Effects of Shocks in
the Exogenous
Variables

Table 5C-1. Effect of a Maintained $1 Billion Increase in FNMA Mortgage Holdings

Periods After Shock	LICs			SLAs				MSBs		CBs	Demand
	MCNI	MFIS	MKIS	MCOS	MFSL	MKSL	MCOM	MFMS	MKMS	MKCB	RM
0	a	a	-.01	-.01	.01	-.01	-.02	a	a	-0.01	-.03
1	a	.01	-.03	-.01	.01	-.03	-.04	-.01	-.01	-0.03	-.06
2	-.01	.01	-.04	-.02	.01	-.05	-.08	-.01	-.02	-0.06	-.09
3	-.03	a	-.06	-.02	.02	-.08	-.11	-.03	-.04	-0.12	-.10
4	-.04	a	-.10	-.02	.03	-.10	-.15	-.04	-.07	-0.19	-.11
5	-.04	-.01	-.13	-.02	.06	-.12	-.18	-.05	-.10	-0.26	-.12
6	-.05	-.02	-.17	-.01	.04	-.14	-.20	-.06	-.15	-0.34	-.12
7	-.05	-.02	-.20	-.01	.04	-.14	-.22	-.07	-.20	-0.42	-.12
8	-.05	-.03	-.24	-.02	.04	-.14	-.23	-.07	-.26	-0.48	-.12
12	-.04	-.03	-.30	-.03	.01	-.18	-.20	-.07	-.42	-0.70	-.11
20	-.03	-.02	-.42	-.03	-.01	-.18	-.12	.01	-.46	-0.98	-.11
32	-.03	-.02	-.45	-.03	-.02	-.19	-.16	-.02	-.43	-1.30	-.09

a Less than |.005|.

Table 5C-2. Effect of a Maintained $1 Billion Increase in Volume of FHLBB Advances

Periods After Shock	LICs			SLAs			MSBs			CBs	Demand
	MCNI	MFIS	MKIS	MCOS	MFSL	MKSL	MCOM	MFMS	MKMS	MKCB	RM
0	a	a	a	a	.19	.19	a	a	a	a	−.01
1	a	a	a	−.03	.29	.42	−.01	a	a	−.01	−.01
2	a	a	−.01	−.07	.60	.63	−.02	a	a	−.01	−.02
3	−.01	a	−.01	−.11	.24	.80	−.02	a	−.01	−.02	−.02
4	−.01	a	−.02	−.16	.18	.89	−.02	−.01	−.01	−.03	−.01
5	−.01	−.01	−.02	−.19	.10	.93	−.02	−.01	−.02	−.04	−.01
6	−.01	−.01	−.02	−.21	.05	.94	−.02	−.01	−.02	−.04	−.01
7	a	a	−.02	−.22	.02	.93	−.02	−.01	−.03	−.05	−.01
8	a	a	−.03	−.21	.02	.92	−.01	−.01	−.03	−.05	a
12	a	a	−.02	−.21	.03	.93	a	a	−.03	−.04	a
20	a	a	−.01	−.23	.02	.95	a	a	−.01	−.03	a
32	a	a	−.01	−.23	.02	.95	a	a	−.01	−.03	a

a Less than |.005|.

Table 5C-3. Effect of a Maintained One Percentage Point Increase in Rate of Interest on FHLBB Advances

Periods After Shock	LICs			SLAs				MSBs		CBs	Demand
	MCNI	MFIS	MKIS	MCOS	MFSL	MKSL	MCOM	MFMS	MKMS	MKCB	RM
0	a	a	a	−.23	−.17	−0.16	a	a	a	a	.01
1	a	a	.01	−.44	−.43	−0.55	.01	a	a	.01	.02
2	a	a	.01	−.58	−.66	−1.09	.02	a	.01	.02	.03
3	.01	a	.02	−.63	−.78	−1.70	.04	.01	.01	.04	.04
4	.02	a	.03	−.63	−.77	−2.11	.05	.01	.02	.06	.04
5	.02	a	.05	−.60	−.66	−2.50	.07	.02	.03	.09	.04
6	.03	.01	.05	−.56	−.51	−2.90	.07	.02	.05	.12	.04
7	.02	.01	.06	−.53	−.35	−3.08	.07	.02	.07	.14	.03
8	.01	.01	.08	−.52	−.24	−3.16	.07	.02	.08	.16	.03
12	.01	.01	.09	−.62	−.23	−3.48	.03	.01	.11	.16	.02
20	.01	a	.08	−.75	−.24	−4.41	.01	a	.07	.18	.02
32	.01	a	.08	−.98	−.23	−5.35	.03	a	.07	.22	.02

a Less than |.005|.

Table 5C-4. Effect of a Maintained One Percentage Point Increase in Interest Rates on Commercial Loans and Corporate Bonds

Periods After Shock	LICs			SLAs			MSBs			CBs	Demand
	MCNI	MFIS	MKIS	MCOS	MFSL	MKSL	MCOM	MFMS	MKMS	MKCB	RM
0	-.04	-.03	.08	.07	-.06	0.11	-.31	-.04	-0.04	-0.15	.35
1	-.30	-.10	.14	.10	-.09	0.28	-.49	-.09	-0.12	-0.27	.56
2	-.40	-.18	.15	.11	-.11	0.48	-.57	-.14	-0.22	-0.62	.67
3	-.40	-.25	.11	.12	-.16	0.66	-.60	-.18	-0.34	-0.87	.74
4	-.38	-.30	.03	.10	-.20	0.80	-.58	-.20	-0.49	-1.06	.78
5	-.33	-.35	-.10	.09	-.25	0.89	-.55	-.20	-0.62	-1.15	.79
6	-.29	-.36	-.23	.08	-.28	0.93	-.49	-.19	-0.73	-1.19	.81
7	-.25	-.35	-.41	.08	-.29	0.93	-.43	-.16	-0.83	-1.22	.82
8	-.20	-.33	-.56	.10	-.26	0.93	-.36	-.12	-0.89	-1.24	.82
12	-.06	-.12	-.93	.17	-.03	0.97	-.17	a	-0.92	-1.36	.80
20	-.05	.01	-.90	.21	.09	1.24	-.27	a	-0.71	-1.97	.77
32	-.09	-.04	-.96	.24	.06	1.50	-.39	a	-1.02	-2.83	.77

a Less than |.005|.

Table 5C-5. Effect of a Maintained $1 Billion Increase in Deposits of Each Intermediary

Periods After Shock	LICs			SLAs			MSBs			CBs	Demand
	MCNI	MFIS	MKIS	MCOS	MFSL	MKSL	MCOM	MFMS	MKMS	MKCB	RM
0	.77	.26	0.24	.16	.51	0.50	.84	.56	0.55	.01	−.04
1	.45	.21	0.39	.16	.38	0.70	.80	.20	0.59	.03	−.05
2	.24	.24	0.58	.12	.33	0.92	.74	.22	0.74	.05	−.05
3	.11	.23	0.76	.08	.24	1.05	.66	.23	0.90	.08	−.05
4	.02	.20	0.91	.04	.14	1.10	.58	.23	1.04	.10	−.05
5	−.03	.18	1.04	.02	.08	1.11	.48	.27	1.15	.12	−.05
6	−.07	.12	1.10	a	.02	1.08	.39	.23	1.40	.15	−.04
7	−.09	.05	1.11	a	−.01	1.03	.19	.17	1.48	.16	−.03
8	−.10	−.02	0.97	.01	−.01	1.00	.19	.11	1.53	.18	−.02
12	−.06	−.09	0.70	.03	.01	1.00	−.08	−.06	1.39	.28	−.01
20	.03	.02	0.47	.02	.02	1.00	−.02	−.03	0.86	.45	a
32	a	.01	0.54	.02	.03	1.00	.08	.03	1.00	.38	a

a Less than |.005|.

Table 5C-6. Effect of a Maintained $1 Billion Increase in Investment in Residential Structures

Periods After Shock	LICs				SLAs		MSBs			CBs	Demand
	MCNI	MFIS	MKIS	MCOS	MFSL	MKSL	MCOM	MFMS	MKMS	MKCB	RM
0	a	a	a	a	a	a	a	a	a	a	a
1	a	a	a	a	a	.01	.01	a	a	a	.01
2	a	a	.01	a	a	.01	.02	a	a	.01	.01
3	a	a	.01	a	a	.02	.03	a	.01	.02	.02
4	.01	a	.01	a	−.01	.02	.03	.01	.01	.02	.02
5	.01	a	.02	a	−.01	.02	.03	.01	.02	.03	.02
6	.01	a	.02	a	−.01	.03	.04	.01	.02	.05	.02
7	.01	a	.03	.01	−.01	.03	.05	.01	.03	.06	.03
8	.01	.01	.04	.01	−.01	.06	.06	.01	.04	.08	.03
12	.01	.01	.08	.01	−.01	.09	.10	.02	.08	.16	.04
20	.02	.01	.17	.02	−.01	.14	.14	.02	.19	.40	.06
32	.03	.01	.31	.02	−.01	.14	.14	.02	.33	.83	.07

a Less than |.005|.

References

[1] Almon, Shirley. "The Distributed Lag Between Capital Appropriations and Expenditures." *Econometrica* 35 (January 1965).

[2] Brainard, William C., and James Tobin. "Pitfalls in Financial Model Building." *American Economics Review* 58 (May 1968).

[3] Cochrane, D., and G. H. Orcutt. "Application of Least Squares Regression to Relationships Containing Auto-Correlated Errors." *Journal of the American Statistical Association* 44 (March 1949).

[4] de Leeuw, Frank. "A Model of Financial Behavior." In James S. Duesenberry, *et al.* (eds.), *The Brookings Quarterly Econometric Model of the United States*, Chicago: Rand McNally, 1965.

[5] de Leeuw, Frank, and Edward M. Gramlich. "The Channels of Monetary Policy." *Federal Reserve Bulletin* 55 (June 1969).

[6] Diamond, A. H. *Mortgage Loan Gross Flows*. U.S. Department of Housing and Urban Development, 1968.

[7] Fair, Ray C., and Dwight M. Jaffee. "Methods of Estimation for Markets in Disequilibrium." *Econometrica*, forthcoming.

[8] Fisher, Robert M. "The Availability of Mortgage Lending Commitments." Staff Economic Study 54, Board of Governors of the Federal Reserve System.

[9] Goldfeld, Stephen M., and Dwight M. Jaffee. "The Determinants of Deposit-Rate Setting by Savings and Loan Associations." *Journal of Finance* 25 (June 1970).

[10] Howrey, Philip, and H. H. Kelejian. "Simulation Versus Analytical Solutions." In Thomas H. Naylor, ed. *The Design of Computer Simulation Experiments*. Durham, N.C.: Duke University Press, 1969.

[11] Huang, David S. "The Short-Run Flows of Nonfarm Residential Mortgage Credit." *Econometrica* 34 (April 1966).

[12] Huang, David S., and Michael D. McCarthy. "Simulation of the Home Mortgage Market in the Late Sixties." *Review of Economics and Statistics* 49 (November 1967).

[13] Hulett, David T. "The Mortgage Market: Alternative Specifications." Mimeographed.

[14] Jorgenson, Dale W. "Anticipations and Investment Behavior." In James S. Duesenberry, *et al.* (eds.). *The Brookings Quarterly Econometric Model of the United States*. Chicago: Rand McNally, 1965.

[15] Klaman, Saul B. *The Postwar Residential Mortgage Market*. Princeton: Princeton University Press, 1961.

[16] Parkin, Michael. "Discount House Portfolio and Debt Selection." *Review of Economic Studies* 112 (October 1970).

[17] Silber, William L. "An Econometric Model of the Mortgage Market." In *Cyclical and Growth Problems Facings the Savings and Loan Industry*, A. W. Sametz, ed., Bulletin No. 46–47, Institute of Finance, New York University.

[18] Smith, Lawrence B. "A Model of the Canadian Housing and Mortgage Markets." *Journal of Political Economy* 77 (September/October 1969).

[19] Sparks, Gordon R. "An Econometric Analysis of the Role of Finanical Intermediaries in Postwar Residential Building Cycles." In *Determinants of Investment Behavior*. NBER, 1967.

[20] Sparks, Gordon R. "A Model of the Mortgage Market and Residential Construction Activity." Paper presented at the 1967 meetings of the American Statistical Association.

[21] Tinsley, Peter A. "Optimal Factor Adjustment Paths: A Generalization of 'Stock Adjustment' Decision Rules." Staff Economic Study, Board of Governors of the Federal Reserve System.

6 A Model of the Housing Sector

JOHN H. KALCHBRENNER

In recent years, renewed interest has been shown in attempts to explain residential construction activity. Perhaps the greatest stimulus to this interest was the adoption of the public policy goal of improvement of the demonstrably inadequate shelter available to lower income households in both rural and urban areas of the United States. The fundamental prerequisite to implementing such a policy is an understanding of the determinants of housing activity. Of particular concern in this area is the pronounced cyclical variability of new residential construction—a fact that poses problems for alleviating the longer-term structural housing problem and may have adverse implications for the efficient utilization of resources devoted to residential construction.

Appraisal of the many proposals offered as bases for public housing policy has been difficult in view of fundamental deficiencies in knowledge concerning the determinants of housing activity. Progress in removing these deficiencies has proven slower than desirable due to data inadequacies and the complexity of the processes involved in housing and related markets. Nevertheless, though students of housing remain unsatisfied with the current state of development of housing models, considerable progress has been made during the past decade. Differences in theoretical approaches have been specified and discussed, models have been estimated which track housing behavior reasonably well, and the areas of disagreement concerning empirical matters have been clarified.[1]

Initially, development of the housing sector of the FMP model reflected

The housing sector of the FMP model represents the work of numerous contributors over a period of several years. During this period, the principal contributors have been Gordon Sparks, Franco Modigliani, Frank de Leeuw, Edward Gramlich, and Albert Ando. It is impossible to disentangle their individual contributions, and those of numerous others, at this point. Nor is it possible to indicate points of disagreement any of the above might have concerning the current form of the sector. The present author, currently responsible for the housing sector, takes full responsibility for any misinterpretations in this paper of the contributions of those named above.

[1] For one critical discussion of current housing models, including the FMP model, see Fromm [3].

somewhat narrower considerations. As is well known by now, the FMP model represents an attempt to specify and estimate a structural model which would provide an explanation of the channels through which monetary policy affects the economy. Given the wide acceptance of the view that monetary policy plays a significant role in influencing short-term cyclical housing behavior, the housing sector was developed in greater detail than would have been required solely for consistency or prediction purposes in the overall model. The resulting sector, within its limitations, is directly relevant to the interest in housing problems per se which subsequently developed at the policy level.

In broad outline, the housing model includes relationships to explain single-family housing starts, multiple-family housing starts, total residential expenditures, and changes in the capital stock of housing. Included in the category "single-family" are one- and two-unit structures and mobile homes. For the present, greater attention has been paid to the factors which determine the demand for housing services than to the supply, or investment, determinants. Specification of the supply determinants remains somewhat rudimentary. A static model is used as a basis for the empirical relationships, with dynamic considerations incorporated largely in an ad hoc manner.

The principal demand component of the housing starts equation is the relationship between the demand for housing services and measures of income, population, and relative prices. This demand is treated conceptually as distinct from demand for houses as an investment asset. Since housing services are not observable directly, it is assumed that they are directly proportional to the existing stock of housing, thereby transforming the unobservable service flow demand into an observable stock demand. In this stock–demand relationship, one of the principal explanatory variables is the unobservable implicit rental price for the service flows. Observable variables are obtained by restating the housing stock demand equation as a price equation.

In addition, the equilibrium price of the housing stock is required in the model to determine residential investment behavior. But, it too is unobservable. The problem is circumvented in this instance by employing a cost-of-capital approach which permits stating the equilibrium price of the stock in terms of the implicit rental price and the housing cost of capital. The latter is defined to include both appropriate interest rates and tax provisions relating to housing.

In terms of actually initiating housing starts, the model relies upon the simple specification that builders respond to variations in the difference between the housing asset price and housing construction costs. The empirical equations are augmented by variables intended to reflect the existence of assumed credit rationing in housing markets and the growth in the scale of the economy over time.

Of the factors which alter the existing housing stock, only housing starts are estimated formally in the model. Depreciation is included as a constant proportion of the stock, while demolitions are ignored due to the absence of data. The additions and alterations rate is estimated in the model, but not as a function of economic variables. Lacking information about this variable and the appropriate specification of the current contribution of past uncompleted housing starts, an iterative scheme is employed to estimate this information in the housing expenditures "identity." Finally, changes in the housing stock are determined by an identity written in terms of housing completions, depreciation, and additions and alterations.

In operation, changes in prices or income affect the implicit rental price of housing services. Changes in the rental rate, given the housing cost of capital, then affect the asset price of housing. Changes in the latter, given construction costs, alter housing starts, which alter the housing stock with a lag. Finally, changes in the housing stock affect the rental price in a direction opposite to the initial change, eventually restoring equilibrium by means of a stock adjustment mechanism.

The data periods for the estimated equations begin with the earliest available necessary data. For multiple-family housing starts and housing expenditures, the data period begins in 1954:4. For single-family housing starts, the period begins in 1956:3. Data period endpoints reflect time constraints which did not permit estimating the entire sector at one time. Housing expenditures were estimated with data through 1968:4, multiple-family starts through 1969:3, and single-family starts through 1970:2.

The two housing starts equations were estimated in log form using ordinary least squares. The expenditure equation was estimated by an iterative procedure employing ordinary least squares at each step. Adjustment for serial correlation was made where appropriate using the Cochrane-Orcutt technique. Distributed lags were estimated using the Almon technique. All data are seasonally adjusted.

The remainder of this paper is organized in the following manner. In an attempt to improve clarity, the basic housing model is presented in its entirety, ignoring discussion of a number of matters related to data problems, dynamics, and disaggregation of housing markets. Following this, a detailed discussion of each of the estimated equations is presented. Included in this discussion are comments concerning the empirical results and some of their implications.

The Basic Housing Model

In this section, we present the basic housing model upon which the empirical equations in the FMP model are based. In order to provide a clear presentation of the fundamental nature of the model, certain simplifying steps are taken. The treatment is largely static, ignoring possible separations of the housing market into component parts. Discussion of most adjustment lags, the possibility of the existence of credit rationing, and a number of empirical problems is deferred until the following section.

The Demand for Housing Services

For purposes of analysis, a distinct separation between the demand for housing services and the demand for the stock of houses as an investment asset is made in the model. The demand for housing services is treated in the framework of the theory of consumer choice. Households are viewed as maximizing utility via choice from among the total array of consumption goods and services, with the demand for aggregate housing services in real terms assumed to depend upon permanent income, the price of housing services relative to the prices of all other goods and services, and population.

Since the flow of housing services is not an observable magnitude, this flow is taken to be proportional to the real value of the housing stock, a specification which ignores the possibility that this stock might be utilized more or less intensively. Further, the price of housing services is also not observable since the true measure includes the implicit rental price of owner-occupied housing. The latter problem is handled by substitution of the assumed determinants of the implicit rental price.

These considerations result in the following expression for the desired real per capita housing stock (desired quantity of housing services), given real per capita permanent income and prices:

$$\frac{K_H^*}{N} = e^{\alpha_0} \left(\frac{Y^p}{N}\right)^{\alpha_1} \left(\frac{P_R}{P_c}\right)^{-\alpha_2} \tag{6-1}$$

where

$\alpha_1, \alpha_2 > 0$
K_H^* = the desired stock of housing
N = population
Y^p = real permanent income
P_R = the implicit rental price index
P_c = the price index for other consumption goods

Given the large size of the existing stock of housing relative to short-run changes in the stock, the short-run stock of housing is taken to be fixed, with market clearing achieved via changes in the implicit rental price. Substituting the actual real housing stock, K_H, for the desired stock, and rewriting (6-1), yields the short-run market clearing solution for the implicit rent index.

$$P_R = e^{\alpha_0/\alpha_2} \left(\frac{K_H}{N}\right)^{-1/\alpha_2} \left(\frac{Y^p}{N}\right)^{\alpha_1/\alpha_2} P_c \qquad (6\text{-}2)$$

Housing Starts

With the exception of additions and alterations to the current real housing stock, housing starts can be viewed as gross investment in residential capital undertaken in the current period. As mentioned at the outset, in the model the decision to invest in residential capital is considered separately from the decision to consume the service flows from the capital stock. The housing starts relationship is treated in a cost-of-capital framework.

Institutionally, the housing market consists of builders who construct houses to be sold upon completion or during construction, and eventual owners who order houses constructed by builders. The decisions of the first group are based upon the prospective profitability of construction with account taken of the availability of mortgage financing for prospective purchasers.[2] The latter is important not only as one of the price components,. broadly construed, facing the purchasers, but also because builders are generally required to obtain permanent mortgage commitments prior to acquiring construction loans.

Prospective owners who initiate new construction should respond to a comparison of the cost of ownership of the durable housing asset, the implicit service flow, the cost of capital, and the cost of acquiring housing service flows from other housing capital owners.

Both of these sets of behavior can be incorporated into a single housing starts relationship based upon the following considerations. Market clearing for holders of the stock of housing requires that the cost of capital be equal to the ratio of the implicit rental price to the price of the housing stock, with allowance made for tax treatment. That is

$$R_H = \frac{P_R(1 - vt)}{P_H} \qquad (6\text{-}3)$$

---

[2] Attempts to include unsold inventories and vacancies in earlier versions of the model were unsuccessful and were dropped.

where

R_H = the cost of capital for housing
P_H = the price of housing
v = the proportion of rent which is taxable
t = the appropriate tax rate

In this expression, it is assumed that the cost of capital for housing should be a weighted average of the land and structure components of depreciation, capital gains, appropriate interest rates, and applicable tax rates.[3] Incorporating these factors, the basic expression for the cost of capital in the model is

$$R_H = (1 - wt)D + (1 - xt)R + (1 - yt)TP + (1 - zt)G \quad (6\text{-}4)$$

where

w, x, y, z = the proportion of each of the four component terms which is taxable or deductible from taxable income
D = the depreciation rate for housing
R = appropriate nominal interest rate(s)
TP = the effective property tax rate
G = expected capital gains
t = the appropriate income tax rate

Equation (6-3) contains two unobservable variables, P_R and P_H. Expressing (6-3) in terms of P_H, and substituting for P_R from (6-2), we have an expression for the price of housing in terms of observable variables.

$$P_H = \left(\frac{P_c}{R_H}\right) e^{\alpha_0/\alpha_2} \left(\frac{K_H}{N}\right)^{-1/\alpha_2} \left(\frac{Y^p}{N}\right)^{\alpha_1/\alpha_2} (1 - vt) \quad (6\text{-}5)$$

where R_H is given by equation (6-4), thus implying equilibrium in the market.

In the derivation of the implicit price of the existing real housing stock, the stock was treated as fixed in the short run. Three factors can alter the real stock: (i) depreciation and removals, (ii) additions and alterations, and (iii) new construction. In terms of relative importance to current economic activity, the latter is the factor of principal interest.

As the model currently stands, specification of the determinants of these factors remains rudimentary. Depreciation and additions and alterations are assumed to be constant proportions of the stock through time, and removals are not considered explicitly.[4] All attempts to include these components in a

---

[3] Equation (6-3) is based upon Jorgenson [5], pp. 45–46. The cost of capital is discussed more specifically in the following section; also, see de Leeuw and Gramlich [2], p. 474.

[4] The means of obtaining an estimate of the unavailable additions and alterations rate involves an iterative estimation process described in the following section.

more satisfactory manner in earlier versions of the model were unsuccessful.

The new construction, or housing starts, component of changes in the capital stock is based upon the cost-of-capital discussion above. Total new construction activity is assumed to respond to variations in the difference between the housing asset price and construction costs, defined to include labor, material, and financial costs. The demand equations in conjunction with the existing stock of housing determine the housing asset price (and the implicit rental price). Investment activity then responds directly to price variations, given construction costs.

During the development of the model, attempts were made to specify and estimate the growth in capacity of the construction industry as the economy grew. Failing this, a trend term is incorporated in the housing starts relationship which has the effect of enlarging the response of construction activity to the price–cost differential as the scale of the economy increases. These factors are combined to form the following housing starts equation:

$$\frac{HS\$/(N \cdot P_{HC})}{K_c e^{rt}} = e^{\beta_0} \left(\frac{P_H}{P_{HC}}\right)^{\beta_1} \tag{6-6}$$

where

$$\beta_1 > 0$$
$HS\$$ = value of housing starts
P_{HC} = the index of construction costs
$K_c e^{rt}$ = real per capita capacity of the housing industry[5]

Since P_H is unobservable, the empirical equation is obtained by substitution from (6-5) to form

$$\frac{HS\$/(N \cdot P_{HC})}{e^{rt}} = e^{\gamma_0} \left(\frac{P_c(1 - vt)}{R_H \cdot P_{HC}}\right)^{\gamma_1} \left(\frac{K_H}{N}\right)^{\gamma_2} \left(\frac{Y^p}{N}\right)^{\gamma_3} \tag{6-7}$$

where

$\gamma_1 = \beta_1 > 0$ the elasticity of housing starts with respect to the price ratio from (6-6), and the elasticity of housing starts with respect to the cost of capital

$\gamma_2 = -\beta_1/\alpha_2 < 0$ and $-\alpha_2$ is the elasticity of demand for housing stock with respect to the rental and consumer price indexes from (6-1)

---

[5] The quarterly rate of growth of real per capita capacity, r, is assumed to be 0.5 percent per quarter, a value consistent with growth of real full employment GNP of 4 percent per year.

$\gamma_3 = \beta_1\alpha_1/\alpha_2 > 0$ and α_1 is the elasticity of demand for the housing stock with respect to real per capita permanent income from (6-1)

As rewritten in (6-7) the arbitrary capacity constant has been incorporated into the constant term. In the regression equations discussed in the following section, various measures of credit rationing are added to this basic equation on the grounds that the interest terms included in the cost of capital understate the true cost of capital and fail to capture rationing in housing markets in the short run.

Housing Expenditures

In the model, the contribution to total current expenditures from residential construction activity is derived from housing starts and additions and alterations to the existing stock. Both current and lagged housing starts generate current expenditures since it takes longer than one quarter to complete housing units on average. Based upon this, we have:

$$EH\$ = \mathscr{L}HS\$ + aKH\$_{-1} \tag{6-8}$$

where

$EH\$$ = current dollar residential construction expenditures
$\mathscr{L}HS\$$ = contribution of current and lagged housing starts to current construction expenditures
a = the additions and alterations rate
$KH\$_{-1}$ = the current dollar value of the existing (i.e., beginning-of-quarter) housing stock
$\mathscr{L}$ = lag operator

Housing Stock

The final relationship in the basic housing model is an identity to update the existing capital stock to reflect losses due to depreciation, and additions from completed housing starts or additions and alterations to the current stock. In constant dollar terms:

$$K_H = (1 - D + a)K_{H-1} + \mathscr{L}HS \tag{6-9}$$

where D is the appropriate depreciation rate, and all other variables are as defined earlier.

Empirical Estimates of the Model

On the basis of the simplified model described above, we next turn to the empirical estimation of the housing sector. For estimation purposes, it is necessary to modify the basic model in several ways to reflect the realities of current housing and related markets. Essentially, there are three modifications: (i) the housing sector is divided into single-family and multiple-family components, (ii) attempts are made to include credit availability or rationing proxy variables, and (iii) certain unavailable data are approximated.

The housing sector is divided into two components to reflect important differences between the markets for single-family houses and multiple-family units. Among these differences are: (i) purchasers of multiple-family units are more likely to be institutional investors rather than owner-occupants of housing space—financing arrangements, tax treatment, and sources of financing differ between the two groups; (ii) the two stocks house different age groups; (iii) an inspection of housing starts data suggests that there was a shift in favor of multiple-family units on the part of consumers beginning in about 1958; and (iv) the two types of units differ in the average length of time required for construction.

Single-Family Housing Starts

The use of the term single-family housing starts is somewhat misleading and requires clarification. In the model, "single-family" units include single-family homes, two-unit structures, and mobile homes. Two-unit structures were included in this category due simply to the fact that single and double units are combined in the data, and there was no way of separating them before 1963.

The current treatment of mobile homes has shortcomings, but hopefully, it represents an interim improvement over previous treatment. In earlier versions of the FMP model, mobile-home expenditures were included as a part of consumption expenditures for durable goods since that is how they are treated in the National Income Accounts. The decision to move mobile homes to the housing sector was made on the basis of the recent very rapid growth of this form of housing. Since the end of World War II, mobile-home sales increased from an estimated annual sales volume of $146 million in 1947 to almost $2.5 billion in 1969, with rapid growth in the 1960s. A comparison of sales of new single-family homes with new mobile-home shipments for 1969 indicates that mobile homes account for almost the entire market under $15,000 and 48 percent of the total, regardless of price, on a unit basis.[6] Consequently, it was felt that mobile homes could no longer be ignored as an explicit component of the housing sector.

However, there are problems associated with attempting to deal with mobile homes explicitly. Foremost is the lack of a quarterly series for mobile homes expenditures. To obtain such a series an approximation was constructed based upon annual expenditure data from the Mobile Homes Manufacturers Association (MHMA) and the quarterly Office of Business Economics (OBE) data for Mobile Homes and Recreation Trailers.

The OBE data, which are at annual rates, were converted to quarterly rates and aggregated to obtain annual figures. The ratios of the MHMA and OBE annual values were then used to obtain interpolated quarterly ratios. These quarterly ratios were applied to the quarterly OBE data at annual rates to obtain the estimated series actually employed in the model. In effect, this adjustment is designed to remove recreational vehicles from the OBE series.

Treating mobile homes as an additive component of total single-family housing starts presents other problems. For example, this procedure ignores the fact that the purchase and financing terms for mobile homes differ considerably from those of conventional single-family dwellings. Until 1969, when savings and loan associations were authorized to finance mobile homes and the FHA was authorized to issue mortgage guarantees for their purchase, mobile homes were typically financed by means of a conditional sales contract with relatively short maturity, much like automobile financing. Sales finance companies typically purchased these contracts from mobile home dealers. More recently, in addition to savings and loan association participation, there have been indications of bank-owned real estate development company interest in financing mobile-home communities.

Other differences might be cited. But, the more important consideration at this stage of development of the model was whether or not the total of single-family, two-family, and mobile-home units could be explained adequately without further disaggregation. Although exploration of possible benefits of separation is desirable, it does not appear that ignoring substitution, financing differences, and other factors seriously affects our ability to explain this total.

Although the single-family housing starts equation is a relatively straight-forward estimation of (6-7), some comments are in order concerning the variables employed. The dependent variable is the log of real per capita single-family housing starts. The population variable employed as a deflator is the adult population most likely to live in single-family dwellings—the population

---

[6] *Flash Facts on Mobile Homes*, Mobile Homes Manufacturers Association, June 1970.

between ages 25 and 65, *NI*. The price deflator is the adjusted Boeckh index of housing construction costs.

The latter was adjusted to take into account increases in productivity, which are ignored in the construction of the index as published. The adjustment was accomplished by assuming growth in construction labor productivity of 3.2 percent, and applying this growth rate to the approximate ratio of labor costs to total costs (0.3) in the contract construction industry, derived from National Income Accounts data. This adjustment reduces the rate of growth of the Boeckh index of housing construction costs by .0025 per quarter.

On the right side of equation (6-7), permanent income is represented by the consumption variable in the FMP model, which includes estimates of the services added by the stocks of consumer durables and is less volatile than OBE consumption. The price series employed are the deflator for consumption in the numerator and the adjusted construction cost index in the denominator. The remaining component of the denominator, the single-family cost of capital, *RCHl*, is constructed as follows:

$$RCHl = (1 - T)(.7RM + .3RCB + .8TP) - 1.46 \qquad (6\text{-}10)$$

where

$$T = \text{the average federal personal income tax rate}$$
$$RM = \text{the mortgage rate}$$
$$RCB = \text{the AAA corporate bond rate}$$
$$TP = \text{the effective property tax rate}$$

This expression is the single-family housing equivalent of (6-4). For this portion of the housing market, the personal tax law allows deductions of interest costs and property taxes, but implicit rent is not taxable, capital gains are generally not taxable, nor is depreciation generally deductible. Consequently, v, w, and z from (6-3) and (6-4) are zero, while x and y are unity. The intercept then represents $(D - G)$.[7]

RM is employed as the direct cost of housing finance, while *RCB* is entered as an opportunity cost measure. The weights on these rates were derived from the average proportions of new mortgages financed by borrowing and own financing. Conceptually, these rates should reflect marginal conditions facing both those who do and those who do not purchase houses, but this information does not exist.

---

[7] The annual rates of depreciation are assumed to be 2.7 percent for houses and zero for land, based upon data in Goldsmith [4]. After unsuccessful attempts to estimate capital gains as a function of past rates of change of prices and other variables the capital gains rates are assumed to be 2 percent for houses and 10 percent for land, based upon the average rate of increase of house prices and fragmentary data on land prices. The weights for land and houses used in determining $(D - G)$ were .2 and .8 respectively.

TP was derived by dividing annual state and local indirect property taxes by the current dollar housing stock and interpolating quarterly. This figure is scaled by .8 to enlarge the denominator since the stock of houses does not include the value of land.

In the empirical equation, housing starts are assumed to respond to changes in the cost of capital with a distributed lag reflecting expectations, inertia, and the time required to initiate housing construction in response to changes in the price–cost differential.

The second term in equation (6-7) is represented by the real stock of single-family houses, *KH1*, deflated by the adult population measure, *N1*. This term is combined for estimation purposes with the proxy for real permanent income, *CON*, deflated by total population, *N*. Constraining the coefficients of these two terms to equality in absolute value assumes that the elasticity of demand for housing services with respect to real per capita permanent income is unity as shown in (6-7). This assumption is based both upon estimation problems and continuing uncertainty concerning the income elasticity in the literature.[8]

In addition to the variables included in (6.7), three other terms are added to the final equation as estimated. These terms are related to the dynamics of financial intermediary behavior, the mortgage market, and the housing market. As indicated in an earlier summary of the FMP model by de Leeuw and Gramlich [2], and elaborated in the other papers in this volume, these sectors exhibit characteristics that lead to the expectation of rationing.[9] Financial intermediary lending and deposit rates change slowly, deposit flows at these institutions are volatile, and there is little control over asset composition. In the mortgage market, the considerations related to the use of advance commitments and the high adjustment costs described by Jaffee in Chapter 5 make it unlikely that the mortgage market clears quarterly. All of these factors, plus the time required to complete new housing units, make it appear unlikely that the housing market is in equilibrium quarterly.

In an attempt to reflect these factors, the change in outstanding mortgage commitments of savings and loan associations ($MCOS/MCOS_{-1}$) is included in the equation.[10] This variable is intended as a proxy for the availability of permanent financing from financial intermediaries, given the assumption that the mortgage rate does not respond sufficiently to clear the mortgage market

---

[8] See de Leeuw [1].

[9] For a more complete description of the meaning of rationing as used here, see de Leeuw and Gramlich [2], p. 483.

[10] In earlier versions of the model, a measure of deposits flows at financial intermediaries was used in this capacity. See de Leeuw and Gramlich [2], p. 483. The logarithmic change in outstanding commitments is used rather than new commitments, the preferable variable, since no data series on the latter is available quarterly.

in the short run. The savings and loan value is used since these institutions are the principal intermediaries in single-family dwelling finance, and multi-collinearity problems plagued attempts to include commitments variables for other intermediaries.

This commitment variable is also intended to reflect the institutional requirement, usually imposed upon construction firms, that they obtain permanent financing commitments prior to obtaining construction loans. Further, in the discussion of (6-6), we defined construction costs to include labor, material, and financing costs. But, the Boeckh index includes only the first two, and there is no suitable variable in the overall FMP model to use for the third (the commercial loan rate would be the closest approximation). The commitment variable is, therefore, interpreted to incorporate this factor as well.

Several critics of the model have argued that a simultaneity problem is present in the use of commitments as an exogenous variable in the housing sector. It can be argued reasonably that the rate of change of commitments reflects interactive behavior of financial intermediaries and builders or purchasers of homes in the mortgage market. If, in fact, commitments are determined jointly by supply and demand, then a current commitment variable should not be treated as an exogenous variable in the housing sector. Two factors mitigate the force of this criticism. First, as explained by Jaffee, it is assumed that excess demand existed in the mortgage market during the period of estimation of the mortgage sector of the model. To the extent that this assumption is correct, commitment changes were determined by the financial intermediaries, and the current housing sector specification is appropriate. Secondly, commitments enter the housing starts equation with lags long enough to becalm any statistical fears of serious simultaneity.

A second additional variable reflecting many of the same considerations is intended to reflect the increased importance of the Federal National Mortgage Association (FNMA) activities in the mortgage market. In the absence of an historical series for FNMA commitments, the arithmetic difference in the stock of mortgages held by FNMA ($\Delta ZMFN$) is currently added to the saving and loan commitment variable to form the availability proxy. The difference in the stock of mortgages held is employed to accord approximately with the commitments stage of the mortgage market. The complete credit availability proxy therefore becomes $(MCOS + \Delta ZMFN)/ (MCOS + \Delta ZMFN)_{-1}$.[11]

---

[11] Attempts were made initially to include the FNMA variable separately without success. In the early part of the data period, FNMA operations were a small factor in the housing sector, but they exhibited large percentage variations which did not correspond closely to housing variations. Combining this variable with the relatively larger commitments variable moderated the early-period large-percentage changes while allowing the growth in importance of FNMA to enter later in the period.

The final additional variable in the single-family housing starts equation represents an attempt to measure ability to meet downpayment requirements, and was suggested by Jared Enzler. The main intent was to devise a variable that would capture personal saving and capital gains on nonphysical assets on the grounds that these accruals could be redistributed into housing. Capital gains on physical assets were excluded in the belief that it was unlikely that quarterly capital gains on these assets would be available readily to use for down payments.

The variable used for this purpose is current household net worth less price changes for the housing stock and the stock of consumer durables, with each of the latter scaled by the appropriate stock. For the housing component, the change in the nominal value of the stock can be expressed as

$$P_t K_t - P_{t-1} K_{t-1} = P \Delta K + K_{-1} \Delta P$$

The first term represents the current addition to the stock of houses, while the second is capital gains on the existing stock. The latter term for both housing and consumer durables is subtracted from current total household net worth V.

In the model, the housing stock is measured at the end of the quarter, but housing prices are measured at mid-quarter. Hence, the price of the existing stock in the current quarter, $KH1_{-1}$, is $(PEH + PEH_{-1})/2$. The relevant capital gains term is then

$$KH1_{-2} \left(\frac{PEH - PEH_{-2}}{2} \right)$$

and similarly for consumer durables. The appropriate complete current-period variable, allowing for consumer durables, is then:

$$V - KH1_{-2} \left(\frac{PEH - PEH_{-2}}{2} \right) - KCD_{-2} \left(\frac{PCD - PCD_{-2}}{2} \right)$$

To measure the change in capital gains on nonphysical assets and savings between the current quarter and the past quarter logarithmically, this variable is expressed as a ratio to V_{-1}. To simplify the notation this ratio is referred to as W.

Both of these credit availability proxy variables are included in the estimated equation with distributed lags to reflect the slow adjustment to equilibrium anticipated in housing and related markets. Since the variables are entered in the form of changes, they have no effect upon the steady-state properties of the model.

Incorporating all of these modifications, the estimated single-family housing starts equation is:

$$\ln\left(\frac{HSI\$}{NI \cdot PHCA}\right) - .005TIME = c_0 + c_1\left[\ln\left(\frac{CON}{N}\right) - \ln\left(\frac{KHI}{NI}\right)_{-1}\right]$$

$$+ \sum w_i \ln\left(\frac{P}{PHCA \cdot RCHI}\right)_{-i}$$

$$+ \sum w_j' \ln\left(\frac{MCOS + \Delta ZMFN}{MCOS_{-1} + \Delta ZMFN_{-1}}\right)_{-j}$$

$$+ \sum w_k'' \ln W_{-k} \qquad\qquad (6\text{-}11)$$

where in addition to the variables already defined

CON = consumption
P = price deflator for consumption
$PHCA$ = adjusted construction cost index

The empirical results for the single-family housing starts equation are shown as equation (6A-1) in chapter Appendix 6A. As indicated by the summary statistics, the equation fits well over the sample period. And, although serial correlation was present in the equation estimated without the lagged error term, the estimated ρ term, 0.55, is not exceptionally large.

In terms of the elasticities discussed in the specification of equation (6-7), the estimated steady state elasticity of housing starts with respect to prices and the cost of capital, $\hat{\gamma}_1$, is 0.95. From either $\hat{\gamma}_2$ or $\hat{\gamma}_3$, the estimated elasticity of demand for housing services with respect to the rental and consumer price indexes is -1.27. This estimate is based upon the assumption of unitary elasticity of demand for housing services with respect to permanent income, and, from (6-1) that the short-run supply of housing services is fixed. It lies within the range of relative price demand elasticities for renters of -0.7 to -1.5 found by de Leeuw [1] using cross-sectional data.

The signs of the individual weights in the distributed lag on the relative-price–cost-of-capital term are positive for the current and earlier three quarters, and negative for the two quarters earliest in time. Further, the weights on current and recent past relative price and interest rate variables are relatively large, and the estimated total lag is short. This implies regressive expectations, or expectations of a return to earlier levels, which leads to rapid postponements in response to adverse relative price or interest movements.[12]

Both of the credit availability proxy variables have the expected sign and are statistically significant, but the length and pattern of the lags on W leads to some suspicion that W captures more than the ability to meet downpayment requirements. Taken at face value, these two variables imply that credit rationing plays a large role in determining single-family residential construction activity in the short run. The large value for $\sum w_k''$, the total impact effect of changes in the constructed net worth variable, caused initial concern. But, since the lag is relatively long and W shows relatively large variability, in any given quarter the impact of current and past W is not so great as the weight sum value of 11.2 suggests. A mixture of negative and positive W tends to moderate the quarter-by-quarter impact of W on the dependent variable.

Nevertheless, it appears that the lag on W is too long. In the limited experience outside the sample period, the actual housing starts turning points have preceded predicted turning points. This appears to be attributable to the relatively large weights on W several quarters back in time.

Two final matters related to this equation should be discussed before moving on. First, since single-family and multiple-family housing have been separated in the model, the cross-price term would be expected to enter each of the component equations. An explicit rental price variable is available in the form of the CPI rental index, and this index is based primarily upon the rental prices of multiple-family units as here defined. However, this index is extremely "sticky," and all attempts to enter this variable or the multiple-family stock were unsuccessful.

Second, the current single-family cost of capital expression implies static price expectations with nominal rather than real interest rates appearing in the equation. Given the inflationary conditions in the economy since the latter part of the 1960s, this assumption did not appear plausible. Several attempts were made to incorporate price expectations explicitly, but none were successful. Work to remedy this deficiency is continuing.

---

[12] A similar response was reported by de Leeuw and Gramlich [2] with respect to the cost of capital in an earlier version of the housing sector. But, that earlier version allowed separate distributed lags on relative prices and the cost of capital, and the distributed lag for relative prices indicated extrapolative expectations, or expectations of further changes in the direction of currently observed changes. Attempts to allow similar flexibility in the current version of the model, after making the indicated modifications and using a longer estimation period, were unsuccessful. The finding of regressive expectations for relative prices, in particular, would appear suspect in the current version.

Multiple Family Housing Starts

The explanation of multiple-family housing starts has proven to be a far more intractable problem than that of explaining single-family starts. To date, all of the versions of the multiple-family starts equation in the model have been disappointing both in terms of goodness of fit and predictive performance.

Given the derivation of the basic housing starts equation, the multiple-family starts equation should be less complex than the single-family equation. From (6-3), the price of multiple-family units is the ratio of the multiple-family rental price to the appropriately defined multiple-family cost of capital. The multiple-family version of (6-6) is then:

$$\frac{HS3\$/(N3 \cdot PHCA)}{K_c e^{rt}} = e^{\beta_0}\left(\frac{PR3}{PHCA \cdot RCH3}\right)^{\beta_1} \tag{6-12}$$

where

$HS3\$$ = value of multiple-family housing starts
$N3$ = the population expected to live in multiple-family units: the population aged 20–25 and those 65 and older
$PR3$ = the implicit deflator for rent in the consumer price index
$RCH3$ = the multiple-family unit cost of capital (defined below)
$K_c e^{rt}$ = the same measure of capacity growth employed in the single-family housing starts equation (6-6)

This basic equation, with the addition of a logistic trend term and a credit rationing variable, appeared in the version of the housing model reported earlier by de Leeuw and Gramlich [2]. But, during the large-scale reestimation of the FMP model, necessitated by NIA data revisions in 1969, a number of changes were made. First, the price variable was not significant using the rental component of the CPI, with the problem stemming from the stickiness of that index. As a consequence, the substitution process for P_R employed in equation (6-5) was adopted. The principal effect of the substitution process is to replace the rental index by the overall consumer price index, permanent income, and the lagged stock of multiple-family units.

The second problem is more serious. During the reestimation process, the multiple-family unit cost of capital variable yielded the incorrect sign and was not significant in the starts equation whether entered separately or combined with the price ratio. Consequently, the cost of capital was deleted from the equation, with the result that interest rates do not currently affect multiple-family housing starts directly in the model. This is clearly an unsatisfactory specification which will require additional work to improve the treatment of the cost of capital in the future.[13]

Two commitments variables are added to the multiple-family starts equation as proxy variables for credit rationing on much the same grounds as discussed above with respect to single-family starts. In this equation, both the change in outstanding commitments of mutual savings banks and new commitments of life insurance companies are included separately.

Finally, a dummy variable is included for the four quarters of 1966. This variable was included to reduce the impact of the 1966 "credit crunch" on the estimated coefficients of the commitments variables due to the sharp divergence of the data from normal variability during that year.

The complete multiple-family starts equation is

$$\ln\left(\frac{HS3\$}{PHCA \cdot N3}\right) - .005TIME = d_0 + d_1\left[\ln\left(\frac{CON}{N}\right) - \ln\left(\frac{KH3}{N3}\right)_{-1}\right]$$

$$+ \sum w_i \ln\left(\frac{P}{PHCA}\right)_{-i}$$

$$+ \sum w'_j \ln\left(\frac{MCOM}{MCOM_{-1}}\right)_{-j}$$

$$+ \sum w''_k \ln MCNI_{-k} + d_2Q \qquad (6\text{-}13)$$

where the newly introduced variables are

$HS3\$$ = multiple-family unit housing starts in value terms
$N3$ = the population aged 20–25 and 65 and older
$KH3$ = stock of multiple-family housing, 1958 dollars
$MCOM$ = outstanding mortgage commitments of mutual savings banks
$MCNI$ = new mortgage commitments of life insurance companies

$$Q = \begin{cases} .5 \text{ in } 1966:3, \ 1967:2 \\ 1.0 \text{ in } 1966:4, \ 1967:1 \\ 0 \text{ otherwise} \end{cases}$$

---

[13] The current multiple-family cost of capital is similar to that for single-family units. The weights on the mortgage rate and the corporate bond rate differ, reflecting the larger average proportion of such units financed by borrowing. The parameters v, x, y, and z are equal to unity, and w is greater than unity to reflect accelerated depreciation provisions. The complete expression is

$$RCH3 = .95RM + .05RCB + .8TP - 2.79$$

The constant term represents $[(1 - wt)/(1 - t)]D - G$, with D and G defined as in footnote 7. The appropriate income tax rate, t, here is assumed to be a weighted average of personal and corporate tax rates with a value of .33; and w is assumed to equal 2 to reflect the double rate declining balance provision afforded multiple-family unit owners except for a short time in late 1966 and early 1967.

The empirical results for the multiple-family housing starts equation are shown as equation (6A-2) in chapter Appendix 6A. Although the equation differs in several respects from the earlier version reported by de Leeuw and Gramlich [2], the summary statistics do not differ greatly. R^2 is improved in the current version from .931 to .963, and the standard error decreased from .098 in the earlier version to .091. Serial correlation is indicated in the results, with an estimated coefficient of .808 using the Cochrane-Orcutt adjustment technique.

According to the results, the elasticity of housing starts with respect to the relative price term is a high 7.51. From this, and the imposition of unitary elasticity of housing services demand with respect to permanent income, the implied elasticity of demand for housing services with respect to relative prices is an algebraically large -2.44, which lies outside the range of the relative price demand elasticity for renters of -0.7 to -1.5 found by de Leeuw [1]. Unlike the single-family starts equation results, the distributed lag of relative prices does not suggest either extrapolative or regressive relative price expectations.

The two credit-availability proxy variables yield results which accord with expectations concerning sign, but the distributed lag on new commitments of life insurance companies is not statistically significant. Without the dummy variable, Q, both of these proxy variables showed greater explanatory power, but it was felt that the estimated weights were distorted by the "credit crunch" experience. For the present, the issue was resolved by opting to include both the dummy variable and the insignificant insurance commitment variable in order to improve the predictive tracking of the equation.

It is apparent from this discussion that the model does not capture multiple-family housing starts behavior in a very satisfactory manner. In addition to the specific estimation difficulties described above, this equation has tended to drift badly outside the sample period for all of the versions that have been employed to date. Consequently, the current equation is viewed essentially as a stop-gap measure to be discarded as soon as time permits further work in this area.

Expenditures on Housing

Determination of the current expenditures on housing is complicated only by the problem of specifying additions and alterations to the existing stock. As indicated by equation (6-8), housing expenditures in the model are a weighted sum of current and lagged combined housing starts, plus additions and alterations to the existing nominal stock.

Edward Gramlich devised the method currently used to obtain an estimate of a, the additions and alterations rate, employing a three-step iterative procedure.[14] The procedure is based upon the following relationships:

$$EH\$ = \sum_j w_j(HS1\$ + HS3\$)_{-j} + a(KH1\$ + KH3\$)_{-1} \quad (6\text{-}14)$$

$$(KH1 + KH3)_{-1} = (1 - D + a)(KH1 + KH3)_{-2}$$
$$+ (\sum w_j)(HS1_{-2} + \tfrac{2}{3}HS3_{-3} + \tfrac{1}{3}HS3_{-4}) \quad (6\text{-}15)$$

These two relationships are simply restatements of (6-8) and (6-9) respectively, in the specific notation of the model.[15] As shown, the housing stock inventory updating relationship is in real terms in the model. In the last term of (6-15), $\sum w_j$ is constrained to be the same as in (6-14) for reasons indicated below. The specific lags and proportions imposed upon the housing starts variables in parentheses were derived from Census data which indicated that an average of one quarter is required to build a single-family unit, and multifamily completions are distributed approximately between two and three quarters after construction begins.

It is not possible to estimate (6-14) directly to obtain empirical estimates of the w_j and a, since the capital stock required in the last term is not available without an estimate of a, as shown in (6-15). An iterative scheme was chosen to obtain estimates of both the w_j and a.

Multiplying (6-15) by PEH_{-1}, the lagged price index for housing expenditures, and employing a back-substitution process, the expression can be rewritten as:

$$PEH_{-1}(KH1 + KH3)_{-1} = (\sum w_j)\left[\sum_{i=0}^{\infty} (1 - D + a)^i PEH_{-1-i}(HS1_{-2-i}\right.$$
$$\left. + \tfrac{2}{3}HS3_{-3-i} + \tfrac{1}{3}HS3_{-4-i})\right] \quad (6\text{-}16)$$

Substituting this expression for the nominal housing stock into (6-14) yields:

$$EH\$ = \sum_j w_j(HS1\$ + HS3\$)_{-j} + a(\sum w_j)\left[\sum_{i=0}^{\infty} (1 - D + a)^i PEH_{-1-i}\right.$$
$$\times (HS1_{-2-i} + \tfrac{2}{3}HS3_{-3-i}$$
$$\left. + \tfrac{1}{3}HS3_{-4-i})\right] \quad (6\text{-}17)$$

---

[14] Conceptually, additions and alterations would be expected to vary with economic conditions rather than remaining a constant fraction of the stock. Lack of data and a desire to avoid the addition of further equations to the model led to the current method of treatment.

[15] In the overall model, mobile homes expenditures are subtracted from single-family housing starts prior to determining housing expenditures. These expenditures are added back into the model in the consumption sector to preserve consistency.

Lagging this expression by one quarter and multiplying by $(1 - D + a)$ yields:

$$(1 - D + a)EH\$_{-1}$$

$$= (1 - D + a)\left[\sum_j w_j(HS1\$ + HS3\$)_{-j}\right]_{-1} + a(\sum w_j)$$

$$\times \left[\sum_{i=1}^{\infty} (1 - D + a)^i PEH_{-1-i}(HS1_{-2-i} + \tfrac{2}{3}HS3_{-3-i} + \tfrac{1}{3}HS3_{-4-i})\right]$$

$$(6\text{-}18)$$

Rewritten in terms of the infinite sum, (6-18) yields an observable expression which is substituted into (6-17) to form:

$$EH\$ - (1 - D + a)EH\$_{-1}$$

$$= \sum_j w_j[(HS1\$ + HS3\$)_{-j} - (1 - D + a)(HS1\$ + HS3\$)_{-j-1}]$$

$$+ a(\sum w_j)PEH_{-1}(HS1_{-2} + \tfrac{2}{3}HS3_{-3} + \tfrac{1}{3}HS3_{-4}) \qquad (6\text{-}19)$$

In the last term of this expression, real housing starts are multiplied by the price deflator used to obtain additions to the capital stock, PEH. This is appropriate since PEH is the price deflator for housing completions (here represented by lagged starts) in the determination of final expenditures. In the actual estimation, there is a minor inconsistency. Lagged nominal housing starts should be deflated by the corresponding $PHCA$ value to obtain real housing starts. The weighted sum of the real starts should then be multiplied by PEH_{-1}. Instead, the nominal lagged values are used. The effect is negligible primarily due to the small magnitude of the coefficient a which multiplies the entire term, the weights imposed on the lagged starts, and the relative stability of the deflator over short time periods.

From these expressions, (6-14) is used to estimate the $\hat{w}_j$, ignoring the capital stock component in the first iteration. The second step involves assuming that $a = D$ in (6-19), and estimating $\hat{a}$, imposing the $\sum \hat{w}_j$ from the first iteration. The final iteration involves a reestimation of (6-19) in which $\hat{a}$ from the second step is imposed only in the term $(1 - D + a)$, using the estimate of D from Goldsmith (.0065 per quarter). The final values which emerge from this process are:

$$\hat{w}_1 = 0.3202 \qquad \hat{a} = .0035$$
$$\hat{w}_2 = 0.6081$$
$$\hat{w}_3 = 0.1298$$
$$\sum \hat{w} = 1.0581$$

The final result is shown as equation (6A-3) in the chapter appendix.

The Stock of Houses

The final relationships in the housing sector are the expressions for the real single-family and multifamily housing stocks. As indicated earlier, the expressions employed in the model are based directly upon (6-15), using the estimates of $(1 - D + a)$ and $\sum w_j$ from the iteration procedure, but separating the total stock by housing type.

Since the two housing stock components are expressed in 1958 dollars in (6-15), real completions of houses are required. Real completions are obtained from lagged nominal starts deflated by the final housing expenditures deflator, *PEH*. This differs from the deflator used in the starts equation, *PHCA*, since starts are measured in terms of construction costs while final sales include value added during construction. This difference, minor for the purpose at hand, plus elements of uncertainty concerning the comparability of the starts and stock data series used in the model, led to the estimation of the weights for housing starts in the expenditures equation and the imposition of the sum of these weights in the stock equation. The housing stock expressions are shown as equations (6A-4) and (6A-5) in the chapter appendix.

**Appendix 6A:
Estimated Equations
for the Housing Sector**

Table 6A. Housing Sector Equations, Estimated Coefficients

Equations	$\bar{R}^2E$	SE	$\bar{R}^2U$	SU	DW
Housing Starts of Single-Family Housing					
(6A-1)	.935	.0428			2.19
		Sample = 1956:3 to 1970:2			
Housing Starts of Multiple-Family Housing					
(6A-2)	.9632	.0909	.8991	.1504	2.01
		Sample = 1954:4 to 1969:3			

Housing Starts of Single-Family Housing

(6A-1)
$$\ln \frac{HSI\$}{N1 \cdot PHCA} - .005TIME = 1.21 + .751\left[\ln\frac{CON}{N} - \ln\left(\frac{KHI}{N1}\right)_{-1}\right]$$
$$(4.4) \quad (1.1)$$
$$+ \sum_{i=0}^{5} b_i \ln\left(\frac{P}{PHCA \cdot RCHI}\right)_{-i}$$
$$+ \sum_{i=0}^{5} c_i \ln\left(\frac{MCOS + \Delta ZMFN}{MCOS_{-1} + \Delta ZMFN_{-1}}\right)_{-i}$$
$$+ \sum_{i=0}^{7} d_i \ln W_{-i} + .545 U_{-1}$$

$b_0 = .7566$ (2.56)
$b_1 = .3882$ (3.33)
$b_2 = .1168$ (2.52)
$b_3 = -.0577$ (−0.56)
$b_4 = -.1354$ (−1.11)
$b_5 = -.1162$ (−1.32)
$\Sigma b_i = .9523^{a}$

$c_0 = .1937$ (3.72)
$c_1 = .1716$ (3.74)
$c_2 = .1454$ (2.97)
$c_3 = .1152$ (2.33)
$c_4 = .0808$ (1.91)
$c_5 = .0425$ (1.62)
$\Sigma c_i = .7492^{a}$

$d_0 = 1.5174$ (2.47)
$d_1 = 1.6927$ (3.73)
$d_2 = 1.7637$ (4.21)
$d_3 = 1.7304$ (3.89)
$d_4 = 1.5928$ (3.45)
$d_5 = 1.3510$ (3.10)
$d_6 = 1.0050$ (2.84)
$d_7 = 0.5546$ (2.65)
$\Sigma d_i = 11.2031^{b}$

Housing Starts of Multiple-Family Housing

(6A-2)
$$\ln \frac{HS3\$}{N3 \cdot PHCA} - .005TIME = 3.43 + 3.08\left[\ln\frac{CON}{N} - \ln\left(\frac{KH3}{N3}\right)_{-1}\right]$$
$$(13.5) \quad (4.6)$$
$$+ \sum_{i=0}^{3} b_i \ln\left(\frac{P}{PHCA}\right)_{-i}$$
$$+ \sum_{i=0}^{5} c_i \ln\left(\frac{MCOM}{MCOM_{-1}}\right)_{-i}$$

$$+ \sum_{i=0}^{5} d_i \ln MCNI_{-i} - .547Q + .808U_{-1}$$
$$(3.8)$$

$b_0 = 1.6753 \ (1.0583)$	$c_0 = 0.2725 \ (1.6244)$	$d_0 = -.0342 \ (-0.3195)$
$b_1 = 2.2521 \ (3.8013)$	$c_1 = 0.3050 \ (2.0639)$	$d_1 = .0206 \ (0.3550)$
$b_2 = 2.1651 \ (2.1799)$	$c_2 = 0.3063 \ (1.9216)$	$d_2 = .0558 \ (1.3129)$
$b_3 = 1.4144 \ (1.6020)$	$c_3 = 0.2765 \ (1.7039)$	$d_3 = .0713 \ (1.4962)$
$\Sigma b_i = 7.5069^c$	$c_4 = 0.2155 \ (1.5414)$	$d_4 = .0672 \ (1.4279)$
	$c_5 = 0.1233 \ (1.4270)$	$d_5 = .0434 \ (1.3620)$
	$\Sigma c_i = 1.4992^a$	$\Sigma d_i = .2242^a$

$$Q = \begin{cases} 0.5 \text{ in } 1966{:}3, 1967{:}2 \\ 1.0 \text{ in } 1966{:}4, 1967{:}1 \\ 0 \text{ otherwise} \end{cases}$$

.119   2.74

Sample = 1954:2 to 1968:4

Expenditures on Residential Construction

(6A-3) $EH\$ = .320(HSI\$ + HS3\$) + .608(HSI\$ + HS3\$)_{-1}$ .810

$\qquad\quad$ (5.9) $\qquad\qquad\qquad\qquad$ (10.8)

$\qquad\quad + .130(HSI\$ + HS3\$)_{-2}$

$\qquad\quad$ (2.30)

$\qquad\quad + .004(HSI\$_{-2} + .67HS3\$_{-3} + .33HS3\$_{-4})$

$\qquad\quad$ (1.0)

$\qquad\quad + .997[EH\$_{-1} - .32(HSI\$ + HS3\$)_{-1}$

$\qquad\qquad\quad - .608(HSI\$ + HS3\$)_{-2} - .130(HSI\$ - HS3\$)_{-3}]$

Stock of Single-Family Houses

(6A-4) $KH1 = 1.06\left(\dfrac{HSI\$}{PEH}\right)_{-1} + .997KH1_{-1}$

Stock of Multiple-Family Houses

(6A-5) $KH3 = 1.06\left[.67\left(\dfrac{HS3\$}{PEH}\right)_{-2} + .33\left(\dfrac{HS3\$}{PEH}\right)_{-3}\right] + .997KH3_{-1}$

Note: The t statistics are in parentheses below or beside coefficients.

a Second degree polynomial, constrained to zero at $t - 6$.
b Second degree polynomial, constrained to zero at $t - 8$.
c Second degree polynomial constrained to zero at $t - 4$.

References

[1] de Leeuw, Frank. "The Demand for Housing: A Review of Cross-Section Evidence." *Review of Economics and Statistics* 53 (February 1971).

[2] de Leeuw, Frank, and Edward Gramlich. "The Channels of Monetary Policy." *Federal Reserve Bulletin* 55 (June 1969).

[3] Fromm, Gary. "Econometric Models of the Residential Construction Sector: A Comparison." Forthcoming in *National Housing Models*. Heath-Lexington, 1972.

[4] Goldsmith, Raymond. *The National Wealth of the United States in the Postwar Period*. Princeton: Princeton University Press, 1962.

[5] Jorgenson, Dale. "Anticipations and Investment Behavior." In J. Duesenberry, et al., (eds.). *The Brookings Quarterly Econometric Model of the United States*. Chicago: Rand McNally, 1965.

[6] Mobile Homes Manufacturing Association, *Flash Facts on Mobile Homes* (June 1970).

7 The Behavior of the Three Sectors Together

EDWARD M. GRAMLICH AND DWIGHT M. JAFFEE

We can now combine the savings deposit, mortgage, and housing sectors to see how the three sectors interact with each other. In this chapter we present a brief summary of the structure of the three sectors, we illustrate the long-run tracking behavior of the sectors, and we describe some multiplier simulation experiments. The multiplier simulations demonstrate the behavior of the three sectors together and determine the quantitative importance of various relationships including the three-sector partial derivatives. They also enable us to evaluate the impact of various policy measures on the three sectors.

Summary of the Model

Savings Deposits

Both versions of the savings deposit sector begin with the identity

$$A_i = a_i V \tag{7-1}$$

where A_i is the appropriate savings deposit asset (non-CD time deposits, savings and loan deposits, mutual savings bank deposits, or life insurance reserves) and V is a concept of net worth. In the Gramlich–Hulett version, V is net worth less prior claims (real capital stocks and money), which means that households have a two-stage decision process and allocate only their unclaimed net worth to savings deposits. In the Modigliani version, V is simply total net worth. The advantage of the prior claim procedure is that if some assets, say real capital stocks and money, are in fact determined before other residual assets, and if they have mathematical forms which are dissimilar to the forms for savings deposits, the two-stage procedure enables one to develop an internally consistent portfolio allocation scheme for all assets and liabilities in net worth.[1] The disadvantage is that if household

---

[1] As an example of the differing mathematical forms, the FMP model explains both stocks of consumer durables and houses by quasi-identities based on past real expenditures, whereas the stock of money is best explained by a logarithmic relationship based on current income and interest rates. It would be virtually impossible to aggregate these diverse expressions without the notion of prior claims.

235

allocation decisions are made simultaneously, the equations are being estimated subject to an inappropriate prior restriction.

In terms of dynamic reactions, both savings deposit versions assume that there is a relatively quick adjustment of deposits to increments in net worth coming from current saving, a more delayed adjustment to increments in net worth in the form of capital gains, and a still more delayed adjustment to changes in interest rates. In the Gramlich–Hulett version, this dynamic structure is represented by making a_i a negative function of recent capital gains along with own and competing interest rates:

$$a_i = f\left(r_i, r_j, \frac{CG}{V}\right) \tag{7-2}$$

where CG refers to recent capital gains, r_i to the own asset rate, and r_j to competing asset rates.

The Modigliani version elaborates on these dynamic relationships. Modigliani first decomposes changes in savings deposit assets into one term representing the asset widening increase as net worth rises and another term representing the asset deepening increase or decrease as rates change:

$$\Delta A = a_{-1}\Delta V + V_{-1}\Delta a \tag{7-3}$$

The increase in net worth is then decomposed into a personal saving component and a capital gains component,

$$\Delta A = a_{-1}(SP + mCG) + V_{-1}\Delta a \tag{7-4}$$

which reflects the fact that only a proportion, m, of current capital gains is immediately reflected in higher savings deposits. Modigliani proceeds to substitute the partial adjustment mechanism

$$\Delta a = g(a^* - a_{-1}), \qquad a^* = f(r_i, r_j) \tag{7-5}$$

into equation (7-4) to capture the long lag on interest rates.

There are also other variables that enter into the determination of savings deposits. Both Gramlich–Hulett and Modigliani find current income (deflated by net worth) an important explanatory variable—in Gramlich–Hulett this variable raises all savings deposits at the expense of other nonliquid assets; whereas in Modigliani it raises time deposits greatly, reduces savings and loan and mutual savings bank deposits, and also reduces other nonliquid assets. In addition, both versions have a nonlinear time trend representing the rapid secular growth of savings and loan deposits over the estimation period—in Gramlich–Hulett at the expense of nonliquid assets, in Modigliani at the expense of mutual savings bank deposits.

The basic allocation structure is also different for the two sectors. Gramlich–Hulett specify each of the four assets in the form of (7-2), add the income and time trend variables, and estimate

$$\frac{MTP}{V} = a_1 = f_1\left(r_1, r_j, \frac{CG}{V}, \frac{YD}{V}\right)$$

$$\frac{MSL}{V} = a_2 = f_2\left(r_2, r_j, \frac{CG}{V}, \frac{YD}{V}, \frac{1}{TIME}\right)$$

$$\frac{MMS}{V} = a_3 = f_3\left(r_3, r_j, \frac{CG}{V}, \frac{YD}{V}\right)$$

$$\frac{MIS}{V} = a_4 = f_4\left(r_4, r_j, \frac{CG}{V}, \frac{YD}{V}\right)$$

(7-6)

The estimating equations are similar for all assets and are estimated simultaneously to insure that substitution effects are the same across all assets (that is, that $\partial a_j/\partial r_i = \partial a_i/\partial r_j$ for all four pairs).

The Modigliani sector separates the allocation decision as follows. The estimating equation for time deposits is derived by combining (7-5) with (7-4), again inserting the income variable, and scaling by net worth.[2]

$$\frac{\Delta MP}{V} = h_1\left(a_{1-1}\frac{SP}{V}, a_{1-1}\frac{CG}{V}, a_{1-1}, F_1[r_1, r_j], \frac{YD}{V}\right)$$

$$\frac{\Delta(MSL + MMS)}{V} = h_2\left(a_{2-1}\frac{SP}{V}, a_{2-1}\frac{CG}{V}, a_{2-1}, F_2[r_2, r_3, r_j], \frac{YD}{V}\right)$$

(7-7)

These two equations, for time deposits and the sum of savings and loan mutual savings deposits, are estimated simultaneously to preserve the cross-substitution effects between r and a combination rate made up by weighting r_2 and r_3, and to give the same coefficient for capital gains, m, the same speed of adjustment for interest rates, g, and the same coefficient for current personal saving.

The partition equation between savings and loan and mutual savings bank deposits is developed in the same manner, though by omitting the capital

---

[2] Modigliani's savings deposit variable, MP, refers to all commercial banks and is not seasonally adjusted.

gains and income terms, moving the first independent variable to the left side, and including the aforementioned nonlinear time trend

$$\frac{\Delta MSL - a'_{2_{-1}} \Delta(MSL + MMS)}{MSL + MMS} = h'_2(a'_{2_{-1}}, F_2[r_2, r_3], TIME, TIME^2)$$

$$\frac{\Delta MMS - a'_{3_{-1}} \Delta(MSL + MMS)}{MSL + MMS} = h'_3(a'_{3_{-1}}, F_3[r_3, r_2], TIME, TIME^2)$$

$$(7\text{-}8)$$

Although only the first of these equations was actually estimated, the speed of adjustment, cross-substitution effect, and time trend implicitly apply to mutual savings bank deposits as well.

Finally, Modigliani explains life insurance reserves through the following entirely separate equation:

$$\frac{\Delta MIS}{CON} = h_4 \left(\frac{MIS_{-1}}{CON}, r_4, r_j, \frac{OASI}{CON} \right) \qquad (7\text{-}9)$$

implying that life insurance reserves are positively related to permanent consumption, CON; negatively related to interest rates and a credit rationing term; and negatively related to $OASI$, Federal social security payments over the period.[3]

The Gramlich–Hulett version (7-6) finds that asset proportions depends on all internal rates (r_1 through r_4) and on the long-term bond rate (for savings and loan deposits), the bill rate (for time deposits), and on the rate of inflation (for savings and loan and life insurance reserves). The latter term measures the tradeoff between savings deposits and common stock. Since real assets and money were omitted by assumption from the definition of net worth, there is no tradeoff between savings deposits and these assets.

Modigliani separates the estimation period into two subperiods, corresponding roughly to the introduction of certificates of deposits at commercial banks. Though only consumer CDs are included in the time deposit dependent variable (large CDs are omitted by assumption), one could still argue that the mere introduction of these instruments changed the nature of time deposit markets. Before the introduction of CDs, Modigliani finds that time deposits competed with bills and money, and afterwards with these two assets and savings and loan and mutual savings bank deposits. Savings and loan and mutual savings bank deposits competed with corporate bonds and to a minor extent bills before the introduction of CDs, and with time

---

[3] CON is defined as expenditures on nondurables and services plus the imputed consumption (interest plus depreciation) on the stock of consumer durables. In equation, (7-9) consumption is expressed in current dollars.

deposits and to a greater extent with bills after CDs. Life insurance reserves competed with real assets (the rate of inflation) and mortgages throughout the period.

Deposit Rates

In both versions of the savings deposit sector, deposit rates are determined consistently with the household demand for savings deposit stocks. Depository institutions are assumed to be price-takers in markets for their assets but to set deposit rates (and the composition of their asset portfolio) so as to induce the profit maximizing level of deposit-stocks. In doing this, these institutions must have some knowledge of the interest elasticity of demand for their deposit stocks. It is assumed that their estimate of the elasticity corresponds to the interest elasticity that is estimated in the deposit stock equations. Since there is no explicit observable variable representing the rate of return on life insurance reserves, only the rates of return on time deposits, savings and loan deposits, and mutual savings bank deposits are explained.

Beginning with time deposits, the Gramlich–Hulett version finds the important rate competition to come from Treasury bills and mutual savings banks and to a lesser extent from savings and loan deposits. These appropriately weighted rates are included as one independent variable in the rate equation, along with the change in the commercial bank loan–deposit ratio which is assumed to force banks to compete more aggressively for deposits by raising time deposit rates. Ceiling rates on time deposits are included in the equation in two ways. Gramlich–Hulett first distinguish between desired and actual rates, using a constraining scheme to insure that actual rates never get above the deposit rate ceiling even if desired rates do. But the Gramlich–Hulett deposit equation also includes, and finds to be very important, a mechanism justified by oligopoly theory whereby the government ceiling in effect becomes a price leader in the time deposit market and influences even desired deposit rates.[4]

The Slovin time deposit equation, estimated to be consistent with the Modigliani asset equation, is somewhat more complicated. Since the interest elasticity switches with the introduction of CDs, there are now two separate rate competition variables, one for the pre-CD period and one for the post-CD period. There is also a more elaborate loan-deposit ratio variable—defined to include mortgage stocks on the loan side, separated between time

---

[4] A similar relationship between changes in the Federal Reserve discount rate and the commercial bank commercial loan rate is discussed by Jaffee [1].

and demand deposits with both allowed to capture their own distributed lags, and included only in the post-CD period. Finally, ceiling rates on time deposits are assumed to have only an impact effect on desired deposit rates.

The other deposit rates are less complicated because there are no ceiling rate problems. The Gramlich–Hulett version makes both savings and loan and mutual savings bank deposit rates a function of the rate competition variable and own asset rates. The Slovin version includes the change in the mortgage deposit ratio and, for savings and loans, the Federal Home Loan Bank advance ratio. Both Slovin equations again switch their rate competition variables for the post-CD period.

Mortgages

Jaffee's mortgage sector distinguishes between the supply activities of the four financial intermediaries discussed above and FNMA and the mortgage demand of households. The intermediary supply model features an intensive examination of the dynamics of the supply process through mortgage commitments and their relationship to mortgage stocks. The household demand then determines the mortgage rate on the basis of stocks of mortgages and houses and mortgage commitments.

On the supply side, Jaffee begins with an equation based on the same maximization principles as the deposit rate equation which makes the desired stock of mortgages for each intermediary a function of deposits and interest rate differentials.

$$M_i^* = b_0 + b_1(RM - RB)A_i \qquad (7\text{-}10)$$

M_i^* is the desired stock of mortgages, RM is the mortgage rate, RB is the long-term bond rate, A_i is the level of intermediary deposits explained above, and for simplicity we have dropped the i subscripts from the coefficients.

The desired net change in mortgages, or the gross change less repayments, is related to M_i^* by a stock adjustment expression,

$$\Delta MG_i - R_i = b_2[b_0 + b_1(RM - RB)A_i] - b_2M_{i-1} + b_3 \Delta A_i \quad (7\text{-}11)$$

where ΔMG_i is the gross change in mortgage stocks, R_i is repayments, and the last term is an impact variable which allows deposits to be invested in mortgages in the first period at a different rate than is dictated by normal stock adjustment considerations.

Jaffee then introduces mortgage commitments to the process by noting that gross mortgage flows can be composed of mortgages flowing from new commitments (b_4NC_i), mortgages flowing from previous stocks of outstanding commitments (b_5OC_{i-1}), and mortgages made entirely outside of the commitments process. If the latter is a constant proportion (b_6) of gross mortgage flows, the relevant identity becomes

$$\Delta MG_i = \frac{1}{1 - b_6}(b_4NC_i + b_5OC_{i-1}) \tag{7-12}$$

The estimating equation for new commitments can be derived by substituting (7-11) into (7-12) to give

$$NC_i = \frac{b_2(1 - b_6)}{b_4}[b_0 + b_1(RM - RB)A_i - M_{i-1}]$$
$$+ \frac{b_3(1 - b_6)}{b_4} \Delta A_i + \frac{1 - b_6}{b_4} R_i - \frac{b_5}{b_4} OC_{i-1} \tag{7-13}$$

The corresponding estimating equation for outstanding commitments can be derived by combining these expressions with the identity that outstanding commitments this period equals outstanding commitments last period plus new commitments less cancellations and take-downs. Assuming that cancellations and take-downs are a constant proportion, b_7, of previously outstanding commitments

$$OC_i = NC_i + (1 - b_7)OC_{i-1} \tag{7-14}$$

which on substitution gives

$$OC_i = \frac{b_2(1 - b_6)}{b_4}[b_0 + b_1(RM - RB)A_i - M_{i-1}]$$
$$+ \frac{b_3(1 - b_6)}{b_4} \Delta A_i + \frac{1 - b_6}{b_4} R_i + \left(1 - b_7 - \frac{b_5}{b_4}\right)OC_{i-1} \tag{7-15}$$

Since the true decision variable for financial institutions is new mortgage commitments, it would be preferable to estimate (7-13) for each institution. The necessary new commitments data are only available for life insurance companies, however, so Jaffee can only estimate (7-13) here. In the case of savings and loan associations and mutual savings banks Jaffee is forced to estimate (7-15) with outstanding commitments data, the only available commitments series. Matters are even worse for commercial banks because here there are no mortgage commitments data at all, and in this case Jaffee estimates (7-11).

Jaffee determines the desired stock of total mortgage liabilities by assuming that households behave in a slightly different manner than in determining their demands for savings deposits. Instead of starting with net worth and allocating this total over all assets, he posits that collateral requirements make households determine mortgage demands on the basis of their housing stock rather than their net worth.

$$MD = (b_8 + b_9 RB - b_{10} RM)KH \qquad (7\text{-}16)$$

where MD is total household mortgage demand and KH is the current dollar value of the housing stock.

In deriving the change in desired mortgages, Jaffee follows Modigliani in decomposing the change into one component, with a very slow speed of adjustment, for refinancing capital gains on old houses, and another component, with a very rapid adjustment, for mortgaging newly purchased houses. The total change in mortgage stocks is the sum of these two components:

$$\Delta MD = b_{11}(b_8 + b_9 RB - b_{10} RM)KH_{-1} \\ - b_{11}M_{-1} + (b_8 + b_9 RB - b_{10} RM)EH \qquad (7\text{-}17)$$

where EH is current dollar housing expenditures.

The expression for the mortgage rate is then derived by letting MD and M refer to the sum of mortgages at all intermediaries and FNMA respectively, by assuming that the actual mortgage rate adjusts gradually to the equilibrium rate, and by letting outstanding commitments also exert a depressing force on the equilibrium rate. Solving (7-17) for the mortgage rate yields

$$RM = \frac{b_{12}}{b_{10}}\left[(b_8 + b_9 RB) - \frac{\Delta MG + b_{11}M_{-1}}{EH + b_{11}KH_{-1}}\right] - b_{13}\frac{OC_{-1}}{EH + b_{11}KH_{-1}}$$

$$+ (1 - b_{12})RM \qquad (7\text{-}18)$$

where ΔMG replaces ΔMD.[5] This expression is estimated for the mortgage rate using a nonlinear technique to determine b_{11}.

Residential Construction

The housing sector of the FMP model distinguishes between the market for rental space and its implicit price, the market for houses as assets and the appropriate asset price, and the behavior of builders in producing homes in

---

[5] The assumption that actual mortgage rates adjust gradually to equilibrium rates implies credit rationing in the short run. It is for this reason that in (7-18) mortgage supply (MG), rather than mortgage demand (MD), is used to determine the mortgage rate. Given the mortgage rate, mortgage demand can then be determined from equation (7-17), and the amount of rationing can be evaluated as $\Delta MD - \Delta MG$.

response to asset prices and construction costs. There are also important credit rationing effects predicated on the inability of builders to begin construction without mortgage commitments and the inability of households to finance down payments when their net worth is falling.

To implement these ideas Kalchbrenner assumes that the implicit rental price clears the market for rental space. Letting the real housing stock KH/PH be proportional to the supply of rental space, and expressing the real demand as a logarithmic function of real permanent income (CON/P) and relative prices yields

$$\frac{KH}{PH} = e^{c_0}\left(\frac{CON}{P}\right)^{c_1}\left(\frac{PR}{P}\right)^{-c_2} \tag{7-19}$$

where PH is housing construction costs, P is the overall price deflator, and PR is the implicit rental price.

The asset price for houses is derived from the proposition that in equilibrium all rates of return, when appropriately discounted for risk, taxes, and other costs, should be equal. For housing this condition is

$$\frac{PR}{PA} = \mathscr{L}\left[c_3 - \left(\frac{\Delta PA}{PA_{-1}}\right)^e + (1 - t)(c_4 RM + c_5 RCB + TP)\right] \tag{7-20}$$

where PA is the asset price, t is the federal personal income tax rate, TP is the state and local property tax rate, c_3 is the rate of depreciation, c_4 and c_5 represent the proportions of new houses financed by mortgages and down payments respectively, the capital gains superscript denotes expected rates of asset price increase, and $\mathscr{L}$ is an undetermined lag operator. The expression reflects the fact that, in housing, some expenses such as interest costs and property taxes are tax deductible and hence should be multiplied by $(1 - t)$ to determine net after tax costs, while capital gains and rental income are generally not taxable and need not be multiplied by $(1 - t)$. After some unsuccessful experimentation with various empirical proxies for the expected rate of price increase, Kalchbrenner has included expected capital gains in the constant term of (7-20). This implies that as the model is presently constituted, nominal and not real interest rates influence investment demand for housing.

The expression on the right side of (7-20) is the net opportunity cost of owning a house. The market equilibrium assumption implies that after a lag the housing asset price will adjust to the implicit price of rental space to satisfy (7-20).

The final part of the housing sector relates real housing starts, deflated by the supply capacity of the economy, to the differential between the asset price and housing construction costs. In a long-run growth context when this proportionate differential is constant, housing starts and the housing stock would grow at the same rate as aggregate capacity. In the short run, starts would rise disproportionately with the implicit asset price and fall with construction costs. In addition, the starts equation includes additional credit rationing terms which depress housing starts on the supply side in periods when builders have difficulty in obtaining new mortgage commitments and on the demand side when household net worth is falling:

$$\frac{HS}{PH} = Y^* \left[e^{c_6} \left(\frac{PA}{PH} \right)^{c_7} \left(\frac{OC}{OC_{-1}} \right)^{c_8} \left(\frac{V}{V_{-1}} \right)^{c_9} \right] \tag{7-21}$$

where Y^* is the supply capacity of the economy.

Converting everything to logarithms and substituting (7-19) and (7-20) into (7-21) gives the estimating equation for housing starts:

$$\ln \frac{HS}{PH} - \ln Y^*$$

$$= c_6 + c_8 \, \Delta \ln OC + c_9 \, \Delta \ln V$$

$$+ c_7 \Big\{ \ln P - \ln PH - \ln \mathscr{L}[c_{10} + (1 - t)(c_4 RM + c_5 RB + TP)]$$

$$+ \frac{1}{c_2} \Big(c_0 + c_1 \ln \frac{CON}{P} - \ln \frac{KH}{PH} \Big) \Big\} \tag{7-22}$$

where c_{10} equals c_3 less the assumed constant value of $(\Delta PA/PA)^e$.

Equation (7-22) is estimated separately for single and multifamily housing starts, with appropriate rationing, cost-of-capital variables, and lags in each. For single-family starts the supply credit rationing variable includes savings and loan commitments and the holdings of FNMA; for multifamily starts it includes mutual savings bank and life insurance commitments. The household net worth rationing variable was omitted from the multifamily equation by assumption and the cost-of-capital variable was found to be empirically unimportant in the multifamily equation.

The housing sector is closed by the identity that

$$KH = (1 - c_3)KH_{-1} + HS \tag{7-23}$$

for both single and multifamily starts. This identity insures that the ultimate effect of a change in either interest rates or income will be to alter the housing stock, the rental price—from (7-19)—and the asset price—from (7-20). Once housing stocks and asset prices have adjusted to their equilibrium level, equation (7-21) shows that there will be no further stimulus to net housing investment over and above that set by the equilibrium rate of growth of the economy.

The Complete Model

In Appendixes A and B the preferred equation estimates and the full set of variable definitions are given. The equations represent the system that is used in the following simulation experiments. Appendix A includes a brief mnemonic guide to the variable names and definitions, which follow the scheme used in the FMP model.

Dynamic Simulations of the Three Sectors Together

We first illustrate the long-run tracking behavior of the sectors described above by a series of dynamic simulations of the three sectors. In these dynamic simulations we have allowed the savings deposits, mortgage, and housing sectors to run over the approximate period of fit, 1957:1–1969:4.[6] For each quarter we use actual values of all exogenous variables (that is, all variables not explained by the three sectors), but only initial values of the endogenous variables. Starting with 1957:1, every endogenous variable is computed simultaneously within the system and these solution variables are used as lagged endogenous variables to compute subsequent solutions to the three sector system. We calculate simulation root mean square errors in the usual way by comparing actual values of endogenous variables with the time path of simulated endogenous variables. We have done each simulation twice, once with the Gramlich–Hulett version of the savings deposit sector and once with the Modigliani–Slovin version.

Table 7-1 below gives the root mean square errors for the most important variables from the two sets of simulations, with each root mean square error compared with the mean of the variable. We can see that both versions of the model do reasonably well in explaining deposit rates and deposits, though in every case the fit of the Modigliani–Slovin version is superior. Much of this improvement in fit is due to the dummy variables which switch the interest elasticities and deposit rate competition variables in the post-CD period, but it is not clear from these numbers how much of an advantage this

---

[6] A few of the mortgage commitments series were not available on a quarterly basis for the fifties, and these equations were fit only for the sixties. In those few cases, initial values for the simulations were derived from annual series.

switch gives the Modigliani–Slovin version nor to what extent this switch makes for an unfair comparison.[7] There are also other differences between the two versions which could lead to differences in performance. In any event, once we leave the savings deposit sector, the lower savings deposit errors in the Modigliani–Slovin version also make for lower errors in mortgage commitments and rates and housing.

Table 7-1. Root Mean Square Errors of the Three Sectors Combined

Variable	Symbol	Mean	RMSE M–S[a]	RMSE G–H[b]
Passbook savings deposits[c]	MP^d, MTP^e	108.54	2.02	4.51
Savings and loan deposits[c]	MSL	87.09	1.27	1.68
Mutual savings deposits[c]	MMS	46.01	0.85	1.27
Life insurance reserves[c]	MIS	111.83	0.15	1.80
Mortgage stock—CBs[c]	$MKCB$	40.65	0.80	0.84
Mortgage commitments—SLAs[c]	$MCOS$	2.43	0.20	0.21
—MSBs[c]	$MCOM$	3.64	0.64	0.75
—LICs[c]	$MCOI$	5.22	1.19	1.26
Mortgage rate[f]	RM	6.27	0.12	0.14
Single-family starts[c]	$HS1\$$	3.78	0.23	0.37
Multifamily starts[c]	$HS3\$$	0.84	0.16	0.20
Housing expenditures[c]	$EH\$$	25.46	1.52	1.71
Mutual savings rate[f]	RMS	4.03	0.12	0.12
Savings and loan rate[f]	RSL	4.27	0.10	0.15
Passbook deposit rate[f]	RTP	3.38	0.07	0.13

[a] Modigliani–Slovin
[b] Gramlich–Hulett
[c] $ billions in current dollars
[d] All commercial banks
[e] Member banks
[f] Percent

Selected graphs for this dynamic simulation are shown in the chapter appendix, Figures 7A-1A, -1B through 7A-12A, -12B. We will consider first the figures charting the Modigliani–Slovin deposit equations. In Figures -1A to -4A, all deposits perform flawlessly until the very end of 1969. At this time there is a slight miss of time deposits on the low side offset by a miss on the high side in both savings and loan and mutual savings bank deposits. But

---

[7] To the extent that the switch in interest elasticities really did occur, which question in some fundamental sense we can never answer, the Gramlich–Hulett version has been remiss in not capturing it. But precisely because we can never tell whether the switch really did occur, we cannot make accurate goodness-of-fit comparisons between the two sectors, for it is always possible to introduce constant and slope dummies in periods that would otherwise have large errors and make apparent improvements in fit.

even though the stocks of these deposits are on target, along with the stock of mortgages (see, for example, Figure -5A for commercial bank mortgages), the level of outstanding commitments for mortgages in savings and loan associations (Figure -6A), mutual savings banks (Figure -7A), and life insurance companies (Figure -8A) tends to drift off for more prolonged periods. This is because outstanding commitments depends in the short run on the flow of deposits, which can be off by large relative amounts even if the stock is on target. The mortgage rate (Figure -9A) depends on the level of mortgages, however, and this behaves very well, at least until the very end of the period, even with the misses in commitments. Housing starts for single-family units (Figure -10A) depend on both the mortgage rate, which is quite accurate, and savings and loan commitments, which are not as accurate, along with some errors of its own. In periods such as 1958 and 1968 the failure to capture the right path of commitments can explain some of the problems of single-family starts; in other periods the starts equation itself is the culprit. The multifamily starts equation (Figure -11A) does much more poorly on its own, but especially in 1969 it would have fared better with a better life insurance commitments performance. Housing expenditures (Figure -12A) follow the path of the two component housing starts equations.

The simulations of the sector using the Gramlich–Hulett deposit equations also demonstrate this interplay between stocks of deposits and mortgages (which work well) and flows which do not work as well. The Figures -1B to -4B show that deposits are quite close, though there are some prolonged drifts in the time deposit equation. Figure -5B indicates that even with the two deposit errors, commercial bank mortgages fit well, but again the level of commitments is off for mutual savings banks and life insurance reserves. The mortgage rate in Figure -9B again tracks well despite the commitments errors, but the housing starts equations and housing expenditures do reflect the cumulative errors generated by mortgage commitments.

Overall the accuracy of these simulation predictions is impressive in both versions of the model. Even after allowing the simulation to run for fifty-two quarters, encompassing a wide variety of economic conditions, making endogenous savings deposits and rates, new and outstanding mortgage commitments, mortgage stocks and repayments, the mortgage rates, various measures of credit rationing, and the housing stock, the Modigliani–Slovin root mean square error for current dollar housing expenditures is only $1.5 billion, or less than 6 percent of its mean over the period. Experienced housing forecasters will attest that it is easy to make errors of this magnitude even projecting only one or two quarters ahead. Errors are similarly small for other important variables. The Gramlich–Hulett version does slightly worse, but still comes within 7 percent of the mean of housing expenditures and is also close on the other variables. The performance of the model would no doubt suffer once the simulations ran further outside of the sample period, but it is nevertheless encouraging that the model has met the within-period tests so well.

Multiplier Simulations

Possibly a more interesting way of examining and comparing the results of the two versions of the extended housing sector is with sectoral multipliers. To compute these sectoral multipliers, we contrast the results of two simulations. The first, or control simulation, is a dynamic simulation of the type described above. The second, or experimental simulation, is the same in all respects except that one or a set of variables exogenous to the three sectors differs from its actual value by specified amount in each quarter of the simulation. Comparison of the two simulations enables us to determine the effect of the specified exogenous change on all the endogenous variables in the sector over the entire simulation period. The sectoral multipliers then are equivalent to three sector partial derivatives with respect to the exogenous changes. Often these three sector responses will illustrate properties of the sector that would not be apparent from a separate examination of single equations.

An Exogenous Increase in Income

The first simulation experiment we present is a $10 billion exogenous increase in real disposable income maintained for the entire period. In this simulation experiment we have added the consumption–net-worth sector of the FMP model to our three sectors in both the control and the experimental run.[8] Hence we allow the increase in income to influence real consumption, the implicit saving to enter net worth, and both income and net worth to affect holdings of savings deposits. We remember also that real consumption is the permanent income measure in the housing sector and by including the consumption equation we allow for an increase in the demand for rental space through this channel.

The results of the simulation are presented in Figure 7-1. The top graphs of the figure show, for both the Modigliani–Slovin and Gramlich–Hulett versions the real expenditure flows for real disposable income, consumption, and housing expenditures. Since the consumption sector is identical for the

---

[8] See de Leeuw and Gramlich [2].

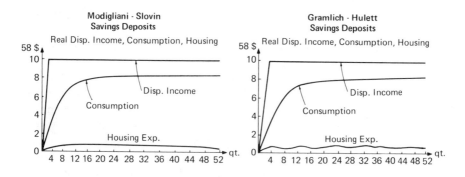

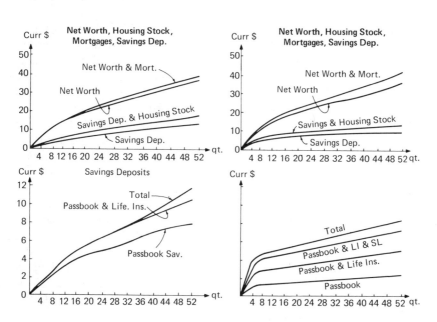

Figure 7-1. Simulation of Maintained $10 Billion Increase in Real Disposable Income, 1957:1 to 1969:4.

two versions, in both cases consumption rises gradually to meet the rise in real disposable income. For the first twelve quarters, consumption is rising because of a long, distributed lag on disposable income; after that it rises because increments to saving add to net worth and provide for additional increments to consumption.

The center graphs in Figure 7-1 show the results for various stocks, all of which are measured in current dollars. As before, the rise in net worth (amounting to $37.0 billion by the end of the period) is identical in the two versions. But the rise in savings deposits is not. In the Gramlich–Hulett version the rise in disposable income immediately increases savings deposits as a proportion of net worth, which proportion is only gradually restored over the long run as net worth slowly catches up. This phenomenon also works in the Modigliani–Slovin sector, though here the immediate rise is less and the long-run rise greater. Because the immediate rise in saving deposits, and hence in mortgage commitments and in the credit rationing variable, is greater in the Gramlich–Hulett sector, the short-run response of housing is somewhat more oscillatory.

The bottom graphs of Figure 7-1 show the composition of savings deposits across the four assets. The Gramlich–Hulett sector has imposed proportionate constraints such that the rise in income is allocated to the four assets in line with their proportionate importance in net worth. Thus, in this version the marginal proportional increase in each asset equals the average proportion of the asset to total savings deposits. The Modigliani–Slovin version, on the other hand, does not make this constraint and allows the rise in income to affect the proportionate composition of savings deposits as well as the total. In the estimated equations this compositional effect turns out to be quite powerful—income raises the share of passbook savings greatly and hurts the share of savings and loan and mutual savings bank deposits. In the simulation, therefore, a large proportion of the rise in net worth ends up in passbook savings and in life insurance reserves. Only a small part of it, about $1 billion, goes into savings and loan and mutual savings bank deposits.[9] Since the deposits of these intermediaries are concentrated in mortgages, the rise in mortgages is less in the Modigliani–Slovin version, and, although interest rates are not shown, the mortgage rate drops and the change in housing expenditures is rather slight—always less than five percent of the initial income change.

The long run in terms of the equilibrium state of the model is substantially

---

[9] This result also highlights one artificial aspect of this experiment, namely, that the increase in income is not allowed to create capital gains in the stock market. The results of the following section indicate that nonbank savings deposits would, in fact, be very responsive to stock market capital gains.

more than the 52 quarters for which the simulation extends. But from the structure of the equations we do know what will happen in this very long run. The rise in consumption relative to disposable income will continue until eventually incremental consumption equals incremental disposable income. At this point, incremental personal saving will no longer be positive and net worth will stabilize. The household portfolio allocation process will then stabilize all savings deposit asset stocks [see equation (7-5) and (7-6)] and, after a slight delay, mortgage stocks [equation (7-10)]. This in turn will set the mortgage rate slightly below, and the housing asset price slightly above, their presimulation values [equations (7-18) and (7-20)]. Housing starts will be increased as long as net worth is rising and the housing asset price is above its presimulation value [equation (7-21)], but this increase in housing starts will eventually raise the real housing stock, lower the price of rental space, raise the demand for mortgages and the mortgage rate, and for both reasons lower the asset price back towards its initial value [equations (7-16) and (7-19)]. The housing stock will stop changing when the asset price finally achieves its presimulation ratio to construction costs—at this point both the housing stock and its asset price stop changing. In the very long run, therefore, the rise in income will have increased net worth, stocks of all savings deposits, mortgages, and houses; but apart from the high replacement demand it will have no permanent effect on the relative asset price for housing, housing starts, or residential construction expenditures.[10]

An Exogenous Fall in Stock Market Values

The next simulation is an exogenous fall in stock market values. We have raised the model's stock market capitalization rate, the dividend–price ratio on common stock, by 1 percent beginning in 1957:1. There ensues a sharp and somewhat erratic fall in stock market values and net worth which then feeds into savings deposits, the mortgage market, and housing. This experiment incorporates a change in net worth resulting from capital gains and thus differs from the previous simulation in which the change in net worth followed a change in income.

The results of this simulation are presented in Figure 7-2. The top graphs show the fall in net worth, which is always large but which varies in size with

---

[10] This simulation has only looked at the demand side of the housing sector. If supply is inelastic in the short run, there will be additional movement in construction costs which will limit the duration of the housing expansion even more, but also bring more resources into the construction industry. In the long run, the asset price will be in the same relation to construction costs as in the demand-only simulation, but the level of both prices depends on the long-run supply elasticity.

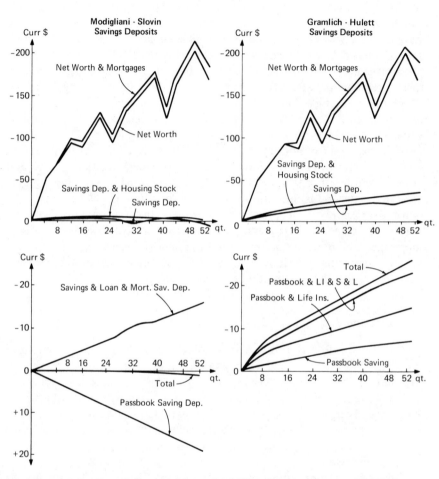

Figure 7-2. Simulation of Maintained One Percent Increase in Dividend–Price Ratio, 1957:1 to 1964:4.

the present level of the dividend–price ratio and dividends. The Gramlich–Hulett savings deposit sector eventually allocates the entire fall in net worth toward a reduction in savings deposits, but precisely because this component of net worth is so volatile, it contains a relatively long delay in the adjustment. Thus, savings deposits decline, but their pattern is not nearly as erratic as the decline in net worth. The decline in savings deposits is again spread proportionately across all assets. It leads to a decline in mortgage stocks at all institutions, and because of the implied rise in mortgage rates and fall in the growth of commitments, to a slight reduction in housing expenditures and the housing stock.

The Modigliani version of the savings deposit sector differs in two respects. In the first place, as equation (7-4) points out, only a portion (m) of the change in net worth in the form of capital gains is immediately subtracted from savings deposits. In the empirical estimates, this proportion turns out to be the relatively small value of 17 percent. Secondly, the passbook savings allocation equation contains a term which increases the proportionate share of passbook savings deposits with income and decreases the share with net worth. Thus an initial fall in net worth will tend to *increase* passbook savings deposits.

These properties are evident in Figure 7-2. From the lower graph we see that the sharp fall in net worth is accompanied by a large rise in passbook savings deposits, which rise actually turns out to be larger than the fall in the other three savings deposits assets. Thus total savings deposits rise very slightly.[11] Since most of the savings deposit reduction comes in savings and loan associations and mutual savings banks, however, the stock of mortgages and the housing stock still fall by roughly the amount in the Gramlich–Hulett version.

In either case, the long-run effect of the reduction in net worth is again to lower the stock of mortgages and houses by a small amount and to leave unchanged the housing asset price, starts, and expenditures net of replacement. Housing expenditures are not shown in the graph, but they are never reduced by more than $1 billion at any time even with this very large change in net worth.

---

[11] In a sense this simulation is artificial because we have reduced net worth without the reduction in consumption and income which would normally accompany this reduction (since consumption depends on net worth). For a reduction in net worth of $150 billion, consumption would fall by about $8 billion which, after the multiplier, would imply a decline in income on the order of $15 billion. The results in Figure 7A–12A indicate that this would lower Modigliani's passbook savings by about $12 billion and life insurance reserves by about $5 billion, with negligible effects on other savings deposits. Thus, in a complete model simulation of an exogenous decline in net worth, passbook savings deposits would still rise, though by less than shown here. (See also footnote 9.)

An Exogenous Decrease in All Market
Interest Rates

For this simulation, we assume that all market interest rates fall by one percentage point (100 basis points). Since the Modigliani–Slovin savings deposit sector has different rate elasticities before and after the introduction of CDs, and since the pre-CD interest elasticities are now a matter of only historical interest, we have run this simulation just for the post-CD period. We have also omitted the year 1969 from the simulation period because at that time the passbook savings rate desired by banks was so far above the government imposed ceiling that even our assumed one percentage point decrease in all market rates would have changed actual time deposit rates by very little. These simulations, therefore, run only for the twenty-four quarter period from 1963:1 to 1968:4.

The results are given in Figure 7-3. The top panel presents the path of interest rates in response to the market rate change. Since market instruments both compete with various types of savings deposits and are among the assets that depository institutions hold, the drop in market rates is promptly reflected in a drop in deposit rates in both versions of the savings deposit sector, though in general this drop is less than the drop in market rates. In the case of life insurance reserves, where the effective deposit rate is fixed, the constant own rate and drop in competing rates leads households to increase their stock by roughly $5 billion in both the Modigliani–Slovin and Gramlich–Hulett sectors. Savings and loan deposits also increase in both versions, because the rate decline of approximately 75 basis points is short of that required to stabilize deposits. But mutual savings bank and passbook savings deposits decline in both versions, though by much larger amounts in the Modigliani–Slovin sector. This discrepancy is partly because the corresponding rates drop more in the Modigliani–Slovin version and partly because the Modigliani passbook savings equation has stronger long-run substitution elasticities.[12]

Since the mortgage rate is somewhat slow to respond to the decrease in market rates, the simultaneous rise in savings deposits and relative decline in market rates leads to a sharp rise in mortgage commitments in both versions. This is the main reason for the temporary boom in housing expenditures, seen in the lower graphs, and for the fact that the mortgage stock initially increases more than the housing stock. But eventually the rise in

---

[12] We would expect passbook savings deposits to fall somewhat when market interest rates fall because demand deposits at commercial banks would simultaneously rise. The rise in demand deposits in the FMP model would probably be somewhat less than the fall in Modigliani's passbook deposits.

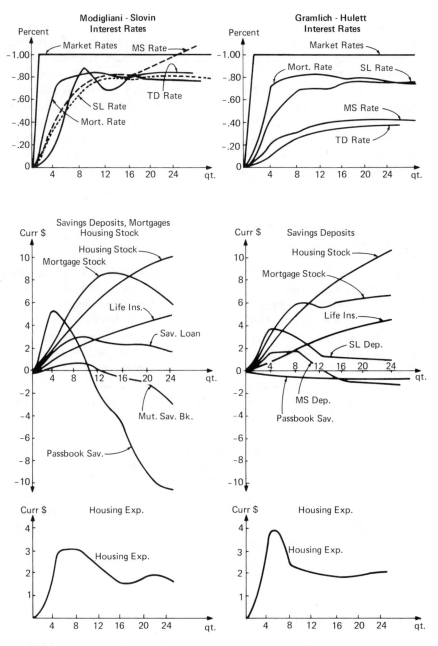

Figure 7–3. Simulation of Maintained One Percentage Point Decrease in all Market Interest Rates, 1963:1 to 1968:4.

mortgages is tempered by the slower growth in savings deposits (especially in the Modigliani–Slovin sector) and the gradual adjustment of mortgages rates to the declining market rates. As these mortgage rates decline, the implicit asset price for houses increases and housing starts and expenditures are stimulated further. Ultimately the housing stock will grow by more than mortgages, with the difference being the aggregate value of housing equity in net worth. As before, the growth in the housing stock will eventually stabilize itself by reducing implicit rents until the implicit asset price restores its former relationship with construction costs. At this point, the housing and mortgages stocks remain at permanently higher levels but the net flow of expenditures returns to its previous level.

An Exogenous Increase in Passbook Ceiling Rates

The final simulation examines the results of an experimental rise in passbook deposit rate ceilings (see Figure 7-4). This simulation again is done for the post-CD period, beginning in 1963:1 when the definitional depressing effect of the ceiling was absent. Thus the rise in passbook deposit rates is solely due to the oligopolistic trigger effect of deposit ceiling rate changes. In the Modigliani–Slovin sector this rise has only an impact effect on passbook savings rates, and hence the ceiling rate change does very little. Passbook savings deposits are increased after a time and they remain high because of the long lag in this equation; all other deposits decline slightly; the mortgage stock declines slightly; and housing expenditures oscillate around zero.

In the Gramlich–Hulett sector the oligopolistic effect of the deposit ceiling change establishes a new rate structure permanently. Passbook savings deposit rates are permanently increased and mutual savings and savings and loan rates are forced to follow to avoid outflows into passbook deposits. Even then, passbook savings deposits rise markedly at the expense of other savings deposits. And since this reallocation of deposits favors commercial banks, which hold less of their assets in mortgages, the overall mortgage stock falls more sharply than in the Modigliani–Slovin sector. The implied decline in mortgage commitments reduces housing expenditures and the stock, but by very small amounts.

Implications for Government Policy

We conclude this study with a discussion of the implications of the model and its simulation for government policies to stimulate or restrict housing

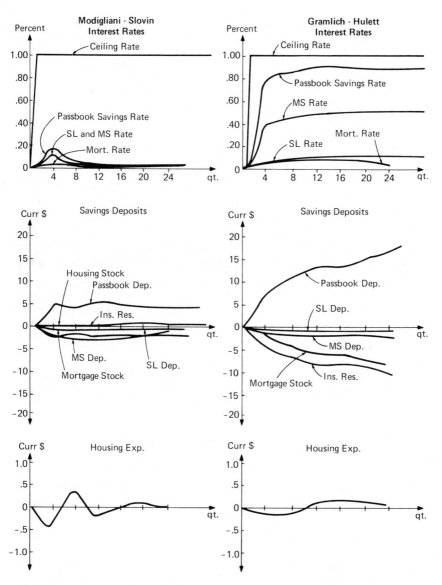

Figure 7-4. Simulation of Maintained One Percentage Point Increase in Passbook Savings Deposit Rate Ceilings, 1963:1 to 1968:4.

expenditures in a macroeconomic setting. The recent volatility of overall housing expenditures, and the consequent ramifications in terms of a national housing policy, have brought this question very much into public debate.

The income simulations show that rises in income definitely stimulate housing expenditures, but by rather small relative amounts. A $10 billion increase in disposable income, which could be brought about by the government through a personal tax cut or expenditure increase on the order of $5 billion, would give rise to short- and intermediate-run increases in housing expenditures of less than $1 billion. Just as consumption takes up the overwhelming fraction of disposable income on the average, so too it would capture most of the marginal increase in disposable income, with very little left over for housing.[13]

The same statement could be made even more strongly for possible government measures taken to alter private wealth, say by actions that influence the rate at which the stock market capitalizes dividend payments. Large changes in private net worth would show up as much smaller changes in the stock of savings deposits, mortgages, and houses. And since the change in the housing stock is relatively small, less than 5 percent of the change in wealth, the first difference of the housing stock, or housing expenditures, is barely changing at all. Even substantial changes in the capitalized value of net worth will, therefore, alter both the flow of housing expenditures and the stock of houses by only small amounts.

The policy leverage of the government is much greater when it comes to monetary policy. If the central bank were to alter the opportunity cost of investment in housing by changing nominal interest rates, there would be a sizeable impact on housing expenditures. In the short run this impact would be mainly attributable to positive or negative credit rationing affecting housing starts through volatile movements in mortgage commitments; in the intermediate run mortgage rates would fall and provide a more lasting stimulus through the cost-of-capital effect. Monetarists argue that the central bank cannot permanently alter the housing opportunity cost because eventually increases or decreases in the rate of inflation will bring real interest rates back to their previous level; but most people would agree that the effect on nominal interest rates would not be erased immediately; and until it is erased there will be an important effect on housing. Whether the real interest rate does return precisely to its previous level or not in the long run is somewhat academic in this case because we have already seen that the basic

---

[13] Although we have not done full model simulations in this chapter, this statement would be even more emphatic if we had, for the rise in income would increase market interest rates and dampen the housing expansion relative to the consumption expansion even more.

structure of the FMP extended housing sector insures that there is no long-run stimulus to housing expenditures whatever happens to the cost of capital in nominal terms.

Whether deposit ceiling rates do or do not permanently affect the rate structure for savings assets, they seem to have a rather minor effect on housing expenditures. Although the pattern and magnitude of this stimulus or destimulus varies according to different assumptions about the passbook deposit market, the impact on housing expenditures is seen never to exceed $\pm\$.5$ billion for a substantial change in the ceiling, and in any case to oscillate around zero according to either assumption. These results indicate that the financial market efficiency implications of an active deposit rate ceiling policy will in all likelihood far outweigh the effects of these ceilings on housing. It may be appropriate social policy to try to stimulate housing, but time deposit rate ceilings are not a very efficient way to do it.

Although we have not done other policy simulations in this chapter, Jaffee's mortgage market simulations (Chapter 5) create doubt as to the effectiveness of other types of governmental quasi-monetary policy measures on housing expenditures. Jaffee finds that FNMA purchases of mortgages, FHLB advances to savings and loan associations, and changes in FHLB advances rates all have very small effects on mortgage rates—not even uniformly in the right direction—and hence on housing expenditures.[14]

The simulations imply, therefore, that the government can influence housing expenditures in the short and intermediate run, but not by very much, not in very many ways, and not in the long run. The only instrument of any potency is the well-known device of changes in the nominal rate of interest. In the long run, even this will not provide a permanent stimulus, both because inflation either partially or fully offsets the nominal rate change and because the adjustment in housing stocks fully dampens the remaining cost-of-capital influence. Changes in disposable income have even less short- and inter-mediate-run influence, and all other quasi-monetary changes or changes in wealth have virtually no influence.

It is perhaps in recognition of the ineffectiveness of the orthodox tools of economic policy for housing that recent discussions have turned to a different set of policy devices, namely the direct subsidization of housing. The particular proposals that have been made are too complex to consider in detail here, but they generally can be classified as tax rebatement, construction cost subsidy, or rent subsidy programs. In most cases policy programs of these types can be directly evaluated within the structure of our model of the

---

[14] We have confirmed these results with three sector simulations. The effects of substantial changes in these instruments on housing expenditures were so small as to be not worth presenting.

housing sector. For example, federal revenue-sharing plans that allow a reduction in property tax rates would stimulate housing investment by causing a reduction in the cost of capital. Similarly, programs that subsidize construction costs would affect the relevant housing price–cost ratio and thus promote a rise in housing starts. Finally, rental subsidies would increase the demand for housing, leading to an increase in the price of houses and finally to an increase in the housing stock. Although we have not attempted here to test any specific proposals with our model, it seems apparent that as a rule the model would indicate that direct subsidization of housing is more effective than the more traditional policy tools.

While the current interest in direct subsidy programs is certainly understandable in view of our results, it should be stressed that the implications of our model remain valid primarily in the context of aggregate macroeconomic questions. Many of the basic issues relating to housing, on the other hand, are perhaps more properly considered on a microeconomic level. For example, although the aggregate quantity and quality of the housing stock remains a valid concern of economic policy, increasing attention is now being paid to the distribution of this housing stock and its quality for lower income groups. The type of model needed to investigate the effectiveness of policy proposals with such an objective in mind is quite different in structure from our macroeconomic form. Some research on models of this type has started, and it is hoped that more will be forthcoming. Perhaps even further in the future, one can look forward to the ultimate merging of micro and macro models of the housing market.

Appendix 7A:
Results of Dynamic
Simulations of the
Three Sectors
Together

(A) with Modigliani–Slovin Deposit Equations (B) with Gramlich–Hulett Deposit Equations.

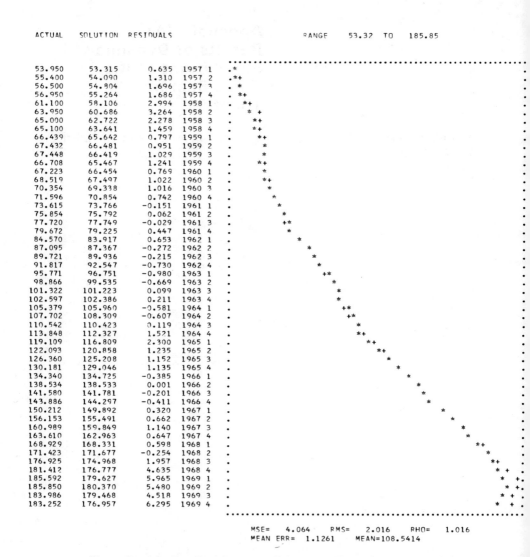

ACTUAL   SOLUTION   RESIDUALS   RANGE   53.32   TO   185.85

ACTUAL	SOLUTION	RESIDUALS		
53.950	53.315	0.635	1957	1
55.400	54.090	1.310	1957	2
56.500	54.804	1.696	1957	3
56.950	55.264	1.686	1957	4
61.100	58.106	2.994	1958	1
63.950	60.686	3.264	1958	2
65.000	62.722	2.278	1958	3
65.100	63.641	1.459	1958	4
66.439	65.642	0.797	1959	1
67.432	66.481	0.951	1959	2
67.448	66.419	1.029	1959	3
66.708	65.467	1.241	1959	4
67.223	66.454	0.769	1960	1
68.519	67.497	1.022	1960	2
70.354	69.338	1.016	1960	3
71.596	70.854	0.742	1960	4
73.615	73.766	-0.151	1961	1
75.854	75.792	0.062	1961	2
77.720	77.749	-0.029	1961	3
79.672	79.225	0.447	1961	4
84.570	83.917	0.653	1962	1
87.095	87.367	-0.272	1962	2
89.721	89.936	-0.215	1962	3
91.817	92.547	-0.730	1962	4
95.771	96.751	-0.980	1963	1
98.866	99.535	-0.669	1963	2
101.322	101.223	0.099	1963	3
102.597	102.386	0.211	1963	4
105.379	105.960	-0.581	1964	1
107.702	108.309	-0.607	1964	2
110.542	110.423	0.119	1964	3
113.848	112.327	1.521	1964	4
119.109	116.809	2.300	1965	1
122.093	120.858	1.235	1965	2
126.360	125.208	1.152	1965	3
130.181	129.046	1.135	1965	4
134.340	134.725	-0.385	1966	1
138.534	138.533	0.001	1966	2
141.580	141.781	-0.201	1966	3
143.886	144.297	-0.411	1966	4
150.212	149.892	0.320	1967	1
156.153	155.491	0.662	1967	2
160.989	159.849	1.140	1967	3
163.610	162.963	0.647	1967	4
168.929	168.331	0.598	1968	1
171.423	171.677	-0.254	1968	2
176.925	174.968	1.957	1968	3
181.412	176.777	4.635	1968	4
185.592	179.627	5.965	1969	1
185.850	180.370	5.480	1969	2
183.986	179.468	4.518	1969	3
183.252	176.957	6.295	1969	4

MSE=   4.064   RMS=   2.016   RHO=   1.016
MEAN ERR=   1.1261   MEAN=108.5414

Figure 7A-1A. Standard Dynamic Solution of Three Sectors Together: Modigliani-Slovin Version. Commercial Bank Passbook Savings Deposits — *MP*.

263

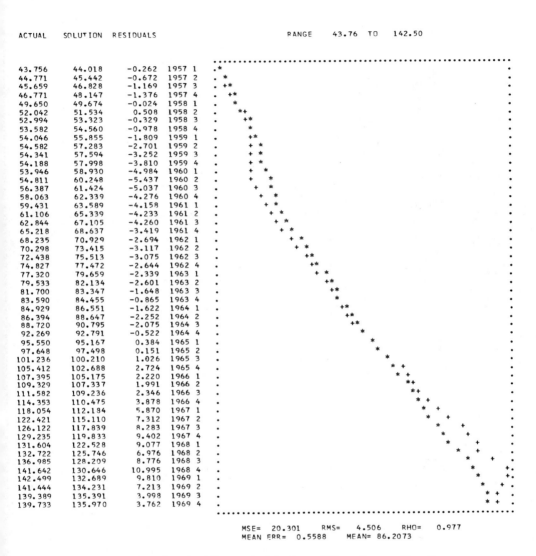

| ACTUAL | SOLUTION | RESIDUALS | | | RANGE | 43.76 | TO | 142.50 |

ACTUAL	SOLUTION	RESIDUALS		
43.756	44.018	-0.262	1957	1
44.771	45.442	-0.672	1957	2
45.659	46.828	-1.169	1957	3
46.771	48.147	-1.376	1957	4
49.650	49.674	-0.024	1958	1
52.042	51.534	0.508	1958	2
52.994	53.323	-0.329	1958	3
53.582	54.560	-0.978	1958	4
54.046	55.855	-1.809	1959	1
54.582	57.283	-2.701	1959	2
54.341	57.594	-3.252	1959	3
54.188	57.998	-3.810	1959	4
53.946	58.930	-4.984	1960	1
54.811	60.248	-5.437	1960	2
56.387	61.424	-5.037	1960	3
58.063	62.339	-4.276	1960	4
59.431	63.589	-4.158	1961	1
61.106	65.339	-4.233	1961	2
62.844	67.105	-4.260	1961	3
65.218	68.637	-3.419	1961	4
68.235	70.929	-2.694	1962	1
70.298	73.415	-3.117	1962	2
72.438	75.513	-3.075	1962	3
74.827	77.472	-2.644	1962	4
77.320	79.659	-2.339	1963	1
79.533	82.134	-2.601	1963	2
81.700	83.347	-1.648	1963	3
83.590	84.455	-0.865	1963	4
84.929	86.551	-1.622	1964	1
86.394	88.647	-2.252	1964	2
88.720	90.795	-2.075	1964	3
92.269	92.791	-0.522	1964	4
95.550	95.167	0.384	1965	1
97.648	97.498	0.151	1965	2
101.236	100.210	1.026	1965	3
105.412	102.688	2.724	1965	4
107.395	105.175	2.220	1966	1
109.329	107.337	1.991	1966	2
111.582	109.236	2.346	1966	3
114.353	110.475	3.878	1966	4
118.054	112.184	5.870	1967	1
122.421	115.110	7.312	1967	2
126.122	117.839	8.283	1967	3
129.235	119.833	9.402	1967	4
131.604	122.528	9.077	1968	1
132.722	125.746	6.976	1968	2
136.985	128.209	8.776	1968	3
141.642	130.646	10.995	1968	4
142.499	132.689	9.810	1969	1
141.444	134.231	7.213	1969	2
139.389	135.391	3.998	1969	3
139.733	135.970	3.762	1969	4

MSE= 20.301 RMS= 4.506 RHO= 0.977
MEAN ERR= 0.5588 MEAN= 86.2073

Figure 7A-1B. Standard Dynamic Solution of Three Sectors Together: Gramlich-Hulett Version. Commercial Bank Passbook Savings Deposits — *MTP*.

264

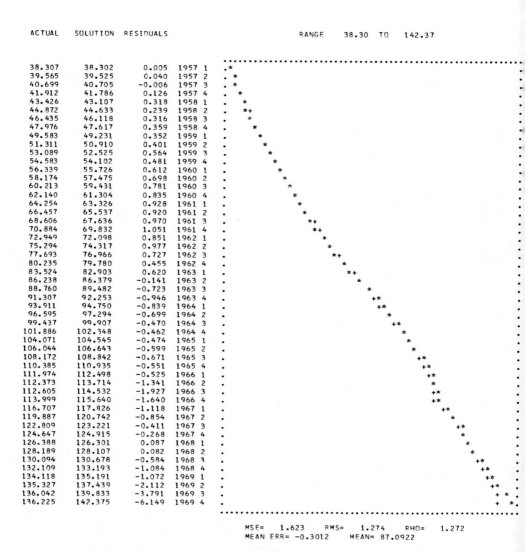

ACTUAL   SOLUTION   RESIDUALS   RANGE   38.30 TO   142.37

ACTUAL	SOLUTION	RESIDUALS		
38.307	38.302	0.005	1957	1
39.565	39.525	0.040	1957	2
40.699	40.705	-0.006	1957	3
41.912	41.786	0.126	1957	4
43.426	43.107	0.318	1958	1
44.872	44.633	0.239	1958	2
46.435	46.118	0.316	1958	3
47.976	47.617	0.359	1958	4
49.583	49.231	0.352	1959	1
51.311	50.910	0.401	1959	2
53.089	52.525	0.564	1959	3
54.583	54.102	0.481	1959	4
56.339	55.726	0.612	1960	1
58.174	57.475	0.698	1960	2
60.213	59.431	0.781	1960	3
62.140	61.304	0.835	1960	4
64.254	63.326	0.928	1961	1
66.457	65.537	0.920	1961	2
68.606	67.636	0.970	1961	3
70.884	69.832	1.051	1961	4
72.949	72.098	0.851	1962	1
75.294	74.317	0.977	1962	2
77.693	76.966	0.727	1962	3
80.235	79.780	0.455	1962	4
83.524	82.903	0.620	1963	1
86.238	86.379	-0.141	1963	2
88.760	89.482	-0.723	1963	3
91.307	92.253	-0.946	1963	4
93.911	94.750	-0.839	1964	1
96.595	97.294	-0.699	1964	2
99.437	99.907	-0.470	1964	3
101.886	102.348	-0.462	1964	4
104.071	104.545	-0.474	1965	1
106.044	106.643	-0.599	1965	2
108.172	108.842	-0.671	1965	3
110.385	110.935	-0.551	1965	4
111.974	112.498	-0.525	1966	1
112.373	113.714	-1.341	1966	2
112.605	114.532	-1.927	1966	3
113.999	115.640	-1.640	1966	4
116.707	117.826	-1.118	1967	1
119.887	120.742	-0.854	1967	2
122.809	123.221	-0.411	1967	3
124.647	124.915	-0.268	1967	4
126.388	126.301	0.087	1968	1
128.189	128.107	0.082	1968	2
130.094	130.678	-0.584	1968	3
132.109	133.193	-1.084	1968	4
134.118	135.191	-1.072	1969	1
135.327	137.439	-2.112	1969	2
136.042	139.833	-3.791	1969	3
136.225	142.375	-6.149	1969	4

MSE= 1.623   RMS= 1.274   RHO= 1.272
MEAN ERR= -0.3012   MEAN= 87.0922

Figure 7A-2A. Standard Dynamic Solution of Three Sectors Together: Modigliani-Slovin Version. Savings and Loan Deposits — *MSL*.

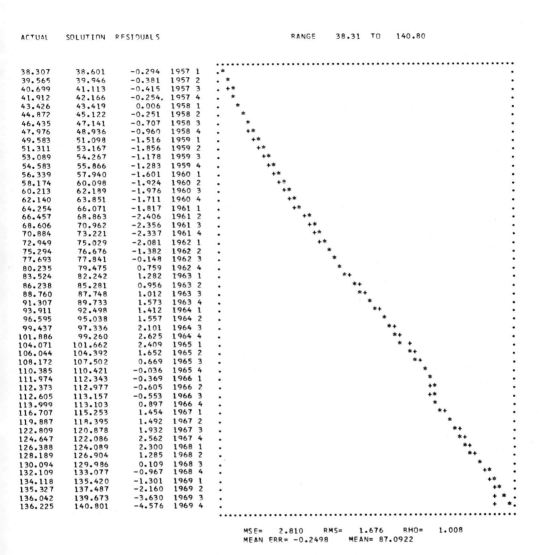

```
ACTUAL    SOLUTION  RESIDUALS                        RANGE    38.31  TO    140.80

38.307     38.601     -0.294   1957 1
39.565     39.946     -0.381   1957 2
40.699     41.113     -0.415   1957 3
41.912     42.166     -0.254.  1957 4
43.426     43.419      0.006   1958 1
44.872     45.122     -0.251   1958 2
46.435     47.141     -0.707   1958 3
47.976     48.936     -0.960   1958 4
49.583     51.098     -1.516   1959 1
51.311     53.167     -1.856   1959 2
53.089     54.267     -1.178   1959 3
54.583     55.866     -1.283   1959 4
56.339     57.940     -1.601   1960 1
58.174     60.098     -1.924   1960 2
60.213     62.189     -1.976   1960 3
62.140     63.851     -1.711   1960 4
64.254     66.071     -1.817   1961 1
66.457     68.863     -2.406   1961 2
68.606     70.962     -2.356   1961 3
70.884     73.221     -2.337   1961 4
72.949     75.029     -2.081   1962 1
75.294     76.676     -1.382   1962 2
77.693     77.841     -0.148   1962 3
80.235     79.475      0.759   1962 4
83.524     82.242      1.282   1963 1
86.238     85.281      0.956   1963 2
88.760     87.748      1.012   1963 3
91.307     89.733      1.573   1963 4
93.911     92.498      1.412   1964 1
96.595     95.038      1.557   1964 2
99.437     97.336      2.101   1964 3
101.886    99.260      2.625   1964 4
104.071    101.662     2.409   1965 1
106.044    104.392     1.652   1965 2
108.172    107.502     0.669   1965 3
110.385    110.421    -0.036   1965 4
111.974    112.343    -0.369   1966 1
112.373    112.977    -0.605   1966 2
112.605    113.157    -0.553   1966 3
113.999    113.103     0.897   1966 4
116.707    115.253     1.454   1967 1
119.887    118.395     1.492   1967 2
122.809    120.878     1.932   1967 3
124.647    122.086     2.562   1967 4
126.388    124.089     2.300   1968 1
128.189    126.904     1.285   1968 2
130.094    129.986     0.109   1968 3
132.109    133.077    -0.967   1968 4
134.118    135.420    -1.301   1969 1
135.327    137.487    -2.160   1969 2
136.042    139.673    -3.630   1969 3
136.225    140.801    -4.576   1969 4
```

```
MSE=    2.810     RMS=     1.676     RHO=    1.008
MEAN ERR= -0.2498      MEAN= 87.0922
```

Figure 7A–2B. Standard Dynamic Solution of Three Sectors Together: Gramlich-Hulett Version. Savings and Loan Deposits – *MSL*.

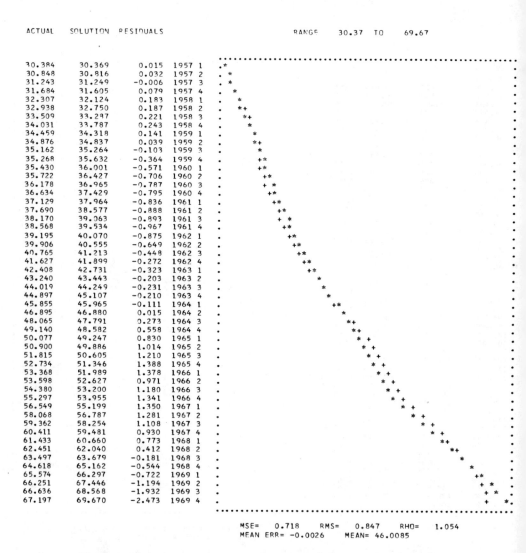

```
ACTUAL     SOLUTION   RESIDUALS                              RANGE    30.37  TO     69.67

30.384     30.369       0.015    1957  1
30.848     30.816       0.032    1957  2
31.243     31.249      -0.006    1957  3
31.684     31.605       0.079    1957  4
32.307     32.124       0.183    1958  1
32.938     32.750       0.187    1958  2
33.509     33.287       0.221    1958  3
34.031     33.787       0.243    1958  4
34.459     34.318       0.141    1959  1
34.876     34.837       0.039    1959  2
35.162     35.264      -0.103    1959  3
35.268     35.632      -0.364    1959  4
35.430     36.001      -0.571    1960  1
35.722     36.427      -0.706    1960  2
36.178     36.965      -0.787    1960  3
36.634     37.429      -0.795    1960  4
37.129     37.964      -0.836    1961  1
37.690     38.577      -0.888    1961  2
38.170     39.063      -0.893    1961  3
38.568     39.534      -0.967    1961  4
39.195     40.070      -0.875    1962  1
39.906     40.555      -0.649    1962  2
40.765     41.213      -0.448    1962  3
41.627     41.899      -0.272    1962  4
42.408     42.731      -0.323    1963  1
43.240     43.443      -0.203    1963  2
44.019     44.249      -0.231    1963  3
44.897     45.107      -0.210    1963  4
45.855     45.965      -0.111    1964  1
46.895     46.880       0.015    1964  2
48.065     47.791       0.273    1964  3
49.140     48.582       0.558    1964  4
50.077     49.247       0.830    1965  1
50.900     49.886       1.014    1965  2
51.815     50.605       1.210    1965  3
52.734     51.346       1.388    1965  4
53.368     51.989       1.378    1966  1
53.598     52.627       0.971    1966  2
54.380     53.200       1.180    1966  3
55.297     53.955       1.341    1966  4
56.549     55.199       1.350    1967  1
58.068     56.787       1.281    1967  2
59.362     58.254       1.108    1967  3
60.411     59.481       0.930    1967  4
61.433     60.660       0.773    1968  1
62.451     62.040       0.412    1968  2
63.497     63.679      -0.181    1968  3
64.618     65.162      -0.544    1968  4
65.574     66.297      -0.722    1969  1
66.251     67.446      -1.194    1969  2
66.636     68.568      -1.932    1969  3
67.197     69.670      -2.473    1969  4

                       MSE=    0.718    RMS=    0.847    RHO=    1.054
                       MEAN ERR= -0.0026    MEAN= 46.0085
```

Figure 7A-3A. Standard Dynamic Solution of Three Sectors Together: Modigliani-Slovin Version. Mutual Savings Bank Deposits – *MMS*.

267

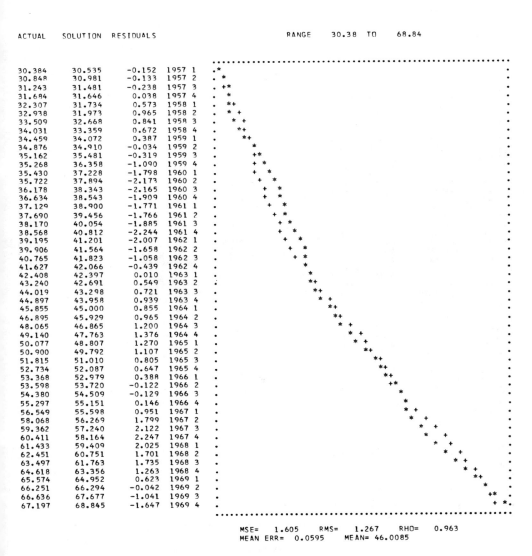

ACTUAL   SOLUTION   RESIDUALS   RANGE   30.38 TO   68.84

ACTUAL	SOLUTION	RESIDUALS		
30.384	30.535	-0.152	1957	1
30.848	30.981	-0.133	1957	2
31.243	31.481	-0.238	1957	3
31.684	31.646	0.038	1957	4
32.307	31.734	0.573	1958	1
32.938	31.973	0.965	1958	2
33.509	32.668	0.841	1958	3
34.031	33.359	0.672	1958	4
34.459	34.072	0.387	1959	1
34.876	34.910	-0.034	1959	2
35.162	35.481	-0.319	1959	3
35.268	36.358	-1.090	1959	4
35.430	37.228	-1.798	1960	1
35.722	37.894	-2.173	1960	2
36.178	38.343	-2.165	1960	3
36.634	38.543	-1.909	1960	4
37.129	38.900	-1.771	1961	1
37.690	39.456	-1.766	1961	2
38.170	40.054	-1.885	1961	3
38.568	40.812	-2.244	1961	4
39.195	41.201	-2.007	1962	1
39.906	41.564	-1.658	1962	2
40.765	41.823	-1.058	1962	3
41.627	42.066	-0.439	1962	4
42.408	42.397	0.010	1963	1
43.240	42.691	0.549	1963	2
44.019	43.298	0.721	1963	3
44.897	43.958	0.939	1963	4
45.855	45.000	0.855	1964	1
46.895	45.929	0.965	1964	2
48.065	46.865	1.200	1964	3
49.140	47.763	1.376	1964	4
50.077	48.807	1.270	1965	1
50.900	49.792	1.107	1965	2
51.815	51.010	0.805	1965	3
52.734	52.087	0.647	1965	4
53.368	52.979	0.388	1966	1
53.598	53.720	-0.122	1966	2
54.380	54.509	-0.129	1966	3
55.297	55.151	0.146	1966	4
56.549	55.598	0.951	1967	1
58.068	56.269	1.799	1967	2
59.362	57.240	2.122	1967	3
60.411	58.164	2.247	1967	4
61.433	59.409	2.025	1968	1
62.451	60.751	1.701	1968	2
63.497	61.763	1.735	1968	3
64.618	63.356	1.263	1968	4
65.574	64.952	0.623	1969	1
66.251	66.294	-0.042	1969	2
66.636	67.677	-1.041	1969	3
67.197	68.845	-1.647	1969	4

MSE=   1.605   RMS=   1.267   RHO=   0.963
MEAN ERR= 0.0595   MEAN= 46.0085

Figure 7A-3B. Standard Dynamic Solution of Three Sectors Together: Gramlich-Hulett Version. Mutual Savings Bank Deposits — *MMS*.

ACTUAL   SOLUTION   RESIDUALS   RANGE   80.25 TO   149.31

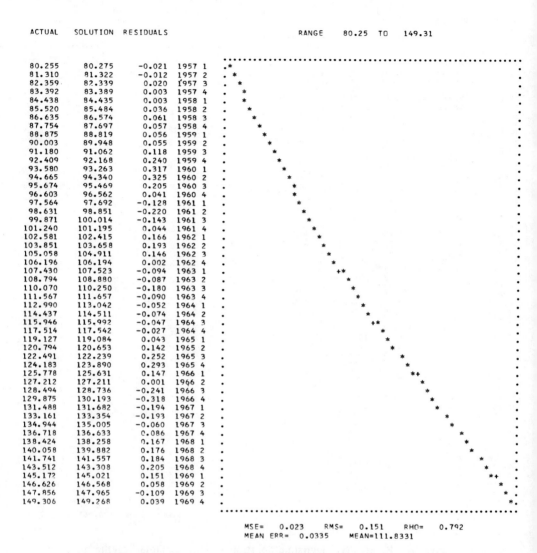

ACTUAL	SOLUTION	RESIDUALS		
80.255	80.275	-0.021	1957	1
81.310	81.322	-0.012	1957	2
82.359	82.339	0.020	1957	3
83.392	83.389	0.003	1957	4
84.438	84.435	0.003	1958	1
85.520	85.484	0.036	1958	2
86.635	86.574	0.061	1958	3
87.754	87.697	0.057	1958	4
88.875	88.819	0.056	1959	1
90.003	89.948	0.055	1959	2
91.180	91.062	0.118	1959	3
92.409	92.168	0.240	1959	4
93.580	93.263	0.317	1960	1
94.665	94.340	0.325	1960	2
95.674	95.469	0.205	1960	3
96.603	96.562	0.041	1960	4
97.564	97.692	-0.128	1961	1
98.631	98.851	-0.220	1961	2
99.871	100.014	-0.143	1961	3
101.240	101.195	0.044	1961	4
102.581	102.415	0.166	1962	1
103.851	103.658	0.193	1962	2
105.058	104.911	0.146	1962	3
106.196	106.194	0.002	1962	4
107.430	107.523	-0.094	1963	1
108.794	108.880	-0.087	1963	2
110.070	110.250	-0.180	1963	3
111.567	111.657	-0.090	1963	4
112.990	113.042	-0.052	1964	1
114.437	114.511	-0.074	1964	2
115.946	115.992	-0.047	1964	3
117.514	117.542	-0.027	1964	4
119.127	119.084	0.043	1965	1
120.794	120.653	0.142	1965	2
122.491	122.239	0.252	1965	3
124.183	123.890	0.293	1965	4
125.778	125.631	0.147	1966	1
127.212	127.211	0.001	1966	2
128.494	128.736	-0.241	1966	3
129.875	130.193	-0.318	1966	4
131.488	131.682	-0.194	1967	1
133.161	133.354	-0.193	1967	2
134.944	135.005	-0.060	1967	3
136.718	136.633	0.086	1967	4
138.424	138.258	0.167	1968	1
140.058	139.882	0.176	1968	2
141.741	141.557	0.184	1968	3
143.512	143.308	0.205	1968	4
145.172	145.021	0.151	1969	1
146.626	146.568	0.058	1969	2
147.856	147.965	-0.109	1969	3
149.306	149.268	0.039	1969	4

MSE=   0.023   RMS=   0.151   RHO=   0.792
MEAN ERR=   0.0335   MEAN=111.8331

Figure 7A–4A. Standard Dynamic Solution of Three Sectors Together:
Modigliani-Slovin Version. Life Insurance Reserves — *MIS*.

```
ACTUAL    SOLUTION   RESIDUALS                    RANGE    84.71  TO    164.64
```

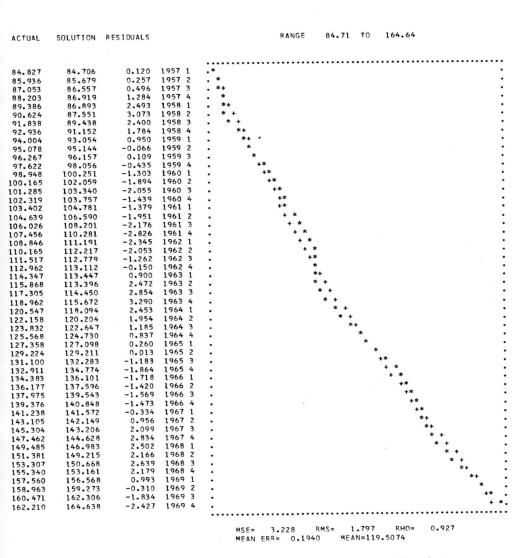

```
 84.827    84.706     0.120    1957 1
 85.936    85.679     0.257    1957 2
 87.053    86.557     0.496    1957 3
 88.203    86.919     1.284    1957 4
 89.386    86.893     2.493    1958 1
 90.624    87.551     3.073    1958 2
 91.838    89.438     2.400    1958 3
 92.936    91.152     1.784    1958 4
 94.004    93.054     0.950    1959 1
 95.078    95.144    -0.066    1959 2
 96.267    96.157     0.109    1959 3
 97.622    98.056    -0.435    1959 4
 98.948   100.251    -1.303    1960 1
100.165   102.059    -1.894    1960 2
101.285   103.340    -2.055    1960 3
102.319   103.757    -1.439    1960 4
103.402   104.781    -1.379    1961 1
104.639   106.590    -1.951    1961 2
106.026   108.201    -2.176    1961 3
107.456   110.281    -2.826    1961 4
108.846   111.191    -2.345    1962 1
110.165   112.217    -2.053    1962 2
111.517   112.779    -1.262    1962 3
112.962   113.112    -0.150    1962 4
114.347   113.447     0.900    1963 1
115.868   113.396     2.472    1963 2
117.305   114.450     2.854    1963 3
118.962   115.672     3.290    1963 4
120.547   118.094     2.453    1964 1
122.158   120.204     1.954    1964 2
123.832   122.647     1.185    1964 3
125.568   124.730     0.837    1964 4
127.358   127.098     0.260    1965 1
129.224   129.211     0.013    1965 2
131.100   132.283    -1.183    1965 3
132.911   134.774    -1.864    1965 4
134.383   136.101    -1.718    1966 1
136.177   137.596    -1.420    1966 2
137.975   139.543    -1.569    1966 3
139.376   140.848    -1.473    1966 4
141.238   141.572    -0.334    1967 1
143.105   142.149     0.956    1967 2
145.304   143.206     2.099    1967 3
147.462   144.628     2.834    1967 4
149.485   146.983     2.502    1968 1
151.381   149.215     2.166    1968 2
153.307   150.668     2.639    1968 3
155.340   153.161     2.179    1968 4
157.560   156.568     0.993    1969 1
158.963   159.273    -0.310    1969 2
160.471   162.306    -1.834    1969 3
162.210   164.638    -2.427    1969 4
```

```
MSE=    3.228    RMS=    1.797    RHO=    0.927
MEAN ERR=   0.1940    MEAN=119.5074
```

Figure 7A–4B. Standard Dynamic Solution of Three Sectors Together: Gramlich-Hulett Version. Life Insurance Reserves — *MIS*.

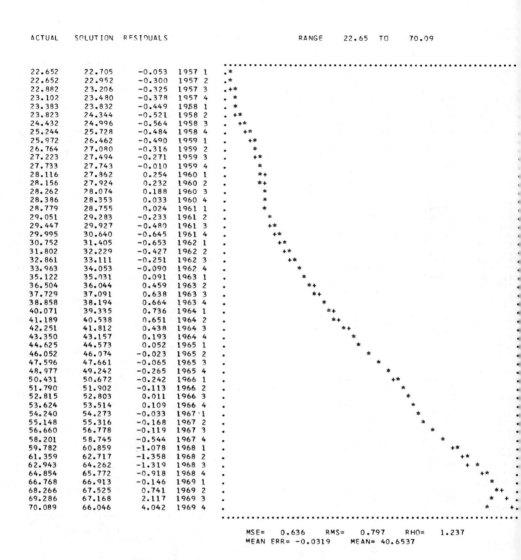

```
ACTUAL    SOLUTION  RESIDUALS                              RANGE    22.65  TO     70.09

22.652    22.705    -0.053   1957 1
22.652    22.952    -0.300   1957 2
22.882    23.206    -0.325   1957 3
23.102    23.480    -0.378   1957 4
23.383    23.832    -0.449   1958 1
23.823    24.344    -0.521   1958 2
24.432    24.996    -0.564   1958 3
25.244    25.728    -0.484   1958 4
25.972    26.462    -0.490   1959 1
26.764    27.080    -0.316   1959 2
27.223    27.494    -0.271   1959 3
27.733    27.743    -0.010   1959 4
28.116    27.862     0.254   1960 1
28.156    27.924     0.232   1960 2
28.262    28.074     0.188   1960 3
28.386    28.353     0.033   1960 4
28.779    28.755     0.024   1961 1
29.051    29.283    -0.233   1961 2
29.447    29.927    -0.480   1961 3
29.995    30.640    -0.645   1961 4
30.752    31.405    -0.653   1962 1
31.802    32.229    -0.427   1962 2
32.861    33.111    -0.251   1962 3
33.963    34.053    -0.090   1962 4
35.122    35.031     0.091   1963 1
36.504    36.044     0.459   1963 2
37.729    37.091     0.638   1963 3
38.858    38.194     0.664   1963 4
40.071    39.335     0.736   1964 1
41.189    40.538     0.651   1964 2
42.251    41.812     0.438   1964 3
43.350    43.157     0.193   1964 4
44.625    44.573     0.052   1965 1
46.052    46.074    -0.023   1965 2
47.596    47.661    -0.065   1965 3
48.977    49.242    -0.265   1965 4
50.431    50.672    -0.242   1966 1
51.790    51.902    -0.113   1966 2
52.815    52.803     0.011   1966 3
53.624    53.514     0.109   1966 4
54.240    54.273    -0.033   1967 1
55.148    55.316    -0.168   1967 2
56.660    56.778    -0.119   1967 3
58.201    58.745    -0.544   1967 4
59.782    60.859    -1.078   1968 1
61.359    62.717    -1.358   1968 2
62.943    64.262    -1.319   1968 3
64.854    65.772    -0.918   1968 4
66.768    66.913    -0.146   1969 1
68.266    67.525     0.741   1969 2
69.286    67.168     2.117   1969 3
70.089    66.046     4.042   1969 4

MSE=    0.636    RMS=    0.797    RHO=    1.237
MEAN ERR= -0.0319    MEAN= 40.6537
```

Figure 7A-5A. Standard Dynamic Solution of Three Sectors Together: Modigliani-Slovin Version. Commercial Bank Mortgage Stock — *MKCB*.

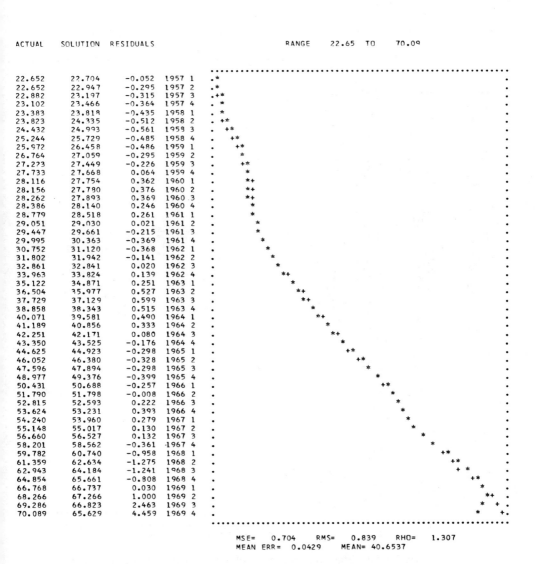

ACTUAL	SOLUTION	RESIDUALS		RANGE 22.65 TO 70.09
22.652	22.704	-0.052	1957 1	
22.652	22.947	-0.295	1957 2	
22.882	23.197	-0.315	1957 3	
23.102	23.466	-0.364	1957 4	
23.383	23.818	-0.435	1958 1	
23.823	24.335	-0.512	1958 2	
24.432	24.993	-0.561	1958 3	
25.244	25.729	-0.485	1958 4	
25.972	26.458	-0.486	1959 1	
26.764	27.059	-0.295	1959 2	
27.223	27.449	-0.226	1959 3	
27.733	27.668	0.064	1959 4	
28.116	27.754	0.362	1960 1	
28.156	27.780	0.376	1960 2	
28.262	27.893	0.369	1960 3	
28.386	28.140	0.246	1960 4	
28.779	28.518	0.261	1961 1	
29.051	29.030	0.021	1961 2	
29.447	29.661	-0.215	1961 3	
29.995	30.363	-0.369	1961 4	
30.752	31.120	-0.368	1962 1	
31.802	31.942	-0.141	1962 2	
32.861	32.841	0.020	1962 3	
33.963	33.824	0.139	1962 4	
35.122	34.871	0.251	1963 1	
36.504	35.977	0.527	1963 2	
37.729	37.129	0.599	1963 3	
38.858	38.343	0.515	1963 4	
40.071	39.581	0.490	1964 1	
41.189	40.856	0.333	1964 2	
42.251	42.171	0.080	1964 3	
43.350	43.525	-0.176	1964 4	
44.625	44.923	-0.298	1965 1	
46.052	46.380	-0.328	1965 2	
47.596	47.894	-0.298	1965 3	
48.977	49.376	-0.399	1965 4	
50.431	50.688	-0.257	1966 1	
51.790	51.798	-0.008	1966 2	
52.815	52.593	0.222	1966 3	
53.624	53.231	0.393	1966 4	
54.240	53.960	0.279	1967 1	
55.148	55.017	0.130	1967 2	
56.660	56.527	0.132	1967 3	
58.201	58.562	-0.361	1967 4	
59.782	60.740	-0.958	1968 1	
61.359	62.634	-1.275	1968 2	
62.943	64.184	-1.241	1968 3	
64.854	65.661	-0.808	1968 4	
66.768	66.737	0.030	1969 1	
68.266	67.266	1.000	1969 2	
69.286	66.823	2.463	1969 3	
70.089	65.629	4.459	1969 4	

MSE= 0.704 RMS= 0.839 RHO= 1.307
MEAN ERR= 0.0429 MEAN= 40.6537

Figure 7A-5B. Standard Dynamic Solution of Three Sectors Together: Gramlich-Hulett Version. Commercial Bank Mortgage Stock — *MKCB*.

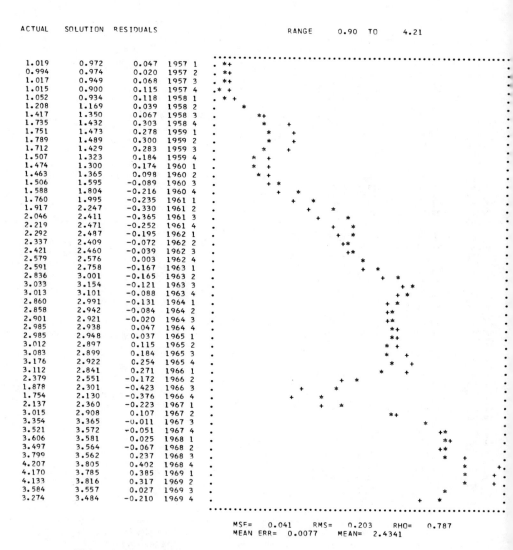

ACTUAL	SOLUTION	RESIDUALS		
1.019	0.972	0.047	1957	1
0.994	0.974	0.020	1957	2
1.017	0.949	0.068	1957	3
1.015	0.900	0.115	1957	4
1.052	0.934	0.118	1958	1
1.208	1.169	0.039	1958	2
1.417	1.350	0.067	1958	3
1.735	1.432	0.303	1958	4
1.751	1.473	0.278	1959	1
1.789	1.489	0.300	1959	2
1.712	1.429	0.283	1959	3
1.507	1.323	0.184	1959	4
1.474	1.300	0.174	1960	1
1.463	1.365	0.098	1960	2
1.506	1.595	-0.089	1960	3
1.588	1.804	-0.216	1960	4
1.760	1.995	-0.235	1961	1
1.917	2.247	-0.330	1961	2
2.046	2.411	-0.365	1961	3
2.219	2.471	-0.252	1961	4
2.292	2.487	-0.195	1962	1
2.337	2.409	-0.072	1962	2
2.421	2.460	-0.039	1962	3
2.579	2.576	0.003	1962	4
2.591	2.758	-0.167	1963	1
2.836	3.001	-0.165	1963	2
3.033	3.154	-0.121	1963	3
3.013	3.101	-0.088	1963	4
2.860	2.991	-0.131	1964	1
2.858	2.942	-0.084	1964	2
2.901	2.921	-0.020	1964	3
2.985	2.938	0.047	1964	4
2.985	2.948	0.037	1965	1
3.012	2.897	0.115	1965	2
3.083	2.899	0.184	1965	3
3.176	2.922	0.254	1965	4
3.112	2.841	0.271	1966	1
2.379	2.551	-0.172	1966	2
1.878	2.301	-0.423	1966	3
1.754	2.130	-0.376	1966	4
2.137	2.360	-0.223	1967	1
3.015	2.908	0.107	1967	2
3.354	3.365	-0.011	1967	3
3.521	3.572	-0.051	1967	4
3.606	3.581	0.025	1968	1
3.497	3.564	-0.067	1968	2
3.799	3.562	0.237	1968	3
4.207	3.805	0.402	1968	4
4.170	3.785	0.385	1969	1
4.133	3.816	0.317	1969	2
3.584	3.557	0.027	1969	3
3.274	3.484	-0.210	1969	4

RANGE 0.90 TO 4.21

MSE= 0.041 RMS= 0.203 RHO= 0.787
MEAN ERR= 0.0077 MEAN= 2.4341

Figure 7A–6A. Standard Dynamic Solution of Three Sectors Together: Modigliani-Slovin Version. Savings and Loan Mortgage Commitments — *MCOS*.

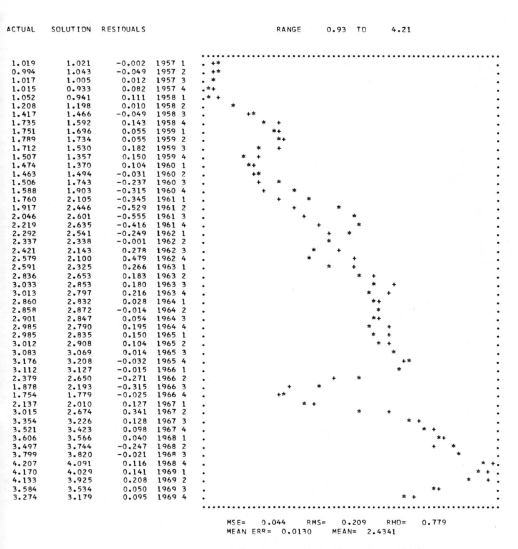

ACTUAL	SOLUTION	RESIDUALS			RANGE	0.93	TO	4.21
1.019	1.021	-0.002	1957	1				
0.994	1.043	-0.049	1957	2				
1.017	1.005	0.012	1957	3				
1.015	0.933	0.082	1957	4				
1.052	0.941	0.111	1958	1				
1.208	1.198	0.010	1958	2				
1.417	1.466	-0.049	1958	3				
1.735	1.592	0.143	1958	4				
1.751	1.696	0.055	1959	1				
1.789	1.734	0.055	1959	2				
1.712	1.530	0.182	1959	3				
1.507	1.357	0.150	1959	4				
1.474	1.370	0.104	1960	1				
1.463	1.494	-0.031	1960	2				
1.506	1.743	-0.237	1960	3				
1.588	1.903	-0.315	1960	4				
1.760	2.105	-0.345	1961	1				
1.917	2.446	-0.529	1961	2				
2.046	2.601	-0.555	1961	3				
2.219	2.635	-0.416	1961	4				
2.292	2.541	-0.249	1962	1				
2.337	2.338	-0.001	1962	2				
2.421	2.143	0.278	1962	3				
2.579	2.100	0.479	1962	4				
2.591	2.325	0.266	1963	1				
2.836	2.653	0.183	1963	2				
3.033	2.853	0.180	1963	3				
3.013	2.797	0.216	1963	4				
2.860	2.832	0.028	1964	1				
2.858	2.872	-0.014	1964	2				
2.901	2.847	0.054	1964	3				
2.985	2.790	0.195	1964	4				
2.985	2.835	0.150	1965	1				
3.012	2.908	0.104	1965	2				
3.083	3.069	0.014	1965	3				
3.176	3.208	-0.032	1965	4				
3.112	3.127	-0.015	1966	1				
2.379	2.650	-0.271	1966	2				
1.878	2.193	-0.315	1966	3				
1.754	1.779	-0.025	1966	4				
2.137	2.010	0.127	1967	1				
3.015	2.674	0.341	1967	2				
3.354	3.226	0.128	1967	3				
3.521	3.423	0.098	1967	4				
3.606	3.566	0.040	1968	1				
3.497	3.744	-0.247	1968	2				
3.799	3.820	-0.021	1968	3				
4.207	4.091	0.116	1968	4				
4.170	4.029	0.141	1969	1				
4.133	3.925	0.208	1969	2				
3.584	3.534	0.050	1969	3				
3.274	3.179	0.095	1969	4				

MSE= 0.044   RMS= 0.209   RHO= 0.779
MEAN ERR= 0.0130   MEAN= 2.4341

Figure 7A–6B. Standard Dynamic Solution of Three Sectors Together: Gramlich-Hulett Version. Savings and Loan Mortgage Commitments — *MCOS*.

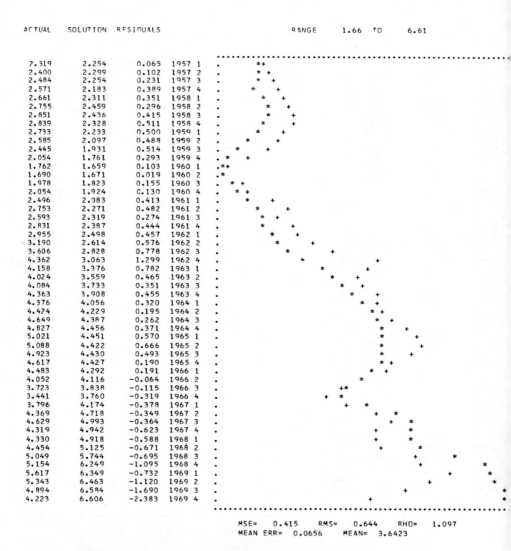

| ACTUAL | SOLUTION | RESIDUALS | | | RANGE | 1.66 TO | 6.61 |

ACTUAL	SOLUTION	RESIDUALS		
2.319	2.254	0.065	1957	1
2.400	2.299	0.102	1957	2
2.484	2.254	0.231	1957	3
2.571	2.183	0.389	1957	4
2.661	2.311	0.351	1958	1
2.755	2.459	0.296	1958	2
2.851	2.436	0.415	1958	3
2.839	2.328	0.511	1958	4
2.733	2.233	0.500	1959	1
2.585	2.097	0.488	1959	2
2.445	1.931	0.514	1959	3
2.054	1.761	0.293	1959	4
1.762	1.659	0.103	1960	1
1.690	1.671	0.019	1960	2
1.978	1.823	0.155	1960	3
2.054	1.924	0.130	1960	4
2.496	2.083	0.413	1961	1
2.753	2.271	0.482	1961	2
2.593	2.319	0.274	1961	3
2.831	2.387	0.444	1961	4
2.955	2.498	0.457	1962	1
3.190	2.614	0.576	1962	2
3.606	2.828	0.778	1962	3
4.362	3.063	1.299	1962	4
4.158	3.376	0.782	1963	1
4.024	3.559	0.465	1963	2
4.084	3.733	0.351	1963	3
4.363	3.908	0.455	1963	4
4.376	4.056	0.320	1964	1
4.424	4.229	0.195	1964	2
4.649	4.387	0.262	1964	3
4.827	4.456	0.371	1964	4
5.021	4.451	0.570	1965	1
5.088	4.422	0.666	1965	2
4.923	4.430	0.493	1965	3
4.617	4.427	0.190	1965	4
4.483	4.292	0.191	1966	1
4.052	4.116	−0.064	1966	2
3.723	3.838	−0.115	1966	3
3.441	3.760	−0.319	1966	4
3.796	4.174	−0.378	1967	1
4.369	4.718	−0.349	1967	2
4.629	4.993	−0.364	1967	3
4.319	4.942	−0.623	1967	4
4.330	4.918	−0.588	1968	1
4.454	5.125	−0.671	1968	2
5.049	5.744	−0.695	1968	3
5.154	6.249	−1.095	1968	4
5.617	6.349	−0.732	1969	1
5.343	6.463	−1.120	1969	2
4.894	6.584	−1.690	1969	3
4.223	6.606	−2.383	1969	4

MSE= 0.415   RMS= 0.644   RHO= 1.097
MEAN ERR= 0.0656   MEAN= 3.6423

Figure 7A-7A. Standard Dynamic Solution of Three Sectors Together: Modigliani-Slovin Version. Mutual Savings Bank Mortgage Commitments — *MCOM*.

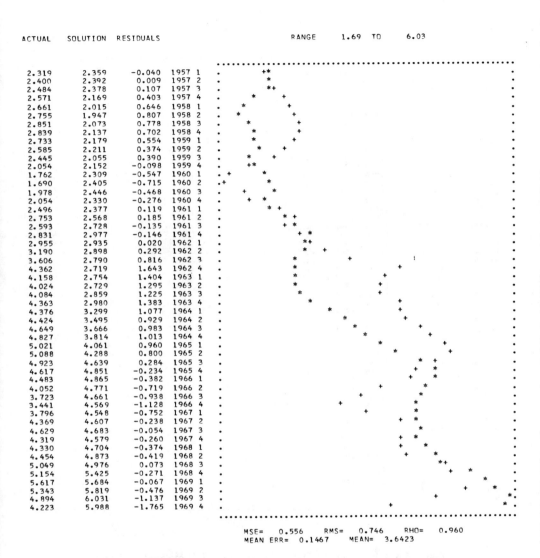

ACTUAL	SOLUTION	RESIDUALS				RANGE	1.69	TO	6.03
2.319	2.359	-0.040	1957	1					
2.400	2.392	0.009	1957	2					
2.484	2.378	0.107	1957	3					
2.571	2.169	0.403	1957	4					
2.661	2.015	0.646	1958	1					
2.755	1.947	0.807	1958	2					
2.851	2.073	0.778	1958	3					
2.839	2.137	0.702	1958	4					
2.733	2.179	0.554	1959	1					
2.585	2.211	0.374	1959	2					
2.445	2.055	0.390	1959	3					
2.054	2.152	-0.098	1959	4					
1.762	2.309	-0.547	1960	1					
1.690	2.405	-0.715	1960	2					
1.978	2.446	-0.468	1960	3					
2.054	2.330	-0.276	1960	4					
2.496	2.377	0.119	1961	1					
2.753	2.568	0.185	1961	2					
2.593	2.728	-0.135	1961	3					
2.831	2.977	-0.146	1961	4					
2.955	2.935	0.020	1962	1					
3.190	2.898	0.292	1962	2					
3.606	2.790	0.816	1962	3					
4.362	2.719	1.643	1962	4					
4.158	2.754	1.404	1963	1					
4.024	2.729	1.295	1963	2					
4.084	2.859	1.225	1963	3					
4.363	2.980	1.383	1963	4					
4.376	3.299	1.077	1964	1					
4.424	3.495	0.929	1964	2					
4.649	3.666	0.983	1964	3					
4.827	3.814	1.013	1964	4					
5.021	4.061	0.960	1965	1					
5.088	4.288	0.800	1965	2					
4.923	4.639	0.284	1965	3					
4.617	4.851	-0.234	1965	4					
4.483	4.865	-0.382	1966	1					
4.052	4.771	-0.719	1966	2					
3.723	4.661	-0.938	1966	3					
3.441	4.569	-1.128	1966	4					
3.796	4.548	-0.752	1967	1					
4.369	4.607	-0.238	1967	2					
4.629	4.683	-0.054	1967	3					
4.319	4.579	-0.260	1967	4					
4.330	4.704	-0.374	1968	1					
4.454	4.873	-0.419	1968	2					
5.049	4.976	0.073	1968	3					
5.154	5.425	-0.271	1968	4					
5.617	5.684	-0.067	1969	1					
5.343	5.819	-0.476	1969	2					
4.894	6.031	-1.137	1969	3					
4.223	5.988	-1.765	1969	4					

MSE=   0.556   RMS=   0.746   RHO=   0.960
MEAN ERR= 0.1467   MEAN=   3.6423

Figure 7A-7B. Standard Dynamic Solution of Three Sectors Together: Gramlich-Hulett Version. Mutual Savings Bank Mortgage Commitments — *MCOM*.

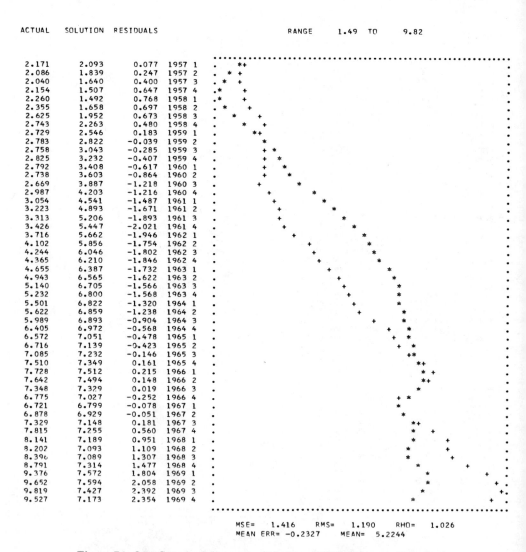

```
ACTUAL    SOLUTION   RESIDUALS                              RANGE    1.49  TO      9.82

2.171      2.093      0.077   1957 1
2.086      1.839      0.247   1957 2
2.040      1.640      0.400   1957 3
2.154      1.507      0.647   1957 4
2.260      1.492      0.768   1958 1
2.355      1.658      0.697   1958 2
2.625      1.952      0.673   1958 3
2.743      2.263      0.480   1958 4
2.729      2.546      0.183   1959 1
2.783      2.822     -0.039   1959 2
2.758      3.043     -0.285   1959 3
2.825      3.232     -0.407   1959 4
2.792      3.408     -0.617   1960 1
2.738      3.603     -0.864   1960 2
2.669      3.887     -1.218   1960 3
2.987      4.203     -1.216   1960 4
3.054      4.541     -1.487   1961 1
3.223      4.893     -1.671   1961 2
3.313      5.206     -1.893   1961 3
3.426      5.447     -2.021   1961 4
3.716      5.662     -1.946   1962 1
4.102      5.856     -1.754   1962 2
4.244      6.046     -1.802   1962 3
4.365      6.210     -1.846   1962 4
4.655      6.387     -1.732   1963 1
4.943      6.565     -1.622   1963 2
5.140      6.705     -1.566   1963 3
5.232      6.800     -1.568   1963 4
5.501      6.822     -1.320   1964 1
5.622      6.859     -1.238   1964 2
5.989      6.893     -0.904   1964 3
6.405      6.972     -0.568   1964 4
6.572      7.051     -0.478   1965 1
6.716      7.139     -0.423   1965 2
7.085      7.232     -0.146   1965 3
7.510      7.349      0.161   1965 4
7.728      7.512      0.215   1966 1
7.642      7.494      0.148   1966 2
7.348      7.329      0.019   1966 3
6.775      7.027     -0.252   1966 4
6.721      6.799     -0.078   1967 1
6.878      6.929     -0.051   1967 2
7.329      7.148      0.181   1967 3
7.815      7.255      0.560   1967 4
8.141      7.189      0.951   1968 1
8.202      7.093      1.109   1968 2
8.396      7.089      1.307   1968 3
8.791      7.314      1.477   1968 4
9.376      7.572      1.804   1969 1
9.652      7.594      2.058   1969 2
9.819      7.427      2.392   1969 3
9.527      7.173      2.354   1969 4

           MSE=    1.416    RMS=    1.190    RHO=    1.026
           MEAN ERR= -0.2327      MEAN=   5.2244
```

Figure 7A–8A. Standard Dynamic Solution of Three Sectors Together: Modigliani-Slovin Version. Life Insurance Company Outstanding Mortgage Commitments — *MCOI*.

ACTUAL   SOLUTION   RESIDUALS   RANGE   0.51   TO   9.84

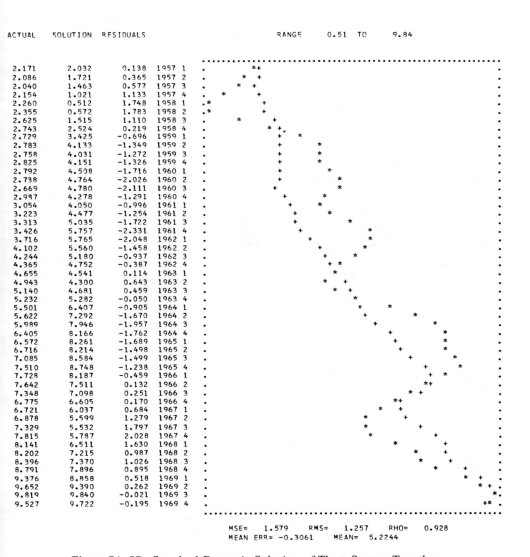

ACTUAL	SOLUTION	RESIDUALS		
2.171	2.032	0.138	1957	1
2.086	1.721	0.365	1957	2
2.040	1.463	0.577	1957	3
2.154	1.021	1.133	1957	4
2.260	0.512	1.748	1958	1
2.355	0.572	1.783	1958	2
2.625	1.515	1.110	1958	3
2.743	2.524	0.219	1958	4
2.729	3.425	-0.696	1959	1
2.783	4.133	-1.349	1959	2
2.758	4.031	-1.272	1959	3
2.825	4.151	-1.326	1959	4
2.792	4.508	-1.716	1960	1
2.738	4.764	-2.026	1960	2
2.669	4.780	-2.111	1960	3
2.987	4.278	-1.291	1960	4
3.054	4.050	-0.996	1961	1
3.223	4.477	-1.254	1961	2
3.313	5.035	-1.722	1961	3
3.426	5.757	-2.331	1961	4
3.716	5.765	-2.048	1962	1
4.102	5.560	-1.458	1962	2
4.244	5.180	-0.937	1962	3
4.365	4.752	-0.387	1962	4
4.655	4.541	0.114	1963	1
4.943	4.300	0.643	1963	2
5.140	4.681	0.459	1963	3
5.232	5.282	-0.050	1963	4
5.501	6.407	-0.905	1964	1
5.622	7.292	-1.670	1964	2
5.989	7.946	-1.957	1964	3
6.405	8.166	-1.762	1964	4
6.572	8.261	-1.689	1965	1
6.716	8.214	-1.498	1965	2
7.085	8.584	-1.499	1965	3
7.510	8.748	-1.238	1965	4
7.728	8.187	-0.459	1966	1
7.642	7.511	0.132	1966	2
7.348	7.098	0.251	1966	3
6.775	6.605	0.170	1966	4
6.721	6.037	0.684	1967	1
6.878	5.599	1.279	1967	2
7.329	5.532	1.797	1967	3
7.815	5.787	2.028	1967	4
8.141	6.511	1.630	1968	1
8.202	7.215	0.987	1968	2
8.396	7.370	1.026	1968	3
8.791	7.896	0.895	1968	4
9.376	8.858	0.518	1969	1
9.652	9.390	0.262	1969	2
9.819	9.840	-0.021	1969	3
9.527	9.722	-0.195	1969	4

MSE=   1.579   RMS=   1.257   RHO=   0.928
MEAN ERR= -0.3061   MEAN=   5.2244

Figure 7A-8B. Standard Dynamic Solution of Three Sectors Together: Gramlich-Hulett Version. Life Insurance Company Outstanding Mortgage Commitments — *MCOI*.

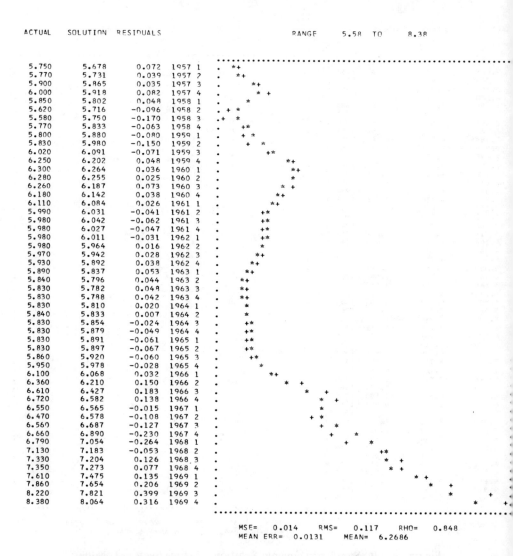

ACTUAL   SOLUTION RESIDUALS   RANGE   5.58 TO   8.38

ACTUAL	SOLUTION	RESIDUALS		
5.750	5.678	0.072	1957	1
5.770	5.731	0.039	1957	2
5.900	5.865	0.035	1957	3
6.000	5.918	0.082	1957	4
5.850	5.802	0.048	1958	1
5.620	5.716	−0.096	1958	2
5.580	5.750	−0.170	1958	3
5.770	5.833	−0.063	1958	4
5.800	5.880	−0.080	1959	1
5.830	5.980	−0.150	1959	2
6.020	6.091	−0.071	1959	3
6.250	6.202	0.048	1959	4
6.300	6.264	0.036	1960	1
6.280	6.255	0.025	1960	2
6.260	6.187	0.073	1960	3
6.180	6.142	0.038	1960	4
6.110	6.084	0.026	1961	1
5.990	6.031	−0.041	1961	2
5.980	6.042	−0.062	1961	3
5.980	6.027	−0.047	1961	4
5.980	6.011	−0.031	1962	1
5.980	5.964	0.016	1962	2
5.970	5.942	0.028	1962	3
5.930	5.892	0.038	1962	4
5.890	5.837	0.053	1963	1
5.840	5.796	0.044	1963	2
5.830	5.782	0.048	1963	3
5.830	5.788	0.042	1963	4
5.830	5.810	0.020	1964	1
5.840	5.833	0.007	1964	2
5.830	5.854	−0.024	1964	3
5.830	5.879	−0.049	1964	4
5.830	5.891	−0.061	1965	1
5.830	5.897	−0.067	1965	2
5.860	5.920	−0.060	1965	3
5.950	5.978	−0.028	1965	4
6.100	6.068	0.032	1966	1
6.360	6.210	0.150	1966	2
6.610	6.427	0.183	1966	3
6.720	6.582	0.138	1966	4
6.550	6.565	−0.015	1967	1
6.470	6.578	−0.108	1967	2
6.560	6.687	−0.127	1967	3
6.660	6.890	−0.230	1967	4
6.790	7.054	−0.264	1968	1
7.130	7.183	−0.053	1968	2
7.330	7.204	0.126	1968	3
7.350	7.273	0.077	1968	4
7.610	7.475	0.135	1969	1
7.860	7.654	0.206	1969	2
8.220	7.821	0.399	1969	3
8.380	8.064	0.316	1969	4

MSE=   0.014   RMS=   0.117   RHO=   0.848
MEAN ERR= 0.0131   MEAN=   6.2686

Figure 7A-9A. Standard Dynamic Solution of Three Sectors Together: Modigliani-Slovin Version. Mortgage Interest Rate − *RM*.

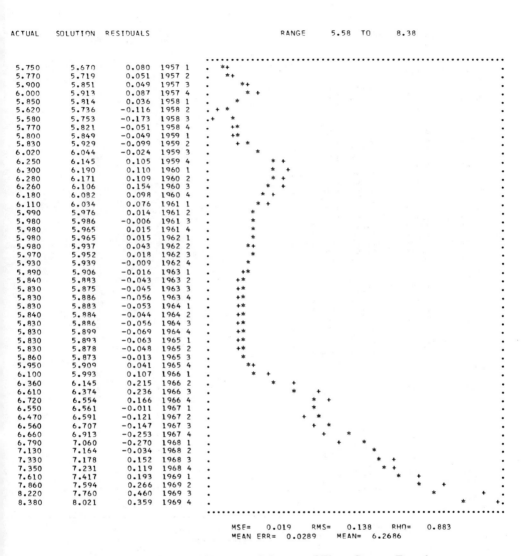

```
ACTUAL    SOLUTION  RESIDUALS                               RANGE      5.58  TO      8.38

5.750     5.670     0.080    1957 1
5.770     5.719     0.051    1957 2
5.900     5.851     0.049    1957 3
6.000     5.913     0.087    1957 4
5.850     5.814     0.036    1958 1
5.620     5.736    -0.116    1958 2
5.580     5.753    -0.173    1958 3
5.770     5.821    -0.051    1958 4
5.800     5.849    -0.049    1959 1
5.830     5.929    -0.099    1959 2
6.020     6.044    -0.024    1959 3
6.250     6.145     0.105    1959 4
6.300     6.190     0.110    1960 1
6.280     6.171     0.109    1960 2
6.260     6.106     0.154    1960 3
6.180     6.082     0.098    1960 4
6.110     6.034     0.076    1961 1
5.990     5.976     0.014    1961 2
5.980     5.986    -0.006    1961 3
5.980     5.965     0.015    1961 4
5.980     5.965     0.015    1962 1
5.980     5.937     0.043    1962 2
5.970     5.952     0.018    1962 3
5.930     5.939    -0.009    1962 4
5.890     5.906    -0.016    1963 1
5.840     5.883    -0.043    1963 2
5.830     5.875    -0.045    1963 3
5.830     5.886    -0.056    1963 4
5.830     5.883    -0.053    1964 1
5.840     5.884    -0.044    1964 2
5.830     5.886    -0.056    1964 3
5.830     5.899    -0.069    1964 4
5.830     5.893    -0.063    1965 1
5.830     5.878    -0.048    1965 2
5.860     5.873    -0.013    1965 3
5.950     5.909     0.041    1965 4
6.100     5.993     0.107    1966 1
6.360     6.145     0.215    1966 2
6.610     6.374     0.236    1966 3
6.720     6.554     0.166    1966 4
6.550     6.561    -0.011    1967 1
6.470     6.591    -0.121    1967 2
6.560     6.707    -0.147    1967 3
6.660     6.913    -0.253    1967 4
6.790     7.060    -0.270    1968 1
7.130     7.164    -0.034    1968 2
7.330     7.178     0.152    1968 3
7.350     7.231     0.119    1968 4
7.610     7.417     0.193    1969 1
7.860     7.594     0.266    1969 2
8.220     7.760     0.460    1969 3
8.380     8.021     0.359    1969 4

                    MSE=    0.019    RMS=     0.138    RHO=      0.883
                    MEAN ERR=  0.0289     MEAN=   6.2686
```

Figure 7A-9B. Standard Dynamic Solution of Three Sectors Together: Gramlich-Hulett Version. Mortgage Interest Rate — *RM.*

ACTUAL   SOLUTION   RESIDUALS   RANGE   2.71   TO   4.62

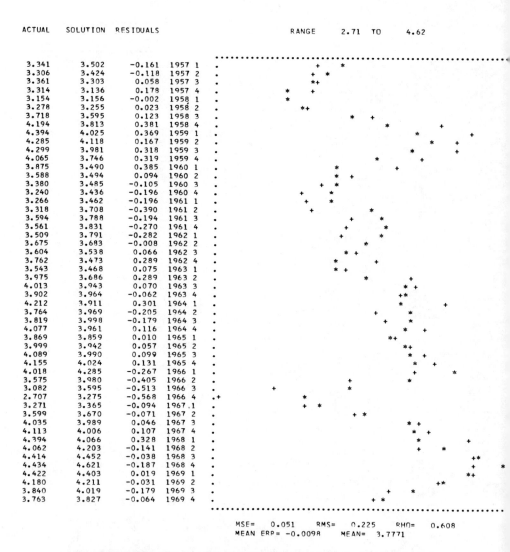

ACTUAL	SOLUTION	RESIDUALS		
3.341	3.502	-0.161	1957	1
3.306	3.424	-0.118	1957	2
3.361	3.303	0.058	1957	3
3.314	3.136	0.178	1957	4
3.154	3.156	-0.002	1958	1
3.278	3.255	0.023	1958	2
3.718	3.595	0.123	1958	3
4.194	3.813	0.381	1958	4
4.394	4.025	0.369	1959	1
4.285	4.118	0.167	1959	2
4.299	3.981	0.318	1959	3
4.065	3.746	0.319	1959	4
3.875	3.490	0.385	1960	1
3.588	3.494	0.094	1960	2
3.380	3.485	-0.105	1960	3
3.240	3.436	-0.196	1960	4
3.266	3.462	-0.196	1961	1
3.318	3.708	-0.390	1961	2
3.594	3.788	-0.194	1961	3
3.561	3.831	-0.270	1961	4
3.509	3.791	-0.282	1962	1
3.675	3.683	-0.008	1962	2
3.604	3.538	0.066	1962	3
3.762	3.473	0.289	1962	4
3.543	3.468	0.075	1963	1
3.975	3.686	0.289	1963	2
4.013	3.943	0.070	1963	3
3.902	3.964	-0.062	1963	4
4.212	3.911	0.301	1964	1
3.764	3.969	-0.205	1964	2
3.819	3.998	-0.179	1964	3
4.077	3.961	0.116	1964	4
3.869	3.859	0.010	1965	1
3.999	3.942	0.057	1965	2
4.089	3.990	0.099	1965	3
4.155	4.024	0.131	1965	4
4.018	4.285	-0.267	1966	1
3.575	3.980	-0.405	1966	2
3.082	3.595	-0.513	1966	3
2.707	3.275	-0.568	1966	4
3.271	3.365	-0.094	1967	1
3.599	3.670	-0.071	1967	2
4.035	3.989	0.046	1967	3
4.113	4.006	0.107	1967	4
4.394	4.066	0.328	1968	1
4.062	4.203	-0.141	1968	2
4.414	4.452	-0.038	1968	3
4.434	4.621	-0.187	1968	4
4.422	4.403	0.019	1969	1
4.180	4.211	-0.031	1969	2
3.840	4.019	-0.179	1969	3
3.763	3.827	-0.064	1969	4

MSE=   0.051   RMS=   0.225   RHO=   0.608
MEAN ERR= -0.0098   MEAN=   3.7771

Figure 7A-10A. Standard Dynamic Solution of Three Sectors Together: Modigliani-Slovin Version. Single-Family Housing Starts — *HS1$*.

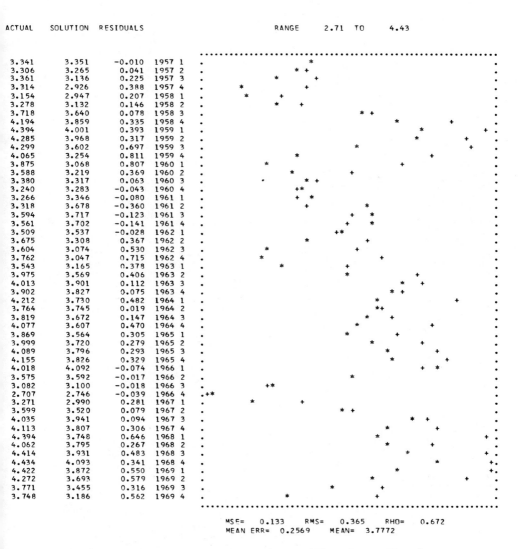

Figure 7A-10B. Standard Dynamic Solution of Three Sectors Together: Gramlich-Hulett Version. Single-Family Housing Starts — *HS1$*.

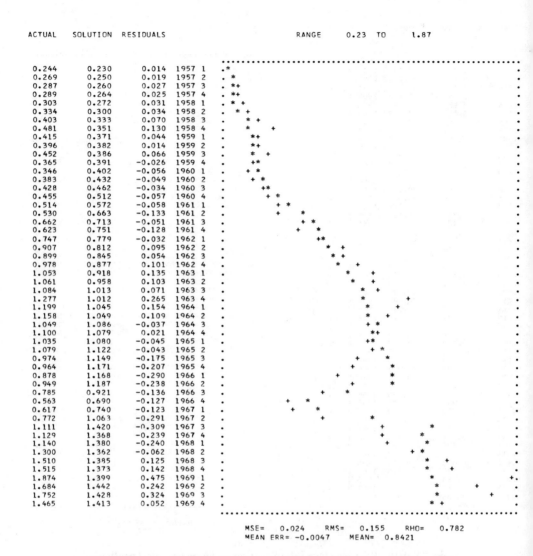

ACTUAL	SOLUTION	RESIDUALS			RANGE	0.23	TO	1.87
0.244	0.230	0.014	1957	1				
0.269	0.250	0.019	1957	2				
0.287	0.260	0.027	1957	3				
0.289	0.264	0.025	1957	4				
0.303	0.272	0.031	1958	1				
0.334	0.300	0.034	1958	2				
0.403	0.333	0.070	1958	3				
0.481	0.351	0.130	1958	4				
0.415	0.371	0.044	1959	1				
0.396	0.382	0.014	1959	2				
0.452	0.386	0.066	1959	3				
0.365	0.391	-0.026	1959	4				
0.346	0.402	-0.056	1960	1				
0.383	0.432	-0.049	1960	2				
0.428	0.462	-0.034	1960	3				
0.455	0.512	-0.057	1960	4				
0.514	0.572	-0.058	1961	1				
0.530	0.663	-0.133	1961	2				
0.662	0.713	-0.051	1961	3				
0.623	0.751	-0.128	1961	4				
0.747	0.779	-0.032	1962	1				
0.907	0.812	0.095	1962	2				
0.899	0.845	0.054	1962	3				
0.978	0.877	0.101	1962	4				
1.053	0.918	0.135	1963	1				
1.061	0.958	0.103	1963	2				
1.084	1.013	0.071	1963	3				
1.277	1.012	0.265	1963	4				
1.199	1.045	0.154	1964	1				
1.158	1.049	0.109	1964	2				
1.049	1.086	-0.037	1964	3				
1.100	1.079	0.021	1964	4				
1.035	1.080	-0.045	1965	1				
1.079	1.122	-0.043	1965	2				
0.974	1.149	-0.175	1965	3				
0.964	1.171	-0.207	1965	4				
0.878	1.168	-0.290	1966	1				
0.949	1.187	-0.238	1966	2				
0.785	0.921	-0.136	1966	3				
0.563	0.690	-0.127	1966	4				
0.617	0.740	-0.123	1967	1				
0.772	1.063	-0.291	1967	2				
1.111	1.420	-0.309	1967	3				
1.129	1.368	-0.239	1967	4				
1.140	1.380	-0.240	1968	1				
1.300	1.362	-0.062	1968	2				
1.510	1.385	0.125	1968	3				
1.515	1.373	0.142	1968	4				
1.874	1.399	0.475	1969	1				
1.684	1.442	0.242	1969	2				
1.752	1.428	0.324	1969	3				
1.465	1.413	0.052	1969	4				

MSE= 0.024   RMS= 0.155   RHO= 0.782
MEAN ERR= -0.0047   MEAN= 0.8421

Figure 7A–11A. Standard Dynamic Solution of Three Sectors Together: Modigliani-Slovin Version. Multifamily Housing Starts — *HS3$*.

| ACTUAL | SOLUTION | RESIDUALS | | | RANGE | 0.23 | TO | 1.81 |

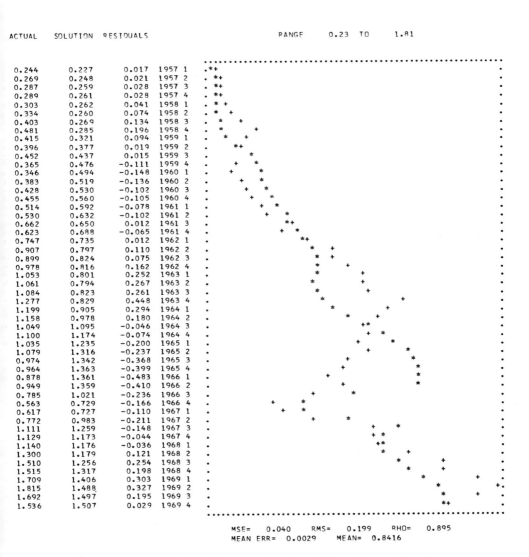

ACTUAL	SOLUTION	RESIDUALS		
0.244	0.227	0.017	1957	1
0.269	0.248	0.021	1957	2
0.287	0.259	0.028	1957	3
0.289	0.261	0.028	1957	4
0.303	0.262	0.041	1958	1
0.334	0.260	0.074	1958	2
0.403	0.269	0.134	1958	3
0.481	0.285	0.196	1958	4
0.415	0.321	0.094	1959	1
0.396	0.377	0.019	1959	2
0.452	0.437	0.015	1959	3
0.365	0.476	-0.111	1959	4
0.346	0.494	-0.148	1960	1
0.383	0.519	-0.136	1960	2
0.428	0.530	-0.102	1960	3
0.455	0.560	-0.105	1960	4
0.514	0.592	-0.078	1961	1
0.530	0.632	-0.102	1961	2
0.662	0.650	0.012	1961	3
0.623	0.688	-0.065	1961	4
0.747	0.735	0.012	1962	1
0.907	0.797	0.110	1962	2
0.899	0.824	0.075	1962	3
0.978	0.816	0.162	1962	4
1.053	0.801	0.252	1963	1
1.061	0.794	0.267	1963	2
1.084	0.823	0.261	1963	3
1.277	0.829	0.448	1963	4
1.199	0.905	0.294	1964	1
1.158	0.978	0.180	1964	2
1.049	1.095	-0.046	1964	3
1.100	1.174	-0.074	1964	4
1.035	1.235	-0.200	1965	1
1.079	1.316	-0.237	1965	2
0.974	1.342	-0.368	1965	3
0.964	1.363	-0.399	1965	4
0.878	1.361	-0.483	1966	1
0.949	1.359	-0.410	1966	2
0.785	1.021	-0.236	1966	3
0.563	0.729	-0.166	1966	4
0.617	0.727	-0.110	1967	1
0.772	0.983	-0.211	1967	2
1.111	1.259	-0.148	1967	3
1.129	1.173	-0.044	1967	4
1.140	1.176	-0.036	1968	1
1.300	1.179	0.121	1968	2
1.510	1.256	0.254	1968	3
1.515	1.317	0.198	1968	4
1.709	1.406	0.303	1969	1
1.815	1.488	0.327	1969	2
1.692	1.497	0.195	1969	3
1.536	1.507	0.029	1969	4

MSE= 0.040   RMS= 0.199   RHO= 0.895
MEAN ERR= 0.0029   MEAN= 0.8416

Figure 7A-11B. Standard Dynamic Solution of Three Sectors Together: Gramlich-Hulett Version. Multifamily Housing Starts — *HS3$*.

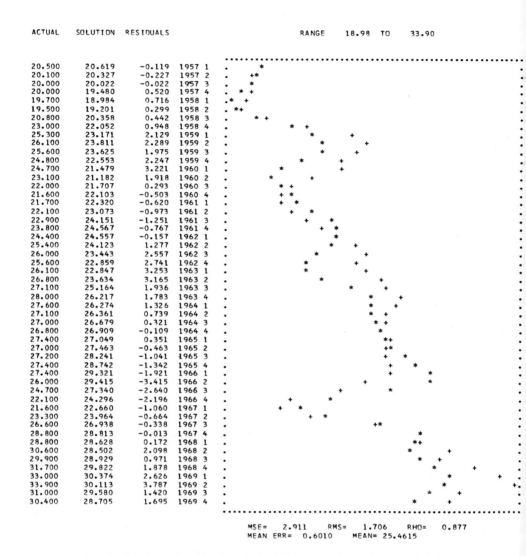

ACTUAL   SOLUTION   RESIDUALS   RANGE   18.98 TO   33.90

ACTUAL	SOLUTION	RESIDUALS		
20.500	20.619	-0.119	1957	1
20.100	20.327	-0.227	1957	2
20.000	20.022	-0.022	1957	3
20.000	19.480	0.520	1957	4
19.700	18.984	0.716	1958	1
19.500	19.201	0.299	1958	2
20.800	20.358	0.442	1958	3
23.000	22.052	0.948	1958	4
25.300	23.171	2.129	1959	1
26.100	23.811	2.289	1959	2
25.600	23.625	1.975	1959	3
24.800	22.553	2.247	1959	4
24.700	21.479	3.221	1960	1
23.100	21.182	1.918	1960	2
22.000	21.707	0.293	1960	3
21.600	22.103	-0.503	1960	4
21.700	22.320	-0.620	1961	1
22.100	23.073	-0.973	1961	2
22.900	24.151	-1.251	1961	3
23.800	24.567	-0.767	1961	4
24.400	24.557	-0.157	1962	1
25.400	24.123	1.277	1962	2
26.000	23.443	2.557	1962	3
25.600	22.859	2.741	1962	4
26.100	22.847	3.253	1963	1
26.800	23.634	3.165	1963	2
27.100	25.164	1.936	1963	3
28.000	26.217	1.783	1963	4
27.600	26.274	1.326	1964	1
27.100	26.361	0.739	1964	2
27.000	26.679	0.321	1964	3
26.800	26.909	-0.109	1964	4
27.400	27.049	0.351	1965	1
27.000	27.463	-0.463	1965	2
27.200	28.241	-1.041	1965	3
27.400	28.742	-1.342	1965	4
27.400	29.321	-1.921	1966	1
26.000	29.415	-3.415	1966	2
24.700	27.340	-2.640	1966	3
22.100	24.296	-2.196	1966	4
21.600	22.660	-1.060	1967	1
23.300	23.964	-0.664	1967	2
26.600	26.938	-0.338	1967	3
28.800	28.813	-0.013	1967	4
28.800	28.628	0.172	1968	1
30.600	28.502	2.098	1968	2
29.900	28.929	0.971	1968	3
31.700	29.822	1.878	1968	4
33.000	30.374	2.626	1969	1
33.900	30.113	3.787	1969	2
31.000	29.580	1.420	1969	3
30.400	28.705	1.695	1969	4

MSE=   2.911   RMS=   1.706   RHO=   0.877
MEAN ERR=   0.6010   MEAN= 25.4615

Figure 7A-12B. Standard Dynamic Solution of Three Sectors Together: Gramlich-Hulett Version. Housing Expenditures — *EH$*.

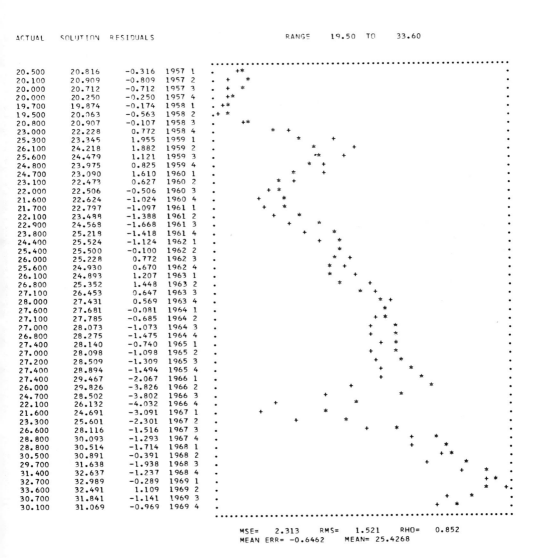

ACTUAL	SOLUTION	RESIDUALS				RANGE	19.50 TO	33.60
20.500	20.816	-0.316	1957	1				
20.100	20.909	-0.809	1957	2				
20.000	20.712	-0.712	1957	3				
20.000	20.250	-0.250	1957	4				
19.700	19.874	-0.174	1958	1				
19.500	20.063	-0.563	1958	2				
20.800	20.907	-0.107	1958	3				
23.000	22.228	0.772	1958	4				
25.300	23.345	1.955	1959	1				
26.100	24.218	1.882	1959	2				
25.600	24.479	1.121	1959	3				
24.800	23.975	0.825	1959	4				
24.700	23.090	1.610	1960	1				
23.100	22.473	0.627	1960	2				
22.000	22.506	-0.506	1960	3				
21.600	22.624	-1.024	1960	4				
21.700	22.797	-1.097	1961	1				
22.100	23.488	-1.388	1961	2				
22.900	24.568	-1.668	1961	3				
23.800	25.218	-1.418	1961	4				
24.400	25.524	-1.124	1962	1				
25.400	25.500	-0.100	1962	2				
26.000	25.228	0.772	1962	3				
25.600	24.930	0.670	1962	4				
26.100	24.893	1.207	1963	1				
26.800	25.352	1.448	1963	2				
27.100	26.453	0.647	1963	3				
28.000	27.431	0.569	1963	4				
27.600	27.681	-0.081	1964	1				
27.100	27.785	-0.685	1964	2				
27.000	28.073	-1.073	1964	3				
26.800	28.275	-1.475	1964	4				
27.400	28.140	-0.740	1965	1				
27.000	28.098	-1.098	1965	2				
27.200	28.509	-1.309	1965	3				
27.400	28.894	-1.494	1965	4				
27.400	29.467	-2.067	1966	1				
26.000	29.826	-3.826	1966	2				
24.700	28.502	-3.802	1966	3				
22.100	26.132	-4.032	1966	4				
21.600	24.691	-3.091	1967	1				
23.300	25.601	-2.301	1967	2				
26.600	28.116	-1.516	1967	3				
28.800	30.093	-1.293	1967	4				
28.800	30.514	-1.714	1968	1				
30.500	30.891	-0.391	1968	2				
29.700	31.638	-1.938	1968	3				
31.400	32.637	-1.237	1968	4				
32.700	32.989	-0.289	1969	1				
33.600	32.491	1.109	1969	2				
30.700	31.841	-1.141	1969	3				
30.100	31.069	-0.969	1969	4				

MSE= 2.313   RMS= 1.521   RHO= 0.852
MEAN ERR= -0.6462   MEAN= 25.4268

Figure 7A-12A. Standard Dynamic Solution of Three Sectors Together: Modigliani-Slovin Version. Housing Expenditures — *EH$*.

References

[1] Jaffee, D. M. *Credit Rationing and the Commercial Loan Market*. New York: Wiley, 1971.

[2] de Leeuw, Frank, and Edward Gramlich. "The Channels of Monetary Policy." *Federal Reserve Bulletin* 55 (June 1969).

Appendix A

Notation and Variable Definitions

The following list provides definitions for the notational variables referred to in the book and used in the equation summary in Appendix B. The notation generally follows the scheme used in the FMP model, the essential features of which are:

Interest rates and related variables begin with R
Balance-sheet variables of financial intermediaries begin with M
Stock variables include a K
Real sector variables are mnemonic

Our notation differs from the FMP model in two respects. First, all variables, unless specifically noted, are in current dollars; in the FMP model, current dollars is specifically indicated by $. Second, in some cases composite variables have been constructed from FMP variables, and have been given new names.

Definitions for the data used in these studies are contained in the FMP model data dictionary and are available upon request. The following conventions have been generally followed.

Dollar magnitudes are measured in billions of current dollars and are seasonally adjusted
Interest rates are measured in percentage points and are not seasonally adjusted
Flows are measured at quarterly rates
Stocks are measured at the end of the quarter

List of Symbols

CG	Capital gains = change in net worth $- SP_{-1}$
CON	Consumption in real terms
$\$C$	Consumption in current dollars
DUM	Dummy variable, 1 starting in 1968:1, 0 otherwise
EH	Residential construction expenditures, real
$EH\$$	Residential construction expenditures, current dollars
$HS1\$$	Single-family housing starts, current dollars
$HS3\$$	Multifamily housing starts, current dollars
$JS1$	Seasonal dummy, first quarter
$JS4$	Seasonal dummy, fourth quarter

KCD	Stock of consumer durables, real
KH	Housing stock, total, beginning of quarter, real
KH1	Housing stock, single-family, beginning of quarter, real
KH3	Housing stock, multiple-family, beginning of quarter, real
KH$	Housing stock, total, beginning of quarter, current dollars
MCL	Commercial and industrial loans at all commercial banks
MCNI	New mortgage commitments, life insurance companies
MCOI	Outstanding mortgage commitments, life insurance companies
MCOM	Outstanding mortgage commitments, mutual savings banks
MCOS	Outstanding mortgage commitments, savings and loan associations
MD	Demand deposits adjusted at all commercial banks
MDS	Demand deposits adjusted at all member banks
MFIS	Gross mortgage flows, life insurance companies
MFMS	Gross mortgage flows, mutual savings banks
MFSL	Gross mortgage flows, savings and loan associations
MIS	Life insurance reserves less policy loans
MKCB	Mortgage stock, commercial banks
MKIS	Mortgage stock, life insurance companies
MKMS	Mortgage stock, mutual savings banks
MKSL	Mortgage stock, savings and loan associations
MMS	Savings deposits, mutual savings banks
$\overline{MMS}$	Savings deposits, mutual savings banks, four-quarter average
MP	Passbook savings deposits, all commercial banks, no seasonal adjustment
MRIS	Mortgage repayments to life insurance companies
MRMS	Mortgage repayments to mutual savings banks
MRSL	Mortgage repayments to commercial banks
MS	Deposits at savings and loan associations and mutual savings banks
MSL	Deposits (shares), savings and loan associations
$\overline{MSL}$	Deposits (shares), savings and loan associations, four-quarter average
MTM	Time deposits, total, member commercial banks
MTP	Passbook savings deposits, member commercial banks
N	Population, millions
N1	Population, between ages 25 and 65
N3	Population between ages 20 and 25, and over 65
OASI	OASI benefits excluding medicare
P	Consumer price deflator
PCD	Price deflator for consumer durables
PDOT	Rate of inflation of *P*
PEH	Housing expenditure (*EH*) price deflator

PHCA   Construction cost index adjusted

RA   Average yield of *RMS* and *RSL*, weighted by four-quarter flows

RCB   Corporate bond yield

RCH1   Cost of capital, single-family houses

RCH3   Cost of capital, multiple-family houses

RCL   Commercial loan rate

RCP   Commercial paper rate

$\overline{RCP - RCL} = RCP + RCP_{-1} - RCL - RCL_{-1}$

RH   Rent index for residential structures

RI   Rate of return on life insurance reserves; assumed constant at 5.00

RM   Mortgage rate

$\overline{RM}$ Mortgage rate, deviation from twelve-quarter average

RMS   Effective rate on deposits, mutual savings banks

RMUN   Municipal bond rate

RSL   Effective rate on deposits, savings and loan associations

RTB   Treasury bill rate

RTP   Effective rate on passbook savings deposits, commercial banks

RTP*   Desired rate on passbook savings deposits, commercial banks

SP   Personal saving

T   Effective rate on personal income tax

TIME   Time trend; 1947:1 = 1, 1947:2 = 2, etc.

TP   Property tax rate

U_{-1} Lagged residual of equation

V   Net worth of households

VU   Unclaimed net worth = net worth − demand deposits − currency − housing stock − consumer durable stock

YD   Disposable income

ZAFH   Advances from Federal Home Loan Bank Board

ZCT   Ceiling rate on passbook savings deposits

ZDRA   Federal Reserve discount rate, quarterly average

ZMFN   Mortgage stock holding, Federal National Mortgage Association

ZRFH   Interest rate on advances, Federal Home Loan Bank Board

Appendix B

Summary of Equations

The following list provides the principle equations used in the simulation experiments in Chapter 7. To provide a more convenient format, only the estimated coefficients and t-statistics (absolute values in parentheses) have been shown. Also, for coefficients estimated as Almon distributed lags, only the sum of the lag coefficients is shown and the length of the lag is indicated by

$$\sum_{i=0}^{n} b_i$$

To obtain more complete summary statistics and the exact lag distribution, reference is made for each equation to the table in which it initially appeared in the individual sectors.

Savings Deposits—A (Gramlich–Hulett Version)

Commercial Bank Passbook Savings (Chapter 2, Appendix 2A, equation 5-A_4)

$$\frac{MTP}{VU} = \underset{(16.0)}{.051} + \underset{(12.3)}{.006}(RTP - RI) + \underset{(.5)}{.001}(RTP - RSL)$$

$$+ \underset{(2.4)}{.003}(RTP - RMS) + \underset{(5.0)}{.002}(RTP - RTB)$$

$$+ \underset{(11.7)}{.396}\frac{YD}{VU} - \underset{(8.8)}{.102}\frac{CG}{VU} + .8U_{-1} \tag{B-1}$$

Mutual Savings Bank Deposits (Chapter 2, Appendix 2A, equation 5-A_3)

$$\frac{MMS}{VU} = \underset{(8.9)}{.018} + \underset{(.1)}{.0004}(RMS - RSL) + \underset{(2.4)}{.003}(RMS - RTP)$$

$$+ \underset{(11.7)}{.214}\frac{YD}{VU} - \underset{(8.8)}{.055}\frac{CG}{VU} + .8U_{-1} \tag{B-2}$$

290

Savings and Loan Association Shares (Chapter 2, Appendix 2A, equation 5-A_2)

$$\frac{MSL}{VU} = .089 + .0004(RSL - RMS) + .001(RSL - RTP)$$
$$\phantom{\frac{MSL}{VU} = } (29.6) \quad (.1) \quad\quad\quad\quad\quad (.5)$$

$$+ .007(RSL - RCB) + .001(RSL - PDOT)$$
$$(5.2) \quad\quad\quad\quad\quad (1.5)$$

$$+ .321 \frac{YD}{VU} - .083 \frac{CG}{VU} - 2.687 \frac{1}{TIME} + .8U_{-1} \quad\text{(B-3)}$$
$$(11.7) \quad\quad (8.8) \quad\quad (15.4)$$

Life Insurance Reserves (Chapter 2, Appendix 2A, equation 5-A_1)

$$\frac{MIS}{VU} = .034 + .006\,(RI - RTP) + .001(RI - RTB)$$
$$\phantom{\frac{MIS}{VU} = } (6.8) \quad (12.3) \quad\quad\quad\quad (1.1)$$

$$+ .001(RI - PDOT) + .608 \frac{YD}{VU} - .158 \frac{CG}{VU} + .8U_{-1} \quad\text{(B-4)}$$
$$(1.9) \quad\quad\quad\quad (11.7) \quad\quad (8.8)$$

Rate Paid on Commercial Bank Passbook Savings—No Ceiling (Chapter 2, Appendix 2B, equation C)

$$RTP^* = -1.596 - .525 \frac{\Delta(MD + MTP - MCL)}{(MD + MTP - MCL)_{-1}}$$
$$ (10.4) \quad (1.1)$$

$$+ .766ZCT - .129\Delta ZCT + .571 \sum_{i=0}^{9} b_{-i}RTPC_{-i} \quad\text{(B-5)}$$
$$(14.2) \quad\quad (2.8) \quad\quad (9.6)$$

where

$$RTPC = \frac{.0009}{.0061} RSL + \frac{.0030}{.0061} RMS + \frac{.0022}{.0061} RTB$$

Rate Paid on Savings and Loan Association Shares (Chapter 2, Appendix 2B, equation A)

$$RSL = -.299 + .561 \sum_{i=0}^{4} b_i RSLC_{-i} + .337 \sum_{i=0}^{9} c_i RM_{-i}$$
$$\quad\;\; (.6) \quad (6.4) \qquad\qquad\qquad (2.5)$$

$$+ .221 \sum_{i=0}^{9} d_i(100)\left(\frac{\Delta MKSL}{MKSL_{-1}} - \frac{\Delta MSL}{MSL_{-1}}\right)_{-i-1}$$
$$(3.5)$$

$$+ 3.666 JQ\left(\frac{ZAFH}{MSL}\right)_{-1} + .029 JQ \qquad\qquad \text{(B-6)}$$
$$(2.0) \qquad\qquad\qquad\;\; (.4)$$

where

$$RSLC = \frac{.0004}{.0089} RMS + \frac{.0009}{.0089} RTP + \frac{.0071}{.0089} RCB + \frac{.0005}{.0089} PDOT$$

$$JQ = \begin{cases} 1 \text{ after } 1962{:}1 \\ 0 \text{ otherwise} \end{cases}$$

Rate Paid on Mutual Savings Bank Deposits (Chapter 2, Appendix B, equation B)

$$RMS = .717 + .142 RM + .047 RM_{-1} + .62 \sum_{i=0}^{5} b_i RMSC_{-i} \quad \text{(B-7)}$$
$$\quad\;\; (3.5) \quad (3.6) \qquad (2.3) \qquad (20.9)$$

where

$$RMSC = \frac{.0004}{.0034} RSL + \frac{.0030}{.0034} RTP$$

Savings Deposits—B (Modigliani–Slovin Version)

Commercial Bank Passbook Savings (Chapter 3, Table 3A-1, equation MP.9)

$$\frac{\Delta MP}{V} = -.009 + .001Q + .002Q(RTP - RA) + .001 RTP - .001 RTB$$
$$\qquad\;\; (3.7) \quad (2.4) \quad (3.3) \qquad\qquad\qquad (7.3) \qquad (9.7)$$

$$+ .043 \frac{YD}{V} - .036\left(\frac{MP}{V}\right)_{-1} + 1.419\left(\frac{MP}{V}\right)_{-1}\left(\frac{SP}{V}\right)$$
$$(3.8) \qquad (1.6) \qquad\qquad (.87)$$

$$+ .1753\left(\frac{MP}{V}\right)_{-1}\left(\frac{CG}{V}\right) + .001 JS1 - .0002 JS4 \qquad \text{(B-8)}$$
$$(2.7) \qquad\qquad\qquad (6.0) \qquad\quad (1.5)$$

where

$$Q = \begin{cases} 1 \text{ after } 1961{:}2 \\ 0 \text{ otherwise} \end{cases}$$

$$RA = \frac{RSL(MSL_{-1} - MSL_{-5}) + RMS(MMS_{-1} - MMS_{-5})}{(MSL_{-1} - MSL_{-5}) + (MMS_{-1} - MMS_{-5})}$$

Savings and Loan Association and Mutual Savings Book Deposits (*Chapter 3, Table 3A-2, equation MS.7*)

$$\frac{\Delta MS}{V} = \underset{(1.5)}{.004} - \underset{(2.4)}{.001Q} + \underset{(3.3)}{.002Q(RA - RTP)} + \underset{(1.0)}{.0002Q(RA - RTB)}$$

$$+ \underset{(2.3)}{.001RA} - \underset{(2.0)}{.001RCB} + \underset{(.64)}{.0001RTB} - \underset{(1.0)}{.012}\frac{YD}{V} - \underset{(1.6)}{.036}\left(\frac{MS}{V}\right)_{-1}$$

$$+ \underset{(.87)}{1.419}\left(\frac{MP}{V}\right)_{-1}\frac{SP}{V} + \underset{(2.7)}{.175}\left(\frac{MP}{V}\right)_{-1}\frac{CG}{V} \qquad \text{(B-9)}$$

where

$$Q = \begin{cases} 1 \text{ after } 1961{:}2 \\ 0 \text{ otherwise} \end{cases}$$

Savings and Loan Association Shares (*Chapter 3, Table 3A-3, equation MSL.2*)

$$\Delta\frac{MSL}{MS} = \underset{(2.3)}{.036} + .021\sum_{i=0}^{11} b_i(RSL - RMS)_{-i} + \underset{(2.5)}{.475(Q_1 \times 10^{-3})}$$

$$- \underset{(2.9)}{.005(Q_1)^2} \times 10^{-3} - \underset{(2.5)}{.074}\left(\frac{MSL}{MS}\right)_{-1} + 1.0\left(\frac{MSL}{MS}\right)_{-1}\left(\frac{\Delta MS}{MS}\right) \qquad \text{(B-10)}$$

where

$$Q_1 = \begin{cases} TIME - 33 \text{ until } 1965{:}4 \\ 43 \text{ after } 1965{:}4 \end{cases}$$

Life Insurance Reserves Net of Policy Loans (Chapter 3, Table 3A-4, equation MIS.2)

$$\frac{\Delta MIS}{\$C} = \underset{(8.6)}{.024} - \underset{(3.2)}{.001JR} - \underset{(3.4)}{.002JR(\overline{RCP - RCL})}$$

$$- \underset{(2.6)}{7.0} \times 10^{-4}RM - \underset{(.85)}{2.7} \times 10^{-4} \sum_{i=1}^{11} b_i RM_{-i}$$

$$- \underset{(1.2)}{7.4} \times 10^{-5} \sum_{i=0}^{7} \left(\frac{\Delta P}{P_{-1}}\right)_{-i} - \underset{(1.9)}{.016}\left(\frac{OASI}{\$C}\right)_{-1} - \underset{(6.0)}{.047}\left(\frac{MIS}{\$C}\right)_{-1}$$

$$\text{(B-11)}$$

where

$$JR = \begin{cases} 1 \text{ if } .5(\overline{RCP - RCL}) > -.7 \\ 0 \text{ otherwise} \end{cases}$$

Rate Paid on Commercial Bank Passbook Savings—No Ceiling (Chapter 4, Table 4C-2)

$$RTP^* = \underset{(15.9)}{-2.01} + \underset{(.59)}{.219Q_2} + \underset{(2.9)}{.170Q_1} \sum_{i=0}^{4} b_i RTB_{-i}$$

$$+ \underset{(2.2)}{.249Q_2} \sum_{i=0}^{2} c_i(.23RTB + .77RA)_{-i}$$

$$+ \underset{(15.5)}{.896} \sum_{i=0}^{8} d_i(.45RCL + .30RM + .25RMUN)_{-i}$$

$$- \underset{(1.8)}{.091}\left[(.45RCL + .30RM + .25RMUN) - ZDRA\right]_{-1}$$

$$+ \underset{(5.3)}{2.30} \sum_{i=0}^{9} e_i(ZCT - ZCT_{-1})_{-i}$$

$$- \underset{(4.3)}{18.07Q_2} \sum_{i=0}^{6} f_i\left[\frac{\Delta MP_{-1}}{MP_{-2}} - \frac{\Delta(MKCB + MCL)_{-1}}{(MKCB + MCL)_{-2}}\right]_{-i}$$

$$- \underset{(3.6)}{14.66Q_2} \sum_{i=0}^{6} g_i\left[\frac{\Delta MD_{-1}}{MD_{-2}} - \frac{\Delta(MKCB + MCL)_{-1}}{(MKCB + MCL)_{-2}}\right]_{-i} \quad \text{(B-12)}$$

where

$$Q_1 = \begin{cases} 1 \text{ after } 1961:2 \\ 0 \text{ otherwise} \end{cases} \qquad Q_2 = \begin{cases} 1 \text{ after } 1961:2 \\ 0 \text{ otherwise} \end{cases}$$

Rate Paid on Savings and Loan Association Shares (Chapter 4, Table 4C-1, equation 1)

$$RSL = -1.09 + .823Q_2 + .563Q_1 \sum_{i=0}^{5} b_i(.51RMS + .43RCB + .06RTB)_{-i}$$
$$ (3.9) \quad (3.2) \quad\quad (8.6)$$

$$+ .462Q_2 \sum_{i=0}^{4} c_i(.203\dot{R}CB + .083RTB + .713RTP)_{-i}$$
$$ (10.6)$$

$$+ .476 \sum_{i=0}^{10} d_i RM_{-i} + 7.62 \sum_{i=0}^{9} e_i \left(\frac{\Delta MKSL_{-1}}{MKSL_{-2}} - \frac{\Delta MSL_{-1}}{MSL_{-2}} \right)_{-i}$$
$$ (7.1) \quad\quad\quad (1.6)$$

$$+ .74U_{-1} \hspace{6cm} \text{(B-13)}$$

where

$$Q_1 = \begin{cases} 1 \text{ after } 1960:4 \\ 0 \text{ otherwise} \end{cases} \qquad Q_2 = \begin{cases} 1 \text{ after } 1960:4 \\ 0 \text{ otherwise} \end{cases}$$

Rate Paid on Mutual Savings Bank Deposits (Chapter 4, Table 4C-1, equation 2)

$$RMS = -.825 - .194Q_2 - .265Q_3$$
$$ (1.5) \quad (.35) \quad\quad (3.1)$$

$$+ .481Q_1 \sum_{i=0}^{5} b_i(.51RSL + .43RCB + .06RTB)_{-i}$$
$$ (3.9)$$

$$+ .711Q_2 \sum_{i=0}^{4} c_i(.203RCB + .083RTB + .713RTP)_{-i}$$
$$ (9.7)$$

$$+ .415 \sum_{i=0}^{10} d_i RM_{-i} + 40.19Q_3 \sum_{i=0}^{9} \left(\frac{\Delta MKMS_{-1}}{MKMS_{-2}} - \frac{\Delta MMS_{-1}}{MMS_{-2}} \right)_{-i}$$
$$ (3.3) \quad\quad\quad\quad (3.6)$$

$$+ .867U_{-1} \hspace{6cm} \text{(B-14)}$$

where

$$Q_1 = \begin{cases} 1 \text{ after } 1960{:}4 \\ 0 \text{ otherwise} \end{cases} \qquad Q_2 = \begin{cases} 1 \text{ after } 1960{:}4 \\ 0 \text{ otherwise} \end{cases} \qquad Q_3 = \begin{cases} 1 \text{ after } 1962{:}1 \\ 0 \text{ otherwise} \end{cases}$$

Mortgage Market

New Commitments of Life Insurance Companies (Chapter 5, Appendix 5A, equation 5A-1)

$$MCNI = -1.63 + .045MIS + .708\Delta MIS + .003(RM_{-1} - RCB_{-1})MIS$$
$$\quad\;\; (2.6) \quad\;\; (2.1) \qquad\;\;\; (3.3) \qquad\qquad (2.3)$$

$$+ .186MRIS - .073MKIS_{-1} + .032MCOI_{-1}$$
$$\qquad (1.9) \qquad\qquad (.46)$$

$$+ .657MCNI_{-1} + .337U_{-1} \qquad\qquad\qquad\qquad \text{(B-15)}$$
$$\quad\; (5.2)$$

Outstanding Commitments of Savings and Loan Associations (Chapter 5, Appendix 5A, equation 5A-2)

$$MCOS = -.749 + .161MSL + .004(RM - ZRFH)MSL + .119MRSL$$
$$\qquad\;\; (4.3) \quad\;\; (6.3) \qquad (2.9)$$

$$- .149MKSL_{-1} + .378MCOS_{-1} + .653U_{-1} \qquad\qquad \text{(B-16)}$$
$$\quad\; (5.9) \qquad\qquad (3.7)$$

Outstanding Commitments of Mutual Savings Banks (Chapter 5, Appendix 5A, equation 5A-3)

$$MCOM = -2.23 + .152MMS + .472\Delta MMS + .012(RM - RCB)MMS$$
$$\qquad\quad (2.8) \quad\;\; (2.6) \qquad\;\; (2.5) \qquad\qquad (2.1)$$

$$+ .060MRMS - .148MKMS_{-1} + .995MCOM_{-1} + .220U_{-1}$$
$$\quad\; (2.5) \qquad\qquad (11.0)$$
$$\qquad\qquad\qquad\qquad\qquad\qquad\qquad\qquad\qquad \text{(B-17)}$$

Outstanding Commitments of Life Insurance Companies (Chapter 5, Appendix 5A, equation 5A-4)

$$MCOI = .763 + 1.00MCNI + .681MCOI_{-1} + .977U_{-1} \quad \text{(B-18)}$$
$$(.84)(8.65)$$

Gross Mortgage Flow of Life Insurance Companies (Chapter 5, Appendix 5A, equation 5A-5)

$$MFIS = .696 - .283DUM + .026MIS + .502MRIS - .047MKIS_{-1}$$
$$(2.1)\quad(3.7)(2.3)(2.8)(2.7)$$

$$+ .922 \sum_{i=0}^{7} b_i MCNI_{-i} + .084U_{-1} \quad \text{(B-19)}$$
$$(15.5)$$

Gross Mortgage Flow of Savings and Loan Associations (Chapter 5, Appendix 5A, equation 5A-6)

$$MFSL = .152 - .830DUM + .118\overline{\Delta MSL} + .260MSL + .190ZAFH$$
$$(.47)\quad(7.1)(2.0)(3.4)(1.7)$$

$$+ .625MRSL - .299MKSL_{-1} + 1.95 \sum_{i=0}^{6} b_i MCOS_{-i}$$
$$(5.3)(3.7)\phantom{MKSL_{-1} +}(11.5)$$

$$+ .741U_{-1} \quad \text{(B-20)}$$

Gross Mortgage Flow of Mutual Savings Banks (Chapter 5, Appendix 5A, equation 5A-7)

$$MFMS = -.779 - .284DUM + .334\overline{\Delta MMS} + .115MMS + .400MRMS$$
$$(2.1)\quad(3.4)(6.1)(3.2)$$

$$- .132MKMS_{-1} + .449 \sum_{i=0}^{6} b_i MCOM_{-i} \quad \text{(B-21)}$$
$$(3.5)\phantom{MKMS_{-1} +}(15.0)$$

Net Mortgage Flow of Commercial Bonds (Chapter 5, Appendix 5A, equation 5A-8)

$$\Delta MKCB = \underset{(.77)}{.005MDS} + \underset{(3.8)}{.072} \sum_{i=0}^{4} b_i MTM_{-i}$$

$$+ \underset{(3.5)}{.016} \sum_{i=0}^{4} c_i(MTM_{-i})(RM - RCL)_{-i} - \underset{(3.3)}{.176MKCB_{-1}}$$

$$+ .632\ U_{-1} \tag{B-22}$$

Mortgage Demand—Mortgage Rate (Chapter 5, Appendix 5A, equation 5A-9)

$$RM = \underset{(3.7)}{1.60} + \underset{(6.6)}{.346RCB} - \underset{(2.5)}{.601}\ \frac{\Delta M_g^T + .03M_{-1}^T}{EH\$ + .03KH\$_{-1}}$$

$$- \underset{(1.5)}{.004}\ \frac{MCOS_{-1} + MCOM_{-1} + MCOI_{-1}}{EH\$ + .03KH\$_{-1}}$$

$$+ \underset{(6.6)}{.549RM_{-1}} + .531U_{-1} \tag{B-23}$$

where

$$\Delta M_g^T = MFIS + MFMS + MFSL + \Delta MKCB + \Delta ZMFN$$

$$M^T = MKIS + MKMS + MKSL + MKCB + ZMFN$$

Mortgage Repayments to Life Insurance Companies (Chapter 5, Appendix 5A, equation 5A-10)

$$MRIS = \underset{(11.9)}{.021MKIS_{-1}} - \underset{(7.5)}{.007(\overline{RM})MKIS_{-1}} + \underset{(3.2)}{.125MFIS_{-1}} + .076U_{-1}$$

$$\tag{B-24}$$

Mortgage Repayments to Savings and Loan Associations (Chapter 5, Appendix 5A, equation 5A-11)

$$MRSL = \underset{(8.6)}{.022MKSL_{-1}} - \underset{(5.0)}{.008(\overline{RM})MKSL_{-1}} + \underset{(5.7)}{.228MFSL_{-1}} + .678U_{-1}$$

$$\tag{B-25}$$

Mortgage Repayments to Mutual Savings Banks (Chapter 5, Appendix 5A, equation 5A-12)

$$MRMS = .012MKMS_{-1} - .001(\overline{RM})MKMS_{-1} + .281MFMS_{-1} \quad (B-26)$$
$$\quad\quad\quad (5.9) \quad\quad\quad\quad\quad (.50) \quad\quad\quad\quad\quad\quad (6.8)$$

Housing Sector

Cost of Capital for Single-Family Housing (Chapter 6, equation 6-10)

$$RCH1 = (1 - T)(.7RM + .3RCB + .8TP) - 1.46 \quad (B-27)$$

Cost of Capital for Multiple-Family Housing (Chapter 6, Footnote 13)

$$RCH3 = .95RM + .05RCB + .8TP - 2.44 \quad (B-28)$$

Housing Starts of Single-Family Housing (Chapter 6, Appendix 6A, equation 6A-1)

$$\ln\left(\frac{HS1\$}{N1 \cdot PHCA}\right) - .005TIME$$

$$= 1.21 + .751\left[\ln\left(\frac{CON}{N} - \ln\frac{KH1}{N1}\right)_{-1}\right]$$
$$\quad (4.4) \quad (1.1)$$

$$+ .952\sum_{i=0}^{5} b_i \ln\left(\frac{P}{PHCA \cdot RCH1}\right)_{-i}$$

$$+ .749\sum_{i=0}^{7} c_i \ln\left(\frac{MCOS + \Delta ZMFN}{MCOS_{-1} + \Delta ZMFN_{-1}}\right)_{-i}$$

$$+ 11.20\sum_{i=0}^{7} d_i \ln(W_{-i}) + .545U_{-1}$$

$$(B-29)$$

where

$$W = [V - KH1_{-2}(PEH - PEH_{-2})(.5) - KCD_{-2}(PCD - PCD_{-2})(.5)]/V_{-1}$$

Housing Starts of Multiple-Family Housing (Chapter 6, Appendix 6A, equation 6A-2)

$$\ln\left(\frac{HS3\$}{N3 \cdot PHCA}\right) - .005TIME$$

$$= \underset{(13.5)}{3.43} + \underset{(4.6)}{3.08}\left[\ln\left(\frac{CON}{N}\right) - \ln\left(\frac{KH3}{N3}\right)_{-1}\right]$$

$$+ 7.51 \sum_{i=0}^{3} b_i \ln\left(\frac{P}{PHCA}\right)_{-i} + 1.50 \sum_{i=0}^{5} c_i \ln\left(\frac{MCOM}{MCOM_{-1}}\right)_{-i}$$

$$+ .224 \sum_{i=0}^{5} d_i \ln(MCNI_{-i}) - \underset{(3.8)}{.547Q} + .808U_{-1} \qquad \text{(B-30)}$$

where

$$Q = \begin{cases} 0.5 \text{ in } 1966{:}3,\ 1967{:}2 \\ 1.0 \text{ in } 1966{:}4,\ 1967{:}1 \\ 0 \text{ otherwise} \end{cases}$$

Expenditures on Residential Construction (Chapter 6, Appendix 6A, equation 6A-3)

$EH\$$

$$= \underset{(5.9)}{.320}(HSI\$ + HS3\$) + \underset{(10.8)}{.608}(HSI\$ + HS3\$)_{-1} + \underset{(2.30)}{.130}(HSI\$ + HS3\$)_{-2}$$

$$+ \underset{(1.0)}{.004}(HSI\$_{-2} + .67HS3\$_{-3} + .33HS3\$_{-4})$$

$$+ .997[EH\$_{-1} - .32(HSI\$ + HS3\$)_{-1} - .608(HSI\$ + HS3\$)_{-2}$$

$$- .130(HSI\$ - HS3\$)_{-3}] \qquad \text{(B-31)}$$

Stock of Single-Family Houses (Chapter 6, Appendix 6A, equation 6A-4)

$$KHI = 1.06\left(\frac{HSI\$}{PEH}\right)_{-1} + .997KHI_{-1} \qquad \text{(B-32)}$$

Stock of Multiple-Family Housing (Chapter 6, Appendix 6A, equation 6-A5)

$$KH3 = 1.06 \left[.67 \left(\frac{HS3\$}{PEH} \right)_{-2} + .33 \left(\frac{HS3\$}{PEH} \right)_{-3} \right] + .997 KH3_{-1} \quad \text{(B-33)}$$

Index

303

About the Contributors

Edward M. Gramlich was born in Rochester, New York, in 1939. He received his B.A. from Williams College in 1961 and his Ph.D. from Yale University in 1965. He worked on the FMP model at the Federal Reserve Board from 1966–1970, supervising the work on the project at the Board in 1969–1970. He was a visiting professor in Monetary Theory at Monash University in Australia in 1970. He is now Director of the Division of Policy Research at the Office of Economic Opportunity. He has written several journal articles on monetary and fiscal policy, state and local governments, and labor markets.

David T. Hulett was born in Washington, D.C., in 1939. He graduated from Princeton University in 1961 and received his Ph.D. from Stanford University in 1966. He taught at Harvard University from 1965–1967 and was at the Federal Reserve from 1967–1970. He is now an economist with the Office of Management and Budget. He has written journal articles on monetary theory and bank portfolio behavior.

Dwight M. Jaffee was born in 1943 in Chicago. He studied economics at Oberlin College and Northwestern University and was graduated from Northwestern in 1964 with highest honors. He received his Ph.D. from the Massachusetts Institute of Technology in 1968. His research interests are primarily in monetary theory and policy and the structure of financial markets. He is author of the book *Credit Rationing and the Commercial Loan Market* and various journal articles. He is currently an associate professor of economics at Princeton University.

John H. Kalchbrenner was born in Chicago in 1937. He received his B.A. from Iowa State in 1958 and his Ph.D. from the University of Wisconsin in 1969. He served in the U.S. Navy from 1960–1964 and at the Federal Reserve from 1968–72. He has written journal articles on monetary and fiscal policy. He is currently an economist with the Federal Reserve Bank of Chicago.

Franco Modigliani was born in Rome, Italy, in 1918. He received a Dr. of Jurisprudence from the University of Rome in 1939, a Dr. of Social Science from the New School for Social Research in 1944, and a LL.D. from the University of Chicago in 1959. He has been a professor of economics at the University of Illinois, Carnegie Institute of Technology, and Northwestern University, and is currently an Institute Professor at the Massachusetts Institute of Technology. He has been a co-director of the FMP econometric model project, has been and is currently on the editorial board of several journals, and has written several books and numerous articles in professional journals. In addition to monetary theory, Professor Modigliani's contributions have been in the field of production theory, international trade, public finance, and macroeconomics.

Myron B. Slovin was born in Providence, Rhode Island, in 1946. He graduated from the University of Michigan in 1968 and attended the London School of Economics in 1966–1967. He received his Ph.D in 1972 from Princeton University with a thesis on intermediary rate setting behavior. He is presently on the staff of the Federal Reserve Board.